W9-AEA-734

LUTHER'S WORKS

American Edition

VOLUME 41

Published by Concordia Publishing House

and Fortress Press in 55 volumes.

General Editors are Jaroslav Pelikan (for vols. 1-30)

and Helmut T. Lehmann (for vols. 31-55)

LUTHER'S WORKS

VOLUME 41

Church and Ministry
III

EDITED BY
ERIC W. GRITSCH

WITH AN INTRODUCTION BY
E. GORDON RUPP

GENERAL EDITOR
HELMUT T. LEHMANN

FORTRESS PRESS / PHILADELPHIA

GENERAL EDITORS'
PREFACE

The first editions of Luther's collected works appeared in the sixteenth century, and so did the first efforts to make him "speak English." In America serious attempts in these directions were made for the first time in the nineteenth century. The Saint Louis edition of Luther was the first endeavor on American soil to publish a collected edition of his works, and the Henkel Press in Newmarket, Virginia, was the first to publish some of Luther's writings in an English translation. During the first decade of the twentieth century, J. N. Lenker produced translations of Luther's sermons and commentaries in thirteen volumes. A few years later the first of the six volumes in the Philadelphia (or Holman) edition of the *Works of Martin Luther* appeared. But a growing recognition of the need for more of Luther's works in English has resulted in this American edition of Luther's works.

The edition is intended primarily for the reader whose knowledge of late medieval Latin and sixteenth-century German is too small to permit him to work with Luther in the original languages. Those who can will continue to read Luther in his original words as these have been assembled in the monumental Weimar edition (*D. Martin Luthers Werke*. Kritische Gesamtausgabe, Weimar, 1883-   ). Its texts and helps have formed a basis for this edition, though in certain places we have felt constrained to depart from its readings and findings. We have tried throughout to translate Luther as he thought translating should be done. That is, we have striven for faithfulness on the basis of the best lexicographical materials available. But where literal accuracy and clarity have conflicted, it is clarity that we have preferred, so that sometimes paraphrase seemed more faithful than literal fidelity. We have proceeded in a similar way in the matter of Bible versions, translating Luther's translations. Where this could be done by the use of an existing English version—King James, Douay, or Revised Standard— we have done so. Where it could not, we have supplied our own.

v

To indicate this in each specific instance would have been pedantic; to adopt a uniform procedure would have been artificial—especially in view of Luther's own inconsistency in this regard. In each volume the translator will be responsible primarily for matters of text and language, while the responsibility of the editor will extend principally to the historical and theological matters reflected in the introductions and notes.

Although the edition as planned will include fifty-five volumes, Luther's writings are not being translated in their entirety. Nor should they be. As he was the first to insist, much of what he wrote and said was not that important. Thus the edition is a selection of works that have proved their importance for the faith, life, and history of the Christian church. The first thirty volumes contain Luther's expositions of various biblical books, while the remaining volumes include what are usually called his "Reformation writings" and other occasional pieces. The final volume of the set will be an index volume; in addition to an index of quotations, proper names, and topics, and a list of corrections and changes, it will contain a glossary of many of the technical terms that recur in Luther's works and that cannot be defined each time they appear. Obviously Luther cannot be forced into any neat set of rubrics. He can provide his reader with bits of autobiography or with political observations as he expounds a psalm, and he can speak tenderly about the meaning of the faith in the midst of polemics against his opponents. It is the hope of publishers, editors, and translators that through this edition the message of Luther's faith will speak more clearly to the modern church.

J. P.
H. T. L.

CONTENTS

ABBREVIATIONS

ANF   —*The Ante-Nicene Fathers*, edited by Alexander Roberts and James Donaldson
(Buffalo and New York, 1885-1896, American reprint of the Edinburgh edition).

CIC   —*Corpus Iuris Canonici*, edited by E. Friedberg
(Graz, 1955).

C.R.   —*Corpus Reformatorum*, edited by C. G. Bretschneider and H. E. Bindseil
(Halle/Saale, 1834-1860).

DRTA. JR —*Deutsche Reichstagsakten unter Kaiser Karl V*,
edited by Historische Kommission bei der
Bayrischen Akademie der Wissenschaften
(Gotha, 1893-   ).

LW   —American Edition of *Luther's Works*
(Philadelphia and St. Louis, 1955-   ).

LWZ   —*The Latin Works of Huldreich Zwingli*, 3 vols.,
translated and edited by S. M. Jackson, *et al.*
(New York, 1912; Philadelphia, 1922, 1929).

MPG   —*Patrologia, Series Graeca*, 161 vols.,
edited by J. P. Migne
(Paris, 1857-1866).

MPL   —*Patrologia, Series Latina*, 221 vols. in 222,
edited by J. P. Migne
(Paris, 1844-1904).

O.C.D.   —*The Oxford Classical Dictionary*, edited by M. Cary
et al.
(2nd ed., Oxford University Press, 1950).

O.D.C.C. —*The Oxford Dictionary of the Christian Church*,
edited by F. L. Cross
(2nd ed., Oxford University Press, 1958).

PE   —*Works of Martin Luther.* Philadelphia Edition.
(Philadelphia, 1915-1943).

PNF	—*The Nicene and Post-Nicene Fathers of the Christian Church.* First Series: edited by Philip Schaff. Second Series: edited by Philip Schaff and H. Wace (New York, 1886-1900).
St. L.	—*D. Martin Luthers sämmtliche Schriften,* edited by Johann Georg Walch. Edited and published in modern German, 23 vols. in 25 (2nd ed., St. Louis, 1880-1910).
WA	—*D. Martin Luthers Werke.* Kritische Gesamtausgabe (Weimar, 1883-).
WA, Br	—*D. Martin Luthers Werke.* Briefwechsel (Weimar, 1930-).
WA, DB	—*D. Martin Luthers Werke.* Deutsche Bibel (Weimar, 1906-1961).
WA, TR	—*D. Martin Luthers Werke.* Tischreden (Weimar, 1912-1921).

INTRODUCTION TO VOLUME 41

The nature and meaning of the Christian church were a theme and preoccupation for Martin Luther throughout his public career. Nearly forty years ago Karl Holl asserted[1] that almost all of Luther's later doctrine of the church was to be found in his lectures on the Psalms (1513-1515); modern studies may have modified, but not discredited this opinion. In them are to be found Luther's enduring stresses on the inwardness of the church as a *communio sanctorum* and the polarity of word and faith. As Ernst Kinder has shown,[2] Augustine was important here. *The City of God*, as the marginal notes in Luther's personal copy attest,[3] was significant for him in the beginning of his teaching, while in his very last lectures, on Genesis, the aging Reformer continued to draw heavily on this massive interpretation of sacred history. On the other hand, Luther's is not, as some critics have thought, the Augustinian dialectic of "visible-invisible" church, and his stress on its inwardness and personal character does not mean for him a Platonic flight from the objective and sacramental. Here his long battle with the Enthusiasts is important, for his "theology of the cross" and his fundamental faith in the Incarnation mean for him that the holy and invisible God will only have commerce with sinners in this fallen world through objective, sensible media. In the famous autobiographical fragment which he wrote in 1545, Luther claimed that, like Augustine, he was one who had learned by writing and teaching.[4] Earlier, he had poignantly written that living, dying, and being damned make the real theologian.[5] Hence

---

[1] Karl Holl, *"Luther und die Schwärmer,"* in *Gesammelte Aufsätze zur Kirchengeschichte* (6th ed.; 3 vols.; Tübingen, 1928-1932), I, 288-325.
[2] Ernst Kinder, *"Gottesreich und Weltreich bei Augustin und bei Luther. Erwägungen zu einer Vergleichung der 'Zwei-Reiche'—Lehre Augustins und Luthers,"* in Friedrich Hübner (ed.), *Gedenkschrift für D. Werner Elert* (Berlin, 1955), pp. 24-42.
[3] WA 9, 24-27.
[4] Cf. LW 34, 338.
[5] WA 5, 163.

the importance of his temptations (*Anfechtungen*) for his theological development. But these were provoked by outward events, and if much of Luther's teaching about the church does antedate the church struggle beginning in 1517, Ernst Bizer has shown that the crowded, fateful events of the next three years provoked him to an even more profound and drastic examination of the theological implications of his position.[6] To a slightly lesser degree these things are true of all of his later life. Much of his most interesting and profound thought is to be found, therefore, imbedded in his "occasional writings."

This volume contains such "occasional" treatises. They are of value for the theologian as well as for the church historian. By 1539 Luther's theology might not have changed very much, but the historical situation was vastly different from that of 1521. Across great areas of Western Europe papal authority had been repudiated, and religious practices and institutions uprooted and replaced by new forms of piety, discipline, and worship. In England and in the cities of Switzerland and of the Rhineland new patterns of reformation had emerged with a different orientation from that of the Lutheran Reformation as it had found embodiment in Germany and Scandinavia, to say nothing of the radical ferment which found its focus in the Anabaptists.

The great game of high politics continued to be dominated by the pope, the emperor, the king of France, and the Turks. In the critical months of 1520-1521 Luther himself had played his part, a pawn of strategic significance. Gerhard Ritter has suggested how near Luther came at this time to becoming the center of a national awakening in Germany.[7] But after the Edict of Worms he was an outlaw, and in the crises of the next decades he had to be an onlooker and an adviser. In the political field, Protestantism was now represented by the princes of the Smalcald League.[8] Our three treatises are related to this background: to

---

[6] Ernst Bizer, *Luther und der Papst* (K. G. Steck and G. Eichholz [eds.], "Theologische Existenz Heute," No. 69 [München, 1958]).

[7] John Riches (trans.), Gerhard Ritter's *Luther, His Life and Work* (New York: Harper and Row, 1963), chap. 4.

[8] The Smalcald League was founded in February, 1531, for the defense of the *Augsburg Confession*, which was presented at the Diet of Augsburg in 1530. Although defeated in the Smalcald War (1546-1547), the members of the

advice given by the reformers to their princes about how to behave in relation to a papal council; to the battle over ecclesiastical property as it came before the courts of the empire; and to the rights of the temporal authorities against papal claims.

It seems important that Luther himself had not grown up in an antipapalist or conciliar milieu. Though after his interview with Cajetan in 1518 he appealed to a general council, his openly expressed view of the fallibility of the Council of Constance[9] provoked the crisis at the Leipzig Debate in the following year; and when, in the days after the Diet of Worms, discussions broke down, it was over the question of the fallibility of councils. The dream of a "free, Christian council" haunted the reformers for two generations, but Luther was one of the first to be disillusioned about the hope of reform from this direction. After 1536 it was apparent that if and when such a great council did meet, it would meet not to hear, or make concessions to, but to condemn the reformers. In this situation Luther drew up an uncompromising but notable document, *The Smalcald Articles,* in which the definition of the church concludes with the words, "Thank God, a seven-year-old child knows what the church is, namely, holy believers, and the sheep who hear the voice of their Shepherd."[10]

This document was followed, in 1539, by the massive treatise *On the Councils and the Church.* In thirty years Luther had read a good deal of church history, down to and including the *Lives of the Popes* by the English exile, Robert Barnes.[11] Luther begins this treatise with a rejection of the humanist hope of a reform based on the teaching of the church fathers. They themselves are a mass of contradictions and cannot be regarded as the norm by which Scripture must be judged, for the fathers themselves insisted they be judged by Scripture. Then there are long discus-

---

league were able to negotiate the Peace of Augsburg in 1555, which gave legal sanction to Protestantism in Germany.

[9] Cf. *LW* 31, 321, n. 22; 322.

[10] Theodore G. Tappert (ed.), *The Book of Concord* (Philadelphia: Muhlenberg Press, 1959), p. 315.

[11] Robert Barnes (1495-1540), involved in the divorce negotiations of Henry VIII of England, studied in Wittenberg, where he met Luther. His *Lives of the Popes* (*Vitae Romanorum Pontificum*) was printed in 1536 by Joseph Klug of Wittenberg with a preface by Luther. Cf. *WA* 50, 3-5.

sions on the great Christological councils of the early church. In the last constructive section of the work Luther repeats his early emphasis: the church consists primarily of people, it is a communion of saints. Here too is the all-important doctrine of the word—"God's word cannot be without God's people, and conversely, God's people cannot be without God's word."[12] This is no purely spiritual, invisible church, but a church whose existence may be known by important outward and objective marks. At the end of the work Luther speaks of the three hierarchies of domestic life, political life, and the spiritual kingdom, and shows that this definition leaves no room for the papacy. He also stresses that the really important work of reformation is not to be looked for in the fuss and flurry of great ecumenical assemblies, but in the quieter, indispensable work of parishes and schools.

The fact that in Saxony a reformation had taken place without tarrying for a council is further stressed in the brilliant polemic *Against Hanswurst*. In justifying the practical claims of the Saxon princes to retain ecclesiastical property, Luther replies—twenty years before John Jewell and Richard Hooker[13]—to the taunt of the Counter Reformation, "Where was your church before Luther?" He claims that the reformers are the "true, ancient (primitive) church" which must always be present on earth, but which now shines clearly, like the sun when it bursts out from behind the clouds. "We for our part have never desired a council to reform our church. God and the Holy Spirit already sanctified our church through his holy word . . . so that we have everything (God be praised) pure and holy—the word, baptism, the sacrament, the keys, and everything which belongs to the true church—without the additions and filth of human doctrine. Life . . . is not lived completely according to our insight and wishes, a fact be-

---

[12] See p. 150.

[13] John Jewell (1522-1571), bishop of Salisbury, is known as the first great apologist of the Anglican church through his *Apologia pro Ecclesia Anglicana* published in 1562. Richard Hooker (1554-1600), a disciple of Jewell, wrote the widely known but unfinished treatise on *The Laws of Ecclesiastical Polity*. Of the five books which appeared in Hooker's lifetime, Books I-IV were published in 1594 and V in 1597. Books VI and VIII appeared in 1648 and VII in 1662.

wailed by the prophets and apostles themselves."[14] The spiritual nature of the church is even more emphatically asserted in the practical setting of the treatise. "The church is a high, deep, hidden thing which one may neither perceive nor see, but must grasp only by faith, through baptism, sacrament, and word."[15]

There is a dire finality about the last treatise, *Against the Roman Papacy, an Institution of the Devil.* Luther believed, as his prince commented when the tract gave offense, that the church of Rome was now incorrigible. Some words of Luther, written solemnly in 1520, may perhaps mark the point at which he hardened his heart against the papal church. "Farewell, unhappy, hopeless, blasphemous Rome. The wrath of God has come upon thee as thou deservest. We have cared for Babylon and she is not healed. Let us then leave her that she may become a habitation of dragons, specters, and witches."[16] More and more he was convinced that the papacy could not be regarded as a neutral institution, but that it was Antichrist, a demonic institution striking at the God-given ordinances of the spiritual and temporal power. Nonetheless, Luther admitted that there had been true Christians in the Roman church in every generation: if the pope would and could go back to being the bishop of the church in Rome, he might still have his place within the Christian church.

What Luther here attacked so fiercely and cruelly was, be it noted, not so much the modern papacy but "popery," the Renaissance papacy in its highly secularized, politically aggressive form, hopelessly entangled in the world and bringing souls into fear and bondage by a legalistic religion which set the traditions of men above the word of God. For Luther the papacy was still what he had seen with his own eyes at Rome as a young monk, and what the hard lessons of his own lifetime had taught him of the diplomacies of the Roman curia. He had little idea of the new spir-

---

[14] See in this volume, p. 223.

[15] See in this volume, p. 211.

[16] Luther wrote these words in 1520 in the margin of a work written against him by Sylvester Prierias (*ca.* 1456-1523), a Dominican monk and official theological adviser to Pope Leo X. Luther did not formally reply to Prierias, but only reprinted the treatise, adding his own comments in the margin. Luther's version was entitled *Responsio ad Martinum Luther (per Fratrem Silvestrum de Prierio).* Cf. WA 6, 329.

itual energies at work in Italy, of the younger generation of Italian Catholics, from which new and great spiritual movements might come, or that provoked in part by his own rebellion, there were to come immense and reputable religious and theological refreshments in the Counter Reformation. For Luther popery was to the end the great *Anfechtung,* and the last months of his life show him to have been preoccupied with the ominous marshaling of sinister forces on the papal side. But also right to the end, and in this treatise with its many faults, there is the same belief in the one holy church, the same confidence in the all-conquering word. Here then is the same Luther who stood firm at the Diet of Worms. Into the roar of this old, wounded lion there enters a fiercer and more agonized note, but, as he threshes about in his wrath, there is also a prophetic note, "The lion has roared; who will not fear? Jehovah has spoken; who can but prophesy?"[17]

E. GORDON RUPP

---

[17] Amos 3:8.

LUTHER'S WORKS

VOLUME 41

ON THE COUNCILS
AND THE CHURCH

1539

Translated by Charles M. Jacobs

Revised by Eric W. Gritsch

INTRODUCTION

Luther's *On the Councils and the Church* represents his final judgment concerning the medieval church as well as the first broad foundation for a new doctrine of the church within nascent Lutheranism. Luther presents his critique of papal and conciliar authority in three parts: Part I argues that the church cannot be reformed according to the decrees of the councils and the church fathers. Part II discusses the historical significance of the apostolic council at Jerusalem (Acts 15) and the first four ecumenical councils—Nicaea (325), Constantinople (381), Ephesus (431), and Chalcedon (451). Luther concludes from his analysis that although councils protect the church from error, they have no authority to create new articles of faith. Part III deals with the true marks of the church according to Holy Scripture. Luther's earlier proposal at the Leipzig Debate in 1519[1] that pope and council be made subject to the word of God becomes an elaborate argument for a radically new concept of the church.

Experience taught Luther to bury all hopes for any reconciliation with Rome—a sad lesson, climaxing in the conviction that "a free, general, Christian council," once his dream, was never to become a reality. In his *Open Letter to the Christian Nobility*[2] of 1520 Luther had already called for such a council, but to no avail. Rome would not listen to the German heretic. After all, the reform councils of the fifteenth century, whose aim it was to curb papal authority, did not leave Rome with happy memories. First through the excommunication of Luther in 1521, then through tedious diplomacy, Rome therefore tried to rebuff all attempts to call a council. And yet, pressure from Charles V (1519-1556) and the German princes could not be endured forever. After years of negotiations, diplomatic artistry, and futile attempts to assemble it earlier, Paul III (1534-1549) finally called a council, which met in 1545 at Trent. Luther, who died shortly after the first conciliar sessions in Trent, became more and more infuriated by

---

[1] *LW* 31, 313-325.
[2] *PE* 2, 61-164.

5

Rome's tactics of delay. Since the Diet of Augsburg in 1530 and the Peace of Nürnberg in 1532 it had become evident that the Protestant cause would not receive a real hearing by pope and emperor. Still, the adherents of the *Augsburg Confession* had declared in 1530 their willingness "to participate in a general, free, and Christian council,"[3] and so in the mid-1530's when papal emissaries, among them Paul Vergerio, papal nuncio to Germany,[4] began to appear in Germany to secure Protestant participation in the council, Protestants had to decide whether or not to attend. Members of the Smalcald League agreed in 1537 to Protestant participation in the council on four conditions: (1) it must be a free, not a papal council; (2) Protestants must be invited as full participants, not as heretics; (3) its decisions must be based upon the authority of Holy Scripture and not upon that of the pope; and (4) it must be held in Germany, if at all possible.[5]

Rome, of course, never accepted these conditions. Furthermore, the hostilities between Charles V and Francis I of France (1515-1547) led to one postponement of the council after another. In June, 1536, Paul III issued a call for a council to meet in Mantua in May, 1537; in April, 1537, he postponed it until November of that same year, then until May 1, 1538, naming Vicenza as the new meeting place. The prelates did not assemble, however, and finally on May 21, 1539, the council was postponed indefinitely because the emperor was at war with France on that date.

It was under these circumstances that Luther prepared *The Smalcald Articles*, published in 1538.[6] He began to write *On the Councils and the Church* at the same time. Since 1533 he had planned to deal extensively with the history of the councils and the church.[7] In 1535 he published a small tract on the Council of

---

[3] Theodore G. Tappert (ed.), *The Book of Concord*, pp. 26-27.

[4] Paul Vergerio (1497/98-1565) visited Wittenberg in November, 1535, and had a conversation with Luther. See the detailed account in Julius Köstlin, *Martin Luther* (3rd ed.; 2 vols.; Elberfeld, 1883), II, 378-384. There is a brief summary of the meeting in E. G. Schwiebert, *Luther and His Times* (St. Louis: Concordia, 1950), p. 740.

[5] *C.R.* 2, 962.

[6] Tappert (ed.), *Book of Concord*, pp. 287-318.

[7] Cf. WA 50, 495.

Constance (1415),[8] followed by a Latin edition of three letters of John Huss and several brief statements concerning conciliar authority in general.[9] Luther's concern for a clear position with regard to conciliar authority was accompanied by a growing interest in the history of the church.[10] In 1538 he published his edited versions of the Apostles' and Athanasian Creeds, the *Te Deum*, and the Nicene Creed,[11] as well as a letter written by Jerome dealing with papal authority.[12] Then he began to work his way through almost all the available sources dealing with the history of the early and medieval church. Most of these sources are used and quoted in the treatise *On the Councils and the Church:* they are the *Ecclesiastical History* of Eusebius of Caesarea, covering the period from the apostles to Constantine the Great (324);[13] its supplementation and elaboration to the year 395 by Rufinus, entitled *The Eleven Books of Ecclesiastical History* (*Historiae Ecclesiasticae Libri XI*);[14] the *Historia Tripartita* of Cassiodorus Senator, who edited and continued these earlier works until *ca.* 560, based upon excerpts from Theodoret of Kyros, Socrates, and Sozomenus of Constantinople;[15] and the collections of the fathers and canon law.[16] In addition, Luther used the newly published two-volume work of Peter Crabbe on the councils[17] and Bartolomeo Platina's *Lives of the Popes*, written between 1471 and 1481.[18] While working on

---

[8] *Theses Against the Council of Constance* (*Sprüche Wider das Concilium Constantiense*). WA 39[1], 13-38.
[9] *Three Letters of John Huss* (*Tres Epistolae Ioannis Hussii*), which includes Luther's brief comments on councils. WA 50, 23-34.
[10] On Luther's interest in church history, see Ernst Schäfer, *Luther als Kirchenhistoriker* (Gütersloh, 1897), and John M. Headley, *Luther's View of Church History* (New Haven, Conn.: Yale University Press, 1963).
[11] *The Three Symbols.* LW 34, 197-229.
[12] *Epistola Sancti Hieronymi ad Evagrium de potestate papae cum praefatione Lutheri.* Cf. WA 50, 339-343; PNF[2] 6, 288-289.
[13] Eusebius' *Ecclesiastical History* is contained in MPG 13, 29-374, and PNF[2] 1, 73-387.
[14] Rufinus' history is contained in MPL 21, 461-540.
[15] The *Historia Tripartita* was the standard Latin textbook on church history in the Middle Ages. It is contained in MPL 69, 879-1214, and PNF[2] 2, 1-178; 2, 236-427; 3, 25-159.
[16] They are contained in MPG, MPL, and CIC.
[17] Peter Crabbe (*ca.* 1470-1553), a Franciscan monk, published his two-volume *Concilia Omnia* with Peter Quentel in Cologne in 1538.
[18] Platina (1421-1481), humanist librarian of Sixtus IV (1471-1484), described the popes from St. Peter to Paul II (d. 1471). Entitled *Historia de Vitis Pon-*

the treatise he became convinced that the flow of reliable historical sources ended at the time of the fourth ecumenical council.[19]
For this reason he treated only the first five centuries.

On March 14, 1539, Luther reported to Philip Melanchthon
that he had finished the treatise, but was not quite happy with
the way it had turned out.[20] Three German editions appeared
during the same year; the first two were printed by Hans Lufft in
Wittenberg, the third by Crafft Müller in Strassburg. A Latin edition, produced by Justas Jonas and printed in 1557 in Basel, became well known during the sixteenth and seventeenth centuries.

Although *Von den Consiliis und Kirchen* was translated *On the
Councils and the Churches* before (*PE* 5, 127), the following reasons compelled the editor to translate *Kirchen* as "church": (1) Luther used the singular in a letter to Melanchthon on March 14,
1539 (*WA*, Br 8, 391, ll. 23-24), announcing that he had finished
the treatise "on the church" (*de ecclesia*). (2) Jonas' Latin edition, which he began immediately after the first German edition
was printed, used the singular (*WA* 50, 506-507). (3) The special
edition of Part III (*Sonderdruck*) in 1540 (*WA* 50, 507) used the
singular, *von der Kirche*, as did the Wittenberg Edition of Luther's
works in 1554. (4) Finally, Luther's doctrine of the church, as he
developed it in the treatise, consistently pointed to the one, ecumenical, Christian church which is represented by all believers
rather than by pope and councils.

I want to take this opportunity to express my appreciation for
the help given by Professor E. Gordon Rupp, who wrote the introduction to this volume. I also wish to thank Frederick C. Ahrens,
who prepared the indexes, and Martin Bertram, who helped re-
translate this treatise.

Two English translations precede this one: C. B. Smyth, *Martin Luther's Authority of Councils and Churches* (London, 1847),
and the one by Charles M. Jacobs in *PE* 5, 131-300, of which this
translation is a revision. The German text is in *WA* 50, 509-653.

---

tificum, his work was incorporated into *Liber pontificalis*, the major source
book for the lives of the popes. Cf. *WA* 50, 502-504. Luther had already used
it against John Eck during the Leipzig Debate. Cf. *LW* 31, 315.

[19] See pp. 106-107.

[20] *WA*, Br 8, 391.

ON THE COUNCILS
AND THE CHURCH

I often joined in the general laughter when I saw someone offer a morsel of bread on the tip of a knife to dogs and then, as they snapped at it, slap their snouts with the knife handle, so that the poor dogs not only lost the bread but also had to suffer pain. That is a good joke. It never occurred to me at that time that the devil could also play his jokes on us and consider us such wretched dogs, until I learned how the most holy father, the pope, with his bulls, books, and daily practices plays the same kind of a dog's joke on Christendom. But, Lord God, with what great harm to the soul and with what mockery of divine majesty! It is just what he is doing with the council now: the whole world has been waiting and clamoring for it; the good emperor and his whole empire have been working to attain it for nearly twenty years;[1] and the pope has always made vain promises and put it off, offering the morsel of bread to the emperor, as to a dog, until, at the opportune moment, he slaps him on the snout while mocking him as his fool and dupe.

Now he is summoning the council for the third time;[2] but he first sends his apostles[3] into all lands to have kings and princes pledge their allegiance to the pope's doctrines. The bishops and their clergy concur in this strategy and absolutely refuse either to yield or to permit a reform, thus the [course of the] council is already determined, before it even convenes, namely, not to undertake any reforms, but to observe everything in accord with what has come to be present practice. Isn't that a splendid council?

---

[1] On November 28, 1518, Luther made his first appeal to a general council. Cf. WA 2, 34, and Schwiebert, op. cit., p. 369. The emperor and various diets had been demanding one since 1523. Thus approximately twenty years had elapsed between these demands and the time Luther wrote this statement.

[2] On October 8, 1537, Pope Paul III called a general council to meet in Vicenza in May, 1538.

[3] Between 1533 and 1538 six papal nuncios appeared in Germany to prepare for the council, including Paul Vergerio. See the Introduction, p. 6, n. 4.

It has not yet convened, and already it has done what it was to do when it met, that is, to slap the emperor on the snout, and even more, to overtake the Holy Spirit and outstrip him by far! Yet I have feared, and often written and said, that they would not and could not hold a council unless they had first captured and controlled the emperor, kings, and princes, so as to have total freedom to decree whatever they pleased, to buttress their tyranny, and to oppress Christendom with far greater burdens than ever before.

In God's name, if you lords—emperor, kings, princes—like the way in which these accursed, damned people trample on your muzzles and rap your snouts, we have to let it happen and remember that they acted much worse in the past: they deposed kings and emperors, anathematized them, drove them out, betrayed them, murdered them, and vented their devilish malice on them, as history testifies; and they intend to go on doing that. Despite this, Christ will know how to find and preserve his Christendom, even against the gates of hell [Matt. 16:18], though emperors and kings neither would nor could help in any way. He can dispense with their help much better than they can do without his. How did he get along before kings and emperors were born? And how would he get along now if no emperor or king existed, even though a whole world of devils raged against him? He is not unused to bitter fare, and he, in turn, can cook up even bitterer fare. Woe to them who must eat it!

But we poor, weak Christians, who must endure being dubbed heretics by such saints, ought to be happy and of good cheer. We ought to praise and thank God the Father of all mercy with great joy for taking such good care of us and for smiting our murderers and bloodhounds with such Egyptian blindness and such Jewish madness that they are determined to yield on no point and to let Christendom perish rather than to allow the most trifling idolatry (with which they are stuffed full and overfull) to be reformed. Of this they boast, and this they do. Cheerful (I say) we ought to be; for thus they make our case better than we could ever have desired, and make theirs worse than they now might think. They know and admit that they are wrong on many points and on top

10

of it have Scripture and God against them, and yet they want to butt their heads against God, and knowingly defend wrong as right. Thus consoled, a poor Christian should indeed be able to take the sacrament even without going to confession, and risk a hundred necks if he had them, when he sees, indeed, when he feels so palpably, that God rules on our side and the devil on theirs.

Thus we now have the final decree of the future council at Vicenza,[4] and the severe verdict of the latest (so estimable) council: the entire world is to despair of a reformation of the church, and there is to be no hearing. Instead (as they boast), they would let Christendom perish, that is, they would have the devil himself as god and lord, rather than have Christ and abandon even a small fraction of their idolatry. Not satisfied with that, they want to coerce us poor Christians with the sword to consciously worship the devil with them and to blaspheme Christ. Such defiance has neither been recorded nor heard of in all of history. Other tyrants at least have the dubious honor of crucifying the Lord of majesty unknowingly, as do the Turks, heathen, and Jews. But here they are, who in Christ's name and as Christians, indeed, as the most select Christians, boast and arm themselves against Christ, saying, "We know that Christ's words and deeds are against us; nevertheless, we refuse to tolerate or yield to his word. Indeed, he must yield to us and tolerate our idolatry; even so we want to be Christians and to be known as such."

So, since the pope, with his following, simply refuses to convoke a council and reform the church, or offer any advice or assistance toward that end, but boastfully defends his tyranny with crimes, preferring to let the church go to ruin, we, so shamefully forsaken by the pope, cannot go on and must seek counsel and help elsewhere and first of all seek and ask our Lord Jesus Christ for a reformation. These desperate tyrants, whose evil forces us to despair of a council and of a reformation, must not drive us also to despair of Christ or to leave the church without counsel and help; we must instead do what we can, and let them go to the devil as they wish.

---

4 See the Introduction, p. 6.

Herewith they testify and cry, to their own perdition, that they are the true Antichrists and "autocatacrites"[5] who condemn themselves and obstinately insist on their own damnation. They thereby exclude themselves from the church and boast publicly that they want to be and to remain the church's most bitter foes. For he who says that he would rather let the church perish than mend his ways or yield on any point confesses clearly and publicly that he is not only no Christian desirous of being in the church (which he would rather allow to founder so that he might survive and not sink with the church), but that he is also willing to contribute to the church's destruction—as they prove so horribly with their deeds over and above their words, permitting hundreds of parishes to lie waste and churches to die without shepherd, sermon, and sacrament.

In times past the bishops, and indeed every Christian (even as at present), let themselves be tortured and went to their deaths gratefully and cheerfully for the dear church. Christ himself died for his church, to preserve and sustain it. But the pope and his following now boast that the church must die for them, so that they may be preserved in their tyranny, idolatry, knavery, and every villainy. What do you think of these fellows? They want to remain, so the church must go. How are we to know what's what? But if the church is to perish, then Christ, upon whom it is built as upon a rock against the gates of hell [Matt. 16:18], must perish first. If Christ is to perish, then God himself, who has established this rock and foundation, must perish first. Who could have suspected these lords to have such great power that the church, together with Christ and God himself, should perish so easily before their threats? They must be far, far mightier than the gates of hell and all devils, against whom the church has prevailed and must now prevail.

Thus they scream (I say) about themselves that they neither want to be the church nor be in the church, but that they want to be the church's worst enemies and help it go to ruin. Yet until now they have pestered and harassed us with the word, "Church! Church!" There has been no limit or end to their shouting and

---

[5] From the Greek *autokatakritos*, "self-condemned." See Titus 3:11.

spitting that they should be regarded as the church; and they charged us miserably with heresy, they cursed us and murdered us because we refused to hear them as the church. Now, I am sure, we are honestly and mightily absolved so that they will not and cannot call us heretics any longer, for they no longer wish to be glorified as the church, but as enemies of the church want to let it be destroyed, even lending a hand in its suppression. It is incongruous for them to be the church and, simultaneously, to let the church perish rather than perish themselves, indeed, to have a hairsbreadth of themselves perish. This is what the passage means, "I will condemn you out of your own mouth, you wicked servant" [Luke 19:22].

If the Last Day were not close at hand, it would be no wonder if heaven and earth were to crumble because of such blasphemy. However, since God is able to endure this, this day cannot be far off.[6] But they laugh about all that, forgetting that God has made them blind, mad, raving, and foolish, esteeming it as great wisdom and manliness. I, too, would feel as secure as they feel, if only their innocent blindness spoke in their actions; but the great wrath of God, revealed in them, terrifies me profoundly. It is high time for all of us to weep and to pray earnestly, as Christ wept over Jerusalem and commanded the women not to weep over him but to weep over themselves and their children [Luke 23:28]. For they do not believe that the time of their affliction is at hand, and they do not want to believe it, even though they can see it, hear it, smell it, taste it, touch it, and feel it.

How should one act in the future, now that the pope will neither accord us a genuine council nor tolerate any reform, but, together with his followers, is willing to let the church perish? He put himself out of the church to save himself and not perish in and with the church. He is gone and has bidden the church farewell! So what (I say) should one do or undertake now that we are to be without a pope? For we are the church, or in the church, which the papists are willing to let go to ruin so that they might survive. We too would like to survive, and are resolved, together with our Lord Jesus and his Father, the God of us all, not

---

[6] On Luther's belief that the Last Day was close at hand, see pp. 244-245.

to go under miserably before the defiance of the papists. We see the necessity for a council or a reformation in the church, for we see such gross abuses that even if we were oxen or asses—not to speak of human beings or Christians—and could not perceive these abuses with our eyes or ears, we should still have[7] to feel them with our paws and hoofs and stumble over them. What if we ourselves, the church destined to perish, were to hold a council against the abiding lords, without the pope and without their consent, and undertook a reformation which would appear quite transitory to these abiding squires, but which they nonetheless would have to put up with?[8] But we want to come to the point of our discussion, since we have now lost the most holy head, the pope, and have to take as much counsel with ourselves as our Lord may grant.

Part I

Many of the papists occupied themselves for years with the councils and the fathers, until they finally gathered all councils into one book, which appeals to me, since I never before found all the councils together.[9] Now there are (in my opinion) several good, pious souls who would have liked to see the church reformed on the pattern of these same councils and fathers, as they too are aware that the present position of the church in the papacy is woefully at variance (as is evident) with the ways of the councils and the fathers. But in this case their good opinion is of no avail, for they undoubtedly have the idea that the pope, with his following, would or should participate in such a reformation. That, however, is fruitless, for here stands the pope, with his abiding lords, declaring obstinately to them as well as to us that they would rather let the church perish than yield on one single point; that is, they would sooner let councils and fathers perish too than give in to them in any way. If councils and fathers were to be obeyed— for God's sake!—what would become of the pope and the present- day bishops? Indeed, they would have to become the church des-

---

[7] *Müsten.*

[8] John Frederick of Saxony (1532-1547) had suggested such a plan. Cf. *C.R.* 3, 141.

[9] I.e., the decisions of the councils, a reference to Peter Crabbe's work on the councils. See the Introduction, p. 7, n. 17.

14

tined to perish, and would no longer be the abiding lords.

I shall pass over the ancient years, the period encompassing a thousand or fourteen hundred years after the birth of Christ, in silence. It is not more than one hundred years ago that the pope adopted the holy practice of bestowing two benefices, such as canonries or parishes, on one priest,[10] about which the Parisian theologians and their associates grumbled and wrote many terrible things.[11] I am not yet sixty years old; nevertheless, I know that within my time it has become customary for a bishop to have more than one diocese.[12] But meanwhile the pope has devoured everything, stolen annates and everything else, distributed dioceses by threes, abbeys and prebends by tens and twenties. How can he regurgitate all this and dissolve his chancellory for the sake of the fathers and the councils? Yes, you say, it is an abuse. Very well, then, take your ancient councils and fathers to heart and reform all this; for it was not like this a hundred years ago, indeed, not even sixty years ago, before you were born.

Now of what use is your reformation according to the fathers and councils? You hear that the pope and the bishops will not tolerate it. And if they cannot tolerate the condition of the church as it existed fifty years ago, when you and I were children, my dear man, how will or can they tolerate our proposal to reform the church by restoring it to its condition of six hundred or a thousand or fourteen hundred years ago? Such a proposal is simply impossible, since the pope is in control and wants to remain unreformed. Therefore we must admit that councils and fathers are powerless in these matters, and so is anything we can say or think about them; for the pope is above councils, above fathers, above kings, above God, above angels. Let me see you depose him and

---

[10] Luther had listed such abuses in *An Open Letter to the Christian Nobility* (1520). See especially *PE* 2, 93-94.

[11] In the fourteenth and fifteenth centuries the University of Paris was the center of conciliarism. Luther may have been referring to John of Paris, who criticized papal authority in *On Regal and Papal Power* (*De Potestate Regia et Papalia*) at the beginning of the fourteenth century. J. Leclercq (ed.), *De Potestate Regia et Papalia* (Paris, 1942). Cf. Walter Ullmann, *The Growth of Papal Government in the Middle Ages* (2nd ed.; London, 1962), p. 385, n. 5.

[12] Cardinal Albrecht of Mainz (1490-1545) held two archbishoprics and one bishopric at the same time. Cf. *LW* 31, 21.

make the fathers and councils his masters! If you do that, I shall gladly join you and assist you. But as long as that does not happen, what is the use of your talking or writing much about councils and fathers? There is no one to take this matter to heart. If the pope, together with his abiding lords, cardinals, bishops, etc., is unwilling to participate in the reformation or to submit to the councils and the fathers with us, there is no use for a council, nor can we hope for a reformation from him, because he will knock down everything anyway and bid us to keep silent.

But do they desire that we, together with them, let ourselves be reformed according to the councils and fathers, and thus help the church, even though the pope with his followers would neither do it nor permit it? To this I give a double answer. Either they are hateful, poisonous, and evil, and do this with bad intent; or they are goodhearted and mean well (as far as this is possible for them). Let the former be told to first take themselves by the nose and remove the log from their own eye [Matt. 7:3-5], then, together with pope and cardinals, or without the pope and cardinals, etc., to grow fond of the councils and fathers and hold to them. When that happens we shall instantly be on hand to emulate such a holy example, and be much better than they are. We are not such accursed people (praise and thank God!) that we would let the church perish rather than yield even on major points, as long as they are not against God; on the contrary, if it depends on our knowledge and ability, we are prepared to perish leaving neither hide nor hair behind, rather than to see the church suffer harm or loss.

But when they themselves pay the fathers and councils no heed and yet would force us to do so, they go too far, and we have to say, "Physician, heal thyself!" [Luke 4:23], and, as Christ says, "They bind heavy burdens, hard to bear, and lay them on men's shoulders; but they themselves will not move them with their finger" [Matt. 23:4]. That leads to nothing, and we have ample reason for refusal, especially since they make such great claims for the sanctity of the fathers and councils, which we do not uphold; nor do they, except with words they speak and write only to flaunt before us. Yet we confess, and must confess, that we are very poor, weak Christians on many points.

16

First, we have so much to do in our faith, day and night, what with reading, thinking, writing, teaching, exhorting, and comforting both ourselves and others that there is indeed neither time nor space left even to wonder whether there ever were councils or fathers, much less to concern ourselves with such sublime things as crowns,[13] chasubles, long robes, etc., and with their profound sanctity. If they have risen so far that they have even become angels, and have so much faith that the devil must leave them alone and cannot let an error loose among them, or terrify a timid conscience, we weak Christians have not yet attained this, and fear that we never shall attain it on earth. That is why they should be gracious and merciful with us and not condemn us because we cannot match their holiness yet. If we should leave our work in matters of faith and, weak as we are, dare their great holiness in dress and food, we might forsake our weak holiness and still not attain their high and splendid holiness, thus sitting down between two chairs.[14]

But if they decline to be gracious and merciful with us, we shall have to let them be angels and dance among the flowers in Paradise as those who have long since mastered faith and no longer experience any temptation from devil, flesh, or world in their celestial sanctity. But we must plague ourselves and wallow in mire and filth, as poor abecedarians and beginners, unable to be such great doctors and masters in faith. For if we had as much faith as they imagine they have, we would bear and hold to crowns, chasubles, councils, and fathers more easily than they do. But this is not so; they bear them easily (for to bear nothing is to bear very easily), meanwhile boasting that we do not want to bear them.

Likewise, the Ten Commandments occupy us poor Christians so much that we are unable to attend to other exalted works that they praise as spiritual, conciliar, and patristic. With utmost diligence we urge and discipline both ourselves and our followers to love God above all things and our neighbor as ourselves, to be

---

[13] *Platten.* Cf. Luther's marginal notes in his edition of the *Donation of Constantine* (1537). WA 50, 72. Cf. also in this volume, p. 287, n. 58.

[14] A German proverb, *"Zwischen Zweien stülen nidersitzen,"* which means roughly "to fall on one's face." Cf. Ernst Thiele, *Luthers Sprichwörtersammlung* (Weimar, 1900), No. 114.

humble and patient, merciful and kind, chaste and sober, neither covetous nor envious, and whatever else God's commandments enjoin. We should be happy if there were no pride, avarice, usury, envy, drunkenness, gluttony, adultery, or wantonness among our people. But there is so much weakness and imperfection among us that we induce but a few to do these good works. The masses remain unchanged and grow worse day by day. Now figure it out: if we are so unsuccessful in doing these necessary works commanded by God, how can we abandon these and devote ourselves to those sublime, splendid, unnecessary works of which they tell us?

If we had done these divine, insignificant, contemptible, or, as they disdainfully call them, "civil" works,[15] then, God willing, we would also begin to do their spiritual, ecclesiastical works having to do with eating meat, dress, certain days, etc.

But it is easy for them because they keep all of God's commandments, love God above all things, are neither avaricious nor usurious, neither adulterers nor whoremongers, neither boozers nor drunkards, neither proud nor envious, etc.; but they perform all these insignificant, good, divine works so easily they are downright idle. Therefore it is only right that they undertake, over and above our "civil" works, stronger and greater works in obedience to the church or the fathers, for they are far too strong to practice such insignificant, good works with us, having outstripped and outdistanced us by far. But according to their profound, great compassion and St. Paul's doctrine, they should nevertheless pity us weak, poor Christians and not condemn or mock us because we, like infants, learn to walk by toddling along holding on to chairs, indeed, we crawl in the mud and cannot skip and dance so nimbly over and around God's commandments as they do—these strong heroes and giants who can tackle greater and sublimer tasks than that of loving God above all things and one's neighbor as oneself, which St. Paul calls the fulfilment of the law in Romans 13 [:10], as Christ also does in Matthew 5 [:19].

But if they will not have pity on us, we nevertheless ask for a

---

15 Cf. *The Augsburg Confession*, Art. XXVI. Tappert (ed.), *Book of Concord*, pp. 63-70.

time of grace until we have carried out God's commandments and the unimportant children's works. After that we will be glad to switch to their sublime, spiritual, knightly, and manly works. For what good would it do to force a child to work and keep pace with a strong man? It wouldn't work—a child is unable to do it. So we poor, weak Christians, who with regard to God's commandments and his insignificant good works totter along the chairs like children and at times can hardly crawl on all fours, indeed, even slide along the ground, and must be held by Christ on leading-strings as a mother or nurse holds a child—we simply cannot keep pace with their strong, manly gait and performance, and may God preserve us from it! Therefore we shall save the ecclesiastical and conciliar holiness (as they call it) until we have no more work to do on God's commandments and divine works, and not bear a reformation we cannot bear. May this be a sufficient answer to the former class of people who with bad intentions ask this reformation of us.

To the others, who mean well and hope, albeit vainly, that a fine reformation such as they have in mind might perhaps still be achieved on the basis of the councils and fathers, even despite an unwilling pope's attempt to thwart it, I reply, also with good intent, that I regard this as an impossible undertaking, and indeed do not know how to go about it. I, too, read the fathers, even before I opposed the pope so decisively. I also read them with greater diligence than those who now quote them so defiantly and haughtily against me; for I know that none of them attempted to read a book of Holy Scripture in school, or to use the writings of the fathers as an aid, as I did. Let them take a book of Holy Scripture and seek out the glosses[16] of the fathers; then they will share the experience I had when I worked on the letter to the Hebrews with St. Chrysostom's glosses, the letter to Titus and the letter to the Galatians with the help of St. Jerome, Genesis with the help of St. Ambrose and St. Augustine, the Psalter with all the writers available, and so on.[17] I have read more than they

---

[16] Comments on biblical passages.

[17] Luther refers here to the period between 1513 and 1517 when he was engaged in an intensive study of biblical and patristic literature. See Köstlin, *Martin Luther*, I, 107-122, and Schwiebert, *op. cit.*, pp. 278-302.

think, and have worked my way through all the books; this makes them appear impudent indeed who imagine that I did not read the fathers and who want to recommend them to me as something precious, the very thing that I was forced to devaluate twenty years ago when I read the Scriptures.

St. Bernard[18] declares that he learned his wisdom from the trees, such as oaks and pines, which were his teachers; that is, he conceived his ideas from Scripture and pondered them under the trees. He adds that he regards the holy fathers highly, but does not heed all their sayings, explaining why in the following parable: he would rather drink from the spring itself than from the brook, as do all men, who once they have a chance to drink from the spring forget about the brook, unless they use the brook to lead them to the spring. Thus Scripture, too, must remain master and judge, for when we follow the brooks too far, they lead us too far away from the spring, and lose both their taste and nourishment, until they lose themselves in the salty sea, as happened under the papacy.

But enough of that! We want to cite reasons such an undertaking is impossible. First, it is obvious that the councils are not only unequal, but also contradictory. The same is true of the fathers. If we should try to bring them into accord with one another, far greater discord and disputes would ensue than we have at present, and we would never get out of it. Since (in these matters) they are very unlike and often contradictory, we should first have to figure a way to cull out the best and let the rest drop. That would provoke an uproar. The one would say, "If we are going to keep them, then we must keep them in their entirety or not at all." The other would say, "Well, you pick out what you like and leave what you dislike." Who would be the judge here?

Look at the decree with which Gratian[19] had proposed to do

18 Bernard of Clairvaux (1090-1153), Benedictine abbot and famed mystic. This passage could not be located in Bernard's works. On Luther's attitude toward Bernard, see Walther Köhler, *Luther und die Kirchengeschichte nach Seinen Schriften* (Erlangen, 1900), pp. 320-333.
19 The *Decretum* of Gratian, a Benedictine canonist at the law school of the University of Bologna. It originated in *ca.* 1140 and represents the first part of Roman Catholic canon law (*CIC* 1), accepted as such by Pope Gregory IX (1228-1241) in 1234, whose *Decretalium* became the second part of canon law

this very thing—the book thus becoming known as *Concordantia Discordantiarum*—that is, he had wanted to compare the discordant statements of the fathers and the councils, to reconcile the contradictions, and to cull out the best. He succeeded, like a crab walks; he often cast aside the best and kept the worst, and yet he neither compared nor harmonized. As the jurists themselves say, it stinks of ambition and avarice, and a canonist is nothing but an ass.[20] How much worse then would we fare if we tried to harmonize all the words and deeds of fathers and councils! All our labor and trouble would be futile, and the evil would only be aggravated.[21] And I do not wish to become involved in such a dispute because I am well aware that it would be interminable and in the end we would be stuck with a vain, uncertain thing, at the expense of wasted time and labor. These young scribblers[22] are much too untried when they think that whatever they read and imagine must be so, and all the world must worship it, although they neither know the *a b c* of Scripture, nor are they versed in the councils and fathers. They shout and sputter without knowing what they are saying or writing.

I shall say no more of Gratian. St. Augustine writes to Januarius[23] that the church in his day, three hundred years after the birth of Christ (for in this year 1539 he has been dead for eleven hundred and two years),[24] was already so encumbered on all sides with the ordinances of the bishops that even the Jewish political system was more tolerable. And he continues clearly and plainly with the words, *"Innumerabilibus servilibus oneribus premunt ecclesiam,"*[25] that is, "They oppress the church with innumerable bur-

---

(*CIC* 2). Luther studied it during his stay in Erfurt and in preparation for the Leipzig Debate in 1519.

[20] The saying cannot be documented. Cf. the poem Luther composed about a similar saying in *WA* 39, 20.

[21] A German proverb, *"Übel erger machen."* Cf. Thiele, *Luthers Sprichwörtersammlung*, No. 478.

[22] *Papirklicker*, i.e., "paper-clippers."

[23] Augustine (354-430), bishop of Hippo, whose writings Luther esteemed. He often cites this letter to Januarius. *Epistola* 82. *MPL* 33, 221; *PNF*[1] 1, 315.

[24] Augustine died in 436 according to medieval chronology. Luther's chronological sources are not quite correct. See p. 23, n. 36, and Schäfer, *op. cit.*, p. 103.

[25] Luther has added *innumerabilibus* and *ecclesiam* to the original text.

dens," while the Jews are burdened only by God and not by men, etc. He also states that Christ desired to have only a few easy ceremonies imposed on his church, namely, baptism and the sacrament;[26] he mentions no more than these two, as every one may read. The books are available, so no one can accuse me of inventing this.

But he also weakens this, saying in the same place, *"Hoc genus habet liberas observationes,"*[27] that is, "No one is obligated to keep all of these, but may ignore them without sin." If St. Augustine is not a heretic here, I never will be one. He who takes the statements of many bishops and many churches and throws the whole pile into the fire, pointing solely to baptism and sacrament, makes certain that Christ did not wish to impose any other burdens on the church—if that which is nothing but comfort and grace could be called a burden—when he says, "My yoke is easy, and my burden light" [Matt. 11:30], that is, my yoke is peace and my burden is joy.

Yet this fine, sensible man does the great, or (as they are called) universal or principal, councils the honor of differentiating them from the other councils and the ordinances of all bishops, saying that one should esteem them, and he writes in the same place that one should reasonably obey the decrees of these great principal councils, since much depends on them; if I may use his own words, *saluberrima autoritas*, that is, it is very useful to regard them as authoritative.[28] But he neither saw any of these great principal councils nor attended any of them, otherwise he would perhaps have written differently, or more, about them. For not more than four great principal councils are famous and well known in all the books. The Roman bishops compare these to the four gospels, as they loudly proclaim in their decretals.[29] The first is the Nicene council, held in Nicaea, in Asia, in the fifteenth year of the reign of Constantine the Great,[30] almost thirty-five years

---

[26] The eucharist. *MPL* 33, 200; *PNF*[1] 1, 300.

[27] *MPL* 33, 200; *PNF*[1] 1, 300.

[28] *MPL* 33, 200; *PNF*[1] 1, 300.

[29] Cf. *Decreti Prima Pars*, dist. V, C. II. *CIC* 1, 35; *MPL* 187, 71-79.

[30] The year 325. Constantine the Great ruled from 306 to 337.

before Augustine's birth.[31] The second was held in Constantinople,[32] in the third year of the emperors Gratian and Theodosius I, who ruled jointly.[33] St. Augustine was still a pagan and
no Christian at that time, a man approximately twenty-six years
old, so he could not concern himself with these matters. He did
not live to see the third council held at Ephesus,[34] still less the
fourth one at Chalcedon.[35] All of this is reliable; it is based on
history and a computation of the years.[36]

I had to say these things in order to make sure that the
meaning of St. Augustine's statement that the great principal councils must be regarded as authoritative by reason of their importance is understood properly; namely, that he was speaking of only
the two councils, held at Nicaea and Constantinople, which he had
not attended, but about which he later learned from writings. At
that time no bishop was superior to any other, for neither the Roman nor the other bishops could ever have brought such councils
about if the emperor had not convoked them, as is well evidenced
by the particular, or small, councils held now and then in the
different countries by the bishops themselves, without a summons
from the emperor. I judge, in my foolishness, that the great principal councils derive their name from the fact that the bishops
were summoned from all the countries by the monarch, the great
chief or universal ruler.[37]

History will have to bear me out, even though all the papists
get mad, that if Emperor Constantine had not convoked the first
council at Nicaea, the Roman bishop Sylvester[38] would have been
obliged to leave it unconvoked. And what could the wretched

[31] Augustine was born in 361 according to medieval chronology. Cf. Schäfer,
op. cit., p. 103; p. 289, nn. 3, 4.
[32] In 381.
[33] Gratian (375-383) and Theodosius I (379-395).
[34] In 431.
[35] In 451.
[36] Luther's chronological computations are based upon the work of John Carion,
a mathematician, who published a chronology of world history with the help of
Philip Melanchthon in 1532 in Wittenberg. In 1541 Luther published his *Supputatio Annorum Mundi*. WA 53, 22-172; cf. Headley, op. cit., pp. 109-111.
[37] Cf. Melanchthon's *Treatise on the Power and Primacy of the Pope*. Tappert
(ed.), *Book of Concord*, pp. 329-330.
[38] Sylvester I (314-337).

bishop of Rome do, since the bishops in Asia and Greece were not subject to him? And even if he could have done it without the power of the emperor Constantine, he would not have had it meet in Nicaea, in Asia, so far across the sea, where no one respected his authority (as he well knew and had experienced), but in Italy, near Rome, or somewhere else nearby; and he would have forced the emperor to come there. I say the same about the other three councils (named above). If the emperors Gratian, Theodosius, Theodosius II,[39] and Marcian[40] had not assembled these three great councils, they would never have been held for the sake of the bishop of Rome or all the other bishops; for the bishops in other countries valued the Roman bishop just as little as the bishops of Mainz, Trier, and Cologne at present value each other in the matter of authority—indeed much less!

Yet one sees in the histories that the Roman bishops have from the first sickened, ailed, wheezed, and gasped for sovereignty over all the bishops, but could not achieve it because of the monarchs. For even before the Nicene council they wrote many letters,[41] sometimes to Asia, sometimes to Africa, and so on, demanding that nothing should be publicly decreed without the Roman See. But no one paid any attention to this at the time, and the bishops in Africa, Asia, and Egypt proceeded as though they had not heard it, although they addressed him with many fine words and humbled themselves, without, however, conceding anything. This is what you will find when you read the histories[42] and compare them diligently. But you must pay no heed to their clamor or that of their adulators; rather, keep eyes and mind fixed on the story and the text.

Since the word "council" now enjoyed the profound respect of Christians throughout the world—partly because of the above-mentioned letter of Augustine—and since these fine monarchs or emperors had died, the Roman bishops constantly strove to associate the name "council" with themselves so that all Christendom

---

[39] Theodosius II (408-450).
[40] Marcian (450-458). Theodosius II and Marcian ruled over the Eastern half of the Roman Empire.
[41] This is specifically mentioned in Peter Crabbe's work on the councils.
[42] The histories used by Luther. See p. 7.

would have to believe what they said, and so that they themselves might secretly become monarchs with the help of this fine name (I wager that I am here hitting the truth and also their own conscience, if they could have a conscience). And it has come to pass; they have brought it about with their ailing and gasping, so that they have now become Constantine, Gratian, Theodosius, Marcian, and much more than these four monarchs and their four great principal councils. For now the pope's councils mean, "I will it; I command it; my will is the reason for it."[43] But [this is not the case] in the entire world, nor in all of Christendom, [it is the case] only in that part of the Roman Empire over which Charles the Great[44] ruled, through whom they attained and accomplished very much, until possessed by all the devils they shamefully murdered, kicked, and in many ways betrayed several emperors—as they still do wherever they can.[45]

But this is enough for now about St. Augustine's comment on the councils. We also want to show what he thought of the fathers. In his letter to St. Jerome, also quoted by Gratian in dist. IX, he says about them: "I have learned to hold the Scriptures alone inerrant. Therefore I read all the others, as holy and learned as they may be, with the reservation that I regard their teaching true only if they can prove their statements through Scripture or reason."[46] Furthermore, in the same section of the *Decretum* is St. Augustine's statement from the preface to his book *On the Trinity:* "My dear man, do not follow my writing as you do Holy Scripture. Instead, whatever you find in Holy Scripture that you would not have believed before, believe without doubt. But in my writings you should regard nothing as certain that you were uncertain about before, unless I have proved its truth."[47]

---

[43] *Sic volo, sic iubeo, sit pro ratione voluntas.* A satirical proverb by Juvenal (*ca.* 60-*ca.* 135), a Roman poet. Cf. *Satura* VI, 223. G. G. Ramsey (trans.), *Juvenal and Persius* ("The Loeb Classical Library" [New York: Putman, 1918]), p. 101.

[44] Charlemagne (768-814).

[45] A reference to the humiliations put upon the Holy Roman emperors by the popes.

[46] Jerome (*ca.* 345-420), translator of the Vulgate and renowned church father. The quotation is found in *MPL* 33, 277; *PNF*[1] 1, 350. Cf. also *Decreti Prima Pars,* dist. IX, C. V. *CIC* 1, 17.

[47] *On the Trinity* (*De Trinitate*), III, 2. *MPL* 42, 869; *PNF*[1] 3, 56.

Many more such statements are found in his other writings; as when he says, "As I read the books of others, so I wish mine read," etc.[48] I shall let the other sayings wait for now; the papists know very well that many similar passages appear here and there in Augustine's writings, and that several of these are contained in the *Decretum*. Yet against their conscience they ignore or suppress these sayings and set the fathers, the councils, indeed, even the bishops of Rome, who by and large were very unlearned men, above all of this. St. Augustine must have felt many a shortcoming in the fathers who preceded him, because he wants to be free, and have all of them, including himself, subjected to the Holy Scriptures. Why should he have needed to be so declinatory toward his forefathers, saying, ". . . as holy and learned as they may be"? He surely could have said, "Indeed, everything they write I put on a level with Holy Scripture because they are so holy and learned." However, he says no, as he also says in the other letter to St. Jerome, who was furious because St. Augustine disapproved of one point in his commentary on Galatians, "Dear brother" (for he was such a fine, friendly man), "I hope that you do not expect your books to be regarded as equal to those of the apostles and prophets," etc.[49] May a pious and good man never write letters to me like those St. Augustine addressed to St. Jerome, asking me not to regard my books as the equal of those of the apostles and prophets! I would be ashamed to death. But it is this with which we are dealing now, and which St. Augustine clearly observed: the fathers were occasionally very human, and had not overcome what is written in the seventh chapter of Romans. Therefore he does not want to trust either his predecessors the holy and learned fathers or himself, and undoubtedly his successors much less, who very likely would be less trustworthy; but instead he wants to have Scripture as master and judge, just as it was related earlier of St. Bernard, that oaks and pines were his masters and that he would rather drink from the spring than from the brook.[50] He would not have spoken like this

---

[48] In the letter to Jerome. *MPL* 33, 277; *PNF*[1] 1, 350.
[49] *MPL* 33, 277. Cf. *Preface to the Wittenberg Edition of Luther's German Writings. LW* 34, 285.
[50] Cf. p. 20.

if he had regarded the books of the fathers the equals of Holy Scripture and had found no flaw in them. Then he would have said instead, "It is the same whether I drink from the Scriptures or from the fathers." He does not do that, but rather lets the brooks flow and drinks from the spring.

What should we do now? If we should take the church back to the teaching and ways of the fathers and the councils, there stands St. Augustine to confuse us and thwart our plan because under no circumstances does he want reliance placed on the fathers, bishops, councils, as learned and holy as they may be, or on himself. Instead, he directs us to Holy Scripture. Outside of that, so he says, all is uncertain, lost, and in vain. But if we exclude St. Augustine, then it conflicts with our purpose, namely, to have a church according to the teachings of the fathers. For when St. Augustine is eliminated from the ranks of the fathers, the others are not worth much. Moreover, it would be senseless and intolerable not to consider St. Augustine one of the best fathers, since he is revered as the best by all of Christendom, and both schools and churches have preserved his memory above that of all others, as is clearly seen. And yet you force on us the endless trouble and labor of holding up councils and fathers against Scripture and living accordingly. Before that is done we shall all be dead and the Last Day will have long since come!

Well, we shall set aside St. Augustine, St. Bernard, and all others who write in the same vein, and take up the fathers and councils ourselves to see whether we can make our lives conform to them. But we shall take up the very best ones, lest we draw this out too long, particularly the first two principal councils praised by St. Augustine, namely, those of Nicaea and Constantinople, although he did not attend them, as we said above. Indeed, to play absolutely safe, and so that we cannot fail or worry, we shall take up the very first council of the apostles,[51] held in Jerusalem, of which St. Luke writes in Acts, chapters 15 [:1-29] and 16 [:4]. It is written there that the apostles boasted that the Holy Spirit had arranged this through them: *"Visum est Spiritui sancto et nobis,"* etc., "It has seemed good to the Holy Spirit and

---

[51] This apostolic council took place in *ca.* 44 or 45.

to us to lay upon you no greater burden than these necessary things: that you abstain from what has been sacrificed to idols and from blood and from what is strangled and from unchastity. If you keep yourselves from these, you will do well" [Acts 15:28-29].

There we hear that the Holy Spirit (as the preachers of councils boast) commands that we eat nothing that has been sacrificed to idols, no blood, and nothing that is strangled. Now if we want to have a church that conforms to this council (as is right, since it is the first and foremost council, and was held by the apostles themselves), we must teach and insist that henceforth no prince, lord, burgher, or peasant eat geese, doe, stag, or pork cooked in blood, and that they also abstain from carp jelly, for there is blood in them, or, as cooks call it, "color."[52] And burghers and peasants must abstain especially from red sausage and blood sausage, for that is not only fluid blood, but also congealed and cooked blood, a very coarse-grained blood. Likewise we are forbidden to eat rabbits and birds, for these are all strangled (according to hunting customs),[53] even if they were only fried, not cooked in blood.

Should we, in obedience to this council, refrain from blood, then we shall let the Jews become our masters in our churches and kitchens; for they have an especially large book on the subject of eating blood,[54] so large that no one could vault over it with a pole. They look for blood so painstakingly that they will not eat meat with any heathen or Christian—even if it is not strangled, but butchered most meticulously (like oxen or calves), drained of blood, and washed—preferring to die. For God's sake, what harried Christians we would become because of that council, just with the two items of eating blood and the meat of strangled animals! Well then, begin, anyone who wants to or can, to bring Christendom into conformity with this council; I shall then be glad to fol-

---

[52] *Farbe.*

[53] A reference to snares.

[54] Luther probably read the Babylonian Talmud, which had been available since 1523 in an edition printed by Daniel Bomburg in Venice. Cf. I. Epstein (trans.), *The Babylonian Talmud* (34 vols.; London, 1935-1948). Examples of the subject are in *Hullin,* chap. 2.

low. If not, I want to be spared the screams of "Councils! Councils! You neither heed the councils nor the fathers!" Or I will counter with the cry, "You yourselves do not heed the councils or the fathers, since you disdain even the supreme council and the supreme fathers, the apostles. Do you think I should or must heed councils and fathers you yourself do not as much as touch with one finger?" I would only say, as I said to the Sabbatarians,[55] that they should keep their Mosaic law first, and then we would keep it too. But now that they neither keep it nor are able to keep it, it is ridiculous that they expect us to keep it.

If you say it is impossible to carry out the decrees of such a council now because the contrary has spread too far, it is of no help, since we resolved to conform to the councils, and it says here that the Holy Spirit has so commanded it. Against the Holy Spirit no spreading or entrenching counts, and no conscience is safe with such a subterfuge. If we wish to be conciliar, we will have to keep this council above all others. If not, we need not keep any of the other councils either, and thus we are rid of all the councils. For in this council there were no ordinary bishops and fathers (as in the others), but the apostles themselves, assured of the Holy Spirit and the most exalted of the fathers. Furthermore, it is not so impossible for us not to eat blood and strangled animals. How would it be if we had to live solely on grain, cabbages, beets, apples, and all the other fruits of the earth and the trees, as our ancestors did before the Deluge, when the eating of meat was not yet permitted?[56] We would still not starve, even though we did not eat meat or fish. How many people have to live today on a diet rare in meat and fish! So the impossibility does not help us at all to strengthen our conscience against the Holy Spirit because we could quite well revert, without harm to body or soul, to a fare not only free of blood or strangled animals, in accordance with the teaching of Moses, but also fishless and meatless, as before the Deluge. I am very surprised anyway that the devil did not bring to light among so many quarrelsome

---

[55] Jews or Christians obeying only Jewish laws. Cf. *Against the Sabbatarians* (*Wider die Sabbather*) (1538). *WA* 50, 312-337.

[56] Gen. 7:11-24. Luther assumed that all animals were prohibited as food before the Flood.

spirits of today these beautiful ideas that have so many fine examples from Scripture on their side!

If we were to say that all these things are not only impossible, but also that they have fallen of themselves, either through disuse or nonuse, or, as I am wont to call the canons no longer applicable, *mortuos*,[57] it would not stand the test either. I know very well that the pope and his followers look for excuses like this to justify themselves, claiming that the church had the authority to alter such a council of the apostles. Yet they lie, for they cannot produce proof of any church that has done this or ordered any change. Therefore it does not behoove the church to alter the ordinances of the Holy Spirit, and it no longer does so.

Besides, these "blind leaders" [Matt. 15:14] do not see that they invite a switch for their own hide with such talk. For if we concede that man has the power to change the Holy Spirit's ordinance and commandment, we shall on the same day swiftly kick the pope with all his encyclicals and bulls, saying, "If the first decree of the apostles is not valid, though we are convinced that it was issued by the Holy Spirit, as they themselves boast, 'it is clear,'[58] how much less valid are the power and the decrees of the pope, since we are nowhere near as certain that the Holy Spirit is with them as he was with the apostles." For we will nevertheless have to grant the apostles some status too; and if they were not above the popes (as the heretic, Dr. Luther, believes), they should at least be assigned a seat next to the popes. And the popes often were truly vile scoundrels, repeatedly repudiating each other's decrees. As the Holy Spirit cannot contradict himself like this, and as the apostles could not have been such popes or scoundrels, it follows that we have to argue differently. Such rotten obscenities will not do it, unless one wished to say that the church is built upon a reed that the wind blows to and fro, depending on the whim of the pope or of other men. The church must not sway on a reed, but should stand on a rock and be firmly founded—Matthew 7 [:25] and 16 [:18].

---

[57] "Dead."

[58] *Visum est.* Luther's opponents often summed up their arguments against him by saying, "It is clear, it is clear."

30

But as we started to say, it fell of itself, with no changes by the church; that is why we don't have to keep it anymore. Well, dear friend, *Male*,[59] says the jurist—should one not keep a law or should it become invalid simply because it is no longer observed or because it has fallen into disuse? Then let us enjoy ourselves and disregard all laws! Let a whore say that she is right because the sixth commandment has fallen and is no longer in use among adulterers and adulteresses. Yes, we children of Adam shall, with the devils, convene and decree a council against God. Do you hear, God, all your commandments have fallen and are no longer in use among us men and devils, so we should no longer keep them, but must oppose them. You must approve this and not damn us, since there is no sin where the law has fallen. So robbers and arsonists may work out their own salvation too, saying, "We no longer owe you princes and lords obedience, but do right in fighting and robbing you; for your law has fallen into disuse among us," etc.

Now advise us here, what should we do? It does not help that the apostolic council has fallen (which is the truth) or that it has been changed by the church (which is a lie). What harm would it do to scratch out the word "Holy Spirit" and attribute the council's work solely to the apostles, without the Holy Spirit—would this help the matter? Is it ridiculous? Well then think of something better! For if the Holy Spirit is not scratched out of the council, one of two things must happen; either both we and the papists must study and obey such a council, or, if it is to be ignored and not obeyed, then we poor heretics should be spared the screams of "Councils! Councils! Councils!" For as already stated, if this council is not to be kept, then none of the others is to be kept either. Otherwise, they, in return, will have to hear the cry, "Physician, heal thyself" [Luke 4:23], "Hans, take hold of your own nose!"[60] Let those who scream like that obey the council first, and we shall be glad to follow in their footsteps. If not, it will be found that they do not cry and spew the word "Coun-

---

[59] "Wrong." It might be a pun on the Latin *male* in terms of a German proverb, *"Mal dir was!"* meaning approximately, "Fooled again!"

[60] I.e., simply a proverbial way of repeating, "Physician, heal thyself." Cf. WA 30III, 378.

cil! Council!" sincerely, but slap people's snouts with it to treacherously and maliciously terrify poor consciences, and to destroy simple souls.

I am pointing out all this about this council because it was the first and foremost, and so that we might reflect on these matters before we permit the church to live or govern according to the councils. If this council confuses us so much, what would happen if we were to take up all the others? It is true, I admit, that the word "council" is easily spoken, and the sermon "one should keep the councils" is easily preached. But what should be our attitude on the question of reinstating their authority? What about that, dear friend? The pope, with his followers, is clever indeed; he extricates himself easily, and says that he is above all councils and may keep what he will and allow others to keep what he wills. Yes, if the problem can be solved in that way, then let us stop using the word "council" and stop preaching (that the councils should be observed) and, instead, scream, "Pope! Pope!" and, "One must obey the pope's doctrine!" Thus we too will all extricate ourselves easily and become as fine Christians as they are. What does the council matter to us if we cannot or will not keep it, but boast only of the name or the letter?

Or what seems even better to me (since we have thus gotten into this conversation, and must also jest a little in this Shrovetide season)[61]—since the letters in the word "council" are after all the main concern, not deeds or results—is to make the professional penmen[62] popes, cardinals, bishops, and preachers; for they could write such letters beautifully, large, small, black, red, green, yellow, and in any way desired. Then the church would be nicely governed in accordance with the councils, and there would be no need to obey what these councils had decreed; instead, the church would be content with the letters c-o-u-n-c-i-l, c-o-u-n-c-i-l. But if the penmen do not please us, then let us take painters, carvers, and printers, who will paint, carve, and print beautiful councils for us. Then the church will be excellently governed! And let us make the painters, carvers, and printers popes, cardinals, and bishops too.

---

[61] *Fastnacht.* In 1539 Shrove Tuesday was on February 19.
[62] *Stulschreiber.*

Why ask further how to keep the decrees of the council? Letters and pictures are enough!

But think a little further. What if all men were blind and could not see these written, painted, carved, or printed councils? How could the church then be governed through the councils? My advice is to take the choristers in Halberstadt and Magdeburg[63] and, instead of singing the *Quicunque*,[64] let them shout, *"Concilium! Concilium!"* until the church shakes to its rafters! We could hear them, even far across the Elbe,[65] though we were all blind. Then the church would be well governed, and these choristers would promptly be made vain popes, cardinals, and bishops, who could easily govern the church, which would otherwise have become impossible for the most holy fathers in Rome. But I shall say more about this council a little later; it is getting too much for me. I must not forget the Council of Nicaea either, which is the best and the first principal council after that of the apostles.

This council decreed, among other things,[66] that apostate Christians shall be readmitted, for seven years of penance.[67] If they died in the meantime, they were to be absolved and not denied the sacrament; today's council-screamers do not keep this, but transgress it and consign the dying Christians to purgatory, thus giving them more penance. If the pope were to observe this decree—the devil!—what poor beggars he and all the monasteries would become if this mine, treasure-trove, and trade, namely, purgatory, masses, pilgrimages, endowments, brotherhoods,[68] indul-

---

[63] The episcopal residences nearest to Wittenberg.
[64] The first word of the Athanasian Creed which, under the synonym *quicunque*, constituted a part of the Roman liturgy sung on Sundays not associated with a particular festival or saint. The creed is also found in Tappert (ed.), *Book of Concord*, pp. 19-21.
[65] The Elbe River is about fifty miles from Magdeburg and Halberstadt.
[66] Luther could find the decrees of Nicaea in several different versions. Besides the edition of Crabbe (see p. 7, n. 17 and *WA* 50, 531, n. *c*), Luther probably used the text preserved by Rufinus (*MPL* 21, 473-475). The decrees are translated in *PNF²* 14, 8-42, from canon law. The text does not always agree with *MPL* 21, 473-475. See, for example, p. 34, n. 70. Luther's citations are not always accurate. On Luther's judgment concerning the Council of Nicaea, see Headley, *op. cit.*, pp. 164-170.
[67] Canon XII in Rufinus' version. *MPL* 21, 474.
[68] *Bruderschafft*. A community of clergymen and laymen committed to works of charity (often in relationship to their "merits"). See, for example, "Hospitalers," *O.D.C.C.*, pp. 658-659.

gences, bulls, etc.,[69] would have to go to ruin. May the devil preserve the pope and all cardinals, bishops, monks, and nuns from having the church ruled according to this council. What would become of them? But since this decree pertains only to me, a man who has until now been agitating against the pope and who can well imagine how they would like to twist the council's words to direct them against me, I shall now drop this subject. I must now deal with matters that affect both parties, to the praise and honor of the council-screamers.

The same council decreed that those who give up warfare for the sake of religion and later go to war again are to spend five years among the catechumens and are then to be admitted to the sacrament after two more years. I am now taking the word "religion"[70] to mean the common Christian faith—but more about that later. In order not to get derailed or interrupted, I shall not argue about such incidental questions as whether the council forbade warfare, or whether it had the power and right to forbid or condemn war (so long as the soldiers do not otherwise deny the faith, to which the preceding statement refers).[71]

We want rather to investigate whether this article, that no soldier can be saved or be a Christian, had been kept before, or whether it can be kept on and on as a matter of law.[72] The pope himself and all his followers will have to testify that this article has fallen and can moreover never possibly be re-established, even less than the apostles' decree about blood sausage, black jelly, and the like, of which we spoke earlier. The council does not speak of murderers, robbers, enemies, but *de militia*, that is, "of regular

---

[69] All these practices were connected with the sacrament of penance and belief in purgatory.
[70] Canon XIII in Rufinus (*MPL* 21, 474). Luther confuses the number of years: Canon XIII states "thirteen years." Luther could easily have made the error by looking up Canon XII instead of Canon XIII. Moreover, Canon XIII does not contain the term "religion." The Latin, *religio*, appears only in canon law, which lists the decrees of Nicaea in various sections. Thus Luther might have used the text of Rufinus (*MPL* 21, 474) and that of *Decreti Secunda Pars, De Penitencia*, dist. V, C. IV (*CIC* 1, 1240-1241), where the term appears in C. V. The editors of *WA* assume that Luther confused the canons in Rufinus and looked up C. V instead of C. IV in canon law. See *WA* 50, 531, n. c.
[71] The "preceding statement" is Canon XII.
[72] Cf. *Whether Soldiers, Too, Can Be Saved* (1526). *PE* 5, 32-74.

wars," in which a prince, king, or emperor may under his banner take to the field, to whom God himself commanded us in Romans 13 [:1-7] to be subject and obedient (like St. Maurice[73] and many others), even if they be heathen, so long as they do not compel us to fight against God.

Well then, let us govern the church according to this council. First of all, we shall unbuckle the emperor's sword and then command the whole world to keep the peace, allowing no one to wage war or to tolerate it, for war is forbidden on pain of seven years' penance, in the Nicene council. What more do we want! The church is governed now; one needs no soldiers; the devil is dead; and all the years since the time of this council have been golden years,[74] indeed, they have been life eternal in profound peace, that is, if the council's statute is legal and enforcible.

But we would have to have unusually good painters here who could portray such churches for us so that we could see them; or if we were blind, we would have to have far greater criers than the choristers of Halberstadt[75] so that we could at least hear it. Perhaps the professional penmen could also write the letters in the word *concilium* because they have more colors available and can make better letters than we poor Christians. And yet, since the work itself is no longer there, we cannot attain salvation through letters, pictures, and shouts. We must speak differently about these things, and leave letters, pictures, and shouts to the papists. As long as we want to be Christians it might behoove us to live according to the councils and not merely to glorify the letters in the word "council."

You may say that the council's decree applies to those Chris-

---

[73] The commander of an Egyptian legion (Theban) which is said to have been exterminated under the Roman emperor Maximinian (286-305) because it would not participate in the persecutions of Christians. Thus sixty-six hundred died. The story of Maurice and the Theban legion is one of the most famous legends of the Middle Ages. Cf. *O.D.C.C.*, p. 877.

[74] "Golden" or "jubilee" years were instituted by Pope Boniface VIII (1294-1303) in 1300 for the purpose of granting special penance to pilgrims worshiping at the shrines in Rome. Though only every hundredth year was to be a jubilee year, the interval between such years was fixed at fifty in 1343, at thirty-three in 1389, and at twenty-five in 1473.

[75] See p. 33, n. 63.

tians who voluntarily run after war for the sake of money,[76] and that one should rightly condemn them. Otherwise, it would be utterly ridiculous for a council to denounce a regular war or obedience to government. For heaven's sake! I am willing to be a senseless fool and an ass, I who certainly also esteem councils very highly. Interpret it as well as you can, and I will be content with it. Only tell me, were you present at the Nicene council when this article was adopted, since you can repeat this interpretation with such certainty? If not, where else did you read this? The article simply says *militia*, "of war"; it says nothing of unjust wars,[77] which did not need to be condemned by councils since they are also thoroughly condemned, according to reason, by all the heathen, who were neither Christians nor councils.

If a king or a prince must fight and defend himself in a just war, he has to take whatever he can get. If, however, mercenaries are to be condemned, how are emperors, kings, and princes going to survive, since there are now only mercenaries available? Tell me, are those lords to fight alone, or are they to weave scarecrows to oppose the foe? Ask the council's advice on whether this could be done! Yes, my dear friend, it is easily said that the council has decreed this, if one looks at the letters like a cow stares at the gate, without reflecting on the implications and on how one should act and comply. And why didn't the popes and bishops later keep this decree themselves—they who have waged so many wars and shed so much blood throughout the world, and still do this unceasingly,[78] meanwhile constantly screaming, "Councils! Councils! Fathers! Fathers!" while reserving the freedom to act contrary to them and culling from them whatever they want us to do?

See here, Luther, this way you will cast the suspicion of sedition upon the Council of Nicaea. If we were now to teach that

---

[76] Cf. Canon XII. *MPL* 21, 1636.

[77] The differentiation between "just" and "unjust" wars grew out of Christian attitudes toward war and peace. Thus the "just war" was defined as an effort to restore peace. Cf. Roland H. Bainton, *Christian Attitudes Toward War and Peace* (New York and Nashville: Abingdon Press, 1960), pp. 89-100.

[78] Luther may have been thinking of the Catholic military league (*Bund*) formed at Nürnberg in 1538 against the Protestant Smalcald League.

the emperor and his soldiers (even though they had a just cause) were condemned, we should rightly be regarded as seditious on the basis of our own writings. I am now (I declare) and must be a good conciliarist; later I shall say more about it and explain myself. Now I repeat that the council cannot be speaking of anything but regular warfare, as it was being conducted at the time throughout the Roman Empire, under the same Emperor Constantine,[79] as well as previously under the heathen. The foot soldiers, called *milites*[80] at the time, were resident citizens then who drew permanent pay, so that whenever the father died or grew too old, his son was compelled to become a soldier in his stead, a custom the Turks still follow today. I am told that the king of France does practically the same thing in Switzerland and gives pay even to children.[81] If this is true, then, it is no lie.[82]

The horsemen, too, were professional and hereditary soldiers and served on salary, being called *equites*.[83] These horsemen were not unlike our noblemen, who must be equipped with mounts and armor, for which they have their fiefs. That the Roman Empire thus always had a certain number both of infantrymen and of cavalrymen receiving permanent pay, etc., I am mentioning to convey a proper understanding of the council, namely, that it cannot have referred to anything but regular warfare, since it had to speak about the Roman soldiery. According to St. Paul's teaching,[84] many Christians were duty-bound to obey orders therein—like St. Mau-

---

[79] See p. 22, n. 30. Known for his wars of succession and his autonomous leadership in the church, Constantine was baptized on his deathbed. The sincerity of his faith, however, has been questioned. Cf. Herrmann Döries, *Das Selbstzeugnis Kaiser Konstantins* (Göttingen, 1954), pp. 397-424.

[80] The technical term for the Roman infantry. Although there were generations of soldiers among the imperial Praetorian guard, Rome's imperial armies had been secured by conscription and voluntary enlistment ever since Emperor Marius (120-70 B.C.).

[81] It was common practice in the late Middle Ages to hire Swiss citizens as soldiers. Occasionally, as among the Turks, entire families were involved. This system of "pensions" was bitterly assailed by Huldreich Zwingli (1484-1531). *LWZ* 1, 68-69.

[82] A proverbial German expression, *"Ists war, so sey es nicht erlogen."* The origin of this proverb is not known.

[83] The technical term for the Roman cavalry.

[84] A reference to Rom. 13:1-7.

rice[85] with his comrades—also Jovian, Gratian, Valentinian, Theodosius, etc., before they became emperors.[86] But if it was right to serve the pagan emperors in war before baptism, why should it have been wrong to serve Christian emperors in the same way after baptism?

Could it be that *religio*[87] here does not refer to the Christian faith, but to monasticism? Then I would be trapped and would, according to this council, have to crawl back into my cowl, even if I wanted to do something else. Furthermore, I should not be able to find St. Peter in heaven, because he was a fisherman before he became an apostle, and after his apostolic office he again plied his trade as a fisherman, although he had left it for Christ's sake.

But even if *religio* now would mean monasticism, the fact remains that neither religious orders nor monasteries or monks existed at that time, although they arose very soon thereafter. St. Anthony and his companions lived about that time; he is called the father of all monks.[88] But at that time a monk was what we today call a recluse or hermit, according to the Greek word *monachos*, [and the Latin] *solitarius*, that is, a solitary person who lives alone, apart from men, in a forest or wilderness or otherwise alone. I know of no such monks today, nor have there been any like that for more than a thousand years,[89] unless we were to call the poor prisoners in towers and dungeons monks, who unfortunately are true monks, for they sit alone, separated from their fellows. The monks of the papacy are more among people and less alone than anyone else; for what class or vocation in the world is more with and among

---

[85] See p. 35, n. 73. Maurice represents an exception since he did not obey his emperor.

[86] Jovian (363-364); Gratian was regent of the Western half of Constantine's empire; he was preceded by Valentinian I (364-375). Theodosius I, who succeeded Valens (364-378) in the East, united the empire in 394. These rulers all distinguished themselves as military leaders.

[87] See p. 34, n. 70.

[88] Luther regarded the origin of monasticism as the end of apostolic times and the beginning of postapostolic times. Anthony (d. 356) took up the life of a hermit in *ca.* 270.

[89] This is correct in so far as there were no hermits, i.e., monks living completely by themselves. Occasionally, however, some monks lived a life of complete seclusion. Cf. *O.D.C.C.*, p. 631.

people and less separated from people than these monks? Unless it be claimed that the monasteries located in the cities and in the country are built neither near nor among people.

But let us forget about grammar, we want to talk about the matter at issue. Does *religio* here mean the monasticism existing at that time? Then why does this council condemn the military, that is, obedience to temporal government, and say that monks who show this obedience cannot be saved? We could still put up with praise of monasticism, but that the regular army is damned, as though St. Anthony could not in good conscience serve the emperor in war, is going too far. Where then would the emperor finally get his soldiers if everybody wanted to become a monk preaching that he was forbidden to serve in war? Tell me, my dear man, how close do you suppose this teaching comes to rebellion, especially if we were to teach it?—particularly since we know that this self-chosen monasticism is not commanded by God, but obedience is commanded. If the monks really wanted to escape from people, they should be honorable and honestly flee, not leave a stench behind them; that is, they should not by their fleeing give other vocations and offices a stench as though these were utterly damned and their own self-chosen monasticism were pure balsam. When a person flees from human society and becomes a monk it sounds as though he were saying, "Shame on you! How these people stink! How accursed is their vocation. I want to be saved and let them go to the devil!" If Christ had fled like this too and had become such a holy monk, who would have died for our sin or atoned for us poor sinners? Do you suppose it would have been the monks with their unsociable and austere mode of life?

True, John the Baptist was also in the wilderness, but he did not withdraw entirely from mankind, for he returned to be among people and preached after he had attained manhood. Christ dwelt (like Moses on Mount Sinai) for forty days in complete solitude among the beasts in the wilderness, and neither ate nor drank. But he too returned to the midst of people. Well then, if we like, let us regard them as hermits and monks. Still, neither condemns the vocation of mercenaries, even though they themselves were not soldiers. On the contrary, John addresses them, saying, "Rob no one by violence or by false accusation, and be content with your wages" [Luke 3:14]. Christ went to the centurion at Capernaum, who undoubtedly also served for wages, to help his servant. Yet Jesus did not bid him to forsake his vocation, but instead praised his faith above all Israel [Matt. 8:10]. And St. Peter allowed Cornelius of Caesarea to remain a centurion after his baptism, together with his troops, who were there in the pay of the Romans [Acts 10]. How much less, then, should St. Anthony and his monks have cast a stench on this order of God with his new and self-appointed holiness, simple layman that he was, wholly unlearned in the vocation of preacher and administrator in the church. To be sure, I do believe that he was a great man in the sight of God, as were many of his disciples; but his undertaking was offensive and dangerous, though he was preserved in it as the elect are preserved amid sin and other offenses. But the example and teaching of Christ and John is to be praised, not the example of his existence.

Now whether *religio* refers to faith or to monasticism, it follows from this council that military service, which at that time represented obedience to temporal government, is to be viewed either as disobedience to God or as stinking obedience to man-chosen monasticism. But the legend of St. Martin[90] indicates that *religio* meant Christian faith; for when he desired to become a Christian, he gave up his hereditary military service, in which his father had been and when his father became too old, had had his son enrolled in his stead—in conformity with the law and custom of the Roman Empire. This act was construed as cowardice and flight from the enemy, as though fear had moved him to become a Christian. We can read this in the legends about him. Thus it is apparent that the illusion had already taken root among the people at that time (not without the preachments of several bishops) that soldiering was an accursed vocation dangerous to the soul, to be eschewed by all who would serve God, for St. Martin lived not

---

[90] Martin of Tours (d. *ca.* 400), one of the most celebrated monks of the West. Luther's source is the legendary account, *The Life of St. Martin, Bishop of Tours* (*Vita S. Martini Episcopi Turonensis*), by Sulpicius Severus (*ca.* 340-410), a well-known early chronicler. MPL 20, 159-176.

long after the Council of Nicaea, since he was a soldier under Julian.[91]

Now if we wish to obey this council or to reinstate it, we have to emulate St. Anthony and flee into the wilderness and make monks of emperors and kings, or say that they can be neither Christians nor saved, or else proclaim that they live in a dangerous and stinking obedience and do not serve God. But if we choose to disobey this council, then we need obey none, for one is as good as another because the same Holy Spirit rules them all in equal measure. Moreover, we want to have councils in fact and consequences, not painted councils or the mere letters of the word "council."[92] But I cannot escape the suspicion that a fraud was committed and that the dear holy fathers never did set up such an article. Surely they would have spared the emperor Constantine this, he who had liberated them from the tyrants, not with St. Anthony's monkery, but with war and sword. It looks as though the other loose bishops pasted it in or smuggled it into the records later.[93]

The same council likewise decreed that the Roman bishop should, in accordance with an old custom, take charge of the suburbicarian churches, just as the bishop in Alexandria had charge of those in Egypt.[94] I cannot and will not explain the word *suburbicariae* because it is not my word; but it seems to mean the churches located up to that time in Italy[95] around the Roman churches, just as the churches in Egypt were adjacent to the churches in Alexandria. Let whoever wants to interpret it do so, but I still understand it to mean that this council gave the bishop of Rome no dominion over his surrounding churches, but en-

---

[91] Julian the Apostate (361-363), so called because he rejected Christianity. He was a nephew of Constantine the Great.

[92] See p. 32.

[93] The acts of the Council of Nicaea, as of the ancient councils in general, had been handed down in various forms, into some of which forgeries had been inserted; there was no authentic text available in Luther's day. Today's modern texts have been established by methods of literary criticism of the kind Luther here employs. For an account of the history of these texts, see *PNF*[2] 14, XVI-XXI.

[94] Cf. Canon VI. *MPL* 21, 473.

[95] Included also were Sicily, Sardinia, and Corsica. Cf. Tappert (ed.), *Book of Concord*, p. 322.

trusted them to his care; and it did not do it as though it had to be done "by divine right,"[96] but because of an old custom. Custom, however, does not mean *scriptura sancta* or God's word. Furthermore, it took the churches of Egypt (also in keeping with an old custom) away from the bishop of Rome and entrusted them to the bishop of Alexandria. Likewise, it is to be assumed that the churches in Syria were entrusted to the bishop of Antioch or Jerusalem, since they are farther away from Rome than Alexandria or Egypt.

Now if this council is to be valid in our churches and go into effect, we must first condemn the bishop of Rome as a tyrant and burn all his bulls and decretals. There is no bull or decretal in which he does not boast vociferously and menacingly that he is the supreme head and lord of all the churches on earth, to whom everyone on earth must be subject, if they wish to be saved.[97] This is exactly as much as saying, "The Council of Nicaea is false, accursed, and damned for taking from me domination over all things and for making the bishop of Alexandria my peer." Anyway, the Turk and the sultan long ago so interpreted and invalidated this article by destroying Alexandria[98] that neither we nor the pope need concern ourselves with it. Thus we learn that the articles of the councils are not all to be kept forever, like articles of faith.

The council likewise decreed that those who emasculate themselves because of the great and unbearable lust of their flesh shall not be admitted to the clergy or to any other office in the church.[99] Furthermore, it decreed that the bishops are to have no women about them or living with them, except mother, sister, aunts (that is, a father's or mother's sister), or other near relative.[100] Here I

---

[96] *Iure divino.*

[97] This is a reference to the bull *Unam Sanctam*, issued in 1302 by Pope Boniface VIII, whose language Luther here imitates. See Ray C. Petry (ed.), *Readings in the Early and Medieval Church* ("A History of Christianity," Vol. I [Englewood Cliffs, N. J.: Prentice Hall, 1962]), pp. 505-506.

[98] Alexandria was destroyed in 641 by the Saracens.

[99] Cf. Canon I. *MPL* 21, 473.

[100] Canon III. *MPL* 21, 473. Luther misinterprets this canon. It does not refer to clerical marriage, but to the presence of women who were neither wives nor relatives. They were called "associates" (*subintroductae*) because they lived in spiritual marriage. On this term, see *O.D.C.C.*, p. 1300.

do not understand the Holy Spirit in this council at all. If those who emasculate themselves because of unbearable passion are not qualified for ecclesiastical office, and those who have a wife or take a wife to ward off such lust, according to St. Paul's suggestion in I Corinthians 7 [:2] are not qualified either, what will be the outcome? Should a bishop or a preacher be stuck in this unbearable passion, and be forbidden to rescue himself from this perilous state by either marriage or emasculation? Why should it be necessary to command a man who has a wife not to have any other women about him, which is, of course, unseemly even for laymen and husbands? Thus the matter of mother, sister, or aunt would take care of itself; if the bishop had a wife, there would be no need for a prohibition. Or does the Holy Spirit have nothing better to do in the councils than to bind and burden his servants with impossible, dangerous, and unnecessary laws?

The histories relate that St. Paphnutius, that excellent man, opposed the bishops in this council who proposed to forbid marriage even to those who had married before their ordination and who wanted to forbid them to discharge their conjugal duties with their own wives. He, however, advised against it, saying that discharging one's conjugal duties was also a mark of chastity.[101] It is recorded that he won out, but these two decrees sound as though the bishops had proceeded to forbid wives anyway, for there were also many incompetent, false bishops in the pious crowd and holy council, such as the Arians[102] and their gang (history clearly shows that), who perhaps contributed to this too. But more of that later. Let us stop talking about the councils for a while and take a look at the fathers—although St. Augustine confuses us because he wants none of them (as was said above)[103] believed, but wants them all held captive and subject to Scripture. We shall nevertheless take a look at them too.

---

[101] *Historia Tripartita*, II, 14. MPL 69, 933; PNF² 2, 256. See in this volume, p. 60. Little is known of Paphnutius (d. 360) save that he was an Egyptian bishop and a member of the Nicene council, and that he opposed the prohibition of clerical marriage.

[102] The Arians derived their name from Arius (d. 336), a presbyter in Alexandria condemned for his Christology. He asserted, contrary to the Nicene Creed, that Christ was not of the same substance with the Father.

[103] See p. 25.

St. Cyprian,[104] one of the earliest fathers, since he lived long before the Council of Nicaea at the time of the martyrs, and was himself one of the outstanding martyrs, taught and staunchly insisted that those who were baptized by heretics had to be rebaptized.[105] He stuck to this until his martyrdom, although he was strongly admonished by other bishops, and St. Cornelius, bishop of Rome,[106] who was martyred at the same time, refused to support him. St. Augustine afterward had great difficulty in excusing him, and finally had to resort to saying that such an error had been washed away by his blood, shed for the love of Christ. Thus spoke St. Augustine, condemning St. Cyprian's doctrine of rebaptism, which has since been condemned again and again (and rightfully so). But we are well content with St. Cyprian, for in him Christ comforts us poor sinners mightily, showing that his great saints are after all still human—like St. Cyprian, this excellent man and dear martyr, who blundered in more serious matters, about which we lack the time to speak now.

But what will we do with the fathers who transmitted this doctrine to St. Cyprian? In the *Ecclesiastical History*, Book VII, pages 1 and 2,[107] you may read what that fine Bishop Dionysius of Alexandria[108] wrote about it to Bishop Sixtus of Rome,[109] saying that this policy had been followed by other great and prominent bishops before the bishops in Africa followed it, that it had been decided upon by the Council of Iconium,[110] and that therefore such important facts should be considered before condemning the practice. But in the Council of Nicaea is clearly written the article that one should rebaptize the heretics, the Paulianists or Photinians.[111] And if this article offends St. Augustine in his *On Here-*

---

[104] Cyprian became bishop of Carthage in 248, and was put to death in 258 because of his faith.

[105] Cf. *Epistola ad Ianuarium. Sententiae episcoporum LXXXVII de haereticis bapizandis; Epistola ad Iubaianum. MPL* 3, 1073-1082; 1089-1116; 1153-1174; *ANF* 5, 375-377; 565-572; 379-386.

[106] Cornelius I (251-253).

[107] Cf. *MPG* 13, 256; *PNF*[2] 1, 294.

[108] Dionysius (d. *ca.* 264) was involved in many controversies over rebaptizing schismatics.

[109] Sixtus II (257-258).

[110] Held in Phrygia, an ancient country of Asia Minor, in *ca.* 235.

[111] Cf. Canon XIX. *MPL* 21, 475; *PNF*[2] 14, 40. This canon is not genuine,

sies[112] because he had plagued himself for a long time with the Anabaptist Donatists,[113] he nevertheless extricates himself for the sake of the Nicene council's decree by saying it must be assumed that the Photinians did not employ the baptismal formula, which other heretics did. If only one could believe it, since there is no proof. For the Photinians did not have, nor did they create, a gospel different from that possessed by the whole church; it thus seems more plausible to assume that they used the common formula, for heretics always like to boast of possessing Scripture. Thus Anabaptism tries to justify itself against St. Augustine and us all, because the Nicene council and other earlier councils and fathers agreed with Cyprian.[114]

Furthermore, the *Constitutions of the Holy Apostles*,[115] the ordinances of the apostles, have now been printed in many editions so that the church may again be properly governed. Among them is this canon: "One should count the heretics' sacrament and baptism as nothing, but should instead rebaptize them."[116] And it can readily be inferred that if the apostles ordained this, it was transmitted (as Dionysius states)[117] by the earlier fathers and councils

---

but is a later addition to the acts of the council. The Paulianists and Photinians are the followers of the heretical bishops Paul of Samosata (d. 269) and Photinus of Sirmium (d. 376). Both rejected Nicene Christology. Cf. *O.D.C.C.*, pp. 1034, 1069.

[112] Cf. *MPL* 42, 34.

[113] A schismatic group named after Donatus (d. *ca.* 355), under whose leadership they established their own church in Carthage. Condemned by a synod in Carthage in 411, they spread throughout North Africa after a debate with St. Augustine, who recommended their persecution by the state. They also became known as Anabaptists (from the Greek "rebaptizers") because they rebaptized converts from the Roman church. Cf. W. H. C. Frend, *The Donatist Church* (Oxford, 1952).

[114] Luther assumes here that the Council of Nicaea settled the question of Anabaptism in favor of Cyprian's position. Yet the council simply acknowledged the Roman practice (with the exception of Paulianism). Cf. Schäfer, *op. cit.*, pp. 272-273.

[115] *Canones apostolorum.* A collection of alleged decrees of synods, claiming apostolic origin. The collection stems from the late fourth or early fifth century and is closely related to the *Apostolic Constitution*. *MPG* 1, 555-591; *ANF* 7, 387-505. In 1524 a new edition was published in Paris by Jacques Merlin, which was followed by others. Cf. *WA* 50, 540, n. *d*. Luther could find them in Crabbe's work on the councils.

[116] Canon XXXVIII.

[117] See p. 44.

to St. Cyprian, and by him to the Council of Nicaea, for Cyprian preceded this council. If the apostles actually decreed this, then St. Cyprian is right, and St. Augustine with all of Christendom and with us who share his view are defeated. For who would teach contrary to the apostles? If the apostles did not decree this, then one should drown and hang all such authors and teachers for circulating, printing, and advertising such books under the apostles' names. They also deserve not to be believed with regard to other books or utterances of theirs henceforth, because they are constantly producing books which they themselves do not believe but nevertheless foist on us, with the letters c-o-u-n-c-i-l, f-a-t-h-e-r-s. If it is only a matter of letters—and their one concern is to fool us with them—a chorister in Halberstadt could cry them out far better than they.

Now if St. Cyprian had such apostles' rules on his side, as well as the Nicene and other councils, how shall we compare the fathers? The apostles and St. Cyprian demand rebaptism; St. Augustine and the whole later church declare this to be wrong. Who is going to preach to Christians in the meantime until this dispute is adjusted and settled? Yes, it is fun to fool around with councils and fathers if one juggles with the letters or constantly postpones the council, as has now been done for twenty years,[118] and does not think of what happens meanwhile to the souls who must be fed with conscientious teaching, as Christ says, "Tend my sheep" [John 21:16].

I excuse St. Cyprian first to the extent that he was not an Anabaptist such as ours are today,[119] for he held that the heretics had no sacrament at all and that therefore they had to be baptized like other heathen. He was honestly mistaken in believing that he was not rebaptizing, but baptizing an unbaptized heathen; for he knows and holds not a rebaptism, but only one single baptism. But our Anabaptists admit that our baptism and that of the papacy is a true baptism, but since it is administered or received by unworthy people, it is no baptism at all. St. Cyprian would never have concurred in this, much less practiced it.

---

[118] See p. 9, n. 1.
[119] Cf. Luther's *Concerning Rebaptism.* LW 40, 229-262.

46

I have a high regard for St. Cyprian's person and faith, and that is why I said the foregoing in his behalf; for doctrine is subject to the words of St. Paul, "Test everything," etc. [I Thess. 5:21]. But we are not interested here in what I may say, but in bringing the fathers into agreement with one another, so that we may become certain of what and how to preach to the poor Christians. Here the apostles and Cyprian are at odds with St. Augustine and the church over baptism. If we obey St. Augustine, then we have to condemn the apostles with their rules and the Nicene council with the earlier fathers and councils, including St. Cyprian. And on the other hand, if St. Cyprian and the apostles are right, then St. Augustine and the church are wrong. Meanwhile, who is going to preach and baptize until we reach an agreement? The papists boastfully quote the canons of the apostles and the councils together with the fathers against us. Some of these, for example, are incorporated in Gratian's canon law.[120] Now if the dam should break and some of these canons and councils were found to be heretical, as the one about rebaptism is, who could prevent the flood from bursting forth irresistibly and proclaiming with a roar, "You lie in everything you write, say, print, vomit, and shout. Not a word of yours can be believed, even though you quote councils, fathers, and apostles"?

However, while we both thus cull from the councils and the fathers, they what they like, and we what we like, and cannot reach an agreement—because the fathers themselves disagree as much as do the councils—who, my dear man, is going to preach to the poor souls who know nothing of such culling and quarreling? Is that tending the sheep of Christ, when we ourselves do not know whether what we are feeding them is grass or poison, hay or dung? And are they to dangle and hang until it is settled and the council arrives at a decision? Oh, how poorly Christ would have provided for the church if this is how things have to go on! No, there must be another way than proving things by means of councils and fathers, or there could have been no church since the days of the apostles—which is impossible, for it is writ-

---

[120] See for example, *Decreti Prima Pars*, dist. XXXV, C. I; dist. XLVII, C. I; dist. LXXXVIII, C. III. *CIC* 1, 131, 151, 307.

ten, "I believe one holy, Christian church,"[121] and, "I am with you always, to the close of the age" [Matt. 28:20]. These words must be the truth, even if all the fathers and councils were wrong! The Man must be called "I am the truth" [John 14:6]; fathers and councils should on the other hand be called "Every man is a liar" [Rom. 3:4] whenever they contradict each other.

I am not saying this for the sake of our people, to whom I will later show what councils, fathers, and church are, if they do not know it (from which God has protected them!), but I am saying this for the sake of the screamers who think that we have never read the fathers and the councils. Although I have not read all the councils—I do not intend to read them all; this would be too great a waste of time since I did read the four principal councils very thoroughly, much more so than any of them did I am sure—I shall also make bold to say that I hold, after the four principal councils, all the others to be of lesser value, even though I would regard several (understand me rightly), I say several, as equally good. I am more familiar with the fathers, I hope, than these screamers who tear out of context whatever they choose and discard the rest if it annoys them. Therefore we must approach the matter differently.

But why should we get excited? If we wish to harmonize the sayings of the fathers let us consult the master of the *Sentences*,[122] who is diligent beyond measure in this task and was way ahead of us, for he too felt this anguish[123] over the disagreement of the fathers and wanted to remedy these things. In my opinion, he did it better than we would, and you will find in no one council, nor in all of the councils, and in none of the fathers, as much as in the book *Sentences*. The councils and fathers deal with several points of Christian doctrine, but none of them deals with them all as this man does; at least, he deals with most of them. And yet, about the real articles, such as faith and justification, he speaks too undecidedly and weakly, even though he gives high

---

[121] The Nicene Creed.

[122] Peter Lombard (*ca.* 1100-1160). His *Four Books of Sentences* (*Sententiarum Libri Quatuor*) was the standard theological textbook of the Middle Ages. The work is contained in *MPL* 192.

[123] *Anfechtung.*

enough praise to the grace of God. Also, as was said above,[124] we might as well have let Gratian do the work of harmonizing the councils for us, something to which he gave much effort, but in which he is not as pure as the master of *Sentences*, for he concedes too much to the Roman bishop, and applies everything to him. Otherwise, he would perhaps have done a better job in harmonizing the councils than we could do now.

If any one wishes further proof that the dear, holy fathers were human beings, he should read the booklet of Dr. Pomer, our pastor,[125] on the four chapters to the Corinthians. He will indeed have to learn from this that St. Augustine was right when he wrote, "My dear man, do not," etc., as was quoted above,[126] namely, that he will believe none of the fathers unless he has Scripture on his side. Dear God, if the Christian faith depended on men or were based on the words of men, what need would there be then for Holy Scripture? Or why should God have given it? Then let us shove it under the bench and, in its stead, lay only the fathers and councils on the desk. Or if the fathers were not human beings, how then shall we human beings attain salvation? If they were human they would also at times have thought, spoken, and acted just as we think, speak, and act, but afterward they would speak (like us) the beloved prayer, "Forgive us our trespasses," etc., especially since they did not have the same promise of the Holy Spirit that the apostles had, but had to be the apostles' disciples.

If the Holy Spirit had been so foolish as to expect or trust that the councils or fathers would do everything well and make no mistakes there would have been no need for him to warn the church against them, saying in I Corinthians 4 [3:12] that one should examine all things and be on one's guard wherever men build with straw, hay, and wood on the foundation. In that way

---

[124] See pp. 20-21.
[125] John Bugenhagen (1485-1528), known as Pomeranus from the place of his birth (Pommern), had been pastor at the town church in Wittenberg since 1523. His *Commentary on Four Chapters of the First Epistle to the Corinthians* (*Ioannis Bugenhagii Pomerani Commentarius, in quatuor capita prioris Epistolae ad Corinthios*) was published in 1530. For the text, see Georg Geisenhof (ed.), *Bibliotheca Bugenhagia* (Leipzig, 1908), No. 266.
[126] See p. 25.

he foretold, not privately and feebly, but openly and mightily, that in the holy church there would be those who build with wood, straw, and hay, namely, teachers who would remain on the foundation and be saved, even though harmed by fire, which cannot be said of the heretics, for they lay a different foundation. The others, however, remain on the foundation, that is, in the faith in Christ, attain salvation, and are called God's saints, even though they too have hay, straw, and wood which must be consumed by the fire of Holy Scripture, albeit without injuring their salvation. As St. Augustine says of himself, *"Errare potero, hereticus non ero,"* "I may err, but I shall not become a heretic."[127] Reason: heretics not only err, but do not want to be corrected; they defend their error as though it were right, and fight against the recognized truth and their own conscience.

St. Paul says of them in Titus 3 [:10-11], "As for a man who is factious, after admonishing him once or twice, have nothing more to do with him, knowing that such a person is perverted and sinful; he is *autokatakritos,*"[128] that is, he wilfully and wittingly persists in remaining condemned in his error. But St. Augustine willingly confesses his error, and lets it be pointed out to him, so he cannot be a heretic even though he has erred. All the other saints do the same and gladly consign their hay, straw, and wood to the fire so that they may remain on the foundation of salvation, as we did too, and still do.

Therefore, because it cannot be otherwise with the fathers (I am speaking of the holy and good ones)—when they build without Scripture, that is, without gold, silver, and precious stones, then they will build with wood, straw, or hay—we must, according to St. Paul's verdict, know how to differentiate between gold and wood, between silver and straw, between precious stones and hay; and we must not be compelled by those obnoxious screamers to believe that wood and silver are the same, that silver and straw are the same, and that emeralds and hay are the same. Or we ought to ask them (if this could be done) first to become so clever themselves as to take wood for gold, straw for silver, and

---

[127] The passage could not be found in Augustine's works.
[128] "Self-condemned"; see p. 12, n. 5.

hay for pearls. Otherwise, they should justly spare us, and not expect such foolishness or childishness of us.

And all of us should also take note of this miracle of the Holy Spirit, namely, that he wanted to give the world all the books of Holy Scripture, of both the Old and the New Testaments, solely through Abraham's people and seed, and that he did not have a single book composed by us Gentiles, just as he did not intend to choose the prophets and apostles from among the Gentiles, as St. Paul says in Romans 3 [:2], the Jews enjoy a great advantage, since they "are entrusted with the oracles of God," and according to Psalm 147 [:19], "He declares his word to Jacob, his statutes and ordinances to Israel." And Christ himself says in John 4 [:22], "We worship what we know, for salvation is from the Jews," and Romans 9 [:4-5] says, "To them belong the covenants, the giving of the law, the patriarchs, and Christ."

Therefore we Gentiles must not value the writings of our fathers as highly as Holy Scripture, but as worth a little less; for they are the children and heirs, while we are the guests and strangers who have come to the children's table by grace and without any promise. We should, indeed, humbly thank God and, like the Gentile woman, have no higher wish than to be the little dogs that gather the crumbs falling from their masters' table [Matt. 15:27]. As it is, we proceed arrogantly and put our fathers and ourselves on a level with the apostles, never thinking that God could break us to pieces more easily, since he did not spare the natural branches and Abraham's seed or heirs for their unbelief, Romans 11 [:21]. And yet, that accursed abomination in Rome usurps the authority to change Scripture arbitrarily solely to suit himself, without any regard for apostles and prophets. That is why St. Augustine is right when he writes to St. Jerome (as related above), "Dear brother, I hope that you do not expect your books to be regarded as equal to those of the apostles and prophets. God forbid that you should desire such a thing."[129]

Moreover, there is neither a council nor a father in which one could find, or from whom one could learn, the whole of Christian doctrine. For example, the Nicene council deals only with the doc-

---

[129] See p. 26, n. 49.

trine that Christ is truly God; the one at Constantinople, that the Holy Spirit is God; the one at Ephesus, that Christ is not two but one person; the one at Chalcedon, that Christ has not one but two natures, the human and the divine. These are the four great principal councils; they deal with no more than these four articles, as we shall hear. But this is still not the complete teaching of the Christian faith. St. Cyprian deals with how one must suffer and die in a firm faith; he rebaptizes heretics; and he also rebukes bad morals and women.[130] St. Hilary[131] defends the Nicene council, states that Christ is true God, and deals with a few psalms. St. Jerome[132] extols virginity and the hermits. St. Chrysostom[133] teaches prayer, fasting, almsgiving, patience, etc., and St. Ambrose[134] deals with many subjects; but St. Augustine treats the greatest number, and that is why the master of the *Sentences* has taken most of his material from him.

In summary, put them all together, both fathers and councils, and you still will not be able to cull from them all the teachings of the Christian faith, even if you culled forever. If it had not been for Holy Scripture, the church, had it depended on the councils and fathers, would not have lasted long. And in proof of this: where do the fathers and councils get what they teach or deal with? Do you think that they first invented it in their own day, or that the Holy Spirit always inspired them with something new? How was the church preserved prior to these councils and fathers? Or were there no Christians before councils and fathers came up? That is why we must speak differently about the councils and fathers and look not at the letters but at the meaning. May that

---

[130] See, for example, *Exhortation to Martyrdom, Addressed to Fortunatus* (*MPL* 4, 678-702; *ANF* 5, 496-506), and *On the Dress of Virgins* (*MPL* 4, 451-478; *ANF* 5, 430-436).

[131] Hilary of Poitiers (*ca.* 315-367), famous for his defense of the Nicene council in his *Against the Emperor Constantius* (*Contra Constantium Imperatorem*). *MPL* 10, 577-606.

[132] In *Epistola 22, ad Eustachium. MPL* 22, 394-425; *PNF*[2] 6, 22-41.

[133] John of Constantinople (*ca.* 354-407), known since the sixth century as Chrysostom ("gold mouth") because of his preaching. See, for example, his *Six Books on the Priesthood. MPG* 26, 623-692; *PNF*[1] 9, 33-83.

[134] Ambrose (*ca.* 340-397) was bishop of Milan. His writings are in *MPL* 15–17; *PNF*[2] 10.

suffice for the first part of this book, so that we can catch our breath too.

Part II

First, concerning the councils, for the letters c-o-u-n-c-i-l afford us stupid people endless difficulty, even more than f-a-t-h-e-r-s and c-h-u-r-c-h. Yet I do not wish to set myself up as judge or master in this matter; I only wish to express my ideas. Grace and luck is wished to anyone who can do better. Amen.

I shall take to heart what St. Hilary says in *On the Trinity*: "*ex causis dicendis summenda est intelligentia dictorum,*"[135] that is, "He who wants to understand what is said must see why or for what reason it was spoken." In the same manner, actions are best understood by understanding that which motivates them.[136] Natural reason also teaches this. I shall illustrate it to make it simpler: if one peasant brings suit against another, saying, "Dear judge, this man calls me a rogue and a rascal," these words and letters, by themselves, convey the idea that the plaintiff has suffered a great wrong, and that they are false and sheer lies. But if the defendant appears and gives reasons for such words, saying, "Dear judge, he is a rascal and a rogue for he was flogged out of the city of N. for his rascality, and he was saved from hanging only through the great efforts and pleading of pious people, and now he wants to do violence to me in my own home," the judge will understand these letters differently than he had before—as daily experience in government shows. For before one learns the reason and the motive for what a man says, it is only letters, the shouts of choristers, or the songs of nuns.

Likewise, Christ says to Peter, "Whatever you bind on earth shall be bound in heaven, and whatever you loose on earth shall be loosed in heaven" [Matt. 16:19]. The pope takes the letters, rides into Never Never Land[137] with them, and interprets them as,

---

[135] Cf. *On the Trinity,* IX, 2. MPL 10, 282; PNF¹ 9, 156. Luther was apparently quoting from memory since his quotation differs from the text in MPL: "*Cum dictorum intelligentia, aut ex praepositis aut ex consequentibus expectatur.*"

[136] Luther switches into Latin here: *Sic ex causis agendi cognoscuntur acta.*

[137] *Schlauraffenland,* from a German fairy tale.

"Whatever I do in heaven and on earth is right. I have the keys to bind and to loose everything and all." Indeed, if we had eaten beets, etc.![138] But if one looks at the sense, one finds that Christ talks about binding and loosing sin, because these are keys to the kingdom of heaven, into which no one can enter unless his sins are forgiven, and from which no one is excluded except him around whom they have been tied because of his impenitent life. Thus these words have nothing to do with St. Peter's power, but apply to the needs of despondent or proud sinners. But the pope converts these keys into two skeleton keys to all the kings' crowns and treasures, to the purse strings, the life, the honor, and the goods of the entire world. For he, like a fool, looks at the letters and pays no heed to the sense.

There are many passages in Holy Scripture that are contradictory according to the letters; but when that which motivates them is pointed out, everything is all right. I should think that all jurists and medical men find a great deal of this in their books too, as I said earlier about the judge. And what is the entire being of man other than sheer antilogies and contradictions, until one hears the facts? That is why my antilogists[139] are admirable, fine, pious sows and asses, who collect my antilogies and discard that which motivates them, indeed, even diligently obscure them; just as though I, too, could not point out antilogies in their books, which cannot even be reconciled by any reason! But enough of this, for they do not deserve that many words.

We shall now take up the Council of Nicaea, which was undertaken for the following reasons: the praiseworthy Emperor Constantine had become a Christian and had given the Christians peace from tyrants and persecutors.[140] He was so filled with strong, earnest faith and sincerity that he warred even against his brother-

---

[138] An allusion to the German proverb, "*Versenge mir die ruben nicht!*" Cf. Thiele, *Luthers Sprichwörtersammlung*, No. 85.

[139] A reference to his opponents who, like John Eck, wrote *Obelisks* against him. Cf. *LW* 31, xvi.

[140] Eusebius, *Ecclesiastical History*, IX, 10. *MPG* 13, 335; *PNF*[2] 1, 366. The subsequent account is based on *Historia Tripartita*, beginning in I, 12. *MPL* 69, 901; *PNF*[2] 23, 251. The reference to the Persians, however, is not contained there. See Schäfer, *op. cit.*, pp. 291-294.

in-law Licinius,[141] to whom he had given his sister Constantia in marriage, and whom he had made co-emperor, and pushed him out of the empire because he would not stop shamefully persecuting Christians, even after several warnings. Now when the good emperor had established this peace for the Christians and done everything for their good, promoting the church in every way he could, all was secure, so he planned a war outside his empire, against the Persians. Into such a fair and peaceful paradise and into such happy days did the old serpent come and arouse Arius, a priest in Alexandria, against his bishop. He wanted to bring up something new against the old faith, and because he coveted fame, he assailed his bishop's doctrine, declaring that Christ was not God. Many priests and great and learned bishops rallied about him, and the malady grew rapidly in many lands, until Arius dared to boast that he was a martyr, having to suffer for the truth's sake at the hands of his bishop Alexander,[142] who did not let him get away with these things and wrote terrible letters against him to all the lands.[143]

When this came to the ears of the good emperor, he acted like a very wise prince; he wanted to douse the flames before the fire grew any bigger. He wrote a letter[144] to both bishop Alexander and priest Arius, admonishing them so kindly and so earnestly that it could not have been better written. He explained to them with what difficulty he had effected peace for the Christians in the empire and if they should now war among themselves it would be a great irritation to the heathen who would perhaps fall from the faith again (which then did happen and he himself complained), and he would thus be hindered from marching against the Persians. To sum up, it was a humble, Christian letter, written by this great emperor to these two men. To me it seems much too humble, for I know my own rough pen so that I could not have drawn such a humble missive from my inkwell, especially if I had been emperor, and an emperor like that!

But the letter did not help. Arius had now gained a large fol-

---

[141] Licinius ruled the Eastern half of the Roman Empire from 314 to 324.
[142] Alexander, bishop of Alexandria (ca. 313-328), who excommunicated Arius.
[143] *Historia Tripartita*, I, 14, 15. *MPL* 69, 914-915; *PNF*[2] 3, 41-42.
[144] *Historia Tripartita*, I, 19. *MPL* 69, 918-920; *PNF*[2] 2, 6-7.

lowing, and wanted to butt his head against his bishop. The pious emperor did not give up either. He sent a personal ambassador, an excellent, world-renowned bishop named Hosius of Cordova, from Spain,[145] to the two in Alexandria, and throughout Egypt, to settle the dispute. This did not help either, and meanwhile the fire kept spreading as though a forest burned. Then the good emperor Constantine made his final move and collected the best and most renowned bishops in every land, ordered that they be brought to Nicaea on the imperial asses, horses, and mules, and asked them to find a satisfactory solution to the matter. Many fine bishops and fathers really did come, especially the famous Jacob of Nisibis[146] and Paphnutius of Ptolemais, bishops who had suffered severe persecution under Licinius and who had performed miracles. But there were also several Arian bishops among them, like mouse-droppings in the pepper.[147]

The emperor was now in good spirits, and hoped for the good ending of the matter; he honored them all. Then several of them came along and handed the emperor a bill of complaint for what one bishop had against the other, and asked for the emperor's judgment. He declined to have anything to do with them, for he was not interested in the bishops' squabbles, but wanted to have this article about Christ judged, and he had not convoked the council for the sake of their bickering. But since they persisted, he bade them to bring him all the bills, and then he cast them, unread, into the fire. However, he sent them away with the kind words that he could not be their judge, they whom God had set as judges over him; and he exhorted them to deal with the main issue.[148] Now then! That is my idea of a wise, gentle, and patient prince. Someone else would have been so irritated by these bishops that he would have knocked the cask to pieces.[149] And

---

[145] *Historia Tripartita*, I, 20. *MPL* 69, 920; *PNF*² 2, 252. Hosius of Cordova (257-ca. 357) was Constantine's ecclesiastical adviser.
[146] A celebrated opponent of Arianism (d. 338); Nisibis is in Mesopotamia.
[147] A German proverb, "*Wie meuse dreck unter pfeffer.*" Cf. Thiele, *Luthers Sprichwörtersammlung*, No. 371.
[148] Here Luther used, besides the *Historia Tripartita*, II, 2 (*MPL* 69, 922-923), Rufinus' translation of Eusebius' *Ecclesiastical History*, I, 2 (*MPL* 21, 468).
[149] *Das fas in einen hauffen gestossen*, an intensification of the German proverb, "*Dem fas den boden ausstossen.*" Thiele, *Luthers Sprichwörtersammlung*, No. 335.

yet he did express his opinion clearly when he burned their complaints, without any regard for their episcopal dignity, thus reproving them for their childish conduct because they had been summoned for a far more important purpose.

Now when the council met, he sat down among the bishops, on a chair lower than theirs.[150] The bishop of Rome, Sylvester, was not present, but (as some say) he had sent two priests.[151] After the bishop of Antioch, Eustathius[152] (who chaired this council), had thanked and praised the emperor for his kindness, Arius' doctrine was publicly read (for it appears that Arius himself was not present, being neither a bishop nor a delegate);[153] it stated that Christ was not God, but was created and made by God, as the histories record at length. At this the holy fathers and bishops arose from their seats in indignation, tore the document to pieces, and declared it was not true; and so Arius was openly condemned by the furious council, so deeply did it hurt the fathers and so unbearable was it for them to hear this blasphemy of Arius. All the bishops signed this condemnation, the Arian bishops too, albeit hypocritically, as the future showed, except two bishops from Egypt who did not sign.[154] So the emperor dissolved the council on the same day, and he himself, and the council too, sent out a written report of this event throughout the world.[155] And the emperor Constantine, very happy that the matter was settled and disposed of, treated the bishops very kindly, especially those who had been persecuted.

This explains why the council met and what they had to do, namely, to preserve this ancient article of faith that Christ is true God against the new cleverness of Arius, who, on the basis of rea-

---

150 *Historia Tripartita*, II, 5. *MPL* 69, 924-925; *PNF*[2] 3, 43-44.

151 *Historia Tripartita*, II, 1. *MPL* 69, 920-921; *PNF*[2] 2, 253. In the *Tripartita* Julius, not Sylvester, is mentioned as bishop of Rome. On the basis of Crabbe's *Concilia Omnia*, Luther named Sylvester. Later scholarship confirmed Luther's historical judgment.

152 Eustathius was bishop of Antioch from *ca.* 324 to *ca.* 330.

153 A peculiar error by Luther. Both the *Historia Tripartita*, II, 5 (*MPL* 69, 924; *PNF*[2] 3, 43), and Rufinus, I, 5 (*MPL* 21, 472), record that Arius was present.

154 *Historia Tripartita*, II, 15, 16. *MPL* 69, 934-935; *PNF*[2] 2, 14, 16. They were Secundus of Ptolemais and Theonas of Marmarica.

155 *Historia Tripartita*, II, 12. *MPL* 69, 931-932; *PNF*[2] 2, 12-13.

son, wanted to falsify this article, indeed, to change it and condemn it; because of this he was himself condemned. The council did not invent this doctrine or establish it as something new as though it had not previously existed in the churches, but rather defended it against the new heresy of Arius. This was demonstrated by the fact that the fathers became upset and tore up the document, thus confessing that since the days of the apostles they had learned and taught differently in their churches. Otherwise, what would have happened to the Christians who for over three hundred years prior to this council, ever since the days of the apostles, had believed in and worshiped the name of Jesus in prayer as true God, who had died in this faith, and had suffered cruel persecution because of it?

I have to point this out in passing, for the pope's hypocrites have lapsed into such gross folly that they think that councils have the power and the right to set up new articles of faith and to alter the old ones. That is not true, and we Christians have to tear up documents like this too. No council ever did it or can do it; the articles of faith must not grow on earth through the councils, as from a new, secret inspiration, but must be issued from heaven through the Holy Spirit and revealed openly; otherwise, as we shall hear later, they are not articles of faith. Thus the Council of Nicaea (as was said) did not invent this doctrine or establish it as something new, namely, that Christ is God; rather, it was done by the Holy Spirit, who came openly from heaven to the apostles on the day of Pentecost, and through Scripture glorified Christ as true God, as he had promised the apostles. It remained unchanged since the days of the apostles until this council, and so on until our own day—it will remain until the end of the world, as he says, "Lo, I am with you always, to the close of the age" [Matt. 28:20].

If we had nothing with which to defend this article except this council we would be in a bad way. Then I myself would not believe the council either, but say, "They were human beings." But St. John, St. Paul, St. Peter, and the other apostles are reliable and offer us a firm foundation and defense; for it was revealed to them and through the Holy Spirit given to them openly from heaven. The churches prior to this council derived it from them and this council has it from them too. For before the council, when Arius first began, as well as in the council and after the council, they defended themselves vigorously with Scripture, especially with St. John's gospel, and disputed sharply, as the books of Athanasius[156] and Hilary testify.[157] The *Historia Tripartita* also says in Book V, chapter 29, "At Nicaea the faith was grounded on the writings of the apostles."[158] Otherwise, if there were no Holy Scripture of the prophets and apostles, the mere words of the council would be meaningless, and its decisions would accomplish nothing. Therefore this article on the deity of Christ was the chief business of this council; indeed, it was the whole council, for that is why it was called and (as I said before) why it was adjourned on the same day on which it was adopted.

But on another day, when the emperor Constantine is not reported to have been present, they met again and dealt with other matters pertaining to the temporal, external rule of the church; among these were undoubtedly also the papers Constantine had previously thrown into the fire when he refused to judge. That is why they had to meet alone to settle these things without the emperor. Most of this was sheer clerical squabbling: there were not to be two bishops in one city; no bishop of a small church was to covet a larger one; clerics or servants of a church were not to leave their own church to wander aimlessly about from one church to another; no one was to consecrate the people of another bishop without his knowledge or consent; no bishop was to accept a person who had been expelled by another bishop; the bishop of Jerusalem should retain his ancient prerogative of pre-eminence before others; and more of such silly prattle.[159] Who could regard such things as articles of faith? And what can one preach about these things to the people in the church? What does

---

[156] Athanasius (*ca.* 295-373), bishop of Alexandria and the most vigorous defender of Nicene theology. For his writings, see *MPG* 16; *PNF*[2] 4.

[157] See p. 52, n. 131.

[158] *Hanc solam fidem, quae Nicaeae apostolorum auctoritate fundata est."* *MPL* 69, 1007a; *PNF*[2] 3, 83.

[159] Luther's source here is Rufinus I, 6. *MPL* 21, 473-475. Luther lists the following canons of Nicaea: X, XVI, XVII, XVIII, V, VIII. On the difference in numbering, see *PNF*[2] 14, 43.

all this have to do with the church or the people—unless one wanted to learn from this, as from a history book, that at this time there were everywhere in the church self-willed, base, disorderly bishops, priests, clerics, and people who were more concerned with honor, power, and wealth than with God or his kingdom, and who in this way had to be held in check!

It is easy to figure out that Constantine did not summon the council for these matters; otherwise, he probably would have done it before Arius ushered in this misery. Why should he have bothered about how these things would be kept? The bishops themselves, each in his own diocese, had to govern his own church and had done so before, as the articles themselves report. Moreover, it would have been a sin and a shame to call such a great council into session for such trivial matters, since God-given reason is quite sufficient to regulate these external matters, and the Holy Spirit, whose mission is to reveal Christ and not to dabble in such matters as are subject to reason, is not needed for this—unless, of course, one would call every act of pious Christians, even their eating and drinking, the work of the Holy Spirit. But the Holy Spirit must have better things to do for the sake of doctrine than these works which are subject to reason.

Not all who were present at this council were pious men; not all were Paphnutiuses, Jacobs, and Eustathiuses, etc. One can count seventeen Arian bishops who were prominent men, although they had to bow and scrape before the others.[160] The history of Theodoret reports[161] that there were twenty articles; Rufinus speaks of twenty-three. Now I cannot say whether the Arians or others afterward added to or subtracted from this number, or whether they substituted others (for the article which St. Paphnutius is said to have had adopted, concerning the wives of priests, is not among them).[162] But I do know well that nearly all of them have long been dead, buried in the books and fallen into decay, never able to rise again, as Constantine indicated and foretold by his act of

---

[160] Rufinus, I, 5. *MPL* 21, 472b.
[161] Although Luther did not read Theodoret's account, he found it quoted in the *Historia Tripartita* (II, 10-30), which usually quotes its sources. See Rufinus, I, 6. *MPL* 21, 473-475. See also Schäfer, *op. cit.*, p. 126, nn. 2, 3.
[162] See p. 43, n. 101.

throwing them into the fire and burning them.[163] They are not kept and cannot be kept. They were hay, straw, and wood (as St. Paul puts it)[164] built on the ground; that is why fire consumed them in time, just as other transitory things disappear. But if they had been articles of faith or commandments of God they would have survived, like the article concerning the divinity of Christ.

However, one ember from these wooden articles has kept on glowing, namely, the one about the date of Easter.[165] We do not observe this article quite correctly either (as the mathematicians and astronomers point out to us) because the equinox in our time is far different than in that time, and our Easter is often celebrated too late in the year.[166] Long ago, shortly after the days of the apostles, the quarrel about the date of Easter broke out; and over this trifling and unnecessary matter the bishops accused one another of heresy and excommunicated one another, which was a sin and a shame. Several advocated observing it on the same day as the Jews, according to the law of Moses; others, lest they be regarded as Jewish, wanted to observe it on the following Sunday.[167] The bishop of Rome, Victor,[168] who also became a martyr, excommunicated all the bishops and churches in Asia approximately one hundred and eighty years before this council for not

---

[163] See p. 56.

[164] I Cor. 3:12.

[165] Rufinus, I, 5 (*MPL* 21, 475*b*) and *Historia Tripartita*, II, 12 (*MPL* 69, 932*c*; *PNF*² 2, 13); IX, 38 (*MPL* 69, 1153-1156; *PNF*² 2, 130-134).

[166] Luther is aware of the difference between the Julian calendar (adopted in 46 B.C.) and the solar year. By A.D. 325 the equinox had moved from March 25 to March 21, the date on which Easter was celebrated. Until the introduction of the Gregorian calendar the equinox was moving forward at the rate of one day in 129 years. Gregory XIII (1572-1585) omitted thirteen days (October 5 to 14) in 1582 and introduced the leap year to balance the Christian calendar with the solar year. The Greek church did not accept the Gregorian calendar, and thus its calendar differs from the Gregorian calendar by thirteen days. For a detailed account of the chronological calculations in the history of the Christian calendar, see *O.D.C.C.*, p. 403; Allan Hauck, *Calendar of Christianity* (New York: Association Press, 1961), pp. 11-26; Albert Hauck (ed.), *Realencyklopädie für protestantische Theologie und Kirche* (3rd ed.; 24 vols.; Leipzig, 1896-1913), XXI, 914-945.

[167] This quarrel took place in 190-191 between the churches of Asia Minor, favoring the Jewish date (the 17th of Nisan), and Rome, advocating the Sunday following.

[168] Victor was bishop from 189 to 198.

adhering to the same Easter date as he did. So early did the Roman bishops make a grab for majesty and power! But Irenaeus,[169] bishop of Lyons, in France, who had known Polycarp,[170] a disciple of St. John the Evangelist, reprimanded him and settled the quarrel so that Victor had to leave the churches in peace.

That is why Constantine also had to take up this matter and help to settle it in the council. He decreed that the same Easter date should be observed throughout the world; read the *Tripartita*, Book IX, chapter 38.[171] I suppose that the present again calls for a reform and correction of the calendar in order to assign Easter its proper place. But no one should undertake that except the exalted majesties, emperors and kings, who would have to unanimously and simultaneously issue an order to all the world saying when Easter is henceforth to be celebrated. Otherwise, if one country were to start without the others, and worldly events, such as markets, fairs, and other business, were governed by the present date, the people of the country would appear at the markets of another country at the wrong time, which would result in wild disorder and confusion in everything. It would be very nice, and easy to do, if the high majesties would want to do it, since all the preparatory work has been done by the astronomers[172] and all that is needed is a decree or command. In the meantime we hold to the flickering ember from the Nicene council that Easter is to be kept on a Sunday; meanwhile the date may wobble back and forth, for they are called "movable festivals";[173] I call them wobbling festivals[174] since the Easter day, with its associated festivals, changes every year, coming early in one year, late in another, and not on a certain day like the other festivals.

This wobbling of the festivals is due to the fact that the an-

---

[169] An ancient church father, Irenaeus was a bishop in *ca.* 177.
[170] Polycarp, bishop of Smyrna, died as a martyr in 155.
[171] *MPL* 69, 1154d-1155a; *PNF²* 2, 131.
[172] The French theologian Peter of Ailly (1350-1420) and the Italian cardinal Nicholas of Cusa (1401-1464) had suggested striking a few days from the Julian calendar. Pope Sixtus IV then asked the astronomer Regiomontanus to undertake a calendar reform which was completed and went into effect under Gregory XIII in 1582.
[173] *Festa mobilia.*
[174] *Schückelfest.*

cient fathers (as was said) in the very beginning wanted to have Easter at the time established by Moses, namely, in the full moon of March, nearest the equinox; and yet they were unwilling to Judaize entirely, or to keep Easter with the Jews on the day of the full moon, so as Christians they dropped the law of Moses and took the Sunday after the March full moon. Thus it happened last year, 1538, that the Jews observed their Easter on the Saturday after Invocavit—as our church calls it—that is, about five weeks before we observed our Easter.[175] Now the Jews laugh about that and ridicule us Christians, saying that we do not keep Easter right and that we do not even know how to keep it right, thus hardening their unbelief. This then irritates our people, and they would gladly see the calendar corrected by the exalted majesties, for without their co-operation this is impossible to do and still less advisable.

In my opinion this experience with Easter is nicely described by Christ in Matthew 9 [:16-17], "No one puts a piece of unshrunk cloth on an old garment, for the patch tears away from the garment, and a worse tear is made. Neither is new wine put into old wineskins; if it is, the skins burst, and the wine is spilled, and the skins are destroyed." They want to retain a part of the old law of Moses, namely, to pay heed to the full moon of March— that is the old garment. Then (as Christians delivered from the law of Moses by Christ) they do not wish to be subject to that same day of the full moon, but, instead want to take the following Sunday—that is the new patch on the old garment. That is why the everlasting squabble and the constant wobbling have to date caused much mischief in the church, and it will have to, until the end of the world, with books appearing without measure or end on this subject. Christ has permitted this to go on for a special reason, as he always proves his strength in weakness and teaches us to recognize our own weakness.

How much better it would have been if they had let Moses' law regarding Easter die altogether and had retained nothing of the old garment. For Christ, to whom this law applied, has an-

---

[175] In 1538 Easter was celebrated on April 21. The Saturday after Invocavit Sunday, the first Sunday in Lent, was March 16.

nulled it completely, killed it, and buried it forever through his passion and resurrection. He rent the veil of the temple and subsequently broke up and destroyed Jerusalem with its priesthood, principality, law, and everything. They should instead have reckoned and noted the days of the passion, the burial, and the resurrection by the course of the sun and set a fixed date for these, as they did with Christmas, New Year's, the day of the Magi,[176] Candlemas,[177] the Annunciation of Mary,[178] the Feast of St. John,[179] and other festivals, which they call fixed, not wobbling festivals. Then one would know every year for certain when the day of Easter and its associated festivals must come, without such great difficulty and disputation.

Well, you say, Sunday should be held in reverence for the sake of Christ's resurrection—it is therefore called *dies Dominica*[180]—and Easter is assigned to that day, since Christ rose on the day after the Sabbath (which we now call Saturday). This is certainly an argument that moved them, but since *dies Dominica* does not mean Sunday, but the Lord's day, why shouldn't any day on which Easter had fallen be called *dies Dominica*, the Lord's day? Is not Christmas also *dies Dominica*, the Lord's day, that is, the day on which the Lord's special event, his birth, is celebrated, which does not fall on a Sunday every year? Yet it is still called Christ's day,[181] that is, the Lord's day, even if it falls on a Friday, because it has a fixed letter[182] in the calendar calculated by the course of the sun. Just so could Easter have a fixed letter in the calendar, whether it came on Friday or Wednesday, as happens with Christmas. That way we would be well rid of the law of Moses with its full moon of March, just as no one asks today whether the moon is full or not at Christmas, but we adhere to the days as calculated by the sun's course and ignore the moon.

---

176 Epiphany, January 6.
177 The Purification of Mary (or the Presentation of Our Lord), February 2.
178 March 25.
179 June 24.
180 "The Lord's day."
181 *Christag.*
182 In the calendar of Luther's time, as well as in ancient Christian calendars, each day was signified by a letter. Beginning with January 1, the letters ran from *a* to *g* and were repeated on the eighth day.

One might argue that since the equinox (as the astronomers point out) is movable, and the years in the calendar move too slowly and so do not keep pace with it, and the more years go by the worse it is, after a while the equinox would move further and further from a fixed Easter day,[183] as it would also move further and further from the day of St. Philip and St. James,[184] and from other festivals. What does it matter to us Christians? Even if our Easter should coincide with the day of St. Philip and St. James (which, I hope, will not happen before the end of the world) and move still further, we still celebrate Easter daily with our proclamation of Christ and our faith in him. It is enough to celebrate Easter once annually on a special day as an obvious, public, and perceptible reminder, not only because it affords an opportunity to discuss more thoroughly the history of the resurrection before the common people, but also because it represents a definite season according to which people may arrange their various business affairs, such as the seasons of St. Michael,[185] St. Martin,[186] St. Catherine,[187] St. John,[188] SS. Peter and Paul,[189] etc.

But this has been neglected from the very beginning; we cannot make any changes because the fathers did not initiate a change. The old garment with its great tear has stayed on and on, and now it may as well stay until the Last Day, which is imminent anyhow. Since the old garment has endured being patched and torn for approximately fourteen hundred years, it may as well let itself be patched and torn for another hundred years; for I hope that everything will soon come to an end.[190] And if the Easters have wobbled back and forth for about fourteen hundred years now, they may as well continue to wobble for the short time still

---

[183] See p. 61, n. 166.
[184] May 1.
[185] September 29.
[186] November 11.
[187] November 25.
[188] June 24.
[189] June 29.
[190] Luther's view is based upon the idea that the world would last for six thousand years, of which only a few were left at his time. He seems to have arrived at the number fourteen hundred on the basis of his estimate for the beginning of the Easter controversies in *ca.* 190 until 1539. See Hauck, *Realencyklopädie*, XXI, 924.

remaining, since no one will do anything about it anyway, and those who would like to do something cannot.

I am entering into this lengthy and needless chatter solely for the purpose of expressing my opinion, in case several sects[191] in the course of time dare arbitrarily to move the Easter festival to another date than that which we now observe. And I believe if the Anabaptists had been sufficiently versed in astronomy to understand these things, they would have rushed in headlong, and (as is characteristic of the sect) introduced something entirely new and observed Easter on a different day than the whole world. But since they were unlearned in the sciences, the devil was unable to employ them as that kind of instrument or tool. Therefore, I advise that one let Easter come as it now comes, and keep it as it is kept now, and let the old garment be patched and torn (as was said); and let Easter wobble back and forth until the Last Day, or until the monarchs, in view of these facts, unanimously and simultaneously change it.

For this is not going to kill us,[192] nor will St. Peter's bark suffer distress because of it, since it is neither heresy nor sin (though the ancient fathers in their ignorance regarded it as such and dubbed each other heretics and excommunicated each other over it), but only an error or solecism in astronomy, which serves temporal government rather than the church. If the Jews mock us, as though we were doing it out of ignorance, then we, in turn, mock them far more because they adhere so rigidly and vainly to their Easter, and do not know that Christ fulfilled, annulled, and destroyed all that fifteen hundred years ago. For we do it willingly, knowingly, not out of ignorance. We would know quite well how to keep Easter according to the law of Moses—far better than they know it. But we will not and must not do it, for we have the Lord over Moses and over all things, who says, "The Son of man is lord of the sabbath" [Matt. 12:8]. How much more

---

191 *Rotten,* a term Luther used frequently to designate the Anabaptists and other opponents of his position. For a survey of the various religious movements opposing the major reformers, cf. George H. Williams, *The Radical Reformation* (Philadelphia: Westminster, 1962).

192 A German proverb, *"Es bricht uns kein bein."* Cf. Thiele, *Luthers Sprichwörtersammlung,* No. 324.

is he the Lord over Easter and Pentecost, which, in the law of Moses, are less than the sabbath, which is on the tables of Moses,[193] while Easter and Pentecost are outside the tables of Moses? Furthermore, we have St. Paul, who flatly forbids any one to be bound to holidays, feasts, and anniversaries of Moses, Galatians 4 [:10] and Colossians 2 [:16].

We therefore have and must have the power and the freedom to observe Easter when we choose; and even if we made Friday into Sunday, or vice versa, it would still be right, as long as it were done unanimously by the rulers and the Christians (as I said before). Moses is dead and buried by Christ, and days or seasons are not to be lords over Christians, but rather Christians are lords over days and seasons, free to fix them as they will or as seems convenient to them. For Christ made all things free when he abolished Moses. However, we will let things remain as they now are, since no peril, error, sin, or heresy is involved, and we are averse to changing anything needlessly or at our own personal whim, out of consideration for others who observe Easter at the same time as we do. We know we shall attain salvation without Easter and Pentecost, without Friday and Sunday, and we know that we cannot be damned—as St. Paul teaches us—because of Easter, Pentecost, Sunday, or Friday.

But to get back to the council, I say that we make too much of this ember from the Nicene council. The pope and his church subsequently made of this not only gold, silver, and precious stones, but also a foundation, that is, an article of faith, without which we could not be saved; and they all call it a commandment of, and an act of, obedience to the church. That makes them far worse than the Jews, for the Jews do have the Mosaic text commanded by God at that time in their favor, while these have nothing but their own fancy on their side; they come along and want to make a new garment out of the old rags of Moses. They claim that they are obeying Moses, though their doctrine is sheer fantasy, a dream about Moses who has long been dead and, as Scripture declares, buried by the Lord himself [Deut. 34:6] (that is, by Christ), so no one has ever found his grave. They

---

[193] The Decalogue.

want to reproduce the living Moses by magic before our eyes, but they fail to see, as St. Paul says in Galatians 5 [:3], that if they wish to keep one part of Moses they must keep all of Moses. Consequently, if they regard it a part of Mosaic law to set the date of Easter according to the full moon in March, they must also keep the whole law concerning the paschal lamb and forthwith become Jews, keeping a bodily paschal lamb with them. If not, they must discard it all, the full moon too, with all the rest of Moses; or in any case not regard this as necessary for salvation like an article of faith, which is what I believe the fathers in this council (especially the best ones) did.

Thus we see that this council dealt primarily with the article that Christ was truly God, for which it was convoked and for which it is and is called a council. They also dealt with several nonessential, physical, external, temporal matters on the side, rightfully to be viewed as temporal and not to be compared with articles of faith; nor are they to be regarded as eternal law (for they are past and expired). But the council found it necessary to attend to such physical matters as were pertinent and needful in their time, which no longer concern us today, and which are neither possible nor profitable for us to observe. And in proof of this, the article prescribing the rebaptism of heretics is false and wrong, even if it was formulated by the true fathers themselves[194] and not patched together by the Arians or the other loose bishops. Thus the apostolic council in Jerusalem also found it necessary for their day to settle, after it had disposed of the important business, several nonessential, external articles, such as that dealing with blood, strangled animals, and the sacrifice to idols; but not with the intention of making this an eternal law in the church, to be kept as an article of faith, for it has fallen into disuse. And why should we not also examine how this council can be understood within the context of the reasons that made it necessary?

This is how it came into being: Gentiles, who had been converted by Barnabas and Paul, had received the Holy Spirit through the gospel just as well as the Jews, and yet they were not under the law like the Jews. Then the Jews insisted very strongly that

---

[194] See pp. 44-46.

the Gentiles be circumcised and commanded to keep the law of Moses; otherwise they could not be saved. These were hard, harsh, and heavy words—no salvation without the law of Moses and circumcision. The Pharisees who had become believers in Christ were especially insistent on this, according to Acts 15 [:5]. Thereupon the apostles and elders met to discuss this matter, and after they had quarreled at length and sharply, St. Peter arose and delivered the powerful and beautiful sermon in Acts 15 [:7-11], "Brethren, you know that in the early days God made choice among you, that by my mouth the Gentiles should hear the word of the gospel and believe. And God who knows the heart bore witness to them, giving them the Holy Spirit just as he did to us; and he made no distinction between us and them, but cleansed their hearts by faith. Now therefore why do you make trial of God by putting a yoke upon the neck of the disciples which neither our fathers nor we have been able to bear? But we believe that we shall be saved through the grace of the Lord Jesus, just as they will."

This sermon sounds as though St. Peter were really angry and disgusted about the harsh words of the Pharisees, who said that those who did not circumcise themselves and keep the law of Moses could not attain salvation, as was said above. He counters with hard, decisive words and says, "You are well aware that the Gentiles heard the Word and were saved through me, like Cornelius and his family; in proof of this, you grumbled against me and chided me because I had gone to the Gentiles, had converted and baptized them"—Acts 10 and 11.[195] "Is it possible that you have forgotten this and are determined to impose burdens on the Gentiles that neither our fathers nor we could bear? What is it but tempting God if we impose impossible burdens on others which we ourselves can carry as little as they can, especially since you know that God has given them the Spirit without this burden, and made them equal to us, since we, together with our fathers, did not receive the same Spirit due to the merit of the burden, but by grace. For because we were unable to bear the

---

[195] Luther here paraphrases Acts 10:1—11:18.

burden, we merited wrath far more than grace, since we were obligated to bear it as we had pledged to do."

This is the substance and the main concern of this council, namely, that the Pharisees wished to establish works or merits of the law, over against the word of grace, as necessary for salvation; that would have nullified the word of grace, including Christ and the Holy Spirit. That is why St. Peter argued so determinedly against it, asserting that one is saved solely by the grace of Jesus Christ, without any works at all. Not satisfied with that, he also dared to say that all their previous fathers—the patriarchs, the prophets, and the entire holy church in Israel—had been saved by nothing but the grace of Jesus Christ, and he condemned as tempters of God everyone who had wanted or still wanted to attain salvation in any other way. I think this is real preaching, and knocks the bottom out of the cask.[196] Shouldn't one burn this heretic who forbids all good works and holds grace and faith alone to be sufficient for salvation—and this for all the saints and all ancestors since the beginning of the world? We must now hear ourselves dubbed heretics and devils, though we simply teach this sermon of St. Peter and the decree of this council, as all the world now knows better than the Pharisees did, whom St. Peter is here chiding.

But St. Peter is far beyond us; and it is weird that he not only preaches the grace of God unto salvation, which everyone is surely glad to hear, but that he also declares that neither they themselves nor their ancestors were able to bear such a burden. In plain German this means, "We apostles and whoever we might be, including our ancestors, patriarchs, prophets, and the whole of God's people, have not kept God's commandments; we are sinners and are damned." He is not just speaking of blood sausage and black jelly here, but of the law of Moses, saying that no one has obeyed it or wanted to obey it. As Christ says in John 7 [:19], "None of you keeps the law." That (it seems to me) is really preaching the law unto damnation and making a damned sinner of oneself too. How then does that self-styled heir to St. Peter's

---

[196] See p. 56, n. 149.

70

throne dare to call himself "most holy"[197] and to elevate whatever saints he wants, by virtue of their works and not by the grace of Christ? And where are the monks who can bear a much heavier burden than that of the law so that they also sell their surplus holiness?[198] We do not have this strange Peter's mind, for we do not dare to regard the patriarchs, prophets, apostles, and holy church as sinners, but must also call the pope the "most holy," meaning "the saint of saints, that is, Christ"![199]

But St. Peter deserves a very gracious and honest absolution, and is no longer to be considered strange, for he preaches in this very great article: first, the law, that we are all sinners. Second, that solely the grace of Christ gives us salvation, including the patriarchs, prophets, apostles, and the entire holy church from its beginning, all of whom he makes and damns as sinners with himself. Third, long before the Nicene council comes into being he teaches that Christ is true God, for he says that all the saints must be damned if they are not saved by the grace of our Lord Jesus Christ. To bestow grace and salvation like a lord, one must be true God, who can remove sin by grace, and death and hell by salvation. No creature can do that, unless it be the "most holy" in Rome—but without harming St. Peter's sermon! Fourth, he who holds otherwise and teaches Christians to attain salvation or obtain mercy through the law or their own works is a tempter of God.

Anyone who will may interpret this burden only in terms of the law of Moses and of circumcision, and not the Ten Commandments or good works. I am satisfied with that; if you can keep the Ten Commandments more easily than the Mosaic ceremonies, go ahead and be holier than St. Peter and St. Paul! I am so weak in keeping the Ten Commandments that it seems to me all Mosaic ceremonies would be far easier for me to observe, if the Ten Commandments would not press me so hard. But there is no time to argue that now; it has been amply discussed in other ways

---

[197] *Sanctissimum.*

[198] A reference to the monastic works of supererogation and to the sale of indulgences based upon the superfluous merits of Christ and the saints. Cf. Luther's *Explanations of the Ninety-five Theses.* LW 31, 83-252.

[199] *Sanctum Sanctorum id est Christum.*

and in other places.[200] But even reason will have to decide and admit that the Ten Commandments or the works of the Ten Commandments neither are nor can be called the grace of Jesus Christ, but are and must be called something entirely different. Now St. Peter asserts here that we must be saved solely by the grace of Jesus Christ; but that grace cannot be received or kept with one's hands, much less with the works of one's hands, but with faith in one's heart, is most certainly true.

It is also strange to see that St. Peter, who as an apostle had the authority and the power, together with the other apostles, to reformulate this article—which is why they are called the cornerstone of the church—nevertheless falls back on the holy church of God in former times, that church of all the patriarchs and prophets from the beginning, and says in effect, "This is not a new doctrine; for this is what our ancestors and all the saints taught and believed. Then how dare we teach a different or a better one, without tempting God and confusing and burdening our brethren's conscience?" That, I say, is the substance or main concern of this council, for which it was convened or convoked; and with which it was settled and adjourned. But the papal ass does not see this main item, and disregards it; instead, he gapes at the other four items added by James,[201] about blood, strangled meat, sacrifices to idols, and fornication, for they want to strengthen their tyranny thereby and claim that since the church has changed such articles, they want to have the power to change the articles of faith and the councils; that is, "We are the church and can decree and do what we like." Listen, papal ass, you are a particularly crass ass, indeed, you are a filthy sow!

The article of this council has neither fallen nor been altered, but, as St. Peter says, has been and will remain in force until the end of the world, for there have always been godly people who were saved solely by the grace of Christ and not by the law.

---

[200] Probably a reference to the controversy with the Antinomians in 1537. This group, whose spokesman was Luther's old friend John Agricola (ca. 1499-1566) of Eisleben, taught that repentance was possible only through the knowledge of God in the gospel, not in the law. Cf. Luther's tract *Against the Antinomians* (*Wider die Antinomer*). WA 50, 461-477.

[201] Acts 15:13-21.

The text and the faith of the gospel, baptism, the sacrament, the office of the keys, the name of Jesus Christ, etc., have survived even under the devil of the papacy, although the pope ranted against them with his accursed lies and shamefully misled the world; just as has been said of the Nicene council, that its decree existed before it and remained after it. For the true conciliar decrees must always remain—as they indeed always have—especially the chief articles, for the sake of which the councils came into being and are called councils.

But what are we to say here about this apostolic council in which James singles out four items—blood, what is strangled, sacrifices to idols, and fornication? Doesn't the council contradict itself, and isn't the Holy Spirit at variance with himself? For these two speeches are plainly and palpably contradictory—not to impose the burden of the Mosaic law, and simultaneously to impose it. Play the sophist, if you will, and say that the council did not speak of the whole law of Moses, but only of portions, several of which might be imposed and others not imposed. But that will not do; for in Galatians 6 [5:3] St. Paul concludes, "He who keeps one part of the law is bound to keep it in its entirety." This is equivalent to acknowledging one's duty to keep the whole law—otherwise, one wouldn't need a part of it either. Here, too, the new patch would be found on an old garment, creating a worse tear [Luke 5:36]. Thus it is quite evident that these items are contained in the law of Moses and nowhere else in the law of the Gentiles, for what need would there be to impose these things on the Gentiles if they were already familiar with them from their native law? How then do we reconcile these two—no law and the whole law?

Well then, if we cannot make them agree, we must dismiss St. James with his article and retain St. Peter with his chief article, for the sake of which the council was held; for without St. Peter's article no one can attain salvation. But, as St. Peter preached in this council, Cornelius and the Gentiles whom St. Peter had baptized along with him in his house were sanctified and saved before St. James came along with his article, etc. I also touched on the question above of whether one may conscientiously let these items go, since the Holy Spirit rules this council and sets all this up. But the dispute on whether the council contradicted itself and disagreed with itself is much sharper. And so, just when they want to relieve us of one impossible burden, they impose a still more impossible one on us, that we do simultaneously nothing and everything. To be sure, now that this has been invalidated we do well to adhere to that one part, namely, to St. Peter's article, that is, to the genuine Christian faith.

Only the fourth item mentioned by St. James, the one regarding fornication, has not been invalidated. To be sure, about twenty years ago courtesans[202] and accursed lords were already beginning to consider fornication not a mortal sin but a venial sin, and advocated the saying, "Nature should have its way,"[203] to which the holiest people in Rome still hold. And, I suppose, those blind leaders were led to this conclusion because St. James set fornication alongside the other three items that have fallen: if the prohibition of blood, strangled meat, and sacrifices to idols is no longer valid, the prohibition of fornication is no longer valid either, since it is listed with these three items, and is furthermore a natural and human act. Let them go their way, they do not deserve anything better.

I shall give my opinion about this; may someone else improve on it. It has now often been said that one should view and also keep the councils according to the chief article which has given the council its purpose; for that is, and in that consists, the real essence of the council, the true body of the council, to which everything else must be adjusted and fitted, like a garment is fitted to the person who wears it or is dressed in it. If the garment doesn't fit, one takes it off and throws it away; then it is no longer a garment. Nor can there be a council (or for that matter an assembly, even a diet or a chapter) after the main business is settled, unless one or two items of secondary importance are found needing to be patched up or settled, as in the Nicene council, when, after it was settled that Christ is true God, the external

---

[202] Members of the papal court. Cf. the *Gravamina* of 1521. DRTA. JR 2, 673. Cf. also *An Open Letter to the Christian Nobility* (1520). PE 2, 88.
[203] *Natura petit exitum.*

matters pertaining to the Easter date and the squabbles of the priests came up—so here St. James's articles come up after the chief article of St. Peter.

Thus the final opinion and verdict of all the apostles and the council was that men must be saved, without the law or the burden of the law, solely by the grace of Jesus Christ. When St. Peter, St. Paul, and their followers had reached this verdict, they were happy and quite satisfied, for they had worked and striven for such a decision against the Pharisees and Jews who had become believers, but still wanted to keep the law. Now when St. James submitted his article, they could put up with it, since it was not imposed as law or a burden of the law, as the council's letter also reports, "To lay upon you no greater burden than these necessary things: that you abstain from blood," etc. [Acts 15:28-29]. They might even have liked St. James to add more items, such as the rule about leprosy or the like, even though they do not affect the Ten Commandments. But these things should not be law or a burden (they say), but items otherwise necessary. Yet when a burden is no longer a burden, it is good to bear; and when a law is no longer law, it is good to keep, like the Ten Commandments. How much more is that true of ceremonies, especially if they are abolished or if very few are retained. But more about this later. For if the pope would relieve us of his burden, so that it need no longer be law, we should readily obey him, especially if he were to retain but a few of his ordinances and drop most of them. Thus St. James and his article must now be interpreted without prejudice to St. Peter's article concerning grace without law, which must remain pure and constant and must rule alone without the law.

However, to understand this council fully we want to take a look at the causes of these secondary issues of St. James. The law of Moses was (so to say) ingrained, born into, suckled into, worked into, and lived into the Jews from their youth, so that it had become almost a part of their nature, as St. Paul says in Galations 2 [:15], "We are Jews by birth," that is, we are born Mosaic. He is here speaking of the law and not merely of birth; this is why they could not tolerate the nature of the Gentiles or be equated with them when they were dispersed among Gentiles in other lands and saw these Gentiles eat blood, strangled meat, and meat sacrifices to idols and still boast that they were God's people or Christians. This moved St. James to guard against such offense, so that the Gentiles did not abuse their freedom too wilfully just to spite the Jews, but acted decently, so that the Jews, rooted so deeply in the law, would not be offended and spurn the gospel. For, dear God, one should have patience with sick and erring men. We drunken Germans too are wise at times and say, "A load of hay must give a wide berth to a drunken man; for no one can win his spurs against sick people, and no one can become an expert among ignoramuses."[204]

Now St. James nevertheless does it very moderately; he disregards the whole Mosaic law concerning sacrifice and all the other items that had to be observed in Jerusalem and in the country and takes up only the four items which offend the Jews dispersed among the Gentiles. These dispersed Jews could not but see the Gentiles' ways, live among them, and at times eat with them; so it was vexing, and also wrong, to place blood sausage, rabbits cooked in blood, blood jellies, and meat sacrifices to idols before a Jew, especially if one knew that he abhorred it and took it as an insult. It would be the same as if I said, "Listen, Jew! Even if I could bring you to Christ by refraining from eating blood sausage or from serving it to you, I would not do it. I would rather scare you away from accepting Christ and chase you to hell with blood sausage." Would that be kind, not to mention Christian? Must not everyone at times keep silent and refrain from an action for the benefit of another human being, when he sees and knows that words and deeds would work his neighbor's harm, especially if this silence does not offend God? Now, at that time, the Gentiles were very antagonistic to the Jews, and very proud because they were their masters. The Jews, on the other hand, were intolerant, believing that they alone were God's people—as many histories clearly testify.

---

[204] Three German proverbs: *"Einem truncken Man soll ein fuder hau weichen"*; *"an krancken Leuten kan niemand kein Ritter werden"*; *"an unverstendigen kann niemand kein meister werden."* They are not contained in Thiele, *Luthers Sprichwörtersammlung.*

Therefore this good advice of St. James was the very best means to peace, indeed, even to the salvation of many; since the Gentiles had attained Christ's grace without law and merit, they should now, on their part, show themselves helpful in a few matters so that the Jews, as the sick and erring folk, might attain the same grace. For it did not harm the Gentiles before God to avoid the external custom of eating blood, strangled meat, and meat sacrifices to idols in public (since grace had liberated their conscience from all that) and to desist, for the benefit and salvation of the Jews, from giving wilful offense; besides, in the absence of the Jews they could eat and drink what they wished, without jeopardy to their conscience. And the Jews, too, would be equally free in their conscience, but could not change the old external customs so suddenly—"Custom is second nature,"[205] especially when it has grown from God's law. Thus fairness and reason also teach that one should not spite nor hinder, but rather serve and help them in accord with the command, "You shall love your neighbor," etc. [Matt. 22:39].

So these two articles, that of St. Peter and that of St. James, are contradictory and yet they are not. St. Peter's deals with faith, St. James's with love. St. Peter's article tolerates no law; it eats blood, strangled meat, meat sacrifices to idols, and the devil in the bargain, without paying much attention, for it feels responsible to God alone and not to man, and does nothing but believe in the gracious God. But St. James's article lives and eats with man; it also directs everything to St. Peter's article, carefully warding off any obstacle that might obstruct the way. Now the office of love is so constituted on earth that since whatever is loved and helped is changeable and transient, love cannot have the same object forever; the one passes away and is replaced by another which it must also love, until the end of the world. Now when the Jews had become upset or stiff-necked and the Gentiles no longer had so much love to give them, everything lapsed—not changed by the power of the church, as the papists lie, but be-

---

[205] *Consuetudo est altera natura.* A proverb preserved by Cicero (106-43 B.C.), famous Roman philosopher, in *De Finibus*, V, 25, 74. See H. Rackham (trans.), *Cicero: De Finibus Bonorum et Malorum* ("The Loeb Classical Library" [New York: Putman, 1921]), p. 476.

cause the cause was removed. So the Christians freely ate blood and black jelly, from which they had abstained for a time out of consideration for the Jews, even though they had not been bound to abstain before God in accordance with their faith. For if St. James had intended to impose these items as law he would have had to impose the entire law, as St. Paul says in Galatians 5 [:3], "He who keeps one law must keep them all"; that would flatly contradict St. Peter's article, which St. James confirms.

But this, I believe, was the reason St. James added fornication, which has always been forbidden in the Ten Commandments, to the other items: fornication was regarded by the Gentiles as a light, indeed, as no sin at all, as one can read in the Gentiles' books and as I pointed out above, which twenty years ago the courtesans and worthless priests also began to say publicly and to believe. Thus among the Gentiles fornication was as great a sin as eating blood sausage, rabbits cooked in blood, blood jellies, or meat sacrifices to idols. Just read in Roman history how unwilling they were to take wives, so that the Emperor Augustus had to compel them to marry; for they thought fornication was right, and to be forced to marry was to suffer violence and injustice.[206] That is why St. James wants to teach the Gentiles that they should gladly abstain from fornication without being forced to by the authorities, and live purely and chastely in the state of marriage, as the Jews did, who were greatly offended by such license in fornication and who could not believe, because of this disparity in food and conduct, etc., that these Gentiles should attain God's grace and become God's people.

The apostles, therefore, did not impose the law on the Gentiles, and yet they permitted the Jews to retain it for some time, meanwhile vigorously preaching grace—as we note in St. Paul when he became a Jew among the Jews and a Gentile among the Gentiles, so that he might win them all, I Corinthians 12 [9:20], and when he circumcised his disciple Timothy, who was already a believer, not because this was prescribed, but, as St. Luke says, "because of the Jews that were in those places" [Acts 16:3], be-

---

[206] Augustus (30 B.C.-A.D. 14) issued this marriage law in A.D. 9 for the third time after two previous attempts (in 28 and 18 B.C.) had failed.

cause he did not want to offend them. Later, in Acts 21 [:26], he let himself be purified in the temple with the Jews and he sacrificed according to the law of Moses, which he did as St. Augustine expressed it in that fine and now famous saying, *"Oportuit synagogam cum honore sepelire,"* "One must give Moses or his church and law an honorable burial."[207]

But how this council and both St. Peter's and St. James's articles were subsequently kept, you can gather amply from St. Paul's epistles,[208] wherein he complains everywhere about the false apostles who insisted on the necessity of the law to the detriment of grace, and who seduced whole clans and countries away from Christ and back to the law, albeit in the name of Christ—just as things became much worse after the Council of Nicaea. After that knave Arius had humbled himself and had even pledged allegiance to the council before Emperor Constantine,[209] for which the emperor reinstated him, he fanned the flames even more. And the bishops of his party pursued the game so abominably, especially after Constantine's death, through his son the emperor Constantius[210] (whom they had won over), that Constantius expelled all true bishops throughout the world except two, Gregory and Basil.[211] Some say that Constantine, the father, had also become an Arian[212] before he died and had in his will commended an Arian priest, strongly recommended by his sister Constantia on her deathbed, to his son Constantius, and that it was through him that the Arians later became so powerful.

These histories admonish us to pray faithfully for great lords, for the devil seeks them out more than others since he can do the greatest damage through them. And they are also a warning to

---

[207] The passage could not be located in Augustine's works.
[208] See for example, I Cor. 1:10 ff.; II Cor. 10:2 ff.; Gal. 5:12.
[209] *Historia Tripartita*, III, 6. MPL 69, 950d; PNF[2] 2, 277. Arius presented a "confession of faith" (*Expositio*) to the emperor.
[210] Constantius was regent in the Orient (337-350) and then emperor (350-361). He supported the Arian party.
[211] *Historia Tripartita*, VII, 22. MPL 69, 1086b; PNF[2] 2, 99. Gregory of Nazianz (*ca.* 329-390), bishop of Constantinople, and Basil the Great, bishop of Caesarea (370-379). Together with Gregory of Nyssa (d. *ca.* 394) they defended the Nicene Creed against Arianism.
[212] This was recorded in the *Chronology* (*Chronicon*) of St. Jerome. See MPL 27, 499-500.

us to be careful and not readily believe the sectarian spirits,[213] even when they humble themselves deeply, as this knave Arius did, and as Saul did with David [I Sam. 24:16 ff.]. "Sometimes even the wicked are defeated" (one says).[214] But they keep in the background until they have enough air and room; then they, like Arius, go ahead and do anyway what they had in mind, so that it really does not surprise me very much that the fathers imposed such severe and long penances on apostate Christians. They must have discovered how false their humility was, and how rarely they sincerely and from the bottom of their hearts humbled themselves or repented—just as Sirach [Ecclus. 12:10] says, "Never trust your reconciled enemy," etc.

To sum up, I let anyone who does not know what *osculum Judae*, "Judas kiss" [Matt. 26:49], means read with me the story of Arius under Constantine, and he will have to say that Arius far outdid Judas. He deceived the good emperor Constantine with these nice words: "We believe in one God, the Father almighty, and in the Lord Jesus Christ, his Son, born of the Father before the whole world, one God, one Word, by whom everything was made," etc.[215] My dear man, what Christian could regard these words as heretical, or think that Arius still viewed Christ as a creature? And yet that he did became quite evident during the hearing. Auxentius,[216] the bishop of Milan, the immediate predecessor of Ambrose, later similarly fooled the people with such beautiful words that at first I really grew angry at St. Hilary when I read the words "Blasphemy of Auxentius" on the title page of Auxentius' *Confessions*.[217] I would have staked my body and soul on Auxentius' oath that he regarded Christ as true God. I also hope that despite such deceptive and crafty words many pious simple

---

213 *Rottengeister.*
214 *"Aliquando compunguntur et mali."* A Latin proverb of unknown origin.
215 Quoted from Arius' *Confession of Faith* (*Expositio*). See p. 79, n. 209.
216 Deposed in 370 by Damasus I, the bishop of Rome (366-384), he kept his bishopric until his death (374).
217 Auxentius stated his position in a letter to the emperor. Hilary of Poitiers added his *Book Against the Arians or Auxentius of Milano* (*Liber Contra Arianos vel Auxentium Mediolanensem*) and entitled the whole *An Example of Auxentius' Blasphemy* (*Exemplum Blasphemia Auxentii*). See MPL 10, 617-618; *Historia Tripartita*, V, 29. MPL 69, 1006; PNF² 3, 83.

folk retained their former belief and were preserved in it, not understanding these words in any way other than that of the faith, as no one could understand them differently who is not informed of the hidden meaning given them by the Arians.

And because it is necessary for Christians to know such an illustration, and since the ordinary reader does not study history so closely and does not realize how useful it is as a warning against all other sectarian spirits whom the devil their god makes so slippery that one cannot catch or grasp them anywhere, I will relate this affair briefly in several items.

First, Arius had taught that Christ is not God, but a creature.[218] Then the good bishops exacted from him the confession that Christ is God; but this he did in a false sense, meaning that Christ was God just like St. Paul, St. Peter, and the angels, who are called "gods and sons of God" in Scripture.[219]

Second, when the fathers became aware of this they again pressed him and his adherents to admit that Christ was true and very God; he used these words for the sake of appearance because it had theretofore been taught like this in all the churches. But among themselves they, particularly Eusebius,[220] bishop of Nicomedia and Arius' highest patron, interpreted these words like this: "Omne factum dei est verum,"[221] "Whatever God creates or makes is true and real; for whatever is false God did not make. Therefore we are willing to confess that Christ is a real, true God (but according to us a created god, like Moses and all the saints)," etc. Here they conceded everything that we still confess in our hymns in church on Sunday and have ever since the Nicene council: "God of God, light of light, very God of very God."[222]

---

[218] *Historia Tripartita*, I, 12. MPL 69, 902b; PNF² 3, 34.

[219] See for example, Job 38:7; Ps. 82:6; John 10:34; I Cor. 8:5.

[220] Eusebius (*ca.* 260-*ca.* 340) was the leader of the middle party (over against orthodoxy and radical Arianism) at the Council of Nicaea. He granted Arius asylum, but did not change his position.

[221] This quotation is not found in the *Historia Tripartita*. Luther probably coined a phrase which may summarize the contents of a letter of Eusebius to Paul, bishop of Tyre, and the statements in a document ascribed to Athanasius; cf. *Historia Tripartita*, I, 16; II, 7. MPL 69, 915-916; 926-927; PNF² 3, 42-43, 44-46.

[222] The Nicene Creed was sung every Sunday following the reading of the gospel.

Third, when the trickery that they with these words still called Christ a creature became known, the dispute became sharper, so that they had to confess that Christ had existed prior to the whole world. Who could here believe otherwise than that Arius and his bishops were genuine Christians and had been unjustly condemned by the Nicene council? For they were playing these tricks soon after the Nicene council (which had made short work of them and formulated the creed as it still exists) because they wanted to ruin the Nicene council and assailed one after another of its points.[223]

Fourth, when this dodge was discovered too, that Christ was still to be and to be called a creature, with the understanding that he had indeed existed before the whole world—that is, that he had been created and made before the whole world or any other creature [Col. 1:15]—they were forced to acknowledge that the whole world, all things, were made by him, as John 1 [:3] declares. However, among their own people they interpreted this to mean that Christ was made first and then all things were made by him.[224]

Fifth, it was now easy for them to confess, "Begotten, not made," born of God, not made, born as all Christians, born of God, are children of God, John 1 [:12-13]; not made among other creatures, but before all creatures.

Sixth, when it came to the core of the matter, that Christ is *homousius*[225] with the Father, that is, that Christ is of one and the same divinity with the Father and has one and the same power with him, they could find no more subterfuges, loopholes, detours, or evasions. *Homousius* means "of one essence or nature" or "of the same and not of a second essence," as the fathers had decreed in the council and as is sung in Latin, *consubstantialis*, and as some afterward called it, *coexistentialis, coessentialis*. This they had accepted in the council at Nicaea, and this they still accepted when they had to speak before the emperor and the fathers; but they fought it bitterly before their own people

---

[223] *Historia Tripartita*, IV, 10. *MPL* 69, 961; *PNF*[2] 2, 38.
[224] *Historia Tripartita*, V, 7. *MPL* 69, 988-990; *PNF*[2] 2, 56-57.
[225] A Latin translation of the Greek "of one substance."

and asserted that such words were not used in Holy Scripture.[226] They held many councils, even during Constantine's lifetime, in order to weaken the Nicene council; they stirred up much trouble, and later frightened our people so much that St. Jerome, dismayed by it, wrote a distressing letter to Damasus, bishop of Rome, suggesting that the word *homousius* be stricken. "For," (he says) "I do not know what sort of poison there is in these letters that the Arians get so upset by them."[227]

A dialogue is still extant in which Athanasius and Arius argue about this word *homousius* before an officer called Probus.[228] When Arius pressed the point that no such word was to be found in Scripture and Athanasius countered in kind, saying that the words *"innascibilis, ingenitus Deus,"* that is, "God is unborn"— which the Arians had employed to prove that Christ could not be God since he was born, while God was unborn, etc.—were not to be found in the Bible either, the official Probus decided against Arius. It is certainly true that one should teach nothing outside of Scripture pertaining to divine matters, as St. Hilary writes in *On the Trinity*, Book I,[229] which means only that one should teach nothing that is at variance with Scripture. But that one should not use more or other words than those contained in Scripture— this cannot be adhered to, especially in a controversy and when heretics want to falsify things with trickery and distort the words of Scripture. It thus became necessary to condense the meaning of Scripture, comprised of so many passages, into a short and comprehensive word, and to ask whether they regarded Christ as *homousius*, which was the meaning of all the words of Scripture that they had distorted with false interpretations among their own people, but had freely confessed before the emperor and the council. It is just as if the Pelagians[230] were to try to embarrass

---

[226] *Historia Tripartita*, V, 8. *MPL* 69, 990-992; *PNF*[2] 2, 57-58.

[227] *Epistola 15*. *MPL* 22, 355-358; *PNF*[2] 6, 18-20.

[228] *Dialogue Against the Arians (Contra Arianos Dialogus)*. *MPL* 62, 155-179. This dialogue passed in the sixteenth century as a work of Athanasius. The author, however, was Vigilius of Thapsus (d. *ca.* 500), whose exact role in the Arian controversy is unknown. Luther already knew of the dialogue during his stay in Erfurt. Cf. *WA* 30[III], 530.

[229] Chapter 18. *MPL* 10, 49; *PNF*[2] 9, 50-51.

[230] The followers of Pelagius (d. *ca.* 418), who opposed Augustine's doctrine

us with the term "original sin" or "Adam's plague" because these words do not occur in Scripture, though Scripture clearly teaches the meaning of these words, that we are "conceived in sin," Psalm 51 [:5], that we are "by nature children of wrath," Ephesians 2 [:3], and that we must all be accounted sinners "because of the sin of one man," Romans [5:12].

Now tell me, if Arius would still today come before you and confess to you the entire creed of the Nicene council, as we sing it today in our churches, could you regard him as heretical? I myself would say that he was right. And if he nevertheless would, like a knave, believe otherwise and subsequently interpret and teach these words differently, wouldn't I have been nicely duped? That is why I do not believe that Constantine became an Arian, but that he adhered to the Nicene council. What happened to him was that he was deceived and believed that Arius agreed with the Nicene council. He also had him take an oath (as was said above) and then demanded that Arius again be received in Alexandria. But as Athanasius refused to do this because he knew the false Arius better than Constantine did, he had to be expelled.[231] It probably occurred to Constantine, as a human being, that Arius, this pious Christian, had been condemned in Nicaea out of envy or jealousy, especially since the Arians, particularly Eusebius of Nicomedia, won the emperor over, filled his ears with gossip, and eulogized Arius. For great kings and lords, though they may be pious, are not always surrounded at court by angels and St. John the Baptist, but often by Satan, Judas, and Doeg, as the Book of Kings clearly testifies [I Kings 22:22; I Sam. 22:9]. It is a good sign that Constantine, before his death, recalled Athanasius, no matter how hard the Arians tried to prevent it, *Tripartita*, III, 11,[232] whereby he indicated that he did not want to have the Nicene council and its doctrines rejected, but that he would have liked to establish unity.

---

of original sin, teaching that sin is not a natural state, but an act of free will. Luther refers here to the Roman theologians who taught Pelagianism or Semi-Pelagianism.

[231] *Historia Tripartita*, III, 6. *MPL* 69, 950d; *PNF*[2] 2, 277.

[232] Actually *Historia Tripartita*, IV, 1-3. *MPL* 69, 957-958; *PNF*[2] 2, 283-284, 301.

That is just what some of our false papist scribblers[233] are doing now; they pretend to teach faith and good works in order to embellish themselves and to besmirch us, as though they had always taught thus and we had unjustly accused them of teaching otherwise, so that, adorned in this sheep's clothing [Matt. 7:15] as though they were exactly like us, they may nicely bring their wolf into the sheep pen again. They do not seriously mean to teach faith and good works; but since they (like the Arians) cannot retain their poison and wolfishness or re-establish it except in this sheepskin of faith and good works, they decorate and hide their wolfskin until they get back into the sheep pen. But one should do to them as they do to our people and demand that they recant their abominations and prove it by casting off all the abuses that have prevailed against faith and good works in their churches among their people, so that one could know them by their fruits [Matt. 7:16]. Otherwise, one cannot believe their mere words and gestures, that is, their sheepskins. Arius, too, should have recanted in the same way, confessed his error, and actually attacked his former doctrine and conduct, as St. Augustine did his Manichaeism,[234] as many people are now doing with their former popery and monkery, among whom, by the grace of God, I can number myself. But they deny that they erred and cannot give God the honor of confessing it, just as the Arians wanted to have their lies defended and did not want people to think that they had been expelled by the council.

We should remember such historical examples well, especially those of us who must be preachers and have the order to feed the flock of Christ, so that we may exercise care and be good bishops, as St. Peter says in I Peter 5 [:2]; for to be an *episcopus,* or bishop, means to be careful, to be alert, to watch diligently, so that the devil does not take us by surprise. Here we see that he is such a master of dissimulation, disguise, and pretense that he becomes far fairer than the "angels of light" [II Cor. 11:14]; and false bishops are holier than true bishops, and the wolf more

---

[233] See p. 21, n. 22.

[234] Named after Manichaeus, a Persian religious philosopher who was executed in Persia in *ca.* 275. It was a syncretistic cult teaching the incompatibility of spirit and matter. Until 384 Augustine was a Manichaean.

pious than any sheep. We are not dealing now with the crude, black, papal poltergeists[235] outside of Scripture. They are now to be found in Scripture and in our doctrine; they want to be like us and yet tear us to pieces. But here only the Holy Spirit can help, and we must pray diligently; otherwise, we shall be badly beaten.

All of this explains quite clearly why the council was held, namely, not for the sake of outward ceremonies, but for the sake of the important article about the divinity of Christ. That was why the dispute arose and was dealt with in the council; afterward it was assailed by the unspeakable raging of the devil, while the other articles were ignored. And this misery lasted for approximately three hundred years among Christians,[236] so that St. Augustine believes that Arius' pain in hell grows worse from day to day as long as that error endures, for Mohammed has come out of this sect. And from what I have presented above one can see clearly that this council neither thought up nor established anything new, but only condemned Arius' new error against the old faith on the basis of Scripture—from which may be inferred that no council (much less the pope in Rome) is authorized to think up or establish new articles concerning faith or good works, as they so falsely boast. This should be enough for the time being about the first principal council of Nicaea.

The second principal council, of Constantinople, about fifty years after the Nicene council, convened under the emperors Gratian and Theodosius,[237] had the following causes: Arius had denied the divinity of Christ and of the Holy Spirit.[238] In the meantime a new heresy was formed—the Macedonians[239] (for one error

---

[235] *Polter Bapst geister.*
[236] The last Arians were converted to the Roman church under the Lombard king Grimoald (d. 671).
[237] See p. 23, n. 33.
[238] The Jena edition of Luther's works (*Jenaer Ausgabe*), which appeared between 1555 and 1558, reads, "and not that of the Holy Spirit" (*und nicht des heiligen Geistes*) (VII, 245b). The doctrine of the Holy Spirit was not discussed in the Arian controversy, but was formulated in the sixth century. Cf. "*Filioque*" in *O.D.C.C.*, p. 504.
[239] Named after Macedonius (d. *ca.* 362), who opposed Bishop Paul of Constantinople (d. 350). Macedonius is linked with a semi-Arian party, later known as Pneumatomachi, from the Greek *pneumatomachoi*, "murderers of the spirit," i.e., those who refused to believe in the divinity of the Holy Spirit.

always begets another and one misfortune another, without end or cessation). They praised the decision of the Nicene council that Christ is true God and vigorously condemned Arius and his heresy; but they taught that the Holy Spirit is not true God, but a creature of God through whom God moves, enlightens, comforts, and strengthens the heart of man, and through whom he does all that Scripture says of him. This heresy also took strong root among many great, learned, and able bishops. This came about because Macedonius was bishop of Constantinople, the largest capital city of the entire Eastern empire and the residence of the imperial court. This same bishop started the heresy; it made quite an impression that the foremost bishop, in the imperial residence in Constantinople at that, taught this. Almost all the lands around Constantinople and those dependent on it hurried to support him, and Macedonius was not idle either; he agitated for his cause energetically, and would have liked to attract the whole world (as the devil is wont to do in all heresies).

Now the good bishops proved themselves too weak to withstand this bishop's heresies; for a bad priest in Alexandria, Arius, had previously aroused such confusion. But here it was not a priest, not even an ordinary bishop, but the bishop of the foremost city of the imperial palace of Constantinople who was arousing such confusion. Here the bishops had once again to call upon the emperor to assemble a principal council against such blasphemy, which the pious emperor Theodosius[240] did, convoking it in Constantinople,[241] in the parish and church in which Macedonius had been bishop, just as Constantine had earlier convoked the Nicene council in Nicaea, where Theogonius was bishop,[242] who had, together with Eusebius of Nicomedia, supported Arius and had later helped to reinstate him.

The next year Damasus, bishop of Rome, also held a council, and would have liked to deal with these matters in Rome so that the Roman See might acquire the authority to call councils and to judge all matters. It was to be known as a principal council, for

---

[240] Theodosius I.
[241] *Historia Tripartita,* IX, 12. *MPL* 69, 1128-1129; *PNF*[2] 2, 121-122.
[242] *Historia Tripartita,* II, 9. *MPL* 69, 928d; *PNF*[2] 2, 10.

as the foremost bishop of the world, he summoned the same fathers who a year before had met in council at Constantinople. But they did not want to come, although they wrote him a very nice Christian letter[243] telling him what they had dealt with in the Council of Constantinople; they informed him, among other things, of how they had condemned Macedonius' heresy and how they had appointed other bishops in Constantinople, Antioch, and Jerusalem. Oh, they should not have done that without the knowledge and consent of the bishop of Rome, who wanted the exclusive right and power to convoke councils (which he, in fact, was powerless to do), to sentence all heresies (which he could not do), and to change bishops (which he was not entitled to do).

They gave him, in addition, some good slaps in the face, telling him that in the new church in Constantinople (for the city had been built recently)[244] they had made Nectarius bishop, and Flavian bishop of Antioch, and Cyril bishop of Jerusalem.[245] These three items were very uncomfortable, indeed, intolerable for the bishop of Rome to hear and read: the first, that they call Constantinople a new church and appoint a bishop there, though no new church and new bishop should have been created without the knowledge and consent of the bishop of Rome; the second is even worse, that they call the church in Antioch the first and the oldest church, in which (as they proved through St. Luke in Acts 11 [:26]) the believers in Christ were called Christians for the first time, and in which St. Peter and St. Paul and many of the greatest apostles had proclaimed the gospel for more than seven years. That, in my German, would be like saying, "Listen, lord bishop of Rome! You are not the first or foremost bishop, but if any particular church should be it, it would more justly be the church in Antioch, which has the Scriptures of St. Luke and actual facts on its side, while Rome can claim neither Scripture nor facts in its behalf."

But these were fine and excellent people, who wished to check the arrogant spirit of Rome gently and mildly, with Christian love

---

243 The letter is quoted in *Historia Tripartita*, IX, 14. *MPL* 69, 1130-1133; *PNF*2 3, 137-138.
244 In 330 Constantine the Great dedicated the city as the "new Rome."
245 *Historia Tripartita*, IX, 14. *MPL* 69, 1132c-1132d; *PNF*2 3, 138.

and humility, and, as Sirach teaches, "To spit on a spark" [Ecclus. 28:12], and to exhort the bishop of Rome to consider that since the gospel had not come to Antioch from Rome but to Rome from Antioch, the church of Antioch as the oldest church should reasonably enjoy precedence over Rome as the younger church; that is, if precedence was to be a question. This ambition (as the words show) rightfully incensed these fine and holy fathers against the Roman bishop (as was just), and if there had been a Dr. Luther in the council and he could have had his way, such a gentle letter would not have been addressed to the bishop of Rome. In a word, there were men in this council with whom all the bishops of Rome of all time could not compare in the least.[246]

The third is the worst, that they call the church in Jerusalem the mother of all churches because Christ the Lord himself had been bishop there, and in proof of this had sacrificed himself on the cross for the sins of the whole world; there the Holy Spirit had been given from heaven on the day of Pentecost; there all the apostles had afterward ruled the church together (not only Peter, of whom the bishop of Rome boasts). Not one of these events had occurred in Rome. Thus they gently admonished the bishop of Rome to consider that he was far from being the bishop of Jerusalem, of the mother church, but that his church in Rome was a daughter church which did not have Christ and the apostles and which did not bring Jerusalem to the faith; but rather, he and his church had been brought to the faith through the church in Jerusalem—so had St. Paul humbled the Corinthians, telling them that the gospel did not come from them, but from others to them [II Cor. 10:14].

But at the end they really overshot the mark and appointed a patriarch to the new church in Constantinople without the previous knowledge and consent of the bishop of Rome, just as though his co-operation in these matters did not matter at all. This is where the eternal quarreling and bickering started (as the pope's hypocrites themselves write)[247] between the bishops of Rome and Constantinople over primacy or supreme authority. When the

---

[246] Proverbial German, *"Nicht kundten das wasser reichen."*
[247] It cannot be established which authors Luther had in mind.

bishop of Constantinople (though he was in a new city) was as patriarch the equal of the bishop of Rome, the one at Rome feared that the other would arrogate the primacy to himself— which afterward actually happened. The bishops of Constantinople asserted that the emperor had his residence or court in Constantinople and not in Rome and that Constantinople was known as "new Rome"; this is why he would have to be the supreme bishop because he was the bishop of the imperial city and court. On the other hand, the one in Rome asserted that Rome was the true Rome, and that the emperor was known as the Roman emperor and not the Constantinopolitan emperor, and that Rome had existed before Constantinople. They indulged in such childish, womanish, and foolish squabbles that it is a sin and a shame to hear and read.

The bickering went on until Phocas[248] became emperor. He had had the pious emperor Maurice (whom history calls a saint), his predecessor and lord (Phocas had been his captain) beheaded, together with his wife and children. This godly Cain confirmed the supremacy of bishop Boniface[249] of Rome over all other bishops. And this kind of supremacy could have been justly certified by no better man than by this shameful murderer of an emperor! So Rome had as good a beginning of papacy as its empire had previously had, when Romulus murdered his brother Remus so that he could rule alone and name the city after himself. Nevertheless, the bishops of Constantinople paid no attention to this, and the squabble continued on and on, although the Roman bishops meanwhile embellished the emperor Phocas' certification with fig leaves [Gen. 3:7], and screamed loudly with great bellowing, Revelation 12 [13:5], that the church of Rome was supreme, not by human command but by Christ's own institution, Matthew 16 [:18], "You are Peter." But the ones in Constantinople saw that

---

248 In 602 Phocas headed a revolution in Constantinople which deposed the ruler of the Eastern half of the Roman Empire, Maurice I (Maurikios), who had been on the throne since 582. He and his entire family were put to death. Pope Gregory I (590-604) hailed the revolution as an act of God against a tyrant. Phocas was emperor until 610, when he was deposed and killed in another revolution, headed by Heraclius. Cf. Schäfer, *op. cit.*, p. 330, n. 3.

249 Boniface III (607) was bishop for only eight months. He had been Rome's diplomatic representative at Constantinople and a friend of Phocas.

those in Rome were quoting the words of Christ falsely and sense-lessly, like uneducated people, and ignored them.

Thus the two churches, Rome and Constantinople, wrangled over the invalid primacy with vain, rotten, lame, and useless squabbles, until the devil finally devoured them both, the ones in Constantinople through the Turks and Mohammed,[250] the others in Rome through the papacy and its blasphemous decretals. I am relating all of this so that one can see what misery was caused by this fine council in Constantinople because the bishop of that city was made patriarch, which would have happened anyway, even if no patriarch of Constantinople had been appointed, for the ambitious devil's head in Rome had already begun to make all kinds of demands of the bishops (as we said above). And if the bishop of Constantinople had not crossed him, he would have rubbed against the bishops of Alexandria, Jerusalem, and Antioch, and he would not have tolerated the decree of the Council of Nicaea, which had made him the equal of the bishop of Alexandria and the inferior of the bishop of Jerusalem. He wants to be supreme without councils and fathers, "by divine right,"[251] instituted by Christ himself—as he bellows, blasphemes, and lies in his decretals.

Well then! There we have the second principal council in Constantinople; it did three things: first, it affirmed that the Holy Spirit is true God, simultaneously condemning Macedonius, who averred and taught that the Holy Spirit was a creature. Second, it deposed the heretical bishops and appointed true bishops, particularly in Antioch and Jerusalem. Third, it made the bishop Nectarius of Constantinople a patriarch, which enraged, incensed, and infuriated the bishops of Rome—although the dear fathers may have done it with the best of intentions. The first is the real, main item and the sole reason for holding the council, from which one can also understand the intention of the council, namely, that it was to do no more and did no more than to preserve the doctrine of the divinity of the Holy Spirit; and with this the council really had finished what it had been summoned to do. The second item, about the deposition

---

[250] A reference to the fall of Constantinople in 1453, when the Christian Byzantine Empire came to an end.
[251] *Iure divino.*

of bishops, is not an article of faith, but an external, tangible work, which reason, too, should and can perform and which does not require either the extraordinary action of the Holy Spirit (as do the articles of faith) or the summoning of a council; and that is why it probably occurred on another day, after the day of the council.

They did not re-establish the churches or bishoprics in Antioch and Jerusalem, but they let them remain as they had been from the beginning. They only put in different persons, which was necessary. These offices must have been in the church from the beginning, and they must remain until the end, but one must always put in different persons, like Matthias, who replaced Judas [Acts 1:26], and living bishops who replace those who die. This is not properly the business of the councils, but it may, indeed it must, be done before the councils, in between the councils, and after the councils, as the needs of the churches demand it. One cannot have councils every day, but one must have persons every day to fill the offices of the churches whenever these become vacant.

The third item is a new one, that they made a patriarch, out of human good intentions. But we have related above what came out of this—what disgraceful quarreling and backbiting these two bishops indulged in—so that one can clearly see that the Holy Spirit did not institute this, for it is not an article of faith, but an external and tangible work of reason, or of flesh and blood. What does the Holy Spirit care about which bishop goes first and which goes last? He has other things to do besides fooling in such worldly child's play! And from this one not only learns that the councils lack the power to create new good works, much less new articles of faith, but one also receives the warning that councils should not create or establish anything new at all. They should know that they did not meet to do this, but to defend the old faith against new teachers although they may put new persons (who cannot be called articles of faith or good works, since they are fallible mortal men) into the old existing offices, which one has to do in the churches, outside the councils, more often than in the councils, indeed, every day.

The fathers of this council themselves also confessed that they did not establish anything new when they (as was said) wrote

Damasus, the bishop of Rome, what among other things they had done in the council, "We know that this is the old true faith that conforms to baptism and teaches us to believe in the name of the Father, the Son, and the Holy Spirit," etc.[252] Indeed, they said nothing at all about the third item, the patriarchate of Constantinople.[253] Perhaps they thought that this was not the item for which they had assembled in the council, and that it would not be heresy if a Christian would not consider it an article of faith to regard the bishop as a patriarch, just as there are many people today who are neither heretics nor lost because they do not regard the pope as the head of the church, despite his councils, decretals, bulls, and bellowing. Or perhaps they did not do it unanimously, but the emperor Theodosius did it, for the other histories report that Theodosius, who had no power to set up articles of faith, suggested and urged it.[254]

Since they themselves now say and confess that it is the old true faith in which we were baptized and in which we were instructed, why should we concede to the councils the great power to establish new doctrines and to burn as heretics all who do not believe them? That would indeed mean misunderstanding the councils and not knowing at all what a council is or what its office and function are; it would be to look merely at the letters and to give the council complete power, even over God! More about that later. We still want to take a brief look at the other two principal councils.

The third principal council was held under Theodosius II,[255] whose grandfather was Theodosius I, mentioned in connection with the second council. This emperor summoned two hundred bishops to Ephesus.[256] And although the Latin writers wanted to weave the

---

[252] *Historia Tripartita*, IX, 14. *MPL* 69, 1131d; *PNF*[2] 3, 138.

[253] *Historia Tripartita*, IX, 13. *MPL* 69, 1129c; *PNF*[2] 2, 121. These records accord the bishop of Constantinople "the next prerogative honor after the bishop of Rome." See in this volume, pp. 89-90.

[254] Rufinus (II, 19), the source Luther used in addition to the *Historia Tripartita*, records the involvement of Theodosius I in ecclesiastical affairs. *MPL* 21, 526.

[255] See p. 24, n. 39. This was the Council of Ephesus in 431.

[256] *Historia Tripartita*, XII, 5. *MPL* 69, 1207-1208; *PNF*[2] 2, 172. The number of bishops is recorded by Crabbe, whom Luther may have regarded as one of the "Latin writers." See *WA* 50, 581, n. *c*.

pope into the story, it is nonetheless true that not the pope but the emperor had to summon this council. Now there was a patriarch in Constantinople of equal rank with the bishop of Rome,[257] so the Eastern bishops paid the bishop of Rome far less heed than before; that is why it was impossible for the bishop of Rome[258] to convoke such a council, especially in Ephesus, far across the sea in Asia. If he had had the power, he would surely have called it closer to Rome, as Damasus did with the former council, that of Constantinople. Yet it is said that he had his delegates there;[259] that may be, but they did not preside.

Here was the reason for this council:[260] the dear fathers and good bishops were gone—St. Ambrose, St. Martin, St. Jerome, St. Augustine (who died that very year), St. Hilary, St. Eusebius, and others like them.[261] In their stead fathers had come up who were not their equals so that even Emperor Theodosius no longer wanted to see a bishop of Constantinople chosen from the priests or clergy of that city because these were usually proud, ambitious, and unruly, managing to cause nothing but trouble. Even St. John Chrysostom was such a person, as the *Historia Tripartita* informs us.[262] Therefore the emperor sent for a "foreigner"[263] (that is what they called him) from Antioch, by the name of Nestorius,[264] who was a man of strict and chaste life, with a pleasing voice, eloquent, an outspoken foe of all heretics. He was to become patriarch and bishop of Constantinople. But here the emperor made a mistake; he tried to escape the rain and plunged into the water.[265]

---

[257] See pp. 87-88, and Schäfer, *op. cit.*, p. 304, n. 1.

[258] Celestine I (422-432).

[259] This reference is contained only in Crabbe. For the exact quotation, see *WA* 50, 581, n. *e*.

[260] Luther's source for the following account is the *Historia Tripartita*, XII, 4. *MPL* 69, 1204-1207; *PNF*[2] 2, 169-172.

[261] Ambrose died in 397; Martin of Tours in *ca.* 400; Jerome in 420; Augustine in 430; Hilary in 367; and Eusebius of Caesarea in *ca.* 340.

[262] *Historia Tripartita*, X, 3. *MPL* 69, 1166*b*; *PNF*[2] 2, 139. See also *Historia Tripartita*, X, 13. *MPL* 69, 1176*b*; *PNF*[2] 2, 148.

[263] *Advena.* See *Historia Tripartita*, XII, 4. *MPL* 69, 1204*a*; *PNF*[2] 2, 169.

[264] Nestorius (d. *ca.* 451), regarded as the founder of the Nestorian heresy, according to which Christ consisted of two completely separate persons, one human and one divine.

[265] A German proverb, "*Wollt dem regen entlauffen und fiel ins wasser.*" Cf. Thiele, *Luthers Sprichwörtersammlung*, No. 478.

This man began to defend his priest Anastasius,[266] who had preached that one should not call the holy Virgin the mother of God, for since she was human she could give birth to no God. This offended all Christians; they understood it to mean that he regarded Christ, born of Mary, not as God but as a mere man, such as we all are. This created such unrest and disturbance that the emperor had to assemble a council to relieve the matter. Then the great bishops assembled (although slowly) in Ephesus, Nestorius with many others like Cyril of Alexandria[267] and Juvenal of Jerusalem.[268] And when John of Antioch[269] delayed his coming, Cyril (who was opposed to Nestorius) and Juvenal proceeded to condemn Nestorius, and he and his followers in turn condemned them. When John of Antioch arrived and found this split, he became furious with Cyril because he had so hotheadedly and hurriedly condemned Nestorius; and these two clashed over it, and each condemned the other and deposed the other from his bishopric.

When Nestorius saw the excitement that had arisen, he said, "Oh, let us remove the cause of this trouble and admit that Mary may be called the mother of God!" But this recantation did not help him; he had to remain under condemnation and in exile. To be sure, the two bishops of Antioch and Alexandria continued to condemn one another after their return home from the council, but in the end they again made peace.[270] It is quite irritating, indeed, saddening, to read that such important men behaved so womanishly and childishly; they really needed a Constantine who would have thrown their bickering letters into the fire too. But those who could have done that were gone.

Now if Nestorius really was in such error that he took Christ to be not God but a mere human being, then he was justly condemned, for his teaching was much worse than that of Arius or Macedonius.

This then is the third principal council; it dealt with no more

---

[266] Anastasius, a presbyter in Constantinople, was sympathetic to Nestorius' cause. He is mentioned only by Socrates in the *Historia Tripartita*, VII, 2.

[267] Cyril (412-414), the most vehement opponent of Nestorius.

[268] Juvenal, bishop of Jerusalem (422-458).

[269] John, bishop of Antioch (429-441).

[270] *Historia Tripartita*, XII, 6. *MPL* 69, 1208; *PNF²* 2, 172.

than this, and we still note that it set up no new doctrine, but defended the old true faith against the new doctrine of Nestorius, if that is really what he taught; thus we cannot grant the councils the power to establish new doctrines. That Christ is true God had been defended previously in the councils of Nicaea and Constantinople, as a true old article, kept from the beginning and proven and authenticated by Holy Scripture against the new heresy of Arius. The other decrees established there apply to bodily matters and are not articles of faith; these we drop.

In order to understand this council thoroughly we shall talk a little more about it. For awhile I myself could not understand just what Nestorius' error was; in any event, I thought that Nestorius had denied the divinity of Christ and had regarded Christ as no more than a mere man, as the papal decretals and all papal writers say.[271] But their own words, when I really looked at them, made me change my mind. They accuse Nestorius of making two persons out of Christ, namely, God and man. Some, who also failed to understand him, thought he had taught that Christ was first born of Mary as mere man and then led such a holy life that the Godhead merged with him, and he thus became God, and their writing is so confused that I think they still do not know today how and why they condemned Nestorius. Remember that they testify that Nestorius took Christ to be both God and man, only he is said to have made two persons of him. Thus it is certain that Nestorius did not take Christ to be a mere man, as we all assumed, for according to their own words he also took him to be God. The only knot that remains is that he is said to have regarded Christ, really and truly God and man, as a dual person, divine and human. That is one fact.

Now he who divides Christ and makes two persons of him fashions two Christs—one divine Christ who is altogether God and not a human being, and a human Christ, who is altogether man and no God at all; otherwise, there could not be two persons. Now it is certain that Nestorius did not believe in two Christs, but in only one single Christ, as their own words convey, that Nestorius re-

---

[271] See for example, *Decreti Tertia Pars, De Consecratione*, dist. V, C. XXXIX. *CIC* 1, 1423; *MPL* 187, 957. See also Crabbe (quoted in *WA* 50, 583, n. *c.*).

garded Christ, that is, the one, sole, same, true Christ and none other, as being two persons. So it must also be false and incorrect to say that Nestorius took Christ to be two persons, for it cannot be that Christ is two persons and yet remains the same one Christ; but rather, as said, if there are two persons, then there are two Christs and not one Christ. But Nestorius holds to no more than one Christ, so he could not have taken Christ to be two persons; otherwise, he would indeed have had to say both yes and no against himself in the same article. Nor do any histories record that Nestorius held Christ to be two persons—except that the pope and their histories imply it, although they themselves admit otherwise when they imputed to Nestorius the teaching that Christ had become God after he was born of Mary or had become united with God into one person. Their conscience or their confused mind forced them to say this, since they had to admit that Nestorius did not believe in more than the one single Christ.

Now the question is: what was it that was condemned about Nestorius and why was this third principal council convoked against him if he did not teach otherwise than that Christ is true God and true man, and one single Christ, not two Christs, that is, one person in two natures—as we all believe and as all Christendom has believed from the beginning? For it appears that the pope and his followers put the words into Nestorius' mouth that he viewed Christ as a mere man and not also as God, and that he took Christ to be two persons or two Christs. This appears (I say) not only from the histories, but also from the very words and documents of the popes and their writers.[272] Now in order to discover the reasons for this council we ask, what was really Nestorius' error?

You may read a page or two of the *Historia Tripartita*, Book XII, chapter 4,[273] which you can do in half of a quarter of an hour, wherein is written everything that one can really know about Nestorius and this council, and see if I hit the mark. The problem was this: Nestorius was a proud and unlearned man, and when he became such a great bishop and patriarch he supposed that he should be looked upon as the most learned man on earth, needing neither

---

[272] *Decreti Secunda Pars,* causa XXIV, ques. 3, C. XXXIX. *CIC* 1, 1005.
[273] *MPL* 69, 1204-1207; *PNF*[2] 2, 169-172.

to read the books of his predecessors and of other people, nor to learn their way of speaking about these things. Instead, since he was eloquent and endowed with a good voice, he wanted to be a self-made doctor or master, and no matter how he expressed it or pronounced something, it should be accounted correct. He approached the statement that Mary was God's mother or the bearer of God with the same pride. Then he, in turn, encountered other proud bishops, whom his pride displeased, especially Cyril of Alexandria; for there was no Augustine or Ambrose at hand. Now Nestorius had learned in the church of Antioch that Christ was true God born of the Father in eternity, as the Nicene council had defended, and afterward born a true man of the Virgin Mary. Nestorius did not question these two items; he himself had preached them for a long time. Indeed, he had even persecuted the Arians at the Council of Nicaea, condemning them so vehemently that he had also instigated many murders and much bloodshed, so staunchly did he regard Christ as true God and man.

Moreover, he also conceded that Christ, God's Son, was born of the Virgin Mary into his humanity, not into his divinity, which we and all Christians also say. But here is where the problem arose: he did not want Mary to be called the mother of God because of this, since Christ was not born of her into his divinity, or, to express it plainly, since Christ did not derive his divinity from her as he did his humanity. There we have the entire bone of contention: God cannot be born of a human being or have his divine nature from one; and a human being cannot bear God or impart the divine nature to a God. This unlearned, uncouth, and proud man insisted on the literal meaning of the words, "God born of Mary," and interpreted "born" according to grammar or philosophy, as though it meant to obtain divine nature from the one who bore him, and the *Tripartita* also says that he viewed these words as an abomination[274]—as we, and all Christians (if that were to be the sense of these words), do too.

One can see from this that Nestorius, as an ignorant, proud bishop, adheres faithfully to Christ, but in his ignorance does not know what and how he is speaking, like one who does not quite

---

[274] *Historia Tripartita*, XII, 4. *MPL* 69, 1206b; *PNF*² 2, 171.

know how to speak of such things, but still wants to speak as an expert. We too know very well that God did not derive his divinity from Mary; but it does not follow that it is therefore wrong to say that God was born of Mary, that God is Mary's Son, and that Mary is God's mother. I have to illustrate this with a plain example: if a woman bears a child, a rotten Nestorius (that is what the *Tripartita* calls him)[275] may be proud and ignorant and puzzle out, "This woman has given birth to the child, but she is not the child's mother because the child's soul is not derived from her nature or blood, but from elsewhere—for instance, from God. Thus this child is, to be sure, born of the woman according to the body; but since the soul is not from her body, she is not the child's mother, for she is not the mother of the child's soul."

A no-good sophist like this does not deny that the two natures, body and soul, are one person, nor does he say that there are two persons or two children, but admits that two natures, like body and soul, form one person or one child; also that the mother has not borne two children, but only one child. However, he fails to see what he is denying or what he is saying. Just such a man was Nestorius, who admits that Christ is God and man in one person; but because his divinity does not come from his mother Mary, she should not be called God's mother. This was rightly condemned in the council, and ought to be condemned. And although Nestorius has a correct view on one point of the principal matter, that Christ is God and man, one should nevertheless not tolerate his other point or mode of expression, that God was not born of Mary and was not crucified by the Jews just as one should not tolerate the sophist (who declares very correctly that a mother cannot bear or impart a child's soul) when he says that a child is not the mother's natural child and a mother is not the child's natural mother.

In summary, the proud, unlearned bishop instigated a bad Greek quarrel, or as the Roman Cicero said of the Greeks, "A controversy has long disturbed the little Greeks, who are fonder of ar-

---

[275] *Historia Tripartita*, XII, 4. MPL 69, 1207a; PNF² 2, 171: *"Non ergo mediocrem concussionem orbiterrarum tepidissima Nestorii ratiocinatio concitant"* ("This idle contention of his has produced no slight ferment in the religious world").

gument than of truth."[276] For whoever admits that a mother bore a child who has body and soul should admit and believe that the mother has borne the whole child and is the child's true mother, even though she is not the mother of the soul; otherwise, it would follow that no woman is the mother of any child, and the fourth commandment, "Honor thy father and thy mother," would have to be abolished. Thus it should also be said that Mary is the true natural mother of the child called Jesus Christ, and that she is the true mother of God and bearer of God, and whatever else can be said of children's mothers, such as suckling, bathing, feeding—that Mary suckled God, rocked God to sleep, prepared broth and soup for God, etc. For God and man are one person, one Christ, one Son, one Jesus, not two Christs, not two Sons, not two Jesuses; just as your son is not two sons, two Johns, two cobblers, even though he has two natures, body and soul, the body from you, the soul from God alone.

Thus Nestorius' error was not that he believed Christ to be a pure man, or that he made two persons of him; on the contrary, he confesses two natures, the divine and the human, in one person—but he will not admit a *communicatio idiomatum*.[277] I cannot express that in one word in German. *Idioma* means that which is inherent in a nature or is its attribute, such as dying, suffering, weeping, speaking, laughing, eating, drinking, sleeping, sorrowing, rejoicing, being born, having a mother, suckling the breast, walking, standing, working, sitting, lying down, and other things of that kind, which are called *idiomata naturae humanae*, that is, qualities that belong to man by nature, which he can and must do or even suffer; for *idioma* in Greek, *proprium* in Latin, is a thing—let us, for the time being, call it an attribute. Again, an *idioma deitatis*,

---

[276] In *De Oratione*, I, 11: "*Iam diu torquet controversia verbi homines graeculos contentionis cupidiores quam veritatis.*" See E. W. Sutton and H. Rackham (trans.), *Cicero: De Oratione, Book I and II* ("The Loeb Classical Library" [2 vols.; Cambridge: Harvard University Press, 1942]), I, 36.

[277] "Communion of the properties," a doctrine propounded by scholastic theology, which states that while the two natures were separated in Christ, the attributes of the one may be predicated by the other, in view of their union in Christ. Luther reinterpreted the doctrine in the context of his own theology. Cf. Paul Althaus, *Die Theologie Martin Luthers* (Gütersloh, 1962), pp. 160-174.

"an attribute of divine nature," is that it is immortal, omnipotent, infinite, not born, does not eat, drink, sleep, stand, walk, sorrow, weep—and what more can one say? To be God is an immeasurably different thing than to be man; that is why the *idiomata* of the two natures cannot coincide. That is the opinion of Nestorius.

Now if I were to preach, "Jesus, the carpenter of Nazareth (for the gospels call him 'carpenter's son' [Matt. 13:55]) is walking over there down the street, fetching his mother a jug of water and a penny's worth of bread so that he might eat and drink with his mother, and the same carpenter, Jesus, is the very true God in one person," Nestorius would grant me that and say that this is true. But if I were to say, "There goes God down the street, fetching water and bread so that he might eat and drink with his mother," Nestorius would not grant me this, but says, "To fetch water, to buy bread, to have a mother, to eat and drink with her, are *idiomata* or attributes of human and not of divine nature." And again, if I say, "The carpenter Jesus was crucified by the Jews and the same Jesus is the true God," Nestorius would agree that this is true. But if I say, "God was crucified by the Jews," he says, "No! For crucifixion and death are *idiomata* or attributes not of divine but of human nature."

Now when ordinary Christians hear this they cannot but think that he regards Christ as a mere man and is separating the persons, which he does not intend to do, though his words lend the impression that he does. From this one can see that he was a very peculiar saint and an injudicious man, for after he concedes that God and man are united and fused into one person, he can in no way deny that the *idiomata* of the two natures should also be united and fused. Otherwise, what could God and man united in one person be? Thus his folly is exactly that against which one teaches in the schools, "One who admits the premise of a good conclusion cannot deny the conclusion."[278] In German we would say, "If the one is true, the other must also be true; if the second is not true, then the

---

[278] *"Qui concedit antecedens bonae consequentiae, non potest negare consequens,"* a proposition that appears in various Roman works; see for example, *De Oratione*, II, 53, in Sutton and Rackham (trans.), *op. cit.*, II, 357. Cf. also C.R. 13, 617, 627.

first is not true either."[279] Whoever admits that Greta is your wife cannot deny that her child (if she is pious) is your child. If one teaches these things in the schools, no one thinks that there could be such crude people; but ask the regents and jurists whether they are not often confronted by such parties, who admit something and still do not want to grant what follows from it.

One might, however, allege that Nestorius had dishonestly confessed that Christ was God and only one person. No, the proud man was not that clever; rather, he was in earnest,[280] for in one of his sermons he cried (says the *Tripartita*), "No, dear Jew, you should not strut! You were not able to crucify God."[281] He means to say with this that Christ is indeed God, but God was not crucified. And in the council, before Bishop Cyril, he said, "Many confess that Christ is God, but I shall never say that God is 'double' or 'triple.' "[282] That is like saying, "Jesus is God, as many of us confess; but I will never teach that God was born two or three times." He had in mind (as the *Tripartita* indicates)[283] that God and death are irreconcilable. It seemed terrible to him to hear that God should die. His meaning was that Christ, in his divinity, was immortal; but he lacked the intelligence to express this thought properly. To add to the trouble the other bishops, also proud men, gave no thought to how one could heal the wounds, but only to tearing them further open.

So although speaking logically it must follow from Nestorius' opinion that Christ is a mere man and two persons, this was not actually his opinion. This crude, unlearned man did not see that he was asserting the impossible when simultaneously he seriously took Christ to be God and man in one person and yet declined to

---

[279] *Ist eines war, so muss das ander auch war sein, ist das ander nicht war, so ist das erst auch nicht war.*

[280] *Historia Tripartita*, XII, 4: *"Nusquam enim Dei verbi subsistentiam perimit . . ."*) ("In these discourses he nowhere destroys the proper personality of the Word of God"). *MPL* 69, 1207a; *PNF*[2] 2, 171.

[281] *Historia Tripartita*, XII, 4: *"Noli gloriari Iudace, non crucifixisti Deum . . . ."* *MPL* 69, 1206d.

[282] *Historia Tripartita*, XII, 5: *Et cum plurimi Deum confiteantur esse Iesum: Ego, inquit Nestorius, bimestrem et trimestrem nequaquam confiteor Deum. MPL* 69, 1207c; *PNF*[2] 2, 172.

[283] *Historia Tripartita*, XII, 4: *"Sermonem tantumodo quasi metuendum exparisse." MPL* 69, 1206b; *PNF*[2] 2, 171.

ascribe the *idiomata* of the natures to the same person of Christ. He wants to hold to the truth of the first, but what follows from the first should not be true—he thereby indicates that he himself does not understand what he is denying.

We Christians must ascribe all the *idiomata* of the two natures of Christ, both persons, equally to him. Consequently Christ is God and man in one person because whatever is said of him as man must also be said of him as God, namely, Christ has died, and Christ is God; therefore God died—not the separated God, but God united with humanity. For about the separated God both statements, namely, that Christ is God and that God died, are false; both are false, for then God is not man. If it seems strange to Nestorius that God dies, he should think it equally strange that God becomes man; for thereby the immortal God becomes that which must die, suffer, and have all human *idiomata*. Otherwise, what would that man be with whom God personally unites, if he did not have truly human *idiomata*? It would be a phantom, as the Manichaeans[284] had taught earlier. On the other hand, whatever is said of God must also be ascribed to the man, namely, God created the world and is almighty; the man Christ is God, therefore the man Christ created the world and is almighty. The reason for this is that since God and man have become one person, it follows that this person bears the *idiomata* of both natures.

O Lord God! We should always rejoice in true faith, free of dispute and doubt, over such a blessed, comforting doctrine, to sing, praise, and thank God the Father for such inexpressible mercy that he let his dear Son become like us, a man and our brother! Yet the loathsome devil instigates such great annoyance through proud, ambitious, incorrigible people that our cherished and precious joy is hindered and spoiled for us. May God have pity! We Christians should know that if God is not in the scale to give it weight, we, on our side, sink to the ground. I mean it this way: if it cannot be said that God died for us, but only a man, we are lost; but if God's death and a dead God lie in the balance, his side goes down and ours goes up like a light and empty scale. Yet he

---

[284] Manichaeism had a place for Jesus as the manifestation of light, which it held to be equivalent with good. Since, however, it regarded matter as evil, Jesus' humanity was denied.

can also readily go up again, or leap out of the scale! But he could not sit on the scale unless he had become a man like us, so that it could be called God's dying, God's martyrdom, God's blood, and God's death. For God in his own nature cannot die; but now that God and man are united in one person, it is called God's death when the man dies who is one substance or one person with God.

This council condemned far too little of Nestorius, for it dealt only with the one *idioma*, that God was born of Mary. Thus the histories relate that it was resolved in this council, in opposition to Nestorius, that Mary should be called *Theotokos*, "bearer of God,"[285] even though Nestorius denied to God in Christ all *idiomata* of human nature such as dying, the cross, suffering, and everything that is incompatible with the Godhead. This is why they should not just have resolved that Mary was *theotokos*, but also that Pilate and the Jews were crucifiers and murderers of God, and the like. That they later condemned him, covering all the *idiomata*, with the words, "Nestorius denies that Christ is God and one person," is certainly correct in effect or according to logic, but is expressed too clumsily and oddly because Nestorius could get no other idea from it than that he had been treated unjustly and wrongly, for he had never taught such words, but on the contrary had always said that Christ was true and very God and not two persons, having for this reason vehemently persecuted the Arians. Such crude people cannot syllogize or draw logical conclusions, namely, that he who denies the *idiomata* or attributes of a nature can be said to deny the substance or nature itself. So the verdict should have been, "Although Nestorius confesses that Christ, true God and true man, is one person, but does not ascribe the *idiomata* of human nature to the same divine person of Christ, he is in error, just as much as if he denied the nature itself." Furthermore, they should not have emphasized only the *idioma* of his mother Mary; then the cause of this council would have been that much easier to understand, which, I think, very few people have understood so far—it is impossible to understand it from Platina[286] and those who follow him.

---

[285] *Historia Tripartita*, XII, 5. *MPL* 69, 1208a; *PNF*² 2, 172.
[286] See p. 7, n. 18, and quotations from Platina in *WA* 50, 583, n. *b*.

I too have been confronted by Nestorians who fought me very stubbornly, saying that the divinity of Christ could not suffer. For example, Zwingli too wrote against me concerning the saying, "The Word became flesh."[287] He would simply not have it that "became" should apply to "Word." He wanted it to read, "The flesh was made word,"[288] because God could not become anything. I myself did not know at that time that this resembled the notion of Nestorius because I did not understand the council either, but recognized it as error on the basis of Holy Scripture, Augustine, and the master of the Sentences.[289] Who knows how many Nestorians may still be in the papacy, praising this council greatly and not knowing what they praise? For reason wants to be clever here and not tolerate that God should die or have any human characteristics, even though it is used to believing, like Nestorius, that Christ is God.

Well then, this council too did not establish anything new in faith, as we said above, but only defended the old faith against the new notion of Nestorius, so one cannot take any examples from it, or give the councils authority to establish new or different articles of faith. This article was in the church from the very beginning and was not newly established by the council, but was preserved through the gospel or Holy Scripture, for it is written in Luke 1 [:32] that the angel Gabriel announced to the Virgin Mary that of her would be born "the Son of the Most High." And St. Elizabeth, "Why is this granted me, that the mother of my Lord should come to me?" [Luke 1:43]. And at Christmas all the angels, "To you is born this day a Savior, who is Christ the Lord" [Luke 2:11]. And in Galatians 3 [4:4] St. Paul, "God sent forth his Son, born of woman." These texts (I am convinced) hold firmly enough that Mary is the mother of God. Thus St. Paul states in I Corinthians 3 [2:8], "The rulers of this world crucified the Lord of glory." Acts 20 [:28], God obtained the church "with his own blood," although

---

[287] John 1:14. Cf. Ulrich Zwingli's tract *Friendly Exposition of the Eucharist Affair, to Martin Luther* (*C.R.* 92, 562 ff.) and Luther's *Confession Concerning Christ's Supper* (1528). *LW* 37, 161-372. On the entire controversy on the eucharist, see Walther Köhler, *Zwingli und Luther* (2 vols.; Leipzig, 1924; Gütersloh, 1953), and *LW* 37, 153-159.

[288] Luther quotes the Vulgate text, *"Verbum caro facta est."*

[289] Peter Lombard in *Four Books of Sentences*, III, dist. XII. *MPL* 192, 1076-1077.

God, to judge by reason, has no blood! And Philippians 2 [:6-7], "Christ, though he was in the form of God, emptied himself, taking the form of a servant, being born in the likeness of men." And the Children's Creed, the Apostles' Creed, says, "I believe in Jesus Christ his only Son our Lord, who was conceived, born of Mary, suffered, was crucified, died, was buried," etc. Here are written, clearly enough, the *idiomata* of human nature, and yet they are ascribed to the only Son and Lord, in whom we believe as we do in the Father, and as in the true God. That should suffice about this council.

The fourth principal council was held in Chalcedon in Pontus or Asia (approximately twenty-two or twenty-three years after the third preceding principal council in Ephesus) through Emperor Marcian, who succeeded Emperor Theodosius II as emperor in Constantinople in the year 455.[290] Thus the four great councils were held within a span of about one hundred and thirty years, for the one at Nicaea was held in the year 327.[291] But many other councils were held previous to, and along with, as well as after them, convoked here and there by the bishops themselves, without the emperors. But these four could not have met without the action of the emperors; the holy fathers were far too weak for that, and one would not easily give way to another, as the histories unfortunately demonstrate. This adds to our special consolation—we should not despair, because the Holy Spirit dwelt in several of these fathers and they were holy and must be called holy, so we too shall be holy and attain salvation.

But I should be glad to learn from someone else why this council met, for no trustworthy history has been transmitted to us. The *Ecclesiastical History*[292] ends with the first council, of Nicaea; the *Tripartita* and Theodoret[293] with the third at Ephesus; and from

---

[290] Marcian actually was emperor from 450 to 457. The chronological difference is due to Luther's using the chronology of John Carion. See p. 23, n. 36.

[291] Luther's *Supputatio* (see p. 23, n. 36) places the Council of Nicaea in 326, that of Constantinople in 376, that of Ephesus in 437, and that of Chalcedon in 458. Accordingly, there is a span of 132 years between the first and the fourth councils. Modern chronology places them in 325, 381, 431, and 451.

[292] Eusebius' *Ecclesiastical History*. Luther read it in the translation of Rufinus. See p. 56, n. 148.

[293] Theodoret's *Ecclesiastical History* ends in 428. The Council of Ephesus was

then on we almost have to depend upon the pope and his histories, in which it is, for sound and obvious reasons, very difficult to believe, for until then they had related everything to themselves and invented their own majesty through such miserable lies, which they still continue to do, that no one's conscience can rely on them. Now advise me, how am I, who does not understand this council or know what it did, going to be saved? And what happened to the dear saints and Christians who throughout these many centuries did not know what this council established? For there must always be saints on earth, and when those die, other saints must live, from the beginning to the end of the world; otherwise, the article would be false, "I believe in the holy Christian church, the communion of saints," and Christ would have to be lying when he says, "I am with you always, to the close of the age" [Matt. 28:20]. There must (I say) always be living saints on earth—they are wherever they can be—otherwise, Christ's kingdom would come to an end, and there would be no one to pray the Lord's Prayer, confess the Creed, be baptized, take the sacrament, be absolved, etc.

Well then, Platina and others say[294] this was the reason: in Constantinople an abbot, or as they called it, an archimandrite, named Eutyches,[295] had advanced another doctrine against Nestorius and had taught that Christ was one person only in the divine nature, against which the fathers in the council resolved that Christ is one person and two natures. That is only right and the Christian faith. But the pope's histories write that he taught that after the deity had assumed humanity and so had become Christ in one person, not more than the deity remained, and that Christ is to be regarded solely as God and not as man.[296] If that is Eutyches' opinion, he is exactly another crude Nestorius, who is said to have

---

held in 431. Luther, who did not read Theodoret's account (see p. 60, n. 161), erred when he assumed that Theodoret recorded this council.

[294] For the section in Platina, see WA 50, 593, n. *b*. Since Pope Leo I (440-461) is mentioned there, "others" may refer to him. Luther refers to Leo's letters below, which had been available in print since 1470 and were contained in Crabbe. Leo's works are contained in MPL 54-56; PNF[2] 12, 1-216.

[295] Eutyches (*ca.* 378-454), archimandrite of a large monastery at Constantinople.

[296] The "pope's histories" refers to Corpus Iuris Canonici, which contains a catalogue of heresies. See Decreti Secunda Pars, causa XXIV, ques. 3, C. XXIX. CIC 1, 1005.

taught that Christ is two persons and yet only one person; thus this one must have taught simultaneously two natures, and yet only one nature, in Christ. For this is what Pope Leo cries in a letter,[297] that Eutyches and Nestorius teach contradictory heresies—and it is certainly true that they who teach that Christ is two and yet one person or nature, and again, that there are two natures and yet only one nature in Christ, surely do contradict each other; indeed, each one contradicts himself.

But if the papists knew that this was not the meaning of Nestorius and of Eutyches, they should, in all fairness, have refrained from such statements, and should have spoken a bit more clearly about the matter and in *terminis propriis,* that is, they should have quoted their own words; otherwise, the heretics will think they are being unjustly and violently attacked with false words and wrong interpretations of their own words, as I said earlier about Nestorius.

That Eutyches did not think there was but one nature in Christ is reflected by the papists' own words when they say that Eutyches confessed that there are two natures in Christ, namely, that the deity has assumed humanity. Whoever confesses this says that Christ has more than one nature. But they do not indicate what Eutyches meant when he said that afterward only the divine nature remained in Christ, not the human; and so they let it rest, as though Eutyches had believed that Christ had two natures, and yet not two, but only one nature. Therefore the later histories are uncertain and obscure too, so that no one can understand what Eutyches or the pope's histories mean, and thus one loses the council, including the reason it was held. Indeed, one can find out through the histories of the councils and the letters of the popes, but, on the other hand, the pope's historians ought not to write so awkwardly and clumsily, nor babble their own words to us; one thing we can certainly gather from this is that they have understood this council exactly as well as I!

I shall give you my ideas; if I hit the mark, good—if not, the Christian faith will not fall herewith. Eutyches' opinion is also (like that of Nestorius) in error regarding the *idiomata,* but in a dif-

---

[297] Leo I. *Epistola 119: ad Maximum Antiochenum episcopum. MPL* 54, 1041*b; PNF*² 12, 85.

ferent way. Nestorius does not want to give the *idiomata* of humanity to the divinity in Christ, even though he maintains that Christ is God and man. Eutyches, on the other hand, does not want to give the *idiomata* of divinity to the humanity, though he also maintains that Christ is true God and true man. It is as though I preached that the "Word," God's Son, is creator of heaven and earth, equal to the Father in eternity, John 1 [:3], and that the "Word," the same Son of God, is true man, John 1 [:14]—Eutyches would grant me that and not doubt it. But if I continue and preach that this same man Christ is creator of heaven and earth, then Eutyches takes offense and is outraged at the words, "A man created heaven and earth," and says, "No! Such a divine *idioma* (as creating heaven) does not appertain to man." But he forgets that he previously conceded that Christ is true God and man in one person and nevertheless refuses to admit the conclusion or "the premise for a good conclusion."[298]

For whoever confesses that God and man are one person must, by reason of such a union of the two natures in one person, also unquestionably concede that this man Christ, born of Mary, is creator of heaven and earth; for he has become this in one person, namely, God who created heaven and earth. Eutyches does not understand such a conclusion, and yet he firmly maintains that Christ is both God and man. Nor does he see that he must deny the human nature of Christ if he rejects the divine *idiomata* of the human nature; for that would divide the person, and Christ would not remain man. And this is what those who write about Eutyches intended to show: he did not allow the human nature in Christ to remain "in his conclusion," though he confesses "in his premise" that the divine and human natures are one Christ, one person, and two natures. To sum up, as was said earlier, whoever confesses the two natures in Christ, God and man, must also ascribe the *idiomata* of both to the person; for to be God and man means nothing if they do not share their *idiomata*. That is why both Nestorius and Eutyches were rightfully condemned because of their error and reason.

---

[298] *Consequens bonae consequentiae.* On the origins of these and other technical terms used by medieval schoolmen, see in this volume, p. 101, n. 278.

It is probably true that Eutyches suffered more anguish[299] than Nestorius, for many of the human *idiomata* were left behind by Christ, such as eating, drinking, sleeping, sorrowing, suffering, dying, being buried, etc. He now sits at the right hand of God and eats, drinks, sleeps, sorrows, suffers, or dies no more in eternity, just as will happen to us when we pass from this life into the other life, I Corinthians 15 [:49, 53]. These are temporal and transient *idiomata;* but the natural ones remain, for instance, that he has body and soul, skin and hair, flesh and blood, marrow and bones, and all the limbs of an ordinary human. That is why one must say that this man Christ, the flesh and blood of Mary, is creator of heaven and earth, has vanquished death, abolished sin, broken hell, all of which are true divine *idiomata,* and yet are rightfully and Christianly ascribed to the person who is flesh and blood of Mary, because it is not two but one person.

It is just like your son Peter being called a scholar, although this *idioma* is only of his soul and not of his body. A Eutyches might quibble and say, "No! Peter is not a scholar; his soul is." And again, a Nestorius might say, "No! I did not flog your son, but his body." That sounds as though one wanted to make two persons out of Peter, or to retain but one nature, though it is not meant that way. It is ignorance and coarseness, and proves that they were bad logicians. Such ignorance, however, is not rare in the world in other matters too; one often admits one thing and yet denies that which must follow from it, as was said, "Admitting the premise and denying the conclusion."[300] There are now, for instance, many great lords and learned people[301] who acknowledge freely and firmly that our doctrine of faith, which justifies by pure grace and without merit, is true. But that one should therefore put an end to and scorn monasticism and the serving of saints and the like, offends them, although it is demanded by the conclusion and is the consequence. No one can be justified without faith; it follows from this that one cannot be justified by a monastic life. Why hold to it then? What good is it?

---

[299] *Anfechtung.*
[300] *Antecedente concessio, negare consequens.*
[301] Luther may have in mind those humanists who agreed with the premises of the Reformation, but were unwilling to agree with the conclusions.

But I shall take myself by the nose too,[302] lest I prove so un-grateful as to forget my own folly. Twenty years ago I taught—[303] as I still do—that faith alone, without works, justifies. But if some-one had arisen at that time and taught that monkery and nunning ought to be called idolatry and the mass a veritable abomination, I, though I would not have helped to burn him, would at least have said that it served him right. And I—thoughtless fool—could not see the conclusion that I would have had to concede, that if faith alone does it, then monkery and mass do not. And still worse, I knew that these were nothing but human works and doc-trine, and yet I did not ascribe such value to the good works commanded by God and performed in faith. Thus I surely proved myself a real Nestorius and Eutyches (albeit in different matters), for I granted one thing but denied the other that followed from it, just as Nestorius admits that Christ is God and man but will not agree that this same God was born and died, which, however, does follow from it.

Moreover, Luther scolds the papists for teaching neither the Christian faith, nor good works, and they on their part do not keep mum either, but in turn rebuke Luther even more vehe-mently for not teaching the Christian faith correctly and for for-bidding good works. What is the obstacle? Why are they not united, although they confess one and the same thing? I shall tell you: a Nestorius has gone astray here on the *idiomata*. Luther wants to have good works, but they should not bear the glorious divine *idiomata*, such as atoning for sin, reconciling God's wrath, and justifying sinners, for such *idiomata* belong to another whose name is "the Lamb of God, who takes away the sin of the world" [John 1:29]. Truly, such *idiomata* must be left to the blood and the death of Christ; good works should have other *idiomata*, other merit and reward. This the papists do not want; instead they give to good works the power to atone for sin and make people pious. Therefore they cry out that Luther does not teach good works, but rather forbids them; but they do not see the conclusion or conse-quence that if one teaches good works that atone for sin, it is tan-

---

[302] Cf. p. 16.
[303] See p. 9, n. 1. This also could be a reference to his *Lectures on Gala-tians 1519.* LW 27, 153-410.

tamount to teaching no good works at all, for such good works are *nihil in rerum natura,* "nothing at all," and cannot be. Consequently, in as much as they so firmly and decisively teach and confess good works, they teach no good works at all.

Here you see Nestorius' logic which admits a "premise" and denies the "conclusion" and thus also falsifies the premise. If the one is true, the other must also be true in any real conclusion or consequence. On the other hand, if the last is false, the first must also be false. They not only admit but absolutely insist that good works atone for sin; yet they condemn that which follows, that such works are not good, indeed, are nothing and no works at all. Now it really follows irrefutably from the former, for good works that atone for sin are as much as no good works, just as this conclusion is irrefutable: *Qui docet id quod non est, docet nihil,* "He who teaches what is not, teaches as much as nothing." One may likewise say of faith, "He who teaches a faith that does not justify alone and without good works teaches as much as no faith at all." For a faith that justifies with or by good works is nothing at all.

I will make it still plainer. Several jurists concede that it is right for priests to marry, but they do not grant the conclusion that their children should be their heirs; that is the same as saying that a priest's marriage must be fornication. If there is a marriage, then the child must also be the heir; if it is not an heir, then there is no marriage. In the schools this is called "denying the conclusion of an admitted premise in a good syllogism" and "retaining the premise when the conclusion has been destroyed"—[304] that is impossible, and those who do it are called crude and ignorant people. But this was the lack in both Nestorius and Eutyches, as happens to many other people in other matters. They both were certainly sincere when they regarded Christ as God and man in one person—as the histories as well as the records of the councils indicate—and yet, they could not reconcile themselves to the conclusion or consequence that the person who is both God and man was really crucified and created heaven; God could not be crucified or man create heaven.

---

[304] *Negare consequens antecedentis concessi in bona consequentia* and *Destructo consequente, retinere antecedens.*

And what shall we say of ourselves? The apostles in Jerusalem, together with many thousands of Jews, had been justified by faith alone, that is, by the grace of Christ. They still had their Nestoriuses and Eutycheses in their system and did not see the conclusion that the laws of Moses did not and could not contribute anything to it, but wanted to ascribe to it the *idiomata* which belong only to the Lamb of God, saying (as we said above) that the Gentiles could not be saved if they were not circumcised and did not keep the law. That was virtually denying Christ with his grace, as St. Paul says in Galatians 2 [:21], "If justification were through the law, then Christ died to no purpose"; and in Romans 11 [:6], "But if it is by grace, it is no longer on the basis of works." But those in Jerusalem said this, "To be sure, it is grace alone, but it must also be works alone, for without the law one cannot be saved, even though one must be saved by grace alone without works." That is, in plain German, boxing one's own ears[305] and not understanding what one says. The schools (as we said) call that "granting the premise and denying the conclusion" or "destroying the conclusion and affirming the premise." No one should at the same time say yes and no about the same thing, unless he be an utter ignoramus or a desperate scoffer.

That is what my Antinomians,[306] too, are doing today, who are preaching beautifully and (as I cannot but think) with real sincerity about Christ's grace, about the forgiveness of sin and whatever else can be said about the doctrine of redemption. But they flee as if it were the very devil the consequence that they should tell the people about the third article,[307] of sanctification, that is, of the new life in Christ. They think one should not frighten or trouble the people, but rather always preach comfortingly about grace and the forgiveness of sins in Christ, and under no circumstances use these or similar words, "Listen! You want to be a Christian and at the same time remain an adulterer, a whoremonger, a drunken swine, arrogant, covetous, a usurer, envious,

---

[305] "*Sich selbs in die backen hauen.*" Cf. Thiele, *Luthers Sprichwörtersammlung*, No. 8.

[306] See p. 72, n. 200.

[307] The third article of the Apostles' Creed. See Luther's *Large Catechism*. Tappert (ed.), *Book of Concord*, pp. 415-420.

vindictive, malicious, etc.!" Instead they say, "Listen! Though you are an adulterer, a whoremonger, a miser, or other kind of sinner, if you but believe, you are saved, and you need not fear the law. Christ has fulfilled it all!"

Tell me, my dear man, is that not granting the premise and denying the conclusion? It is, indeed, taking away Christ and bringing him to nought at the same time he is most beautifully proclaimed! And it is saying yes and no to the same thing. For there is no such Christ that died for sinners who do not, after the forgiveness of sins, desist from sins and lead a new life. Thus they preach Christ nicely with Nestorian and Eutychian logic that Christ is and yet is not Christ. They may be fine Easter preachers, but they are very poor Pentecost preachers, for they do not preach *de sanctificatione et vivificatione Spiritus Sancti,* "about the sanctification by the Holy Spirit," but solely about the redemption of Jesus Christ, although Christ (whom they extoll so highly, and rightly so) is Christ, that is, he has purchased redemption from sin and death so that the Holy Spirit might transform us out of the old Adam into new men—we die unto sin and live unto righteousness, beginning and growing here on earth and perfecting it beyond, as St. Paul teaches.[308] Christ did not earn only *gratia,* "grace," for us, but also *donum,* "the gift of the Holy Spirit," so that we might have not only forgiveness of, but also cessation of, sin. Now he who does not abstain from sin, but persists in his evil life, must have a different Christ, that of the Antinomians; the real Christ is not there, even if all the angels would cry, "Christ! Christ!" He must be damned with this, his new Christ.

Now see what evil logicians we are in sublime matters that are so far beyond or remote from us that we simultaneously believe and disbelieve something. But in lowly matters we are exceedingly keen logicians. No matter how stupid a peasant is, he soon understands and figures out this: he who gives me a groschen is not giving me a gulden. This follows as a matter of course, and he sees the logic of it clearly. But our Antinomians fail to see that they are preaching Christ without and against the Holy Spirit because they propose to let the people continue in their old ways

---

[308] In, for example, Romans 6 and 7.

and still pronounce them saved. And yet logic, too, implies that a Christian should either have the Holy Spirit and lead a new life, or know that he has no Christ. Nevertheless, these asses presume to be better logicians than Master Philip[309] and Aristotle—I must not mention Luther because the pope was made to feel only their logic—they soar far too high for me! Well, then, the logic of Nestorius and Eutyches is a common plague, especially with reference to Holy Scripture; but in other matters it acquits itself better, although it plagues jurists and rulers enough in subtle matters, where they have to hear a yes and no at the same time and have difficulty in distinguishing the two.

Now if Nestorius and Eutyches stubbornly and proudly clung to their opinion (as I neither can nor should judge from the histories I read) after the bishops had instructed them, they were justly condemned not only as heretics but also as silly fools. But if they did not stubbornly cling to their opinion, as the acts of the councils themselves report, especially about Eutyches,[310] and the bishops neglected to instruct in a spirit of gentleness those who erred—in conformity with St. Paul's teaching [Gal. 6:1]—they will one day have to answer to the true judge for their pride and rash action,[311] although they themselves may have judged the case aright (for by now the councils had acquired a great reputation, and there were, I suppose, all of six hundred and thirty bishops in attendance here).[312]

I remember how Master John Wesel,[313] who was pastor in Mainz and who with his books dominated the University of Erfurt, from which I also received my master's degree, had to be

---

[309] Philip Melanchthon (1497-1560).

[310] *Historia Tripartita*, XII, 5. *MPL* 69, 1208a; *PNF*[2] 2, 172.

[311] A reference to the actions of the Council of Ephesus in 449, labeled the "robbers' synod" by Pope Leo I, in which Bishop Dioscur of Alexandria condoned tyrannical procedures and mob action. Its decisions have never been accepted by the Roman Catholic Church.

[312] Recorded by Platina, but not by Rufinus. See *WA* 50, 600, n. *c.*

[313] John of Wesel (*ca.* 1400-1481), an ecclesiastical reformer who attacked indulgences on the basis of Holy Scripture. He was tried before a Dominican commission employed by the inquisition, accused of heresy, and condemned to life imprisonment in a monastery. The quotation Luther attributes to him does not appear in the records of the trial. Cf. Robert Menties (trans.), Karl Ullmann's *Reformers Before the Reformation* (2 vols.; Edinburgh, 1855), I, 217-276.

condemned by those accursed, arrogant murderers called "inquisitors of heretical depravity"[314] (I should say "inventors") the Dominicans, only because he would not say, "I believe that there is a God," but said, "I know that there is a God"; for all the schools held that "the existence of God is known of itself,"[315] as St. Paul also says in Romans 1 [:19]. And you will find related in the *Apology* how the murdering Franciscans dealt with John Hilten in Eisenach.[316]

Suppose that an honorable man would unexpectedly approach you and me, his coarse expression giving a peculiar cast to the matter, saying, "I must tell you that a new prophet has arisen who teaches that if a man becomes perfectly holy he is able not only to perform miracles but also to create heaven and earth, angels, and whatever inhabits heaven and earth, out of nothing"— as several scholastics have also argued, Book IV [of the *Sentences*][317]—and, what is even worse, he says, "The old true God had died," etc. Here you and I would say, "He must be the devil and his mother." Scripture says, "I the Lord do not change" [Mal. 3:6]; and St. Paul, "Who alone has immortality" [I Tim. 6:16]. Why waste many words? God alone lives, and he himself is life. Then he would begin, "Why, you yourself teach and say that Christ is a man, perfectly holy, the creator of heaven and earth, furthermore, true God, who died for you on the cross." Behold how suddenly we become blasphemous Nestoriuses and Eutycheses, confessing simultaneously that Christ is God and man, one person, that he died for us, that he created heaven and earth, though we have just said it must be the devil and his mother who say that a man created heaven and earth and that God died! And yet, logical consistency compels us to believe that Christ is God and man in one person. Here you see how the *idiomata* can take unthinking people unawares and confuse and perplex them. In such an instance one should proceed with gentle instruction and

[314] *"Haereticae pravitatis inquisitores,"* the official title for those Dominicans who were employed by the inquisition, instituted by Pope Gregory IX in 1232.
[315] *"Deum esse, per se notum sit."*
[316] The story is told in Philip Melanchthon's *Apology of the Augsburg Confession,* Art. XXVII. Tappert (ed.), *Book of Concord,* pp. 268-269.
[317] Book IV deals with the seven sacraments and with the last things. Cf. *MPL* 192, 839-962.

refrain from any arrogant condemnation of those who err. May God grant that I lie; but I fear that on the Last Day some of the heretics will be the judges, condemning the bishops who sat in judgment over them. God is strange and inscrutable in his judgments [Rom. 11:33]. However, we know that he "opposes the proud, but gives grace to the humble" [I Pet. 5:5]. Especially in the councils and in the church one should never act from *zelos*,[318] that is, from envy and pride, for that is intolerable to God.

That is my opinion about Eutyches. If I did not hit the mark, I missed it,[319] and it is their fault. Why did they not give a better account of the matter and report on it with greater care, so that it might be clearly understood? And what should we do if the acts of this council were lost? The Christian faith would not have to perish because of that! Other and far more useful things than the acts of this council have been lost. St. Augustine himself bemoans the fact that he could find but very little in his predecessors to aid him against Pelagius, though such an important subject must have been much discussed.[320] I have formed my opinions on the basis of the words of the Roman bishop Leo, who writes that the heresies of Nestorius and Eutyches are inconsistent or contradictory and in opposition to one another.[321] Now the *Tripartita* leaves no doubt that Nestorius confessed that Christ is true God and true man, very emphatically so, and that he was not an Arian, simply denying the divinity of Christ.[322] On the contrary, he banished and persecuted the Arians, even to the point of murder and slaughter. But his heresy consists in that he, confused and led astray by the *idiomata*, could not understand how God could be born of a woman and be crucified. Therefore Eutyches' heresy must be regarded contradictory because he regards Christ as God and man, but refuses to ascribe the *idiomata* of the divine nature to the human nature; just as Nestorius, on the other hand,

---

[318] From the Greek for "zeal."
[319] A German proverb of unknown origin, "*Hab ichs nicht troffen, so hab ich gefeilet.*"
[320] The passage could not be located in Augustine's writings. Cf. Schäfer, *op. cit.*, p. 314, n. 3.
[321] Leo I. *Epistola 165: ad Leonem Augustum*, C. II. *MPL* 54, 1155-1157; *PNF*[2] 12, 107-108.
[322] *Historia Tripartita*, XII, 4. *MPL* 69, 1204-1205; *PNF*[2] 2, 169.

would not ascribe the *idiomata* of the human nature to God in the one person of Christ. That is what is meant by saying that the two are in opposition to one another or contradictory.

If, however, it was his intention simply to deny the human nature in Christ, then his heresy does not contradict that of Nestorius; then he must have been raving mad to believe that the divinity is united with humanity in Christ, and that at the same time only one nature, namely, the divine, remained or came into being. That would not only be opposed to Nestorius, but also to all believers and unbelievers, to all heretics and true Christians, to all heathen and all of mankind, for no man ever taught a thing like that. But since they gave such an account of this matter and themselves testified that Eutyches had admitted that divinity and humanity are merged into one person in Christ, and yet also made the other statement, as though they intended that no one should understand it, we will not understand it either. Why should we care, since we ourselves have a better conception of it? In the council Eutyches says that he had not stated his position in the words of which they accused him, namely, that he had denied the human nature in Christ.[323] From this one can infer that he was in error and that he did not want to deny the humanity in Christ. But if I were Dr. Luther, I would like to hear from these popish writers how they could believe their own words when they made bold to say that Nestorius held that there were two persons in Christ and yet only one person, and that Eutyches held that there were two natures in Christ and yet only one nature. I surely believe that they, too, are Nestorian and Eutychian dialecticians. I say nothing of their theology; perhaps they are compelled to be antilogicians.

But to return to the council—we find that this council too did not establish any new article of faith; again it furnishes no proof that councils are vested with the authority to foist new doctrines on Christendom, for this article is far more abundantly and firmly grounded in Scripture, John 5 [:27], "The Father has given him authority to execute judgment, because he is the Son of man." If Christ had adapted himself to Eutyches' opinion, he would have

---

[323] *Historia Tripartita,* XII, 4. *MPL* 69, 1208a; *PNF²* 2, 172.

been obliged to say, "because he is the Son of God," for to execute judgment is an *idioma* of divine, not of human, nature. Christ, however, imputes this power to his human nature, namely, to the Son of man, that is, the Son of the Virgin Mary. And in Matthew 22 [:43-45] Christ asks the Pharisees how they explain the fact that David calls Christ his Lord, though he had to be his Son and seed. If he is David's Son or seed, how then can he sit at the right hand of God? Here Eutyches would have had to say that not David's seed, but only God's Son can sit at the right hand of God. And yet he confesses that God's Son and David's Son are one person; but where the person sits, there sits God's Son and David's. Eutyches did not see this conclusion; therefore it was inferred that he did not regard Christ as man, but only as a divine person and nature, though this was not what he meant.

In summary, all the prophets, all of Scripture, ascribing to Christ or the Messiah an everlasting kingdom, redemption from sin, death, and hell, oppose Eutyches, for they all say that the seed of the woman shall bruise the serpent's head, Genesis 3 [:15], that is, shall vanquish sin, death, devil, and hell; these too are *idiomata* of divine nature and not of the woman's seed. And all the world is to be blessed through the seed of Abraham, Genesis 22 [:18], that is, sin, death, hell, the curse of God, are to be removed. These too are *idiomata*, not of Abraham's seed, but of divine nature. And later there followed the glorious and mighty prophecies of David, Isaiah, Jeremiah, and all the other prophets declaring that David's seed shall establish eternal righteousness, that is, abolish sin, death, and hell.[324] All of these are clearly *idiomata* of divine majesty and nature, yet are ascribed throughout Holy Scripture to the Son of David, Christ, the Son of the Virgin Mary. Even if I do not have this council or any proper understanding of it, I still have Scripture and a proper understanding of it. The council too is bound to hold to it; and for me Scripture is far more reliable than all councils.

Whoever is thus disposed may read more of the history of the councils; I read myself into a bad humor with it. Such bickering, confusion, and disorder prevailed there that I am really inclined

---

[324] For example, Jer. 23:5.

to believe Gregory of Nazianz, the teacher of St. Jerome, who, having lived before this time and having witnessed better councils and fathers, still wrote, "To tell the truth, I believe it advisable to flee all the councils of bishops; for I saw nothing good resulting from the councils, not even the abolition of evil, but rather sheer ambition and quarreling over precedence," etc.[325] I am surprised that they, in view of these words, did not long ago brand him as the worst heretic. But he speaks the truth when he says that the bishops are ambitious, haughty, quarrelsome, and vehement in the councils; you will find that corroborated in this council. By the same token, not all who teach correctly or uphold the true doctrine are necessarily holy. For Balaam also is a true prophet [Num. 24:16], and Judas is a true apostle [Matt. 10:4], and the Pharisees occupy the seat of Moses and teach the truth [Matt. 23:2-3]. Thus we too must have something else and something more reliable for our faith than the councils. That "something else" and "something more" is Holy Scripture.

The truth of his statement that he saw no good results come from the councils is strongly borne out by the histories. For before the Council of Nicaea the heresy of Arius was a jest compared with the misery evoked after the council, as was said above. The same applies to the other councils, as in the cases of Macedonius and Nestorius; for the faction that was condemned held together all the more firmly, trying to justify itself and to be exonerated. They fanned the flames more vigorously than before against the councils that had not understood them rightly. That is the way we Germans fared at the Council of Constance:[326] there the pope was made subject to the council and was deposed, and his tyranny and simony[327] were strongly condemned. Yet ever since that time he is possessed by seven more devils [Matt. 12:45] and his tyranny and simony have gotten off to an even better start. He devours, robs, and steals all convents, cloisters, churches; he sells indulgences, grace, law, God, Christ, the Holy Spirit; he betrays,

---

[325] *Epistola 130: ad Procopium. MPG* 37, 225-226.

[326] This council was held from 1414 to 1418. For more of Luther's reactions to this council, see Headley, *op. cit.*, pp. 225-228.

[327] Simony, meaning the sale of spiritual things for money, gets its name from Acts 8:18-24. Ecclesiastical offices frequently were bought in the Middle Ages.

ruins, confuses emperors and kings; he wages wars, sheds blood, assassinates body and soul, so that it becomes quite evident what god it is that keeps house in Rome. That is the reward we Germans have for deposing and reforming the popes at the Council of Constance. Indeed, I think that this was the appropriate end for this council. If seven devils do not suffice for them, then depose and reform more popes the next time, and you may have seventy-seven legions warring against you—provided there is still room for even more devils to inhabit them and they are not already full of them. Such was the reformation of the Council of Constance.

These then are the four principal councils and the reasons they were held. The first, in Nicaea, defended the divinity of Christ against Arius; the second, in Constantinople, defended the divinity of the Holy Spirit against Macedonius; the third, in Ephesus, defended the one person of Christ against Nestorius; the fourth, in Chalcedon, defended the two natures in Christ against Eutyches. But no new articles of faith were thereby established, for these four doctrines are formulated far more abundantly and powerfully in St. John's gospel alone, even if the other evangelists and St. Paul and St. Peter had written nothing about it, although they, together with the prophets, also teach and bear convincing witness to all of that. Since these four principal councils (which the bishops of Rome, according to their decretals, put on a level with the four gospels, as though these matters together with all articles of faith were not contained far more richly in the gospels, or as if the councils had not taken them from there—so nicely do these episcopal asses understand the essence of the gospels and of the councils) neither intended nor were able to create and establish anything new in matters of faith, as they themselves confess, how much less then can one assign such power to the other councils, which are to be regarded lower, if these four are and are to be called principal councils.

All the other councils too must be viewed in this way, be they large or small. Even though there were many thousands of them, they do not introduce anything new either in matters of faith or of good works; but they defend, as the highest judges and greatest bishops under Christ, the ancient faith and the ancient good works in conformity with Scripture. To be sure, they may also deal with temporal, transient, and changeable things in order to meet the need of their particular time; this, however, must also be done outside the councils in every parish and school. But if they establish anything new with regard to faith or good works, you may rest assured that the Holy Spirit had no hand in it, but only the unholy spirit with his angels. For in that instance they must act without and outside of Holy Scripture, indeed, in opposition to it, as Christ says, "He who is not with me is against me" [Matt. 12:30]. The Holy Spirit can neither know nor do anything more than St. Paul when he says in I Corinthians 2 [:2], "I decided to know nothing among you except Jesus Christ and him crucified." The Holy Spirit has not been given to teach or instill in us anything except Christ, but he is to teach and remind us of all that is in Christ "in whom are hid all the treasures of wisdom and knowledge" [Col. 2:3]. He is to make him clear to us, as Christ says [John 16:13], and not exalt our reason and notions or make an idol of these.

This is why these councils are outside Scripture and are councils of Caiphas, Pilate, and Herod; as the apostles say in Acts 4 [:26], "They were gathered against the Lord." They take counsel, or hold councils, against God and his Christ [Ps. 2:2]. And all the evangelists relate[328] that the chief priests and Pharisees conferred, or assembled councils, deliberating how they might kill Christ— as David had foretold in Psalm 2 [:2-3] that they would take counsel together against God and his anointed, calling Christ's preaching "bonds" and "cords" which they would burst asunder and cast from them. Such are the majority of the pope's councils, in which he sets himself up in Christ's stead as head of the church, makes Holy Scripture subject to himself, and tears it asunder. His decretals show how he condemned the sacrament in both kinds at Constance[329] after he had already rent marriage asunder, forbidden it and condemned it, and virtually crucified and buried Christ.

---

[328] Matt. 26:4; Mark 14:1-2; Luke 22:2; John 11:47-53.
[329] Cf. Luther's treatment of the decrees of the Council of Constance in WA 39ᴵ, 13-39.

This brings us to the main question prompting me to write this booklet: what, then, is a council? Or, what is its task? If it is not the function of a council to establish new articles of faith, then all the world has to date been fooled terribly because it neither knows nor believes anything other than that a decision of a council is an article of faith or at least a work necessary for salvation, so that he who does not keep the decree of a council cannot be saved because he does not obey the Holy Spirit, the council's master. Well then, I think that my conscience is clear when I say that no council (as I said before) is authorized to initiate new articles of faith, because the four principal councils did not do that. Consequently, I will state my opinion here and reply to this main question as follows.

First, a council has no power to establish new articles of faith, even though the Holy Spirit is present. Even the apostolic council in Jerusalem introduced nothing new in matters of faith, but rather held that which St. Peter concludes in Acts 16 [15:11], and which all their predecessors believed, namely, the article that one is to be saved without the laws, solely through the grace of Christ.

Second, a council has the power—and is also duty-bound to exercise it—to suppress and to condemn new articles of faith, in accordance with Scripture and the ancient faith, just as the Council of Nicaea condemned the new doctrine of Arius, that of Constantinople the new doctrine of Macedonius, that of Ephesus the new doctrine of Nestorius, and that of Chalcedon the new doctrine of Eutyches.

Third, a council has no power to command new good works; it cannot do so, for Holy Scripture has already abundantly commanded all good works. What good works can one think of that the Holy Spirit does not teach in Scripture, such as humility, patience, gentleness, mercy, faithfulness, faith, kindness, peaceableness, obedience, self-discipline, chastity, generosity, readiness to serve, etc., and in summary, love? [Gal. 5:22-23]. What good work could one imagine that is not included in the commandment of love? What sort of a good work would it be if it were not motivated by love? For love, according to St. Paul's teaching, is the fulfilment of the whole law [Gal. 5:14]—as Christ himself says in Matthew 5.

123

Fourth, a council has the power—and is also duty-bound to exercise it—to condemn evil works that oppose love, according to all of Scripture and the ancient practice of the church, and to punish persons guilty of such works, as the Nicene council's decree rebuked the ambition and other vices of bishops and deacons. But here one should speak of two kinds of evil works: some that are, and are called clearly wicked, such as greed, murder, adultery, ambition, and the like. These we find condemned by the councils, as they are also condemned, outside the councils, in Holy Scripture and are, moreover, also punished by civil law. But besides these there are other, new good works which are not called evil, but are seemingly good, refined vices, holy idolatries invented by strange saints, or even mad saints; in summary, they are the white devil and a glittering Satan. Such evil, I should say new, good works should be condemned by the councils most sharply and severely, for they pose a danger to the Christian faith and an offense to Christian life and are a caricature or mockery of both.

For instance, when a weak Christian hears or sees a holy hermit or monk leading a special kind of life, more austere than that of the ancient, ordinary Christian way and vocation, he stumbles over this and supposes that the life of all the ancient Christians was nothing, or even worldly and dangerous, in comparison with that of this new saint. That gave rise to the abomination throughout the world of a Christian burgher or peasant who believes in Christ with a true and pure faith and practices the genuine, ancient good works commanded by God in Holy Scripture—such as humility, gentleness, patience, chastity, charity, and faithfulness toward his neighbor, industry, and application to his work, office, calling, and station—thinking such a man a true old saint and Christian, whereas he himself is a stench and a cipher compared to the new saint with his special garb, food, fasting, bed, mien, and other similar new good works, who is a conceited, ambitious, angry, impatient, hateful, lustful, presumptuous, false Christian. St. Paul himself calls such people arrogant and egotistic saints who choose a new mode of life for themselves and a new way of serving God not commanded by God, over and above the Christian church's old, true, common way of life and service to God, ordained and commanded by him.

124

The elect may have been preserved amid these offensive new works, but they had to shed this new skin and be saved in the old Christian skins, just as happened to St. Anthony[330] when he had to learn that a cobbler or tanner in Alexandria was a better Christian than he was with his monkery. He also conceded that he had not advanced as far as this cobbler had. So it was with the great St. John too, the "first hermit,"[331] who was also a prophet for the emperor Theodosius and highly lauded by St. Augustine.[332] When the people, among them St. Jerome, admired the severity of his life, he replied, "Why do you look for anything extraordinary among us? After all, you are more fortunate in your parishes, where the writings and the precepts of apostles and prophets are preached to you." That is what I call taking off the cowl and subjecting oneself to Holy Scripture, praising solely the ordinary Christian way of life. Paphnutius[333] too had to learn that he was on the same level with a fiddler who had been a murderer, and with two wives who had lain with their husbands that same night. Thus he was constrained to remark, "Alas! One must not despise any estate." The same thing also happened to St. Bernard, to Bonaventure,[334] and undoubtedly to many other pious men. In the end, when they realized that their new holiness and monkery could not stand the test against sin and death, they crawled and were saved in the ancient Christian faith, without such new holiness— as the words of St. Bernard testify in many places.[335]

In none of the councils, especially not in the four principal councils, do we find these new good works condemned, except that one or two small councils—for instance, the one that met at Gangra and was composed of twenty bishops (the proceedings of

---

[330] This story is recorded in the *Lives of the Fathers* (*Vitae Patrum*), III, 130, which passed as the work of Jerome, but is now ascribed to Rufinus. See *MPL* 73, 785.

[331] *Primus Eremita*, known as John the Hermit. See Rufinus, II, 20, 32. *MPL* 21, 526c; 538c.

[332] Augustine's praise is found in *The City of God* (*De Civitate Dei*), V, 26. *MPL* 41, 172; *PNF*[1] 2, 105.

[333] See p. 43, n. 101. Paphnutius was a disciple of Anthony. See Rufinus, *History of the Monks* (*Historia Monachorum*), XVI. *MPL* 21, 436.

[334] Bonaventure (1221-1274), a Franciscan theologian known as "the seraphic doctor" because of his mysticism. He taught at the University of Paris.

[335] Cf. Schäfer, *op. cit.*, pp. 441 ff.

which recently appeared in print)[336]—did do something about it. On the contrary, they let the new holiness get the upper hand until the Christian church was hardly recognizable any longer. They acted like lazy gardeners who permit the vines to grow so rampant that the old true tree has to suffer or perish. Even before St. Anthony's day monasticism had made such headway that by the time of the fourth council there was an abbey near Constantinople, of which the aforementioned Eutyches was abbot—although the monasteries of that day were not such imperial castles of stone as they afterward became. For they called him *Archimandrita*.[337] *Mandrae* is said to mean a fence or hedge, made of bushes, shrubs, and boughs, used as an enclosure for animals or as a fold for sheep. And Eutyches, as the head of it, lived with his followers in such an enclosure and led a secluded life. From this one can gather what a monastery was like at the time, before it was enclosed with walls. But just as happens in a garden, where the weeds grow much higher than the true fruit-bearing shoots, so it also happens in the garden of the church: these new saints, who sprout and grow out from the side and yet want to be Christians, nourished by the sap of the tree, grow far better than the true old saints of the Christian faith and life. And since I have touched on the subject, I must relate what I noticed in the histories. St. Bernard was an abbot for thirty-six years, during which time he founded one hundred and sixty monasteries of his order.[338] Now, one knows what kind of monasteries the Cistercians have. At that time, perhaps, they may have been smaller, but today they are regular principalities. And I will say even more: at that time, that is, under the reign of the emperors Henry III, IV, and V,[339] within the span of twenty years, four different princely monastic orders

---

[336] The little synod of Gangra, in Paphlagonia, held in 343, adopted a series of canons directed against extreme asceticism. John Kymaeus, pastor in Homberg, used these canons in 1530 in an attack on the Anabaptists. The book was published in 1537 with a preface by Luther (WA 50, 46-47). The canons to which Luther here refers are noted in WA 50, 609, n. c.

[337] This term means "sheep-tender"; cf. John 21:16.

[338] Cf. Luther's *Supputatio*. WA 53, 156. Cf. also the analysis of his sources in WA 53, 9-15.

[339] Henry III (1039-1056); Henry IV (1065-1106); Henry V (1106-1125).

came into being—the Grandmontines,[340] the Reformed Regular Canons,[341] the Carthusians,[342] and the Cistercians.[343] And what do you suppose happened in the four hundred years since then? I truly believe that one could well say it rained and snowed monks— and it would be no wonder if there were no city or village today without a monastery or two, or at least a terminary or stationary.[344] The histories chide Emperor Valentinian[345] because he used the monks for service in war. Alas, my dear man, these idle folks were multiplying too fast. One also reads that several kings of France forbade men, especially serfs, to become monks, for everybody flocked to the monasteries in search of freedom under the cowl.

The world wants to be fooled. If you wish to catch many robins and other birds, you must place an owl or a screech owl on the trap or lime-rod, and you will succeed. Similarly, when the devil wants to trap Christians, he must put on a cowl, or (as Christ calls it) a sour, hypocritical expression [Matt. 6:16]. Thus we stand in greater awe of such owls and screech owls than of the true suffering, blood, wounds, death, and resurrection, which we see and hear of in Christ, our Lord, endured because of our sin. So we fall, in throngs and with all our might, away from our Christian faith and into the new holiness, that is, into the devil's trap and lime-rod. For we always must have something new. Christ's death and resurrection, faith and love, are old and just ordinary things; that is why they must count for nothing, and so

---

[340] The Order of Grandmont, originally located in Normandy, was formed in 1073. It disappeared after the French Revolution in 1789.
[341] The Augustinian Canons, founded after 1059. They are to be distinguished from the Augustinian Eremites, the order Luther joined in 1505. See *O.D.C.C.*, p. 109.
[342] Founded by Bruno of Cologne in 1084 in the mountainous region near Grenoble in France. They were known for their almost total seclusion from the world.
[343] Founded at Cîteaux in 1098 by Robert of Molesme. A more radical form of Benedictine monasticism, the Cistercian Order became famous through Bernard of Clairvaux.
[344] Terms originally used to designate the houses of mendicant orders and later applied to other monasteries.
[345] Luther confuses Valentinian I with his brother Valens; see p. 38, n. 86. It was Valens who, according to Platina, compelled Egyptian monks to enter the army and to return to the civic duties they had abandoned through their decision to become monks.

we must have new wheedlers (as St. Paul says). And this serves us right since our ears itch so much for something new that we can no longer endure the old and genuine truth, "that we accumulate,"[346] that we weigh ourselves down with big piles of new teachings. That is just what has happened and will continue to happen. For the subsequent councils, especially the papal ones (for afterward they are almost all papal), did not merely refrain from condemning these new good works, but exalted them throughout the world far above the good old works, so that the pope canonized or elevated many saints from the monastic orders.

At first it was rather nice to look at—and still is—but in the end it becomes an abominable, monstrous thing, since everyone adds to it from day to day. Thus, the beginning of St. Francis' order[347] looked fine, but now it has become so crude that they even put cowls on the dead so that the dead might be saved in them. Isn't it terrible to hear that? Well, that is the way it goes: if one starts to fall away from Christ and gets into the habit of falling, one can no longer stop. That has happened in our own time in the Netherlands, when Madame Margaret[348] ordered that she be made a nun after her death. It was done; she was dressed in a nun's garb, placed at a table, and offered food and drink served as for a true princess. Thus she atoned for her sin and became a holy nun. But after this had lasted a few days, the pious Emperor Charles heard of it, and he had it stopped. Had he not done that, I believe such an example would have flooded the whole world. That is what the new holiness does and must do because it wants to do better than the true, old Christian holiness, which does not fool like this, but remains constant and always exercises itself in faith, love, humility, discipline, patience, etc.; one sees in it nothing abominable, but only lovely, charming, peaceful, kind, and useful examples that please God and man. But the new holiness blusters with a peculiar, new demeanor to entice unsteady

---

[346] *Ut acervemus,* II Tim. 4:3.

[347] Francis of Assisi (*ca.* 1182-1226), whose real name was Giovanni Bernardone. Originally a mendicant order, the Franciscans had gained so much wealth by the thirteenth century that the debate about it resulted in a schism within the order in 1250.

[348] Margaret of Austria (1507-1530), aunt of Charles V and regent of the Netherlands.

souls to itself. It makes a great ado, but there is nothing to it,[349] as St. Peter writes [II Pet. 2:14-22].

Likewise, Gerson writes that the Carthusians are right when they apply their rule so rigorously that they eat no meat even if they should have to die.[350] Well then, if a pious physician here notices that the sick man could be helped by nothing but chicken broth or a bite of meat, then one does not obey the physician, but rather the sick man must die. There I praise St. Augustine, who writes in his *Rule*[351] that one should ask the physician's advice saying, "Not all people have the same capability, hence one should not regard all as equal." This is a true and beautiful "meekness";[352] moreover, it does not force them to remain forever, for the monastery was not a prison but a voluntary association of a few priests. Dr. Staupitz[353] once told me that he had heard from the bishop of Worms, who was a Dahlberg,[354] that if St. Augustine had written nothing but the *Rule*, one would still have to say that he was an excellent, wise man. This is certainly true; for he would have utterly condemned those Carthusians as murderers, and their monasteries as veritable, physical dens of murderers (which in truth they are). I myself saw a sick man, who was still young, walking with a crutch in the Carthusian monastery in Erfurt;[355] I asked him whether he was excused from the choir and the watch. "No," he replied sadly, "I must perish."

But we got our just desserts. God sent us his Son to be our teacher and savior. Not satisfied with that, he himself preaches from his high, heavenly throne to us all, saying, *"Hunc audite,"*

---

[349] A German proverb, *"Ist doch nichts dahinden."* Cf. Thiele, *Luthers Sprichwörtersammlung*, No. 6.

[350] John Gerson (1363-1429), a professor at the University of Paris and a cardinal. He asserted the authority of the general council over the pope at the various "reform councils" held in the beginning of the fifteenth century. See *Concerning the Carthusians' Abstention from Meat* (*De non esu carnium Carthusiensium*) in *Gersonis Opera* (2nd ed.; 4 vols.; Basel, 1488), II, 39.

[351] *The Rule of St. Aurelius Augustine* (*Regula S. Aurelii Augustini*), IX. *MPL* 32, 1383.

[352] *Epieikeia* in Greek. Cf. II Cor. 10:1.

[353] John von Staupitz, Luther's superior in the monastery; *LW* 31, XVI.

[354] John of Dahlberg, bishop of Worms (1482-1503).

[355] Luther stayed in Erfurt as a student and as a monk in the Augustinian monastery there, from 1501 until 1508, and was undoubtedly familiar with the nearby Carthusian monastery.

"Listen to him" [Matt. 17:5]. Thus we should drop to our knees with the apostles and believe that we hear nothing else in the whole world. But we let the Father and the Son preach in vain, do things on our own, and invent our own sermon. This then is the way it goes, as Psalm 81 [:11-12] says, "My people did not listen to my voice; so I gave them over to their stubborn hearts." Thence come such fine *etelothreskiae* and *apheidiae*, Colossians 2 [:23], "self-chosen spirituality" and "merciless severity to the body," so that we kill ourselves despite God's command that one should care for, not kill, the body. Don't you think that if in accordance with St. Augustine's *Rule* and St. Paul's teaching, one had let the physicians give advice about the bodies of those in the religious orders, especially the women, many a fine person would have been helped who otherwise has had to go mad or has died—as daily experiences have indeed taught us? However, this was the time of wrath, when the new and mad holiness had to reign for the punishment of the world.

Fifth, a council has no power to impose new ceremonies on Christians, to be observed on pain of mortal sin or at the peril of conscience—such as fast days, feast days, food, drink, garb. But if they do this, St. Augustine confronts them with the words addressed to Januarius, "Observance of these things is free. Christ instituted few ceremonies."[356] Because they have the power to command them, we have the power to ignore them; indeed, we are forbidden to observe them by St. Paul in Colossians 2 [:16], "Let not your conscience be troubled over certain days, over fasting, food, or drink," etc.

Sixth, a council has the power and is bound to condemn such ceremonies in accordance with Scripture; for they are un-Christian and constitute a new idolatry or worship, which is not commanded by God, but forbidden.

Seventh, a council has no power to interfere in worldly law and government, etc.; for St. Paul says, "He who wants to serve God in spiritual warfare should refrain from engaging in civilian pursuits" [II Tim. 2:4].

Eighth, a council has the power and is bound to condemn

---

[356] *Epistola 54. MPL* 33, 200; *PNF*[1] 1, 300.

such arbitrary ways or new laws, in accordance with Holy Scripture, that is, to throw the pope's decretals into the fire.

Ninth, a council has no power to create statutes or decretals that seek nothing but tyranny, that is, statutes on how the bishops should have the power and authority to command what they will and everybody should tremble and obey; but it has the power and is bound to condemn this in accordance with Holy Scripture, I Peter 5 [:3], "Not as domineering over those in your charge," and as Christ says, "But not so with you; rather let the leader become as one who serves" [Luke 22:26].

Tenth, a council has the power to institute some ceremonies, provided, first, that they do not strengthen the bishops' tyranny; second, that they are useful and profitable to the people and show fine, orderly discipline and conduct. Thus it is necessary, for example, to have certain days, and also places where one can assemble; also certain hours for preaching and for the public administration of the sacraments, for praying, singing, praising and thanking God, etc.—as St. Paul says, I Corinthians 14 [:40], "All things should be done decently and in order." Such items do not serve the bishops' tyranny, but only the people's need, profit, and order. In summary, these must and cannot be dispensed with if the church is to survive.

But if someone is occasionally hindered by some emergency, sickness, or whatever it may be from observing this, it need not be sin. For it is done for his benefit and not for the bishops'. If he is a Christian, he thereby will not harm himself. What difference does it make to God if someone does not want to belong to such a group or participate in this way? Everyone will find out for himself. In summary, he who is a Christian is not bound to such order; he would rather do it than let it go if he is not forced into it. Here, therefore, no law can be laid down for him; he would want to do and would prefer to do more than such a law demands. But he who haughtily, proudly, and wilfully despises it—let him go his way, for such a person will also despise a higher law, be it divine or human.

Perhaps you might say here, "What do you finally want to make of the councils if you clip them so close? At that rate a pastor, indeed a schoolteacher (to say nothing of parents), would have greater power over his pupils than a council has over the church." I answer: Do you think then that the offices of the pastor and the schoolteacher are so low that they cannot be compared with the councils? How could one assemble a council if there were no pastors or bishops? How could we get pastors if there were no schools? I am speaking of those schoolteachers who instruct the children and the youth not only in the arts, but also train them in Christian doctrine and faithfully impress it upon them; I also speak in the same manner of pastors who teach God's word in faithfulness and purity. For I can easily prove that the poor, insignificant pastor at Hippo, St. Augustine, taught more than all the councils (to say nothing of the most holy popes in Rome, whom I fear to mention). I will go further than that: there is more in the Children's Creed[357] than in all the councils. The Lord's Prayer and the Ten Commandments also teach more than all the councils. Moreover, they not only teach, but also guard against anything new that opposes the ancient doctrine. For heaven's sake! How the papists will pluck these words of mine from their context, shout them to bits, torture them to death, and prove them illogical; but meanwhile they will not mention the reasons I have spoken in this manner. For they are pious and honest people, who cannot do anything but calumniate and lie, something I should indeed be afraid of! But may God forgive me, I really cannot do it; I would rather let them go on with their slander and their lies.

But let us, you and me, discuss this subject together. What then can a council do, or what is its task? Listen yourself to their own words. *Anathematizamus* is the name of their office—"We condemn." Indeed, they speak even more humbly and do not say, "We condemn," but *anathematizat ecclesia,* "The holy Christian church condemns." The council's condemnation would not terrify me, but the holy church's condemnation would slay me in an instant because of the Man who says, "I am with you always, to the close of the age" [Matt. 28:20]. Oh, this Man's condemnation is not to be endured. But the councils, since they appeal to the holy Chris-

---

[357] The Apostles' Creed.

tian church as to the true and supreme judge on earth, testify that they cannot judge according to their own discretion, but that the church, which preaches, believes, and confesses Holy Scripture, is the judge—as we shall hear. Just as a thief or a murderer would be secure from the judge as far as his person is concerned, but law and country are united in the judge, their servant, and of these two he must be afraid.

A council, then, is nothing but a consistory, a royal court, a supreme court,[358] or the like, in which the judges, after hearing the parties, pronounce sentence, but with this humility, "For the sake of the law," that is, "Our office is *anathematizare*, 'to condemn'; but not according to our whim or will, or newly invented law, but according to the ancient law, which is acknowledged as the law throughout the entire empire." Thus a council condemns a heretic, not according to its own discretion, but according to the law of the empire, that is, according to Holy Scripture, which they confess to be the law of the holy church. Such law, empire, and judge must surely be feared on pain of eternal damnation. This law is God's word, the empire is God's church; the judge is the official or servant of both.

Not only the council, but every pastor and schoolteacher is also the servant or judge of this law and empire. Moreover, a council cannot administer this judicial office forever without intermission; for the bishops cannot forever remain assembled together, but must gather only in times of certain emergencies and then anathematize, or be judges. Thus, if an Arius in Alexandria grows too strong for his pastor or bishop, attracts the people, and also urges other pastors and people in the country to join him, so that the pastor in Alexandria is defeated and his judicial office can no longer defend the law of the empire, that is, the true Christian faith—in such an emergency and at such a time the other pastors and bishops should rally with all their might around the pastor of

---

[358] *Consistorium, Hofegericht, Camergericht.* These terms were borrowed from Roman law and represent names for courts in sixteenth-century Germany. The first Protestant *Consistorium,* not unlike a modern denominational synod, was formed in Saxony in 1539. The *Consistorium* was originally the supreme court in ancient Rome, and later the highest ecclesiastical court within the medieval church.

Alexandria and help him defend the true faith against Arius and condemn Arius to save the others, so that this misery does not get the upper hand. And if the pastors are unable to come, the pious Emperor Constantine should add his power to help assemble the bishops. It is just like when a fire breaks out; if the man of the house cannot extinguish it alone, all the neighbors should hurry over and help quench it. And if they do not hurry over, the government should help and command that they must gather to anathematize or condemn the fire, in order to save the other houses.

Thus the council is the great servant or judge in this empire and law. Yet when the emergency has passed, it has done its duty—just as, in temporal government, the supreme, great judges have to help when the lower, secondary courts prove too weak to cope with an evil, until the case is at last brought before the highest, greatest court, the diet, which cannot meet forever either, but must adjourn after the emergency is over and again leave matters to the lower courts. At the diet, however, it happens that occasionally new or additional laws have to be enacted, or that old laws have to be amended, improved, or even abolished; justice cannot forever be administered according to an eternal law, for this is a temporal government which rules over temporal, changeable, and variable things. Therefore the laws that are made for these changeable things must also change. If that for which the law was made no longer exists, then the law no longer represents anything, just as the city of Rome no longer has institutions and ways of life it had had before; and therefore the laws that were passed for these are also dead and invalid. Transient things have transient laws.

But in this empire of the church the rule is, "The word of our God will stand for ever" [Isa. 40:8]. One has to live according to it and refrain from creating new or different words of God and from establishing new and different articles of faith. That is why pastors and schoolteachers are the lowly, but daily, permanent, eternal judges who anathematize without interruption, that is, fend off the devil and his raging. A council, being a great judge, must make old, great rascals pious or kill them, but it cannot produce any others. A pastor and a schoolteacher deal with small, young rascals and constantly train new people to become bishops and councils, whenever it is necessary. A council prunes the large limbs from the tree or extirpates evil trees. But a pastor and a schoolteacher plant and cultivate young trees and useful shrubs in the garden. Oh, they have a precious office and task, and they are the church's richest jewels; they preserve the church. Therefore all the lords should do their part to preserve pastors and schools. For if indeed we cannot have councils, the parishes and schools, small though they are, are eternal and useful councils.

One can see quite well how earnestly the ancient emperors regarded parishes and schools,[359] since they endowed the monasteries so richly. That they were primarily schools is evidenced by these names: provost, dean, *scholasticus,* cantor, *canonici,* vicars, custodians, etc.[360] But what has become of these? O Lord God! If they were at least willing to do something, remain what they were, keep what they had, were princes and lords, and again introduced hours of study and compelled the canons, vicars, and choir pupils to listen to a daily lesson from Holy Scripture so that they would again, in some sense, look like a school, and so that one could have pastors and bishops and thus help to rule the church. O Lord God, what immeasurable benefit they could be to the church! And God would not begrudge them their wealth or power, but let them have them, if they but amended their shameful lives. But all our sighs and complaints are in vain. They neither hear nor see; they allow the parishes to lie waste and the people to become rude and wild without the word of God. I have heard it from people whom I must believe that in many dioceses there are two, three, and four hundred good parishes vacant. Isn't it dreadful and terrible to hear of such conditions among Christians? May God in heaven have mercy and give ear to our pitiable sighs and lamentations. Amen.

And to finish this matter of the councils at last, I hold that one should now be able to understand what a council is, its rights, power, office, and task; also, which councils are genuine and which false: namely, that they should confess and defend the ancient faith,

---

[359] Luther refers here to the educational reforms of Charlemagne. Cf. WA 50, 7.
[360] Cf. *The Smalcald Articles,* Part II, Art. III. Tappert (ed.), *Book of Concord,* pp. 297-298.

and not institute new articles of faith against the ancient faith, nor institute new good works against the old good works, but defend the old good works against the new good works—because he who defends the old faith against the new faith also defends the old good works against the new good works. For as the faith is, so are also the fruits or good works, though the two councils[361] did not see this conclusion. Otherwise, they would have condemned the archimandrite Eutyches not only because of the faith (which they did in earnest), but also because of his monkery (which they did not); on the contrary, they affirmed it, thereby proving that they were poor logicians, stating a premise but not drawing the conclusion—a common evil throughout the world. They just made the error with regard to good works that Nestorius and Eutyches made with regard to faith. That is to say: God not only wants to make us children in the faith, but also wants to show us up as fools in logic and regards us as simple Nestoriuses and Eutycheses, in order to humble us. For even if the theology of Nestorius and Eutyches is condemned, their rotten logic still remains in the world for all time, as it was there from the beginning, namely, that one states the premise, but does not draw the conclusion. How much can one say about it? If you have all the councils you are still no Christian because of them; they give you too little. If you also have all the fathers, they too give you too little. You must still go to Holy Scripture, where you find everything in abundance, or to the catechism, where it is summarized, and where far more is found than in all the councils and fathers.

Finally, a council should occupy itself only with matters of faith, and then only when faith is in jeopardy. For public evil works can be condemned and the good ones maintained at home by the temporal government and by pastors and parents. But the false good works also belong to matters of faith, since they vitiate the true faith. Therefore they too are part of the business of a council, if the pastors are too weak to deal with them. The councils (as was already said) did not pay any attention to them, with the exception of one or two small councils, such as that of Gangra mentioned above.[362] Ceremonies ought to be completely disre-

---

[361] Ephesus (431) and Chalcedon (451).
[362] See p. 126, n. 336.

garded by the councils and should be left at home in the parishes, indeed, in the schools so that the schoolmaster, along with
the pastor, would be "master of ceremonies."[363] All others will
learn these from the students, without any effort or difficulty. For
instance, the common people will learn from the pupils what, when,
and how to sing or pray in church; they will also learn what to
sing by the bier or at the grave. When the pupils kneel and fold
their hands as the schoolmaster beats time with his baton during
the singing of "And was made man,"[364] the common people will
imitate them. When they doff their little hats or bend their knees
whenever the name of Jesus Christ is mentioned, or whatever other
Christian discipline and gestures they may exercise, the common
people will do afterward without instruction, moved by the living
example. Even under the pope all the ceremonies originated in
the schools and the parishes, except where the pope was bent on
exercising his tyranny with measures regarding food, fasts, feasts,
etc. However, here too moderation must be applied, so that there
do not get to be too many ceremonies in the end. Above all, one
must see to it that they will not be considered necessary for salvation, but only serve external discipline and order, which can be
changed any time and which must not be commanded as eternal
laws in the church (as the popish ass does) and embodied in books
with tyrannical threats, for this is something entirely external, bodily, transitory, and changeable.

Accordingly, we would have enough matters today that are
sufficiently important and weighty to warrant the summoning of a
council. For we poor, wretched Christians of small faith and, unfortunately, real *Misergi*,[365] that is, Christians who hate work—
those of us who are still left—would have to put the pope on trial,
together with his followers, because of the aforementioned article
of St. Peter which says that it is tempting God if one encumbers
the faithful with unbearable burdens "which neither we nor our
forefathers have been able to bear" [Acts 15:10] (and which especially the pope and his ilk will not touch with one finger). St.

---

[363] *Magister Ceremoniarum.*
[364] *"Et homo factus est."* From the Nicene Creed.
[365] A Latin term meaning "those who feel miserable about work."

137

Peter indeed speaks of the law of Moses, which God himself commanded; but the papal ass oppressed us with his own filthy, foul, and stinking burdens, so that the holy church was forced to be his privy—and whatever issued from him above and below, we had to worship as God. Furthermore, he set fire to and burned down not one or two churches, as Arius and his kind did, but the whole Christian church when he destroyed, as far as he could, St. Peter's ancient, true article of faith; for that we must be saved by the grace of God alone (as St. Peter testifies [Acts 15:11]), as all of Christendom since the beginning of the world was saved, all the patriarchs, prophets, kings, saints, etc.—this he calls heresy, and he has consistently condemned this same article from the beginning, and cannot desist from doing so.

At this point we ask and cry for a council, requesting advice and help from all of Christendom against this arch-arsonist of churches and slayer of Christians, so that we can again have this article of St. Peter. But we also demand that no Nestorian or Eutychian logic be employed in it, which states or confesses one point but denies the conclusion or other point. We demand the whole article, full and pure, as it was instituted by St. Peter and taught by St. Paul, namely, that everything be condemned whose condemnation follows from this article—or, as St. Peter calls it, "the unbearable, impossible burden," and St. Augustine, "the countless burdens imposed on the church by the bishops."[366] What good does it do to admit the truth of the first part, that we are to be truly justified and saved solely by the grace of Christ, and still not let the second part, its necessary conclusion, follow? Thus St. Paul says, "But if it is by grace, it is no longer on the basis of works; otherwise, grace would no longer be grace" [Rom. 11:6], and St. Peter, "If it is grace, it is not the intolerable burden; if it is the intolerable burden, then it is not the grace of Christ, and it is tempting God."[367] St. Augustine, too, says, "Since Christ did not wish to burden the church with many ceremonies—indeed, wanted it to be free—it was not his will to have it oppressed by the innumerable

[366] In the frequently quoted letter to Januarius. *Epistola 54. MPL* 33, 201; *PNF*[1] 1, 300.
[367] Luther's own translation of Acts 15:10-11.

burdens of the bishops, making the lot of the church worse than that of the Jews, who were burdened with God's laws and not (like the church) with human, presumptuous, arbitrary ordinances."[368]

This dialectic of St. Peter, St. Paul, and St. Augustine is what we want to have, for it is the logic of the Holy Spirit, a logic which treats matters in their entirety rather than breaking them up in Nestorian fashion, allowing one thing alone to be true, but not the other that must also be true because it follows from the first. Otherwise, it would be like the stories recorded about several kings of Israel and Judah, who, to be sure, re-established the worship of God, but failed to do away with the high places or other altars and worship. This the prophet Elijah called "limping with two different opinions" [I Kings 18:21]. We Germans call it "trying to make two brothers-in-law with one sister."[369] Thus they tried to give one nation two different gods—or, even if they did institute any reforms at all, they still permitted a strange, different god to remain alongside the true one. They too were stupid Nestorian logicians who confessed that only one God should be worshiped and yet did not see and did not permit the logical conclusion that all other gods had to be removed; otherwise, they could not have the one God either. That is why we will not tolerate in the council which we demand a Nestorius, who gives us one thing, yet takes another from us, with whom we cannot even retain the one thing given to us. He is a regular Indian giver.[370] If the council grants us that the grace of Christ alone saves us and does not also grant us the conclusion and deduction that works do not save us, but maintains that works are necessary for satisfaction or for righteousness, then the first that was granted to us is thereby again taken from us, namely, that grace alone, without works, saves us. Thus we keep nothing, and the evil is made worse.

I will speak German:[371] the pope should not only abolish his tyranny of human ordinances in the council, but also hold with us that even the good works performed in accordance with God's com-

---

[368] Epistola 54. MPL 33, 200; PNF[1] 1, 300.
[369] Zween schweger mit einer schwester machen wollen. Cf. Thiele, Luthers Sprichwörtersammlung, No. 9.
[370] Gebers Nemers. Cf. ibid., No. 290.
[371] I.e., frankly.

mandments cannot help to achieve righteousness, to blot out sin, to attain God's grace—only faith can do this, faith in Christ, who is a king of righteousness in us through his precious blood, death, and resurrection, with which he blotted out our sin for us, made satisfaction, reconciled God, and redeemed us from death, wrath, and hell. Therefore he should condemn and burn all his bulls, decretals, books on indulgence, purgatory, monasteries, saint worship, and pilgrimages, together with all his countless lies and idolatries, since they rant directly against this article of St. Peter. He should also return everything he bought, stole, robbed, plundered, or acquired through it, especially his false primacy, which he extols as being so necessary that no one can be saved who is not subject to him. The pope's hat did not die for my sin, nor is its name Christ—and all Christians before and under him were sanctified and saved without his hat.

This, I think, is indeed an important enough matter about which to hold an impressive, decisive, and mighty council. The emperor and kings should lend a hand here and force the pope into it, if he is unwilling, as the emperors did in the four principal councils. But not all the bishops, abbots, monks, doctors, and worthless riffraff, or the large number of hangers-on, should come to it. Otherwise, it will be a council that spends its first year in arriving and in quarreling over who shall sit at the head, and who is to walk ahead of whom; the second year in reveling, banqueting, racing, and fencing; the third year in other matters and also in burning, perhaps a John Huss[372] or two—and meanwhile incurring expenses so vast that one could indeed finance a campaign against the Turks.[373] On the contrary, it would be necessary to summon from all lands people who are thoroughly versed in Holy Scripture and who are also seriously and sincerely concerned with God's honor, the Christian faith, the church, the salvation of souls, and the peace of the world. Among them there should also be a few intelligent and reliable laymen (for this is also a matter that con-

---

[372] John Huss (ca. 1369-1415), reformer of Bohemia who was martyred during the Council of Constance.

[373] Pope Paul III issued a bull on June 15, 1537, *De Indulgentiis Contra Turcam,* asking for assistance against the Turks. Cf. Luther's comments on the bull in *The Bull of Paul III* (*Bulla Papae Pauli III*). WA 50, 113-116.

cerns them). For instance, if Sir Hans von Schwarzenberg[374] were living, he and men like him could be trusted. And it would suffice if there were a total of three hundred select men to whom the fate of the country and the people could be entrusted—just as the first council[375] had only three hundred and eighteen members, summoned from all the lands the Turks and our monarchs now rule, and seventeen of them were false and Arians anyway. The second at Constantinople had one hundred and fifty; the third at Ephesus, two hundred; the fourth at Chalcedon, six hundred and thirty, almost as many as the others combined, and yet these men were quite unlike the fathers in Nicaea and Constantinople.[376]

Moreover, the affairs of all countries that no one else can or cares to judge, as well as old, superannuated, and bad quarrels should not be unearthed and dumped into the lap of the council. A Constantine should be there to rake up all these matters and cast them into the fire, ordering that they be judged and decided at home in the respective countries; he should order them to attack instead the questions at issue and dispose of these as quickly as possible. Then the pope's heresies, indeed, abominations, would be read in public, one by one, and all would be found in opposition to St. Peter's article and to the ancient, true Christian faith of the church, which has adhered to St. Peter's doctrine from the beginning of the world; and they would be promptly condemned, etc.

"Well," you say, "it is futile to hope for such a council." I myself think so too. But if one wants to talk about it and asks and wishes for a council, one would have to wish for a council like that, or forget about it completely, desire none, and say nothing at all. For the first council in Nicaea, and the second one in Constantinople, were councils like that—whose examples could indeed be easily followed. And I point this out to show that it would be the duty of emperors and kings, since they are Christians, to summon such a council for the salvation of the many thousands of souls

---

[374] John Freiherr von Schwarzenberg (1463-1528), a supporter of the Reformation, was imperial chamberlain in 1521 and later an adviser of Margrave George of Ansbach. He was an influential adviser of the emperor during the diets in Nürnberg in 1522 and 1524.
[375] Nicaea (325).
[376] Luther derived this information from the work of Crabbe. Cf. WA 50, 605, n. b.

that the pope, with his tyranny and avoidance of a council (as far as he is concerned), allows to perish, even though they all could be restored to St. Peter's article and to the true, ancient Christian faith. Otherwise, they would have to be lost, for they cannot obtain this doctrine of St. Peter's because they neither hear nor see anything of it.

And even if other monarchs declined to do anything toward a principal council, emperor Charles and the German princes could still hold a provincial council in Germany. Some think that this would result in a schism, but who knows? If we did our part in it and sincerely sought God's honor and the salvation of souls, God might yet touch and turn the hearts of the other monarchs so that they would, in time, approve and accept the judgment of this council. It could not happen suddenly; but if Germany were to accept it, it would also have an echo in other countries, whither it cannot or can hardly reach without a great preacher such as the council is, and without a strong voice heard from afar.

Well then, if we must despair of a council let us commend the matter to the true judge, our merciful God. Meanwhile we shall promote the small and the young councils, that is, parishes and schools, and propagate St. Peter's article in every way possible, preserving it against all the accursed new articles of the faith and of the new good works with which the pope has flooded the world. I shall comfort myself when I see the children wearing bishop's masks, thinking that God makes and will make genuine bishops of these play-bishops; on the other hand, I shall regard as play-bishops and mockers of God's majesty those who, according to their title, ought to be real bishops—as Moses says, "They have stirred me to jealousy with what is no god. . . . So I will stir them to jealousy with those who are no people; I will provoke them with a foolish nation" [Deut. 32:21]. It will not be the first time that he repudiates bishops. In Hosea he threatened, "Because you have rejected knowledge, I reject you from being a priest to me" [Hos. 4:6]. And so it came, and so it comes to pass.[377]

May that suffice regarding the councils. In conclusion, we shall now also speak about the church.

---

[377] *Et factum est ita, et fit ita.*

142

Part III

Just as they scream about the fathers and the councils, without knowing what fathers and councils are, only to drown out our voices with mere letters, so they also scream about the church. But as for saying what, who, and where the church is, they do not render either the church or God even the service of asking the question or thinking about it. They like very much to be regarded as the church, as pope, cardinals, bishops, and yet to be allowed, under this glorious name, to be nothing but pupils of the devil, desiring nothing more than to practice sheer knavery and villainy.

Well then, setting aside various writings and analyses of the word "church," we shall this time confine ourselves simply to the Children's Creed, which says, "I believe in one holy Christian church, the communion of saints." Here the creed clearly indicates what the church is, namely, a communion of saints, that is, a crowd[378] or assembly of people who are Christians and holy, which is called a Christian holy assembly, or church. Yet this word "church" [379] is not German and does not convey the sense or meaning that should be taken from this article.

In Acts 19 [:39] the town clerk uses the word *ecclesia* for the congregation or the people who had gathered at the market place, saying, "It shall be settled in the regular assembly." Further, "When he said this, he dismissed the assembly" [vs. 41]. In these and other passages the *ecclesia* or church is nothing but an assembly of people, though they probably were heathens and not Christians. It is the same term used by town councilmen for their assembly which they summon to the city hall. Now there are many peoples in the world; the Christians, however, are a people with a special call and are therefore called not just *ecclesia*, "church," or "people," but *sancta catholica Christiana*, that is, "a Christian holy people" who believe in Christ. That is why they are called a Christian people and have the Holy Spirit, who sanctifies them daily, not only through the forgiveness of sin acquired for them by Christ (as the Antinomians foolishly believe), but also through the abolition,

---

378 *Hauffe.*
379 *Kirche.*

the purging, and the mortification of sins, on the basis of which they are called a holy people. Thus the "holy Christian church" is synonymous with a Christian and holy people or, as one is also wont to express it, with "holy Christendom," or "whole Christendom." The Old Testament uses the term "God's people."

If the words, "I believe that there is a holy Christian people," had been used in the Children's Creed, all the misery connected with this meaningless and obscure word ("church") might easily have been avoided. For the words "Christian holy people" would have brought with them, clearly and powerfully, the proper understanding and judgment of what is, and what is not, church. Whoever would have heard the words "Christian holy people" could have promptly concluded that the pope is no people, much less a holy Christian people. So too the bishops, priests, and monks are not holy, Christian people, for they do not believe in Christ, nor do they lead a holy life, but are rather the wicked and shameful people of the devil. He who does not truly believe in Christ is not Christian or a Christian. He who does not have the Holy Spirit against sin is not holy. Consequently, they cannot be "a Christian holy people," that is, *sancta et catholica ecclesia.*

But since we use this meaningless word "church" in the Children's Creed, the common man thinks of the stone house called a church, as painted by the artists; or, at best, they paint the apostles, disciples, and the mother of God, as on Pentecost, with the Holy Spirit hovering over them. This is still bearable; but they are the holy Christian people of a specific time, in this case, the beginning. *Ecclesia,* however, should mean the holy Christian people, not only of the days of the apostles, who are long since dead, but to the end of the world, so that there is always a holy Christian people on earth, in whom Christ lives, works, and rules, *per redemptionem,* "through grace and the remission of sin," and the Holy Spirit, *per vivificationem et sanctificationem,* "through daily purging of sin and renewal of life," so that we do not remain in sin but are enabled and obliged to lead a new life, abounding in all kinds of good works, as the Ten Commandments or the two tables of Moses' law command, and not in old, evil works. That is St. Paul's teaching. But the pope, with his followers, has applied both the name and the image of the church to himself and to his vile, accursed mob, under the meaningless word *ecclesia*, "church," etc.

Nevertheless, they give themselves the right name when they call themselves *ecclesia* (that is, if we interpret this term to agree with their way of life), either *Romana* or *sancta*, but do not add (as, indeed, they cannot) *catholica*. For *ecclesia* means "a people"; that they are, just as the Turks too, are *ecclesia*, "a people." *Ecclesia Romana* means "a Roman people"; that they are too, and indeed much more Roman than the heathen of ancient times were. *Ecclesia Romana sancta* means "a holy Roman people"; that they are too, for they have invented a holiness far greater than the holiness of Christians, or than the holy Christian people possess. Their holiness is a Roman holiness, *Romanae ecclesiae*, a holiness "of the Roman people," and they are now even called *sanctissimi, sacrosancti*, "the most holy," as Virgil speaks of a "holy thirst for gold,"[380] and Plautus of "the most holy one of all";[381] for they cannot stand Christian holiness. Therefore they are not entitled to the name "Christian church" or "Christian people," if for no other reason than that "Christian church" is a name and "Christian holiness" an entity common to all churches and all Christians in the world; therefore it is called "catholic." But they have little, if any, regard for this common name and holiness; instead, they invented a special, higher, different, better holiness than that of others. This is to be known as *sanctitas Romana et ecclesiae Romanae sanctitas*, that is, "Roman holiness and the holiness of the Roman people."

For Christian holiness, or the holiness common to Christendom, is found where the Holy Spirit gives people faith in Christ and thus sanctifies them, Acts 15 [:9], that is, he renews heart, soul, body, work, and conduct, inscribing the commandments of God not on tables of stone, but in hearts of flesh, II Corinthians 3 [:3]. Or, if I may speak plainly, he imparts true knowledge of God, accord-

---

380 *Sacra fames, sacra hostia*. Virgil (70-19 B.C.), a Roman poet, in *Aeneid*, III, 57. See H. Rushton Fairclough (trans.), *Virgil: Eclogues, Georgics, Aeneid I-III* ("The Loeb Classical Library" [2nd ed., rev.; Cambridge: Harvard University Press, 1956]), p. 352. Luther, quoting from memory, leaves out the term "gold" (*auri*).
381 *Omnium sacerrumus*. Plautus (d. 184 B.C.), another Roman poet, in *Mostellaria*, IV, 2, 67. Henry T. Riley (trans.), *The Comedies of Plautus* (2 vols.; London, 1884), II, 500.

ing to the first table, so that those whom he enlightens with true faith can resist all heresies, overcome all false ideas and errors, and thus remain pure in faith in opposition to the devil. He also bestows strength, and comforts timid, despondent, weak consciences against the accusation and turmoil of sin, so that the souls do not succumb or despair, and also do not become terrified of torment, pain, death, and the wrath and judgment of God, but rather, comforted and strengthened in hope, they cheerfully, boldly, and joyfully overcome the devil. He also imparts true fear and love of God, so that we do not despise God and become irritated and angry with his wondrous judgments, but love, praise, thank, and honor him for all that occurs, good or evil. That is called new holy life in the soul, in accordance with the first table of Moses. It is also called *tres virtutes theologicas*, "the three principal virtues of Christians,"[382] namely, faith, hope, and love; and the Holy Spirit, who imparts, does, and effects this (gained for us by Christ) is therefore called "sanctifier" or "life-giver."[383] For the old Adam is dead and cannot do it, and in addition has to learn from the law that he is unable to do it and that he is dead; he would not know this of himself.

In accordance with the second table, He also sanctifies the Christians in the body and induces them willingly to obey parents and rulers, to conduct themselves peacefully and humbly, to be not wrathful, vindictive, or malicious, but patient, friendly, obliging, brotherly, and loving, not unchaste, not adulterous or lewd, but chaste and pure with wife, child, and servants, or without wife and child. And on and on: they do not steal, are not usurious, avaricious, do not defraud, etc., but work honorably, support themselves honestly, lend willingly, and give and help wherever they can. Thus they do not lie, deceive, and backbite, but are kind, truthful, faithful, and trustworthy, and do whatever else the commandments of God prescribe. That is the work of the Holy Spirit, who sanctifies and also awakens the body to such a new life until it is perfected in the life beyond. That is what is called "Christian

---

[382] They became principal topics in scholastic theology after Augustine. Cf. I Cor. 13:13.

[383] *Sanctificator* or *vivificator*.

holiness." And there must always be such people on earth, even though it may be but two or three, or only children. Unfortunately, only a few of them are old folks. And those who are not, should not count themselves as Christians; nor should they be comforted with much babbling about the forgiveness of sins and the grace of Christ, as though they were Christians—like the Antinomians do.

For they, having rejected and being unable to understand the Ten Commandments, preach much about the grace of Christ, yet they strengthen and comfort only those who remain in their sins, telling them not to fear and be terrified by sins, since they are all removed by Christ. They see and yet they let the people go on in their public sins, without any renewal or reformation of their lives. Thus it becomes quite evident that they truly fail to understand the faith and Christ, and thereby abrogate both when they preach about it. How can he speak lightly about the words of the Holy Spirit in the first table—about comfort, grace, forgiveness of sins— who does not heed or practice the works of the Holy Spirit in the second table, which he can understand and experience, while he has never attempted or experienced those of the first table? Therefore it is certain that they neither have nor understand Christ or the Holy Spirit, and their talk is nothing but froth on the tongue, and they are as already said, true Nestoriuses and Eutycheses, who confess or teach Christ in the premise, in the substance, and yet deny him in the conclusion or *idiomata*; that is, they teach Christ and yet destroy him through their teaching.

All this then has been said about Christian holiness, which the pope does not want. He has to have one that is much holier, name-ly, that found in the prescription of chasubles, tonsures, cowls, garb, food, festivals, days, monkery, nunning, masses, saint-worship, and countless other items of an external, bodily, transitory nature. Whether one lives under it without faith, fear of God, hope, love, and whatever the Holy Spirit, according to the first table, effects, or in misbelief, uncertainty of heart, doubts, contempt of God, im-patience with God, and false trust in works (that is, idolatry), not in the grace of Christ and his merit, but in the atonement by works, even selling the surplus ones to others and taking in exchange all the goods and wealth of the world as well earned—all that is of no

147

consequence because a man may be holier than Christian holiness itself.

Thus, in the second table it matters not that they teach disobedience toward parents and rulers, that they even murder, make war, set people against each other, envy, hate, avenge, are unchaste, lie, steal, are usurious, defraud, and indulge in every villainy to the utmost. Just throw a surplice over your head and you are holy in accordance with the Roman church's holiness, and you can indeed be saved without the Christian holiness. But we will pay no attention to these filthy people, for any effort expended on them will be futile. "God's wrath has come upon them at last," as St. Paul says [I Thess. 2:16]. Instead, we shall discuss the church among ourselves.

Well then, the Children's Creed teaches us (as was said) that a Christian holy people is to be and to remain on earth until the end of the world. This is an article of faith that cannot be terminated until that which it believes comes, as Christ promises, "I am with you always, to the close of the age" [Matt. 28:20]. But how will or how can a poor confused person tell where such Christian holy people are to be found in this world? Indeed, they are supposed to be in this life and on earth, for they of course believe that a heavenly nature and an eternal life are to come, but as yet they do not possess them. Therefore they must still be in this life and remain in this life and in this world until the end of the world. For they profess, "I believe in another life"; thereby they confess that they have not yet arrived in the other life, but believe in it, hope for it, and love it as their true fatherland and life, while they must yet remain and tarry here in exile—as we sing in the hymn about the Holy Spirit, "As homeward we journey from this exile. Lord, have mercy."[384] We shall now speak of this.

First, the holy Christian people are recognized by their possession of the holy word of God. To be sure, not all have it in equal measure, as St. Paul says [I Cor. 3:12-14]. Some possess the word in its complete purity, others do not. Those who have the pure word are called those who "build on the foundation with

---

[384] The fourth line of a pre-Reformation hymn adapted by Luther in 1524, "Now Let Us Pray to the Holy Ghost." LW 53, 263-264.

gold, silver, and precious stones"; those who do not have it in its purity are the ones who "build on the foundation with wood, hay, and straw," and yet will be saved through fire. More than enough was said about this above. This is the principal item, and the holiest of holy possessions,[385] by reason of which the Christian people are called holy; for God's word is holy and sanctifies everything it touches; it is indeed the very holiness of God, Romans 1 [:16], "It is the power of God for salvation to every one who has faith," and I Timothy 4 [:5], "Everything is consecrated by the word of God and prayer." For the Holy Spirit himself administers it and anoints or sanctifies the Christian church with it rather than with the pope's chrism, with which he anoints or consecrates fingers, garb, cloaks, chalices, and stones. These objects will never teach one to love God, to believe, to praise, to be pious. They may adorn the bag of maggots,[386] but afterward they fall apart and decay with the chrism and whatever holiness it contains, and with the bag of maggots itself.

Yet this holy possession is the true holy possession, the true ointment that anoints unto life eternal, even though you cannot have a papal crown or a bishop's hat, but must die bare and naked, just like children (in fact, all of us), who are baptized naked and without any adornment. But we are speaking of the external word, preached orally by men like you and me, for this is what Christ left behind as an external sign, by which his church, or his Christian people in the world, should be recognized. We also speak of this external word as it is sincerely believed and openly professed before the world, as Christ says, "Every one who acknowledges me before men, I also will acknowledge before my Father and his angels" [Matt. 10:32]. There are many who know it in their hearts, but will not profess it openly. Many possess it, but do not believe in it or act by it, for the number of those who believe in and act by it is small—as the parable of the seed in Matthew

---

[385] *Heiligthum* or *Heilthum*. These words recur continually in the following section. The term "holy possession" (used in *PE* 5, 270) conveys both the meaning of "sanctuary" and "relic." Luther plays constantly on the idea of wonder-working objects of reverence when he speaks of the marks of the church.

[386] *Madensack*, i.e., the body that goes to decay.

13 [:4-8] says that three sections of the field receive and contain the seed, but only the fourth section, the fine and good soil, bears fruit with patience.

Now, wherever you hear or see this word preached, believed, professed, and lived, do not doubt that the true *ecclesia sancta catholica*, "a Christian holy people" must be there, even though their number is very small. For God's word "shall not return empty," Isaiah 55 [:11], but must have at least a fourth or a fraction of the field. And even if there were no other sign than this alone, it would still suffice to prove that a Christian, holy people must exist there, for God's word cannot be without God's people, and conversely, God's people cannot be without God's word. Otherwise, who would preach or hear it preached, if there were no people of God? And what could or would God's people believe, if there were no word of God?

This is the thing that performs all miracles, effects, sustains, carries out, and does everything, exorcises all devils, like pilgrimage-devils, indulgence-devils, bull-devils, brotherhood-devils, saint-devils, mass-devils, purgatory-devils, monastery-devils, priest-devils, mob-devils, insurrection-devils, heresy-devils, all pope-devils, also Antinomian-devils, but not without raving and rampaging, as is seen in the poor men mentioned in Mark 1 [:23-26] and 9 [:17-29]. No, he must depart with raving and rampaging as is evidenced by Emser,[387] Eck,[388] Snot-nose,[389] Schmid,[390] Wetzel,[391]

---

[387] Jerome Emser (1478-1527), a humanist who became an adviser to Duke George of Saxony, Catholic ruler of Saxony and an enemy of Luther. Cf. Luther's polemic tract *To the Leipzig Goat* (1521). *PE* 3, 275-286.

[388] John Eck (1486-1543), known for his debate with Luther at Leipzig in 1518. Cf. *LW* 31, 309-325.

[389] *Rotzleffel*, a German term for "impudent young rascal" and Luther's name for John Cochlaeus (1479-1552), a Catholic theologian who was a fanatic opponent of the Reformation and the author of *Memoirs on the Actions and Writings of Martin Luther* (*Commentaria de Actis et Scriptis M. Lutheri*) (1549), a polemic biography of Luther. See Adolf Herte, *Die Lutherkommentare des Johannes Cochlaeus* ("Religionsgeschichtliche Studien und Texte," Vol. XXXIII [Münster, 1935]).

[390] John Faber (1478-1541), the son of a smith (*faber* in Latin) and bishop in Vienna. He had been writing polemic tracts against Luther since 1521.

[391] Used as a name for dogs and as a pun on George Wetzel (1501-1573), who was originally a follower of Luther, but since 1533 had been an opponent of the Reformation and a protege of Duke George of Saxony.

Bumpkin, Boor, Churl, Brute, Sow, Ass,[392] and the rest of his screamers and scribes. They all are the devil's mouths and members, through whom he raves and rampages. But it does them no good. He must take his leave; he is unable to endure the power of the word. They themselves confess that it is God's word and Holy Scripture, claiming, however, that one fares better with the fathers and the councils. Let them go their way. It is enough for us to know how this chief holy possession purges, sustains, nourishes, strengthens, and protects the church, as St. Augustine also says, "The church is begotten, cared for, nourished, and strengthened by the word of God."[393] But those who persecute and condemn it identify themselves by their own fruits.

Second, God's people or the Christian holy people are recognized by the holy sacrament of baptism, wherever it is taught, believed, and administered correctly according to Christ's ordinance. That too is a public sign and a precious, holy possession by which God's people are sanctified. It is the holy bath of regeneration through the Holy Spirit [Titus 3:5], in which we bathe and with which we are washed of sin and death by the Holy Spirit, as in the innocent holy blood of the Lamb of God. Wherever you see this sign you may know that the church, or the holy Christian people, must surely be present, even if the pope does not baptize you or even if you know nothing of his holiness and power—just as the little children know nothing of it, although when they are grown, they are, sad to say, estranged from their baptism, as St. Peter laments in II Peter 2 [:18], "They entice with licentious passions of the flesh men who have barely escaped from those who live in error," etc. Indeed, you should not even pay attention to who baptizes, for baptism does not belong to the baptizer, nor is it given to him, but it belongs to the baptized. It was ordained for him by God, and given to him by God, just as the word of God is not the preacher's (except in so far as he too hears and believes it) but belongs to the disciple who hears and believes it; to him is it given.

---

[392] Probably names suggested by the sound of "Wetzel," which lose their force in translation.
[393] *Ecclesia verbo dei generatur, alitur nutritur, roboratur.* The saying could not be located in Augustine's writings.

Third, God's people, or Christian holy people, are recognized by the holy sacrament of the altar, wherever it is rightly administered, believed, and received, according to Christ's institution. This too is a public sign and a precious, holy possession left behind by Christ by which his people are sanctified so that they also exercise themselves in faith and openly confess that they are Christian, just as they do with the word and with baptism. And here too you need not be disturbed if the pope does not say mass for you, does not consecrate, anoint, or vest you with a chasuble. Indeed, you may, like a patient in bed, receive this sacrament without wearing any garb, except that outward decency obliges you to be properly covered. Moreover, you need not ask whether you have a tonsure or are anointed. In addition, the question of whether you are male or female, young or old, need not be argued—just as little as it matters in baptism and the preached word. It is enough that you are consecrated and anointed with the sublime and holy chrism of God, with the word of God, with baptism, and also this sacrament; then you are anointed highly and gloriously enough and sufficiently vested with priestly garments.

Moreover, don't be led astray by the question of whether the man who administers the sacrament is holy, or whether or not he has two wives.[394] The sacrament belongs to him who receives it, not to him who administers it, unless he also receives it. In that case he is one of those who receives it, and thus it is also given to him. Wherever you see this sacrament properly administered, there you may be assured of the presence of God's people. For, as was said above of the word, wherever God's word is, there the church must be; likewise, wherever baptism and the sacrament are, God's people must be, and vice versa. No others have, give, practice, use, and confess these holy possessions save God's people alone, even though some false and unbelieving Christians are secretly among them. They, however, do not profane the people of God because they are not known; the church, or God's people, does not tolerate known sinners in its midst, but reproves them and also makes them holy. Or, if they refuse, it casts them out from

---

[394] See pp. 154-164.

the sanctuary by means of the ban and regards them as heathen, Matthew 18 [:17].

Fourth, God's people or holy Christians are recognized by the office of the keys exercised publicly.[395] That is, as Christ decrees in Matthew 18 [:15-20], if a Christian sins, he should be reproved; and if he does not mend his ways, he should be bound in his sin and cast out. If he does mend his ways, he should be absolved. That is the office of the keys. Now the use of the keys is twofold, public and private. There are some people with consciences so tender and despairing that even if they have not been publicly condemned, they cannot find comfort until they have been individually absolved by the pastor. On the other hand, there are also some who are so obdurate that they neither recant in their heart and want their sins forgiven individually by the pastor, nor desist from their sins. Therefore the keys must be used differently, publicly and privately. Now where you see sins forgiven or reproved in some persons, be it publicly or privately, you may know that God's people are there. If God's people are not there, the keys are not there either; and if the keys are not present for Christ, God's people are not present. Christ bequeathed them as a public sign and a holy possession, whereby the Holy Spirit again sanctifies the fallen sinners redeemed by Christ's death, and whereby the Christians confess that they are a holy people in this world under Christ. And those who refuse to be converted or sanctified again shall be cast out from this holy people, that is, bound and excluded by means of the keys, as happened to the unrepentant Antinomians.

You must pay no heed here to the two keys of the pope, which he converted into two skeleton keys to the treasure chests and crowns of all kings. If he does not want to bind or reprove sin, whether it be publicly or privately (as he really does not), let it be reproved and bound in your parish. If he will not loose, or forgive it, let it be loosed and forgiven in your parish, for his retaining or binding, his remitting or releasing, makes you neither holy nor unholy, since he can only have skeleton keys, not the true

---

[395] Luther had previously discussed this subject at length in his treatise *The Keys* (1530). *LW* 40, 325-377.

keys. The keys belong not to the pope (as he lies) but to the church, that is, to God's people, or to the holy Christian people throughout the entire world, or wherever there are Christians. They cannot all be in Rome, unless it be that the whole world is there first—which will not happen in a long time. The keys are the pope's as little as baptism, the sacrament, and the word of God are, for they belong to the people of Christ and are called "the church's keys"[396] not "the pope's keys."[397]

Fifth, the church is recognized externally by the fact that it consecrates or calls ministers, or has offices that it is to administer. There must be bishops, pastors, or preachers, who publicly and privately give, administer, and use the aforementioned four things or holy possessions in behalf of and in the name of the church, or rather by reason of their institution by Christ, as St. Paul states in Ephesians 4 [:8], "He received gifts among men . . ."[398]—his gifts were that some should be apostles, some prophets, some evangelists, some teachers and governors, etc. The people as a whole cannot do these things, but must entrust or have them entrusted to one person. Otherwise, what would happen if everyone wanted to speak or administer, and no one wanted to give way to the other? It must be entrusted to one person, and he alone should be allowed to preach, to baptize, to absolve, and to administer the sacraments. The others should be content with this arrangement and agree to it. Wherever you see this done, be assured that God's people, the holy Christian people, are present.

It is, however, true that the Holy Spirit has excepted women, children, and incompetent people from this function, but chooses (except in emergencies) only competent males to fill this office, as one reads here and there in the epistles of St. Paul that a bishop must be pious, able to teach, and the husband of one wife[399]—and in I Corinthians 14 [:34] he says, "The women should keep silence in the churches." In summary, it must be a competent and chosen man. Children, women, and other persons are not qualified for this

---

[396] *Claves Ecclesiae.*
[397] *Claves Papae.*
[398] Luther is as usual quoting from memory, and confuses Eph. 4:8 with Ps. 68:18, from which the Ephesian passage quotes.
[399] For example, I Tim. 3:2; Titus 1:6.

office, even though they are able to hear God's word, to receive baptism, the sacrament, absolution, and are also true, holy Christians, as St. Peter says [I Pet. 3:7]. Even nature and God's creation makes this distinction, implying that women (much less children or fools) cannot and shall not occupy positions of sovereignty, as experience also suggests and as Moses says in Genesis 3 [:16], "You shall be subject to man." The gospel, however, does not abrogate this natural law, but confirms it as the ordinance and creation of God.

Here the pope will object through his loudmouths and brawlers of the devil, saying, "St. Paul does not speak only of pastors and preachers, but also of apostles, evangelists, prophets, and other high spiritual vocations; that is why there must be higher vocations in the church than those of pastors and preachers. What, Sir Luther, do you have to say now?" What do I have to say now? This is what I have to say: if they themselves would become apostles, evangelists, prophets, or would show me at least one among them—oh, what nonsense I am talking!—who is worth as much as a schoolboy or who is as well versed in Holy Scripture and in Christian doctrine as a seven-year-old girl, I shall declare myself caught. Now I know for certain that an apostle, an evangelist, a prophet knows more, or indeed as much, as a seven-year-old girl. (I am speaking about Holy Scripture and about faith.) For I thoroughly believe, more firmly than I believe in God, that they are acquainted with more human doctrine, and also with more villainy, because they are proving it before my very eyes by the things they are doing, and so they are apostles, evangelists, and prophets just as little as they are the church; that is to say, they are the devil's apostles, evangelists, and prophets. The true apostles, evangelists, and prophets preach God's word, not against God's word.

Now, if the apostles, evangelists, and prophets are no longer living, others must have replaced them and will replace them until the end of the world, for the church shall last until the end of the world [Matt. 28:20]. Apostles, evangelists, and prophets must therefore remain, no matter what their name, to promote God's word and work. The pope and his followers, who persecute God's

155

word while admitting that it is true, must be very poor apostles, evangelists, and prophets, just like the devil and his angels. But why do I keep coming back to these shameful, filthy folk of the pope? Let them go again, and bid them not to return, or etc.

Just as was said earlier about the other four parts of the great, divine, holy possession by which the holy church is sanctified, that you need not care who or how those from whom you receive it are, so again you should not ask who and how he is who gives it to you or has the office. For all of it is given, not to him who has the office, but to him who is to receive it through this office, except that he can receive it together with you if he so desires. Let him be what he will. Because he is in office and is tolerated by the assembly, you put up with him too. His person will make God's word and sacraments neither worse nor better for you. What he says or does is not his, but Christ, your Lord, and the Holy Spirit say and do everything, in so far as he adheres to correct doctrine and practice. The church, of course, cannot and should not tolerate open vices; but you yourself be content and tolerant, since you, an individual, cannot be the whole assembly or the Christian holy people.

But you must pay no attention to the pope,[400] who bars any married man from being called to such an office. With Nestorian logic he declares that all must be chaste virgins; that is to say, all the clergy must be chaste, while they themselves may, of course, be unchaste. But look here! You bring up the pope again, and yet I did not want you any more. Well then, unwelcome guest that you are, I will receive you in Luther-like fashion.

The pope condemns the marriage of bishops or priests; that is now plain enough. Not content with that, he condemns bigamy[401] even more severely. Indeed, to express myself clearly, he distinguishes four, if not five, kinds of bigamy.[402] I will now call one who marries twice or who takes another's widow to wife a biga-

---

[400] This whole section repeats the ideas of a sermon preached by Luther on March 2, 1539. Cf. WA 47, 671-678.

[401] Luther calls it *digamia* (from the Greek *digamos*).

[402] See *Decreti Prima Pars*, dist. XXVI, C. I-III (*CIC* 1, 95-96); dist. XXXIII, C. II (*CIC* 1, 123); dist. XXXIV, C. IX-XVIII (*CIC* 1, 128-130); *Decretalium D. Gregorii Papae IX*, lib. i, tit. XXI (*CIC* 2, 146-148).

mist. The first kind of bigamist is one who marries two virgins successively; the second, one who marries a widow; the third, one who marries the betrothed whose deceased groom left her a virgin. The fourth acquires the name shamefully because he is the one who marries a "virgin," unknowingly or unwillingly, and later discovers that she is not at all pure or a virgin. And yet, in the pope's judgment this person must be more of a bigamist than the third type who married the virgin bride. All of these men stink and have an evil smell in canon law. They are not allowed to preach, baptize, administer the sacrament, or hold any office in the church, even if they were holier than St. John and their wives holier than the mother of God. So marvelously holy is the pope in his decretals!

However, if someone had ravished a hundred virgins, violated a hundred honorable widows, and lain with a hundred whores before that, he may become not only pastor or preacher but also bishop or pope. And even if he were to continue this kind of life, he would nonetheless be tolerated in those offices. But if he marries a bride who is a virgin, or a make-believe virgin, he cannot be a servant of God. It makes no difference that he is a true Christian, learned, pious, competent. He is a bigamist; thus, he must leave his office and never return to it. What do you think of that? Is that not a higher holiness than that of Christ himself, together with that of the Holy Spirit and his church? Christ spurns neither men with one wife or two successive wives, nor women with one husband or two successive husbands, if they believe in him. He lets them remain members of his holy, Christian people. He also make use of them for whatever work they are adapted. Scripture uses the term "bigamist" for one who, like Lamech, has two wives living at the same time [Gen. 4:19]. The pope, however, is more learned and calls one who marries two women successively a bigamist. He applies the same rule to women, for he is far more learned than God himself.

Better still, the pope himself admits that a bigamous marriage is a true marriage and does not constitute a sin against God, nor against the world or the church,[403] and that such a marriage is a

---

[403] *Decreti Prima Pars*, dist. XXVI, C. II. *CIC* 1, 95; *MPL* 187, 149c.

sacrament of the church; and yet such a man must be barred from holding an ecclesiastical office—as must the third or fourth type of bigamists, who really should be called husbands of one wife or husbands of virgins. Why? Well, here is the rub: such a marriage cannot be a sacrament or an image of Christ and his church, for Christ had but one bride, the church, and this bride has but one husband, Christ, and both remain virgins. So much sheer nonsense has been talked about this subject that it is impossible to relate it at all. The canonists should rightly be called lawyers for asses. First, if marriage is to be a sacrament of Christ and his church, then no marriage can be a sacrament unless both bridegroom and bride remain virgin, for Christ and the church remain virgins. But how will we get children and heirs under those conditions? What will become of the estate of marriage, instituted by God? In summary, there will be no marriage, other than that of Mary and Joseph and others like it. All the remaining marriages cannot be a sacrament, and may perhaps even be harlotry.

Second, who taught or decreed this, that we must keep it? St. Paul says (they say) in Ephesians 4 [5:31-32] that husband and wife are a great sacrament. I say, "Yes, in Christ and the church." My dear man, can you gather from these words of St. Paul that marriage is the kind of a sacrament of which they speak? He says that husband and wife are one body, which is a great sacrament. Then he interprets himself, saying, "I speak of Christ and the church, not of husband and wife." But they say that he is speaking of husband and wife. Paul envisages Christ and the church as a great sacrament or "mystery";[404] so they say that husband and wife are a great sacrament. Why then do they regard it as virtually the least of the sacraments, indeed, as sheer impurity and sin, in which one cannot serve God? Moreover, can you also deduce from St. Paul's words that men and women in bigamous marriages are not husband and wife or one body? If they are one body, why then are they not a sacrament of Christ and the church? After all, St. Paul is speaking generally about husbands and wives who become one body, whether they were single or widowed be-

---

[404] *Mysterium* (from the Greek *mysterion* used in Eph. 5:32).

fore, and calls them a sacrament (as you understand "sacrament"). Whence then are you so clever as to differentiate in marriage, taking only the single marriage as a sacrament of Christ and the church—that is, the marriage of a man with a virgin—and excluding all others? Who ordered you to martyr and force St. Paul's words in this manner?

Furthermore, you do not even call such a marriage a sacrament. For bridegrooms do not let their brides remain virgins, nor do the latter marry men in order that they may stay virgins; this they could do far better without husbands. No, they want and should bear children, for which God created them. What now becomes of the sacrament of Christ and the church, both of whom remained virgins? Is this the best argument "from image to historical fact or, conversely, from historical fact to image?"[405] Where did you learn such logic? Christ and the church are married, but remain virgins in the body; therefore husband and wife shall also remain virgins in the body. Furthermore, Christ is married to only one virgin; therefore a Christian or a priest shall also be married to only one virgin; otherwise, you say, there is no sacrament. Why, then, do you admit and say that the marriage of a widow is also a sacrament because it is a marriage, and again it is not a sacrament because the wife was not a virgin? Are you not mad, and crazy, and crass Nestorians, not knowing when you say yes and when you say no, stating one thing in the premise and another in the conclusion? Away with you stupid asses and fools!

Another crass error stemmed from the fact (unless, indeed, the former grew out of this) that they called and regarded bishops and popes as the bridegrooms of the church.[406] In verification of this view they cite the saying of St. Paul, "A bishop must be the husband of one wife" [I Tim. 3:2], that is to say, he must be the bishop of one church, as Christ is the bridegroom of one church; therefore they should not be bigamists. Popes and bishops, indeed,

---

[405] A figura ad historiam, vel econtra, ab historia ad figuram. A reference to the "dialectical" method of exegesis. Cf. Philip Melanchthon, Dialectical Questions (Erotemata Dialectices) (1527), VII, 653, 705. C.R. 13, 734. See also Clyde L. Manschreck, Melanchthon (New York and Nashville: Abingdon Press, 1958), p. 151.

[406] Decreti Prima Pars, dist. XXVI, C. II. CIC 1, 95; MPL 187, 149c.

are fine fellows to be bridegrooms of the church—yes, if she were a brothel-keeper or the devil's daughter in hell. True bishops are servants of this bride, and she is lady and mistress over them. St. Paul calls himself *diaconus*, a "servant of the church" [I Cor. 3:5]. He does not claim to be the bridegroom or the lord of this bride, rather, the true and only bridegroom of this bride is called Jesus Christ, God's Son. St. John does not say, "I am the bridegroom," but, "I am the friend of the bridegroom, who stands and hears him, and who rejoices greatly at the bridegroom's voice," for "he who has the bride" (he says) "is the bridegroom" [John 3:29]. One should gladly give ear to such speech and then conduct oneself as a servant.

But how nicely they themselves keep even this crass asininity and folly. A bishop may have three bishoprics, and yet he must be called husband of one wife. And even if he has but one bishopric, he still has one hundred, two hundred, five hundred, or more parishes or churches; yet he is the bridegroom of one church. The pope claims to be the bridegroom of all churches, both large and small, yet he is called the husband of one church. They are not bigamists or men with two wives, though they have all these brides at the same time. But he who marries a virgin who was betrothed to another is a bigamist. God will inflict gross, monstrous folly like this on us if we despise his word and want to do everything better than he commanded.

Indeed, they have an *acutius*[407] in their *Decretum*, in which St. Augustine holds, against St. Jerome, that he who had a wife before baptism and also one after baptism had two wives. Dear asses, does it therefore follow that St. Augustine, even though he views such a man as the husband of two wives (something Scripture does not do), wishes to have him condemned and barred from serving God, as you do? And even though this should follow, do you not have a strong *noli meis*[408] in dist. IX against it? How is it that you hold so fast to the *acutius* (though it is against Scripture) and pass so lightly over the *noli meis* and other chapters?

---

[407] A quotation from Augustine in *Decreti Prima Pars*, dist. XXVI, C. II: *Acutius intelligunt* .... *CIC* 1, 95; *MPL* 187, 149c.
[408] Augustine, *On the Trinity*, III, 2. *MPL* 42, 869; *PNF*[1] 3, 57. See also in this volume, p. 25.

This is, of course, your idea: you want to be lords of the church; whatever you say should be accepted as right. Marriage shall be right and a sacrament, if you will it so; on the other hand, marriage shall be an impurity, that is, a defiled sacrament that cannot serve God, if you will it so. Marriage shall bear children, and yet the wife shall remain a virgin or it is not a sacrament of Christ and the church, if you will it so. The bigamists are blameless and have a true marriage and sacrament, if you will it so; on the other hand, they are condemned and barred from serving God and have no sacrament of Christ and the church, if you will it so. Behold how the devil, who teaches you this nonsense, makes you reel and sway back and forth.

Why should I regard St. Augustine's statement as an article of faith if he himself does not wish to do so and if he himself does not even want to accept the sayings of his predecessors as articles of faith? Suppose that the dear fathers' opinion and teaching about a bigamist was such (as described)—what does it matter to us? It does not obligate us to hold and to teach that view. We must found our salvation on the words and works of man as little as we build our houses of hay and straw. But the canonists are such stupid asses and fools, with their idol in Rome, that they convert the words and deeds of the dear fathers into articles of faith against their will and without their consent. It should be proved by Scripture that such men may be called bigamists or trigamists; then their exclusion from the ministry of the church would be right and stand approved by St. Paul's instruction in I Timothy 3 [:2], "A bishop shall be the husband of one wife." But this frequently happened to the fathers—they sewed old patches on new cloth.[409] This is the case here: no bigamist shall be a servant of the church; that is right and that is the new cloth. But that this or that man is really a bigamist, that is the old patch of their own opinion because Scripture does not say it. Scripture regards the man who has two wives living at the same time as a bigamist; and it is assumed that St. Paul had had a wife, Philippians 4 [:3],[410] and that she died. So he too must have been a

---

[409] See p. 63.
[410] Luther interprets the term "yokefellow" as an indication of Paul's marriage

man with two wives, obliged to give up his apostolic office; for in I Corinthians 7 [:8] he counts himself among the widowed, and yet in I Corinthians 9 [:5] he, along with Barnabas, claims the right to be accompanied by a wife. Who will assure us that the poor fishermen, Peter, Andrew, and James, were married to virgins and not to widows, or that they did not have two wives in succession?

These blockheads do not have the same idea of chastity that the fathers had, but would like to confuse the poor souls and jeopardize them, if only their stinking and filthy book[411] is regarded as right and their "science" is not found to err or to have erred. Otherwise, they would indeed see what chastity is—since, with regard to other "opinions"[412] (and what is their best and foremost but a matter of mere opinion?), they can say nicely, "It is not held; but hold this."[413] Why can they not do it here, especially since they do not hesitate to repudiate not only one father, but all of them, in "the cases to be decided,"[414] as their idol sputters and bellows? But they would like to rule the church, not with trustworthy wisdom, but with arbitrary opinions, and again confuse and perplex all the souls in the world, as they have done before. But just as they reject all the fathers and theologians in their petty canons, so do we, in turn, reject them in the church and in Scripture. They shall neither teach us Scripture nor rule in the church; they are not entitled to it, nor do they have the competence for it. But they shall attend to their trifling canons and squabbles over prebends—that is their holiness. They have cast us poor theologians, together with the fathers, from their books; for this we thank them most kindly. Now they propose to throw us out of the church and out of Scripture; and they themselves are not worthy to be in them. That is too much, and rips the bag

---

and assumes (on the basis of I Cor. 7:8) that he became a widower. Modern biblical scholarship does not agree. Cf., for example, George A. Buttrick *et al.* (eds.), *The Interpreter's Bible* (12 vols.; New York and Nashville: Abingdon, 1952-1957), IX, 107-108; X, 78-79.

[411] Canon law.

[412] *Opiniones.*

[413] *Non tenetur; hoc tene.*

[414] *Causis decidendis.* Here Luther mocks the slogans of medieval canonists who were frequently involved in court cases concerning ecclesiastical property.

wide open.[415] And furthermore, we shall not put up with it.

I truly believe that in accordance with their wisdom no man could marry a virgin and, after her death, become a priest among them, for who can guarantee or vouch that he is actually getting a virgin? "The road runs past the door"[416] (as they say). Now if he would find her not a virgin—and that is a chance he must take—he would, through no fault of his own, be a stinking bigamist. And if he wants to be certain that he can become a priest, he dare not marry a virgin either, for what assurance does he have that she is one? However, he may ravish virgins, widows, and wives, have many whores, commit all sorts of secret sins—he is still worthy of the priestly office. The sum and substance of it all is that the pope, the devil, and his church are averse to the estate of matrimony, as Daniel [11:37] says; therefore he wants it viewed as such a defilement that a married man cannot fill a priest's office. That is as much as to say that marriage is harlotry, sin, impure, and rejected by God. And even though they say, at the same time, that marriage is holy and a sacrament, that is hypocrisy and a lie, for if they would sincerely regard it as holy and a sacrament they would not forbid a priest to marry. But since they do prohibit it, it follows that they consider it impure and a sin—as they plainly say, "You must be clean, who bearest [the vessels of the lord]"[417] or (if some really are that pious) they must be stupid Nestorians and Eutychians, affirming a premise and denying the conclusion. May this be the reception that we, for the time being, accord the papal ass and the asinine papists, as we return to our own people.

Therefore do not worry (as was said) about the papists' talk concerning the personal qualifications for an ecclesiastical office, for these asses do not understand St. Paul's words, nor do they know what St. Paul's language calls a sacrament. He says [Eph. 5:31-32] that Christ and the church are a sacrament, that is, Christ and the church are one body, as husband and wife are, and that

---

[415] A German proverb, "Das zurreisset den sack." Cf. Thiele, *Luthers Sprichwörtersammlung*, No. 39.

[416] Another proverb, "*Der weg gehet fur der thür ruber.*" Cf. *ibid.*, No. 10.

[417] *Mundamini, qui fertis [vasa Domini].* A reference to the formula used at the ordination of priests.

this is a great mystery, to be apprehended by faith. It is not visible or tangible; therefore it is a sacrament, that is, something secret, a mystery, invisible, hidden. But since not only virginal but also widowed people entering matrimony are one body, every marriage is a figure or symbol of this great sacrament or mystery in Christ and the church. St. Paul speaks of neither virgins nor widows; he speaks of marriage, in which husband and wife are one body. Now wherever you find these offices or officers, you may be assured that the holy Christian people are there; for the church cannot be without these bishops, pastors, preachers, priests; and conversely, they cannot be without the church. Both must be together.

Sixth, the holy Christian people are externally recognized by prayer, public praise, and thanksgiving to God. Where you see and hear the Lord's Prayer prayed and taught; or psalms or other spiritual songs sung, in accordance with the word of God and the true faith; also the creed, the Ten Commandments, and the catechism used in public, you may rest assured that a holy Christian people of God are present. For prayer, too, is one of the precious holy possessions whereby everything is sanctified, as St. Paul says [I Tim. 4:5]. The psalms too are nothing but prayers in which we praise, thank, and glorify God. The creed and the Ten Commandments are also God's word and belong to the holy possession, whereby the Holy Spirit sanctifies the holy people of Christ. However, we are now speaking of prayers and songs which are intelligible and from which we can learn and by means of which we can mend our ways. The clamor of monks and nuns and priests is not prayer, nor is it praise to God; for they do not understand it, nor do they learn anything from it; they do it like a donkey, only for the sake of the belly and not at all in quest of any reform or sanctification or of the will of God.

Seventh, the holy Christian people are externally recognized by the holy possession of the sacred cross. They must endure every misfortune and persecution, all kinds of trials and evil from the devil, the world, and the flesh (as the Lord's Prayer indicates) by inward sadness, timidity, fear, outward poverty, contempt, illness, and weakness, in order to become like their head, Christ.

And the only reason they must suffer is that they steadfastly adhere to Christ and God's word, enduring this for the sake of Christ, Matthew 5 [:11], "Blessed are you when men persecute you on my account." They must be pious, quiet, obedient, and prepared to serve the government and everybody with life and goods, doing no one any harm. No people on earth have to endure such bitter hate; they must be accounted worse than Jews, heathen, and Turks. In summary, they must be called heretics, knaves, and devils, the most pernicious people on earth, to the point where those who hang, drown, murder, torture, banish, and plague them to death are rendering God a service. No one has compassion on them; they are given myrrh and gall to drink when they thirst. And all of this is done not because they are adulterers, murderers, thieves, or rogues, but because they want to have none but Christ, and no other God. Wherever you see or hear this, you may know that the holy Christian church is there, as Christ says in Matthew 5 [:11-12], "Blessed are you when men revile you and utter all kinds of evil against you on my account. Rejoice and be glad, for your reward is great in heaven." This too is a holy possession whereby the Holy Spirit not only sanctifies his people, but also blesses them.

Meanwhile, pay no heed to the papists' holy possessions from dead saints, from the wood of the holy cross. For these are just as often bones taken from a carrion pit as bones of saints, and just as often wood taken from gallows as wood from the holy cross. There is nothing but fraud in this. The pope thus tricks people out of their money and alienates them from Christ. Even if it were a genuine holy possession, it would nonetheless not sanctify anyone. But when you are condemned, cursed, reviled, slandered, and plagued because of Christ, you are sanctified. It mortifies the old Adam and teaches him patience, humility, gentleness, praise and thanks, and good cheer in suffering. That is what it means to be sanctified by the Holy Spirit and to be renewed to a new life in Christ; in that way we learn to believe in God, to trust him, to love him, and to place our hope in him, as Romans 5 [:1-5] says, "Suffering produces hope," etc.

These are the true seven principal parts of the great holy possession whereby the Holy Spirit effects in us a daily sanctification and vivification in Christ, according to the first table of Moses. By this we obey it, albeit never as perfectly as Christ. But we constantly strive to attain the goal, under his redemption or remission of sin, until we too shall one day become perfectly holy and no longer stand in need of forgiveness. Everything is directed toward that goal. I would even call these seven parts the seven sacraments, but since that term has been misused by the papists and is used in a different sense in Scripture, I shall let them stand as the seven principal parts of Christian sanctification or the seven holy possessions of the church.

In addition to these seven principal parts there are other outward signs that identify the Christian church, namely, those signs whereby the Holy Spirit sanctifies us according to the second table of Moses; when he assists us in sincerely honoring our father and mother, and conversely, when he helps them to raise their children in a Christian way and to lead honorable lives; when we faithfully serve our princes and lords and are obedient and subject to them, and conversely, when they love their subjects and protect and guard them; also when we bear no one a grudge, entertain no anger, hatred, envy, or vengefulness toward our neighbors, but gladly forgive them, lend to them, help them, and counsel them; when we are not lewd, not drunkards, not proud, arrogant, overbearing, but chaste, self-controlled, sober, friendly, kind, gentle, and humble; when we do not steal, rob, are not usurious, greedy, do not overcharge, but are mild, kind, content, charitable; when we are not false, mendacious, perjurers, but truthful, trustworthy, and do whatever else is taught in these commandments—all of which St. Paul teaches abundantly in more than one place. We need the Decalogue not only to apprise us of our lawful obligations, but we also need it to discern how far the Holy Spirit has advanced us in his work of sanctification and by how much we still fall short of the goal, lest we become secure and imagine that we have now done all that is required. Thus we must constantly grow in sanctification and always become new creatures in Christ. This means "grow" and "do so more and more" [II Pet. 3:18].

However, these signs cannot be regarded as being as reliable as those noted before since some heathen too practice these works and indeed at times appear holier than Christians; yet their actions do not issue from the heart purely and simply, for the sake of God, but they search for some other end because they lack a real faith in and a true knowledge of God. But here is the Holy Spirit, who sanctifies the heart and produces these fruits from "an honest and good heart," as Christ says in the parable recorded in Matthew 13 [Luke 8:15]. Since the first table is greater and must be a holier possession, I have summarized everything in the second table. Otherwise, I could have divided it too into seven holy possessions or seven principal parts, according to the seven commandments.

Now we know for certain what, where, and who the holy Christian church is, that is, the holy Christian people of God; and we are quite certain that it cannot fail us. Everything else may fail and surely does, as we shall hear in part. Men should be selected from this people to form a council; that might be a council ruled by the Holy Spirit. Thus Lyra, too, writes that the church is not to be assessed by the high or spiritual vocations in it, but by the people who truly believe.[418] I am surprised that he was not burned at the stake for these words, for denying that popes, cardinals, bishops, and prelates compose the church; this amounts to abominable heresy, intolerable and offensive to the holy Roman church. More about this elsewhere.[419]

Now when the devil saw that God built such a holy church, he was not idle, and erected his chapel beside it, larger than God's temple. This is how he did it: he noticed that God utilized outward things, like baptism, word, sacrament, keys, etc., whereby he sanctified his church. And since the devil is always God's ape,

---

[418] Nicholas of Lyra (1270-1340), a Franciscan theologian and famous interpreter of the Bible. Luther frequently quotes him, as does Melanchthon, who quoted this statement of Lyra's in the *Apology of the Augsburg Confession,* Arts. VII, VIII. Tappert (ed.), *Book of Concord,* p. 172. The quotation Luther cites is found in *Comments on Matthew XVI* (*Annotationes in Matth. XVI*). See WA 50, 644, n. *a.* Five volumes of Lyra's works were published in 1471-1472 in Rome. *O.D.C.C.,* p. 957.

[419] Cf. *The Smalcald Articles,* Art. IV. Tappert (ed.), *Book of Concord,* pp. 298-301.

trying to imitate all God's things and to improve on them, he also tried his luck with external things purported to make man holy— just as he tries with rain-makers, sorcerers, exorcists of devils, etc. He even has the Lord's Prayer recited and the gospel read over them to make it appear a great holy possession. Thus he had popes and papists consecrate or sanctify water, salt, candles, herbs, bells, images, *Agnus Dei*,[420] pallia,[421] chasubles, tonsures, fingers, hands—who can tell it all?—finally the monks' cowls to a degree that many people died and were buried in them, believing that thereby they would be saved. Now it would have been fine indeed if God's word or a blessing or a prayer were spoken over these created things, as children do over their food or over themselves when they go to bed and when they arise. St. Paul says of this, "Everything created by God is good, and is consecrated by the word of God and prayer" [I Tim. 4:4-5]. The creature derives no new power from such a practice, but is strengthened in its former power.

But the devil has a different purpose in mind. He wants the creature to derive new strength and power from his aping tomfoolery. Just as water becomes baptism by the power of God, a bath unto eternal life, washing away sin and bringing salvation, a power which is not inherent in water; just as bread and wine become the body and blood of Christ; just as sins are remitted by the laying on of hands in accordance with God's institution—so the devil too wants his mummery and aping tomfoolery to be strong and imbued with supernatural power. Holy water is to blot out sin, exorcise devils, fend off evil spirits, protect women in childbed, as the pope teaches us in the *Aquam sale, de pe*;[422] consecrated salt is to have the same effect. An *Agnus Dei* consecrated by the pope is to do more than God himself can do, as this is described in verses that I should some day publish with marginal

---

[420] Luther refers to amulets usually made of wax and stamped with the image of a lamb.

[421] A woolen shoulder cape with the insignia of the archbishop's office on it.

[422] *Aquam sale*, a section in canon law dealing with consecration, according to which holy salt is used in rites of purification. *De pe* is either a slip of the pen for *de co* (*de consecratione*) or Luther's abbreviation for *de poenitentia*, the title of the chapter on penitence. Cf. *Decreti Tertia Pars: De Consecratione*, dist. III, C. XX. *CIC* 1, 1358; *MPL* 187, 1787c.

notes.[423] Bells are to drive away devils in thunderstorms. St. Anthony's knives stab the devil; consecrated herbs expel venomous worms; some blessings heal cows, keep off milk thieves,[424] and quench fire; certain letters give security in war and at other times against iron, fire, water, wild beasts, etc.;[425] monasticism, masses, and the like are said to confer more than ordinary salvation. Who can tell it all? There was no need so small that the devil did not institute a sacrament or holy possession for it, whereby one could receive advice and help. In addition, he had prophetesses, soothsayers, and sages able to reveal hidden things and to retrieve stolen goods.

Oh, he is far better equipped with sacraments, prophets, apostles, and evangelists than God, and his chapels are much larger than God's church; and he has far more people in his holiness than God. One is also more inclined to believe his promises, his sacraments, and his prophets than Christ. He is the great god of the world. Christ calls him "ruler of the world" [John 12:31; 14:30; 16:11] and Paul "the god of this world" [II Cor. 4:4]. With this aping tomfoolery he estranges men from faith in Christ and causes the word and the sacraments of Christ to be despised and almost unrecognizable because it is easier to perceive such things than to blot out sin, help in time of need, receive salvation through the devil's sacraments rather than through Christ's. For it is Christ's will to make people holy and pious in body and soul through the Holy Spirit and not let them remain in unbelief and sin. This is too hard for those who do not wish to be pious or to desist from sin. They can readily dispense with this work of the Holy Spirit after they learn how they can be saved more easily without him— for example, by holy water, *Agnus Dei,* bulls and breves, masses and cowls—thus making it unnecessary to seek or heed anything else.

But not only that! The devil has armed himself with these

---

[423] Cf. Luther's notes *On the Blessed Water and the Agnus Dei of the Pope* (*Von dem Geweihtem Wasser und des Papstes Agnus Dei*) (1539). WA 50, 668-673.

[424] I.e., witches who make cows go dry.

[425] In 1518 Luther dealt with these ecclesiastical customs more favorably. Cf. for example, *The Decalog, Preached to the People of Wittenberg* (*Decem Praecepta, Wittenbergensi Praedicata Populo*) (1518). WA 1, 401.

things in order to abolish God's word and sacraments with them. This is his line of thought: if someone arises to attack my church, sacraments, and bishops, saying that external things do not save, then God's word and sacraments shall perish with them, for these too are external signs and his church and bishops are also human beings. If mine do not stand approved, his will stand approved even less, especially because my church, bishops, and sacraments work promptly and help now and in this life, visibly and tangibly, for I am present in them and help quickly, as soon as it is desired. Christ's sacraments, however, work spiritually and invisibly and for the future so that his church and bishops can only be smelled, as it were, faintly and from afar, and the Holy Spirit behaves as though he were absent, permitting people to endure every misfortune and making them appear as heretics in the eyes of my church. Meanwhile, my church is not only so close that one can actually grasp it, but also my works follow very quickly; so everyone assumes that it is the true church of God. This is the advantage I have.

And that is what happened. When we began to teach, on the basis of the gospel, that these external things do not save, since they are merely physical and creatural and are often used by the devil for the purpose of sorcery, people, even great and learned people, concluded that baptism, being external water, that the word, being outward human speech, that Scripture, being physical letters made with ink, that the bread, being baked by the baker, and the wine were nothing more than outward, perishable things. So they devised the slogan, "Spirit! Spirit! The Spirit must do it! The letter kills!" So Münzer[426] called us Wittenberg theologians scribes of Scripture and himself the scribe of the Holy Spirit, and many others followed his example. There you see how the devil had armed himself and built up his barricades. If anyone were to attack his outward doctrine and sacraments (which afford quick, visible, and mighty aid), then the outward words and sacraments

---

[426] Thomas Münzer (1489-1525), labeled the "restless spirit of Allstedt" by Luther, became a leader of the rebellious peasants in the Peasants' War of 1525. The passage is found in Hans J. Hillerbrand, "Thomas Münzer's Last Tract Against Martin Luther," *The Mennonite Quarterly Review*, XXXVIII (1964), 26.

of Christ (attended by tardy or, at least, by invisible and feeble help) must go down to far worse destruction along with them.

Therefore the *ecclesia*, "the holy Christian people," does not have mere external words, sacraments, or offices, like God's ape Satan has, and in far greater numbers, but it has these as commanded, instituted, and ordained by God, so that he himself and not any angel will work through them with the Holy Spirit. They are called word, baptism, sacrament, and office of forgiveness, not of angels, men, or any other creature, but of God; only he does not choose to do it through his unveiled, brilliant, and glorious majesty, out of consideration for us poor, weak, and timid mortals and for our comfort, for who could bear such majesty for an instant in this poor and sinful flesh? As Moses says, "Man shall not see me and live" [Exod. 33:20]. If the Jews could not endure even the shoes of his feet on Mount Sinai, that is, the thunder and the clouds, how could they, with their feeble eyes, have endured the sight of the sun of his divine majesty and the clear light of his countenance? No, he wants to work through tolerable, kind, and pleasant means, which we ourselves could not have chosen better. He has, for instance, a godly and kind man speak to us, preach, lay his hands on us, remit sin, baptize, give us bread and wine to eat and to drink. Who can be terrified by these pleasing methods, and wouldn't rather delight in them with all his heart?

Well then, that is just what is done for us feeble human beings, and in it we see how God deals with us as with beloved children and not, as he surely would have a right to, in his majesty. And yet, in this guise he performs his majestic, divine works and exercises his might and power, such as forgiving sin, cleansing from sin, removing death, bestowing grace and eternal life. Indeed, these things are missing in the devil's sacraments and churches. No one can say there, "God commanded it, ordered it, instituted it, and ordained it; he himself is present and will do everything himself"; but one must say, "God did not command, but forbade it, that man, or rather that ape of God, invented it and misled the people with it." For he effects nothing except that which is temporal, or, if it purports to be spiritual, it is sheer

171

fraud. He cannot forgive sin eternally and save, as he lyingly claims, by means of holy water, masses, and monkery, even though he may restore a cow's milk which he had first stolen from her by his prophetesses and priestesses. Among Christians these are called the devil's harlots and, when apprehended, are rightfully burned at the stake, not because of the theft of milk, but because of the blasphemy with which they fortify the devil, his sacraments, and his churches against Christ.

In summary, if God were to bid you to pick up a straw or to pluck out a feather with the command, order, and promise that thereby you would have forgiveness of all sin, grace, and eternal life, should you not accept this joyfully and gratefully, and cherish, praise, prize, and esteem that straw and that feather as a higher and holier possession than heaven and earth? No matter how insignificant the straw and the feather may be, you would nonetheless acquire through them something more valuable than heaven and earth, indeed, than all the angels, are able to bestow on you. Why then are we such disgraceful people that we do not regard the water of baptism, the bread and wine, that is, Christ's body and blood, the spoken word, and the laying on of man's hands for the forgiveness of sin as such holy possessions, as we would the straw and feather, though in the former, as we hear and know, God himself wishes to be effective and wants them to be his water, word, hand, bread, and wine, by means of which he wishes to sanctify and save you in Christ, who acquired this for us and who gave us the Holy Spirit from the Father for this work?

On the other hand, what good would it do you even if you went to St. James,[427] clad in armor, or let yourself be killed by the severe life of the Carthusians, Franciscans, or Dominicans in order to be saved, and God had neither commanded nor instituted it? He still knows nothing about all this, but you and the devil invented them, as special sacraments or classes of priests. And even if you were able to bear heaven and earth in order to be saved, it would still all be lost; and he who would pick up the straw (if this were commanded) would do more than you, even if you

---

[427] I.e., to the shrine of St. James of Compostella in Spain, where according to Spanish tradition the apostle was martyred in 44. See Acts 12:2.

could carry ten worlds. Why is that? It is God's will that we obey his word, use his sacraments, and honor his church. Then he will act graciously and gently enough, even more graciously and gently than we could desire; for it is written, "I am the Lord your God; you shall have no other gods before me" [Exod. 20:2-3]. And, "Listen to him and to no other" [Matt. 17:5]. May that suffice on the church. More cannot be said unless each point is elaborated further. The rest must deal with different ideas, about which we want to speak too.

Besides these external signs and holy possessions the church has other externals that do not sanctify it either in body or soul, nor were they instituted or commanded by God; but, as we said at length above, they are outwardly necessary or useful, proper and good—for instance, certain holidays and certain hours, forenoon or afternoon, set aside for preaching or praying, or the use of a church building or house, altar, pulpit, baptismal font, candlesticks, candles, bells, priestly vestments, and the like. These things have no more than their natural effects, just as food and drink accomplish no more by virtue of the grace the children say at the table,[428] for the ungodly or rude folk who don't say it, that is, who neither pray to God nor thank him, grow just as fat and strong from food and drink as Christians do. To be sure, Christians could be and remain sanctified even without these items, even if they were to preach on the street, outside a building, without a pulpit, if absolution were pronounced and the sacrament administered without an altar, and if baptism were performed without a font—as happens daily that for special reasons sermons are preached and baptisms and sacraments administered in the home. But for the sake of children and simple folk, it is a fine thing and conducive to good order to have a definite time, place, and hour to which people can adapt themselves and where they may assemble, as St. Paul says in I Corinthians 14 [:40], "All things should be done decently and in order." And no one should (as no Christian does) ignore such order without cause, out of mere pride or just to create disorder, but one should join in observing such order for the sake of the multitude, or at least should not disrupt or hinder

---

428 These prayers are called *Benedicite* and *Gratias*.

it, for that would be acting contrary to love and friendliness.

Nevertheless, there should be freedom here: for instance, if we are unable, because of an emergency or another significant reason, to preach at six or seven, at twelve or one o'clock, on Sunday or Monday, in the choir or at St. Peter's, one may preach at a different hour, day, or place, just as long as one does not confuse the people, but properly apprises them of such a change. These matters are purely external (as far as time, place, and persons are concerned) and may be regulated entirely by reason, to which they are altogether subject. God, Christ, and the Holy Spirit are not interested in them—just as little as they are interested in what we wish to eat, drink, wear, and whom we marry, or where we want to dwell, walk, or stand; except that (as was said) no one should, without reason, adopt his own way and confuse or hinder the people. Just as at a wedding or other social event no one should offend the bride or the company by doing something special or something that interferes, but one should join the rest, and sit, walk, stand, dance, eat, and drink with them. For it is impossible to order a special table for each individual, and also a special kitchen, cellar, and servant. If he wants anything, let him leave the table without disturbing the others. Thus here too everything must be conducted peacefully and in order, and yet there must be freedom if time, person, or other reasons demand a change; then the masses will also follow harmoniously, since (as was said) no Christian is thereby made any more or less holy.

The pope, to be sure, has scribbled the whole world full of books about these things and fashioned them into bonds, laws, rights, articles of faith, sin, and holiness so that his decretal really deserves, once again, to be consigned to the fire.[429] For we could do well without this book[430] that has caused so much great harm. It has pushed Holy Scripture aside and practically suppressed Christian doctrine; it has also subjected the jurists, with their imperial law, to it. Thus it has trodden both church and emperor underfoot; in their stead it presented us with these stupid asses, the canonists, these will-o'-the-wisps who rule the church with it

---

[429] On December 10, 1520, in Wittenberg, Luther burned copies of the canon law along with the bull, *Exsurge, Domine,* excommunicating him.

[430] I.e., canon law.

and, still more deplorable, left the best parts in it and took the worst out, foisting them on the church. Whatever good there is in it, one can find much better and more richly in Holy Scripture, indeed, also in St. Augustine alone, as far as teaching Christendom is concerned; and then, as far as temporal government is concerned, also in the books of the jurists. For the jurists themselves once contemplated throwing this book out of jurisprudence and leaving it to the theologians. However, it would have been far better to throw it into the fire and reduce it to ashes, although there is something good in it, for how could sheer evil exist unless there was some good with it? But there is too much evil, so much that it crowds out the good, and (as was said) a greater measure of good is to be found in Scripture and also in the fathers and among the jurists. Of course, it might be kept in the libraries as evidence of the folly and the mistakes of the popes, some of the councils, and other teachers. That is why I am keeping it.

We will regard these externals as we do a christening robe[431] or swaddling clothes in which a child is clad for baptism. The child is not baptized or sanctified either by the christening robe or by the swaddling clothes, but only by the baptism. And yet reason dictates that a child be thus clothed. If this garment is soiled or torn, it is replaced by another, and the child grows up without any help from swaddling clothes or christening robe. Here too one must exercise moderation and not use too many of these garments, lest the child be smothered. Similarly, moderation should also be observed in the use of ceremonies, lest they become a burden and a chore. They must remain so light that they are not felt, just as at a wedding no one thinks it a chore or a burden to conform his actions to those of the other people present. I shall write on the special fasts when I write about the plague of the Germans, gluttony and drunkenness, for that properly belongs in the sphere of temporal government.[432]

---

[431] *Westerhemd* (from the Latin *vestis*, meaning "garment"). The robe was usually white (in accordance with Rev. 6:11) and was used in the early church to dress those to be baptized. Cf. WA 50, 651, n. *a*.

[432] Luther wrote about this in 1518 in his *Explanations of the Ninety-five Theses*. LW 31, 86-88.

Above and elsewhere[433] I have written much about the schools, urging firmness and diligence in caring for them. Although they may be viewed as something external and pagan, in as much as they instruct boys in languages and the arts, they are nevertheless extremely necessary. For if we fail to train pupils we will not have pastors and preachers very long—as we are finding out. The school must supply the church with persons who can be made apostles, evangelists, and prophets, that is, preachers, pastors, and rulers, in addition to other people needed throughout the world, such as chancellors, councilors, secretaries, and the like, men who can also lend a hand with the temporal government. In addition, if the schoolteacher is a godly man and teaches the boys to understand, to sing, and to practice God's word and the true faith and holds them to Christian discipline, then, as we said earlier, the schools are truly young and eternal councils, which perhaps do more good than many other great councils. Therefore the former emperors, kings, and princes did well when they showed such diligence in building many schools, high and low, monastic schools and convents, to provide the church with a rich and ample supply of people; but their successors shamefully perverted their use. Thus today princes and lords should do the same, and use the possessions of the cloisters for the maintenance of schools and provide many persons with the means for study.[434] If our descendants misuse these, we at least have done our duty in our day.

In summary, the schools must be second in importance only to the church, for in them young preachers and pastors are trained, and from them emerge those who replace the ones who die. Next, then, to the school comes the burgher's house, for it supplies the pupils; then the city hall and the castle, which must protect the schools so that they may train children to become pastors, and so that these, in turn, may create churches and children of God (whether they be burghers, princes, or emperors). But God must be over all and nearest to all, to preserve this ring or circle against

---

[433] See Luther's *To the Councilmen of All Cities in Germany that They Establish and Maintain Christian Schools* (PE 4, 101-130) and *A Sermon on Keeping Children in School* (PE 4, 133-178).

[434] Cf. *The Smalcald Articles*, Art. III. Tappert (ed.), *Book of Concord*, pp. 297-298.

the devil, and to do everything in all of life's vocations, indeed, in all creatures. Thus Psalm 127 [:1] says that there are only two temporal governments on earth, that of the city and that of the home, "Unless the Lord builds the house; unless the Lord watches over the city." The first government is that of the home, from which the people come; the second is that of the city, meaning the country, the people, princes and lords, which we call the secular government. These embrace everything—children, property, money, animals, etc. The home must produce, whereas the city must guard, protect, and defend. Then follows the third, God's own home and city, that is, the church, which must obtain people from the home and protection and defense from the city.

These are the three hierarchies ordained by God, and we need no more; indeed, we have enough and more than enough to do in living aright and resisting the devil in these three. Just look only at the home and at the duties it alone imposes: parents and landlords must be obeyed; children and servants must be nourished, trained, ruled, and provided for in a godly spirit. The rule of the home alone would give us enough to do, even if there were nothing else. Then the city, that is, the secular government, also gives us enough to do if we show ourselves really obedient, and conversely, if we are to judge, protect, and promote land and people. The devil keeps us busy enough, and with him God gave us the sweat of our brow, thorns and thistles in abundance [Gen. 3:18-19], so that we have more than enough to learn, to live, to do, and to suffer in these two governments. Then there is the third rule and government. If the Holy Spirit reigns there, Christ calls it a comforting, sweet, and light burden [Matt. 11:30]; if not, it is not only a heavy, severe, and terrible task, but also an impossible one, as St. Paul says in Romans 8 [:3], "What the law could not do," and elsewhere, "The letter kills" [II Cor. 3:6].

Now why should we have the blasphemous, bogus law or government of the pope over and above these three high divine governments, these three divine, natural, and temporal laws of God? It presumes to be everything, yet is in reality nothing. It leads us astray and tears us from these blessed, divine estates and laws. Instead, it dresses us in a mask or cowl, thereby making us the

177

devil's fools and playthings, who are slothful and no longer know these three divine hierarchies or realms. That is why we no longer want to put up with it, but acting in conformity with St. Peter's, St. Paul's, and St. Augustine's teaching, want to be rid of it and turn the words of Psalm 2 [:3] against them, "Let us burst their bonds asunder, and cast their cords from us." Indeed, we shall sing with St. Paul, "Even if an angel from heaven should preach a gospel contrary to that, let him be accursed" [Gal. 1:8]; and we shall say with St. Peter, "Why do you make trial of God by putting such a yoke upon the neck?" [Acts 15:10]. Thus we shall again be the pope's masters and tread him underfoot, as Psalm 91 [:13] says, "You will tread on the lion and the adder, the young lion and the serpent you will trample under foot." And that we shall do by the power and with the help of the woman's seed, who has crushed and still crushes the serpent's head, although we must run the risk that he, in turn, will bite us in the heel [Gen. 3:15]. To this blessed seed of the woman be praise and honor, together with the Father and the Holy Spirit, to the one true God and Lord in eternity. Amen.

AGAINST HANSWURST

1541

Translated by Eric W. Gritsch

INTRODUCTION

Henry of Braunschweig/Wolfenbüttel, since 1514 ruler of a duke-dom frequently divided by family feuds, was a bitter enemy of the Reformation.[1] A personal friend of Emperor Charles V, whom he assisted in a war against the Venetian aristocrats, he was the first to oppose the German peasants when they revolted in 1525; and in 1531 he joined the Catholic Union that opposed the Smal-cald League. But Henry was unable to prevent the infiltration of Protestantism into his territory. While he was away participating in the imperial wars against Italy, John Bugenhagen, one of Lu-ther's personal friends and a fiery adherent to the cause of the Reformation, managed to persuade most of the magistrates of Braunschweig/Wolfenbüttel to introduce the Reformation into their territories; when Henry returned in 1528, he found most of his lands infected with the new movement. He tried to rid his dukedom of Protestants through legislation, diplomacy, and fre-quently through brute force. But the newly founded Smalcald League, under the leadership of Landgrave Philip of Hesse,[2] as-sisted the Protestants, and open warfare between the Catholic Union and the league became imminent.

When the princes of the Smalcald League arranged to meet in Braunschweig in the spring of 1538, Henry refused to grant Philip of Hesse and Elector John Frederick of Saxony safe-conduct to ride through his territory. When the Protestant party nevertheless went through, they were fired upon. The landgrave retaliated at the end of the same year by seizing one of Duke Henry's secre-taries and confiscating letters containing plans of action against the Smalcald League. He published these plans, in order to ex-pose Henry as a traitor to the Protestant cause. Quite a few Ger-man princes, afraid of open warfare between Catholics and Prot-estants, disapproved of such harsh action. Duke George of Saxony,[3]

[1] For a detailed analysis, see Friedrich Koldewey, *Heinz von Wolfenbüttel. Ein Zeitbild aus dem Jahrhundert der Reformation* (Halle, 1883).
[2] Philip of Hesse (1504-1567).
[3] See p. 221, n. 57.

a supporter of the Catholic Union but also Philip's father-in-law, advised him to publish a defense of his action. Philip did so, and Henry replied to it, seeing a chance to avenge himself publicly. Then the elector joined the dispute, and each side hurled violent charges and countercharges at the other.

Luther at first took no part in the controversy. But when in *Rejoinder Against the Elector of Saxony*,[4] dated November 2, 1540, Duke Henry referred to Elector John Frederick as "one whom Martin Luther has called his dear and reverent Hanswurst,"[5] Luther felt compelled to answer. He did so—applying the term "Hanswurst" not to the elector but to Henry—and thereby produced one of his most violent attacks upon the opponents of his cause. "Hanswurst" refers to a German carnival figure, carrying a long leather sausage around his neck and wearing a colorful clownlike costume. He was a stock character in comedies of Luther's time, "a broadly farcical or burlesque" character, as Merriam-Webster's dictionary defines him. He appeared first in Sebastian Brant's *Ship of Fools*, a satire written in Low German dialect. It was printed in Basel in 1494 and became one of the most popular works of the sixteenth century.

Luther not only attacked Duke Henry in *Against Hanswurst*, but he also discussed the life and doctrine of the church, distinguishing between the true ancient, and the false new, church. It is this part of the treatise that is most valuable for us today.

Duke Henry's position in this controversy was severely compromised by several misdeeds associated with his name: he was accused by princes and common people alike of arson, immoral conduct, and tyranny. The town of Einbeck, for example, had been burned to ashes, and several other Protestant towns reported cases of arson, charging that the fires had been set by the duke's hirelings. Moreover, Henry's behavior toward his brother William, whom he had imprisoned for twelve years to rid himself of opposition in his bid for absolute territorial rule, cost him the friend-

---

[4] *Duplik Wider den Kurfürsten von Sachsen* (hereafter cited as the *Rejoinder*). The full title as well as a more detailed account of the circumstances of its publication are recorded in WA 51, 462.

[5] Cf. *Rejoinder*, Bl. A4^b. WA 51, 462.

ship of many a Catholic prince. Finally, the duke's affair with a young lady at his court, Eva von Trott—sometime before the death of his wife in 1541—virtually ruined his reputation among friend and foe. A father of eleven children, born during a seemingly happy marriage with Mary of Württemberg between 1515 and 1541, Henry became the target of vicious attacks. In defense he spread rumors that Eva had taken ill and had died in one of his hideouts; actually, she had been taken to the Castle Stauffenberg, where Henry continued his affair with her, fathering several children. All these things were discovered in 1542, after the publication of Luther's tract, when the Smalcald League invaded Braunschweig/Wolfenbüttel and drove Henry from his territory. Henry, who had charged Philip of Hesse with the same crimes because the landgrave had committed bigamy,[6] fled to France.

The Smalcald League was defeated in 1547 in a battle with the Catholic forces and was compelled to negotiate a peace treaty. Henry returned to his territory during the ensuing brief period of peace and regained all his possessions. In 1556 at the age of sixty-seven he married Princess Sophia, the daughter of the Polish king Sigismund. He died in 1568, a successful defender of the old religion.

Luther's language in *Against Hanswurst* is as violent as that of Duke Henry in the *Rejoinder*. Such violence, however, is not uncommon in the polemical literature of the sixteenth century. "Luther delighted less in muck than many of the literary men of his age; but if he did indulge, he excelled in this as in every other area of speech."[7] Men like Ulrich von Hutten, John Eck, St. Thomas More, William Shakespeare—to mention only a few—used words that sound peculiar, if not shocking, to the modern reader. "Nobody ever wore his heart more on his sleeve than Luther, and there for all to see are his fun and tenderness, his deep love of his family and his home, his mighty prayers, and the vulgarity which

---

[6] For the complex story of Luther's involvement in Philip's bigamy, see E. S. G. Potter (trans.), Heinrich Boehmer's *Luther in the Light of Recent Research* (Grand Rapids: Zondervan, 1930), pp. 213-224.

[7] See Roland H. Bainton, *Here I Stand* (New York and Nashville: Abingdon-Cokesbury Press, 1950), p. 298.

prevents us thinking of him as some stained-glass figure, or cloying his memory with sickly romanticism.[8]

Against Hanswurst was written between February 19 and April 4, 1541.[9] The original German manuscript is deposited at the Kaiser-Friedrich-Wilhelm Museum in Magdeburg. Four German editions appeared in 1541, the first printed by Hans Lufft, the other three by printers in Marburg. In 1543 a Latin and German *Excerpt (Auszug)* followed, which was combined with the second edition of *The Smalcald Articles*.[10]

The text of the first German edition, which is the basis of this translation, is given in WA 51, 469-572. A special word of thanks is due Peter Stephens, who helped in the preparation of the translation.

---

[8] See E. Gordon Rupp, *Luther's Progress to the Diet of Worms* (New York: Wilcox and Follett, 1951), p. 106.

[9] See *WA* 51, 462-464.

[10] See *WA* 51, 466-467.

AGAINST HANSWURST

Von Braunschweig of Wolfenbüttel has now published another libel in which he has set out to rub his scabby, scurvy head against the honor of my gracious lord, the elector of Saxony. He has also twice attacked and baited me: first, when he writes that I have called my gracious lord Hanswurst, and then when he attacks the whole essence of the faith, of which I must confess I am one of the foremost exponents at the present time. He curses, blasphemes, shrieks, struggles, bellows, and spits, so that, if people really heard him utter these words, they would gather with chains and bars, just as if (like the man in the gospels [Mark 5:1-10]) he were possessed by a legion of devils and had to be seized and bound. And though I do not think that this vile fellow is worth a syllable's reply, I will nevertheless—since he is not alone—give our people something to talk about.

Speaking for myself, I am very glad that such books[1] are written against me, for it makes me tingle with pleasure from head to toe when I see that through me, poor wretched man that I am, God the Lord maddens and exasperates both the hellish and worldly princes, so that in their spite they would burst and tear themselves to pieces—while I sit under the shade of faith and the Lord's Prayer, laughing at the devils and their crew as they blubber and struggle in their great fury. And yet, they achieve nothing except to make their case worse every day and mine (that is God's) better and stronger. And if they could endure or understand it, I would have thanked them and asked them to go on writing such books against me without interruption, and blubber and writhe along with all the devils in hell. How better could I plague them? For thus I become young and vigorous, strong and gay.

For all such books, even if there were as many as thousands

---

[1] A reference to the *Rejoinder*. See p. 182, n. 4.

of them written every day and every hour as von Wolfenbüttel has vices and lies, are very easily refuted with the single word, "Devil, you lie," just as that haughty beggar Dr. Luther sings so proudly and boldly in those words of his hymn, "One little word shall fell him."[2] Therefore, since the devil rages in his Harry of Wolfenbüttel and seeks every opportunity to lie so that he may win his spurs against me with this word "Hanswurst," I do not propose to answer his damned bond slave Harry, either at length or in detail, for he is not worthy of my attention. On the contrary, I shall let him seek his honor as best he can; and he would indeed have to search a thousand years before he could find the slightest trace of it. But first I want to say something about Hanswurst.

How the devil, with all his powers, likes lying is indicated by the fact that he is really trying so unusually hard in his Harry of Wolfenbüttel. I had not supposed or expected this arrogant spirit to seek such a ridiculous and childish reason for lying; he should have better reasons. But it must be as people say, "He who likes laughing tickles himself,"[3] or as Chrysippus says, "He who likes lying must lie even when he speaks the truth."[4] For you know quite well, you angry little spirit, and so does your possessed Harry, as well as your poets and scribes, that this phrase "Hanswurst" is not mine, nor was it invented by me, but it is used by other people[5] about those boors and blockheads who, though they want to be clever, are nevertheless clumsy and ridiculous in all that they say or do. In this sense I have often used it too, especially in preaching.[6] But in my conscience I cannot recall that I have ever meant a particular person, whether friend or foe; though I have used the term as occasion demanded.

---

[2] "A Mighty Fortress Is Our God," stanza 3. *Service Book and Hymnal of the Lutheran Church in America* (Philadelphia, 1958), No. 150; LW 53, 283-285.

[3] A German proverb, "*Wer gern lachet, der kutzelt sich selbs.*" Cf. Thiele, *Luthers Sprichwörtersammlung*, No. 232.

[4] Chrysippus (*ca.* 282-209 B.C.) is regarded as one of the founders of the Stoic school of philosophy. The saying is found in C. G. Yonge (trans.), Diogenes Laertius' *The Lives and Opinions of Eminent Philosophers* (London, 1891), V, 11.

[5] A reference to Sebastian Brant's *Ship of Fools*. See the Introduction, p. 182.

[6] Cf., for example, WA 36, 88; 41, 433; 49, 429.

I would not hesitate to say whom I had meant if I were aware of it, even if it had been Harry of Wolfenbüttel with all his crew. By God's grace, I would defend it before you all in court.

From this it follows then, since you and your Harry lie so shamelessly and take every opportunity to do so, that your book is for the most part nothing but sheer lies from start to finish. It is just like our Lord's saying, "He who is dishonest in a very little is dishonest also in much" [Luke 16:10]. How can he who cannot keep himself from little unnecessary lies, keep himself from big ones? Indeed, since you and your Harry are such vulgar blockheads that you think such lewd and stupid gossip will harm me or bring you honor, you are the real Hanswursts—blockheads, boors, and dunderheads. And I would answer you with this, that you are, both father and son, incorrigible, shameless, and perjuring scoundrels in saying that I have called my most gracious lord "Hanswurst." Such wurst-tricks require no further answer. Some people probably suppose that you regard my gracious lord as Hanswurst because by God's (that is, your enemy's) grace he is strong, plump, and somewhat round. But think what you will, so make in your pants, hang it round your neck, then make a jelly[7] of it and eat it like the vulgar sows and asses you are!

That is enough about Hanswurst. The other things that are said in this libel about the safe-conduct and the public peace, etc., do not concern me now.[8] They are answered both by my gracious lord and the landgrave, so that Hanswurst of Wolfenbüttel will try in vain to seek and to save his honor, as all reasonable people testify; and the *Rejoinder* proves beyond the shadow of a doubt that in the future no one will be able to write a slanderous (as they say) book against him. And if the book were so long as to reach to the ends of the earth, it could not say a thing that redounded to his honor. What does not exist cannot be praised! Harry of Wolfenbüttel might wish that he could keep this honor of being called Hanswurst. But I do not call him Hanswurst to honor him, but out of sheer grace and mercy, of which he is not worthy.

---

[7] *Galreden*, i.e., *Gallerte*.
[8] See pp. 181-182.

Third, where his pride gets the best of him and he attacks at the very center and slanders my gracious lord by calling him a heretic, an apostate, a rebel, a monster, a Nabal, a Cain, and the like without measure,[9] in which I and all of us are to be included, I answer, as I did before, that for my part I could wish nothing dearer for this possessed Hanswurst (as long as it did not lead to his or anyone else's destruction, for that would neither help me nor the cause) than that he and his followers would have to go on writing such books without interruption. Meanwhile, I would sit still and blithely watch how the devil, and his Hanses and Harrys, his sausages and his tripes,[10] vainly fretted and tormented themselves, and blubbered and writhed, achieving nothing except to make us laugh and make their own case worse. Indeed, I would like to see them say aloud what they write, for if they did, people would gather with chains and bars (as I have said above) and out of sympathy would seize and bind them as demoniacs. And if people did not do this, then, perhaps at God's prompting, oxen and swine would trample them to death with their horns and hoofs.

For in answer to all such words of libel, since it is just poor, naked, and unadorned slander, bawled out without cause or reason and without stating a single point, we—while they shout till they are hoarse and fit to drop dead—just answer with one simple little word, "Devil, you lie!" Hanswurst, how you lie! Oh, Harry Wolfenbüttel, what a shameless liar you are! You spout a lot, but you say nothing. You slander, but you prove nothing. This kind of art is performed by the arch-prostitute in the street when she calls an honest virgin a drab, a whore, a harlot, and a strumpet, though she has no grounds for it and, in fact, knows the contrary to be true. Hence she makes herself malicious and the girl loved and esteemed. It would cause such a prostitute no great effort to give utterance to a book like the one our Hanswurst of Wolfenbüttel has written.

But if, however, the devil and his Hanswurst could write and state, "For such and such a reason the elector is a heretic, an

---

[9] Cf. the passages from the *Rejoinder* quoted in *WA* 51, 471, n. 10.
[10] *Würste* and *Caldaunen,* a pun on "Hanswurst."

apostate," etc., then he would not be a Hanswurst, and one could then deal with the matter. But that is too big and impossible a task, not only for Hanswurst and his father, but also for the pope, the whole world, and all the devils. They have tried now for twenty years, and the more they have tried, the more they have failed. That is my answer to this poor Harry and Hanswurst who, like the spiteful whore, can do no more than spew out mere invective. For if they could do more, they would mix it in now and then and not just shout empty and futile slander.

Generally, in addition to what we have just said, we answer all devils, papists, and all their crew that they, as befits devils and the devil's lot, lie shamelessly in such books and speeches. We give them the answer the Holy Spirit gave us all long ago in Proverbs 26 [:2], "Like a sparrow in its flitting, like a swallow in its flying, a curse that is causeless does not alight." Here Solomon teaches us that we ought not to heed vilifications or curses that come to us undeserved, without cause or reason, since they pass by and do not alight. This is proved by all of history and its examples. Where are the vilifications that Arius and all the heretics made against the church? Where are the slanderers of our own time—Emser, Eck, the snot-nose,[11] and Wetzel? Their books have vanished and come to nothing, but the word of God remains forever [Isa. 40:8].

Our Lord expresses himself much more gloriously in the judgment and comfort he gives in Matthew 5 [:11-12] when he says, "Blessed are you when men revile you and persecute you and utter all kinds of evil against you falsely on my account. Rejoice and be glad, for your reward is great in heaven." Without doubt the reverse is true: fear and mourn, you who lie and revile Christ and his followers, for your damnation is great in hell. Here we have the true judgment and command that we are to rejoice when we are reviled for the sake of Christ, and we ought to say confidently that they lie. Now all the devils and all the world could not deny that it is not for murder, adultery, or some other vice that we are so basely slandered and called heretics. Moreover, there is nothing about that in Harry's book—and I defy them to

---

[11] John Cochlaeus.

mention such. But it is for the gospel's sake that we are slandered. For they themselves admitted at the Diet of Augsburg[12] that our confession of faith cannot be refuted by Holy Scripture. And some of their princes said of their theologians, "How well our theologians defend us; they declare that their [opponents'] case is grounded in Scripture, but ours is not!" This is true. Even today they condemn us because we do not accept the councils, the fathers, and the decretals of their church above and in addition to Scripture.

Well then, this is our foundation and our bastion, and these are not (like Hanswurst's) empty, futile words. The Bible and the word of God and their own testimony are on our side. But on their side is something other than the word of God, namely, the words of men, which we do not want to have and which are indeed strictly forbidden by Christ himself and the apostles: Matthew 15 [:9], "They worship me in vain with human doctrine," and Galatians 1 [:8], "But whoever preaches to you another gospel, even if it be an angel from heaven, let him be accursed." These are not (I say) simply our own empty, naked words of slander, as are those of the devil, of Wolfenbüttel, of Schmid,[13] of Snot-nose, and the like. You can see in this one of the true signs of who and where the true holy church is, namely, that it is and must be basely perjured, reviled without reason, and derided by the devil's donkeys and his senseless Harrys. This is called "bearing abuse for Christ,"[14] since there is no other way if we wish to be true Christians.

St. Paul says to us, "Do not be frightened in anything by your opponents. This is a clear omen to them of their destruction, but of your salvation, and that from God. For it has been granted to you that for the sake of Christ you should not only believe in him but also suffer for his sake, engaged in the same conflict which you saw and now hear to be mine" [Phil. 1:28-30]. If, then, we are to be slandered, someone must do it. St. Peter and

---

[12] In 1530. The statement, attributed to Duke William of Bavaria, is contained in George Spalatin's *Something Historical* (*Etliche Historica*). St. L. 16, 879-880.

[13] John Faber; see p. 150, n. 390.

[14] *Improperium Christi probantes.* Cf. Heb. 13:13.

St. John will not do it, nor will any Christian or intelligent heathen. Clearly it must be done by mad, possessed people like
Harry of Wolfenbüttel, Schmid, the snot-nose, Eck, Münzer, the
Anabaptists,[15] the pope, the cardinals, the devil and his mother,
and other lackeys of the devil in the papacy. Such a fine work
and office as this belongs to saints like these in the most holy
church of the pope.

Let slanderous books be published, and let it rain and snow
slander. It is written that we should rejoice over it as the surest
sign that we are the true, blessed church. Moreover, Christ and
St. Peter judge our slanderers and call them liars and damned enemies of God. What more could we want? How could they do us
greater honor, give us greater joy and stronger comfort, than by
reviling us without cause, solely for the sake of Christ and because of their own devilish and murderous hate (for this is Christ's
judgment)? They are shameless and damned liars, who make our
faith stronger and our salvation more certain, while at the same
time cursing and damning themselves. Therefore I have said above
that it is not only easy to answer their books of slander, but also
comforting to hear that they slander us. And the more bitterly
and violently they vilify us, the better they make it, not for themselves, but for us. They cannot make it worse for themselves; they
drive themselves into God's judgment, and they want to be damned
by him as thieves and murderers of his fold [John 10:1], that is,
his church (as I have just said)—something I neither wish for them
nor for myself, for they help me so much with their slanders.

But now, since Harry's book either is produced by all the
devils and papists or at least gives them all pleasure (which is
the same, Romans 1 [:32], "They not only do them but approve
those who practice them"),[16] and is so exceedingly poisonous, bitter, and malicious, I regard it as the finest book that the devils
and the papists have produced for many years. For Christ, who is
the Lord over blessing and cursing, has such skill that he turns
Balaam's curse into a blessing [Numbers 23–24]; similarly, Psalm
109 [:28], "Let them curse, but do thou bless!" and Matthew 5
[:11], "How blessed you are when you suffer insults." Therefore,

---

15 See p. 45, n. 113.
16 *Faciens et consentiens.*

to tell the truth, Hanswurst with all his devils and papists could not have done my gracious lord, the elector of Saxony, and us a greater honor before God, particularly when he calls us heretics, apostates, etc. With such vilifications and curses he gives our Lord Christ cause to bless and comfort us and, on the other hand, cause to curse and damn them as liars, thieves, and murderers of God and his holy church. So when Harry says that the elector is a heretic, it has no other effect on Christ than this, "Harry, you are a damned liar and scoundrel, and your papacy with you."

That was what they wanted. Now understand what is said in Psalm 37 [:15], "Their sword shall enter their own heart." Very likely Harry's libel is regarded by them as a sharp sword against the elector and us, which should devour us in a moment; but according to the true understanding of Christ the meaning is (as I have already said): his libel is a sharp sword which pierces Harry's heart, and with it the devil's and the papists', but it does not touch a hair on our heads. Although, like a madman, he does not feel it yet, he will feel it soon. If you would like a gloss for every slander in Harry's book, then write this, "Here, before God, Hanswurst pierces his own heart and the hearts of all the papists, and thereby most highly blesses and honors the elector of Saxony and the holy Christian church."

May the merciful God protect my most gracious lord (and, indeed, all reasonable men), that they may never do or say anything that pleases or seems good to Harry and his lot! For even when he calls my gracious lord a drunkard and a Nabal [I Samuel 25], he does not do it because he hates vice, but because he hates the person and the creature of God. It grieves him not to find as many vices in him as he had hoped so that he could satisfy his devilish hate with slander and reproach. For he would gladly make a speck of sawdust into a log, and his own logs into specks [Matt. 7:3-5]. One can easily discover the reason: where he cannot find vices he looks for them, taking Christian and princely virtues and slandering them, hoping to transform them into vices with lies against his own conscience. But he cannot do it. That is the way with the children of the devil, who for this reason is called *diabolus, calumniator*, that is, "devil" or "slanderer."

For the devil, their god and father, does not dislike men because they have sin and vice, but he dislikes the creatures of God and God himself, and, as he has fallen into disgrace, he desires them also to fall into disgrace by vilifying, accusing, and damning them. Thus, when he cannot make them sin, or find sin in them, it pains him bitterly; and it annoys him that they are godly. Then he proceeds to attack what is good and virtuous, vilifying and reviling it and wishing to make into sin what is not sin, as Scripture everywhere says of him. If, however, he happens to find a sin, he laughs up his sleeve.[17] Then he takes pains to see how he can make it bigger and more heinous, so that one may really say that Harry's book is a true copy and document straight from the devil's workshop. When godly people find sin in others, they are sorry for them, for they hate sin and would that it had not happened. These are the children of God who reprove public evil out of compassion; or, if men will not listen to them, but prefer to be devils, they let them go, condemning them to hell or consigning them to the devil [I Cor. 5:5].

However, so that we may not completely waste our time with Harry's devilish dirt, but may offer the reader something better and more useful—though not for the sake of Harry or those who incite him, for they are "self-condemned; they have ears, but hear not"[18]—we will come to the point at issue, namely, why the papists, through their Harry, call us heretics. And the point is that they allege that we have fallen away from the holy church and set up a new church. This then is the answer: since they themselves boast that they are the church, it is for them to prove that they are. If they can prove it with a single reason (I don't ask for more), then we shall give ourselves up as prisoners, willingly saying, "We have sinned, have mercy upon us."[19] But if they cannot prove it, they must confess (whether they like it or not) that they are not the church and that we cannot be heretics since we have fallen away from what is not the true church. Indeed, since there is nothing in-between, we must be the church of Christ and they

---

[17] A German proverb, *"Da lachet er in die faust."*
[18] *Suo iudicio condemnati, aures habent, et non audiunt.* Cf. Titus 3:11; Ps. 135:17.
[19] *Peccavimus, miserere nostri.*

the devil's church, or vice versa. Therefore it all turns on proving which is the true church.

As long as there is no proof it is vain for one part to boast of being the church and call the other part heretics. One part must be false and untrue. For there are two kinds of churches stretching from the beginning of history to the end, which St. Augustine calls Cain and Abel.[20] The Lord Christ commands us not to embrace the false church; and he himself distinguishes between two churches, a true one and a false one, in Matthew 7 [:15], "Beware of false prophets, who come to you in sheep's clothing," etc. Where there are prophets, there are churches in which they teach. If the prophets are false, so also are the churches that believe and follow them. We have been unable up to now to get the papists to willingly prove why they are the true church, but they insist that according to Matthew 18 [:17] one must listen to the church or be lost. Yet Christ does not say there who, where, or what the church is; only that where it is, it ought to be listened to. We confess and say that as well, but we ask where the church of Christ is, and who it is. We are concerned *non de nomine*, "not with the name" of the church, but with its essence.

It is just as if I asked a drunkard or a fool or someone half-asleep, "Tell me, friend, who or where is the church?" and he answered me, ten times over, nothing but, "One should listen to the church!" But how am I to listen to the church when I do not know who or where the church is? "Well," they say, "we papists have remained in the ancient and original church ever since the time of the apostles. Therefore we are the true church, for we have come from the ancient church and have remained in it; but you have fallen away from us and have become a new church opposed to us." Answer: "But what if I prove that we have remained faithful to the true ancient church, indeed, that we are the true ancient church and that you have fallen away from us, that is, the ancient church, and have set up a new church against the ancient one?" Let us hear that!

First, nobody can deny that we, as well as the papists, have received holy baptism and because of that are called Christians.

---

[20] *On the Trinity*, XV, 1. *MPL* 41, 438; *PNF*[1] 2, 285.

Now baptism is not something new, invented by us in our own day, but it is the same ancient baptism instituted by Christ, in which the apostles and the early church and all Christians have been baptized. If then we have the same baptism as the original, ancient (and, as the creed says, "catholic," that is, "universal") Christian church, and are baptized in it, then we belong to the same ancient universal church; and they like us, and we like them, are baptized with one baptism; and therefore there is no difference between us as to baptism. But baptism is the first and most important sacrament, without which the others are all nothing, as they must admit. This is why the papists cannot truthfully call us a different or a new or a heretical church, since we are children of the ancient baptism, together with the apostles themselves and all of Christendom, Ephesians 4 [:5], "one baptism."

Second, nobody will deny that we have the holy sacrament of the altar, just as Christ himself instituted it and the apostles and the whole of Christendom have since practiced it. Thus we eat and drink with the whole of ancient Christendom from one table, and we receive with them the same one ancient sacrament; we have done nothing new or different. Consequently, we are one church with them, or as St. Paul says in I Corinthians 11 [10:17], "one body" and "one loaf" since we eat of one loaf and drink of one cup. So the papists cannot call us heretics or a new church, unless they first call Christ, the apostles, and the whole of Christendom heretics, as in truth they do, for we are one church with the ancient church, in one sacrament.

Third, nobody can deny that we have the true and ancient keys, and do not use them in any other way than to bind and loose sins, committed against the command of God. This we do in accordance with Christ's institution [Matt. 16:19; John 20:23] and the practice of the apostles and the whole of Christendom until the present day. We have therefore one kind of keys and one common practice with the ancient church. Hence we are this same ancient church, or are, in any event, in it; for we make no new keys, we make no new laws, nor do we exclude kings and lords from, or admit them to, temporal power, but it is only sinners that we exclude from, or admit to, the kingdom of heaven. This we do just as the ancient church did at the Lord's command, so that the papists libel us once more, indeed, slander us and in us make the ancient church, the apostles, and Christ himself heretical.

Fourth, nobody can deny that we have in fulness and purity the preaching office and the word of God, that we teach and preach diligently, without adding any new, sectarian, or human doctrine, and in this we do just as Christ commanded [Matt. 28:19-20] and as the apostles and all of Christendom have done. We invent nothing new, but hold and remain true to the ancient word of God, as the ancient church had it. Therefore we are, together with the ancient church, the one true church, which teaches and believes the one word of God. So the papists once more slander Christ himself, the apostles, and all of Christendom when they call us innovators and heretics. For they find nothing in us but what belongs to the ancient church—that we are like it, and are one church with it.

Fifth, nobody can deny that we, like it, do indeed hold, believe, sing, and confess the Apostles' Creed, the ancient creed of the ancient church, and neither make nor add anything new to it. Hence we belong to the ancient church and are one with it. There is, therefore, in this matter also, no reason the papists should really call us heretics or a new church, for whoever believes as the ancient church did and holds things in common with it belongs to the ancient church.

Sixth, nobody can deny that we have the same prayer as the ancient church, the same Lord's Prayer. We have not invented a new or different one; we sing the same psalms and praise and thank God with united heart and voice according to the teaching of Christ, the practice of the apostles and the ancient church, and their command to us to follow their example. And so again the papists cannot call us heretics or a new church, unless they first call Christ himself such, together with his beloved ancient church, etc.

Seventh, nobody can deny that with the ancient church we hold and teach that one should honor and not curse the temporal powers and should not compel them to kiss the pope's feet. This is also not something which we have newly devised, for St. Peter in II Peter 2 [:10] curses those who would invent and in the future do such new things. And St. Paul is with us in Romans 13 [:1-7], as is the whole of ancient Christendom, so that in this we are not, nor may we be called, innovators—as the papists call us, thereby not only slandering us, but God himself. But we are and belong to the ancient, holy, and apostolic church, as its true children and members. For we have always most faithfully taught obedience to our temporal authority,[21] be it emperor or princes. We ourselves have lived accordingly and prayed for them with all our heart.

Eighth, nobody can deny that we praise and honor marriage as a divine, blessed, and well-pleasing ordinance of God's creation for the procreation of children and the prevention of carnal unchastity. We have not newly invented it, nor have we of ourselves newly devised it, much less have we forbidden it, like innovators. But just as God from the beginning instituted it, and Christ confirmed it [Matt 19:4-6], and the apostles and the ancient church honored and taught it, so have we remained in this same ancient rule and ordinance of God. In this we have been like the ancient church and have indeed been its true and proper members. So you can see that here again the papists accuse us falsely of innovation.

Ninth, nobody can deny that we experience the same suffering (as St. Peter says [I Pet. 5:9]) as our brethren in the world. We are persecuted in every place, strangled, drowned, hanged, and tormented in every way for the sake of the word. Our lot is like that of the ancient church, and in this we are beyond measure like it, so that we may well say we are the true ancient church, or at least its companions and copartners in suffering; for this is not something we have newly invented, but something we really experience. Indeed, we (like this same ancient church) are like the Lord Christ himself on the cross: there are Annas and Caiaphas, together with the priests, standing in front of the cross, vilifying the Lord after crucifying him. The pope, the cardinals, and the monks have likewise condemned, damned, and murdered us, shedding our blood and reviling us as well. The soldiers, that is, some of the temporal powers, stand there and also revile us. In addition, there is

---

[21] *Oberkeit.*

that criminal on the left, Harry of Wolfenbüttel, with his crew, whom God has already judged and hanged in chains in hell. He must add his vilification, so that this mark of the ancient church may also be fully seen in us.

Tenth, nobody can deny that we have not shed blood, murdered, hanged, or avenged ourselves in return, as we could often have done and could still do. But as Christ, the apostles, and the ancient church did, we endure, admonish, and pray for others. And, indeed, we do this publicly in church, in the litany and in sermons, just as Christ our Lord did and taught and as the ancient church also did, so that in this we all act according to the ancient practice of the ancient church.

Since the papists know that in all these and other things we are like the ancient church and may truly be called the ancient church—for these things are not new or invented by us— it is amazing that they should deceive and damn us so shamelessly, calling us apostates and founders of a new church; for they cannot find anything in us which was not held in the ancient and true church at the time of the apostles. Thus I really think that this is the time of which Daniel 7 [:8-9] says, "One that was ancient of days took his seat" after the little horn had spoken blasphemously, and sat in judgment. For the original and ancient church shines forth once more (like the sun emerging from the clouds behind which it was shining, but where it could not be seen), and the horn which speaks blasphemies will perish and everything come to an end, as it is written and is evident in the result—but there is no time to speak of that now.

Yet someone might say, "You lack one thing, namely, fasting, because you heretics do not fast" (they say). Lord God, if there is one thing we have from the ancient church, it is unfortunately fasting. If there is one thing the papists have from the new church, it is that they do not fast but live riotously and on fast days even more than on feast days. Indeed, we do not just fast, but (with St. Paul [I Cor. 4:11]) we suffer hunger. We see it daily in our poor ministers, their wives and children, and in many other poor people, whose hunger stares at you out of their eyes.[22] They

---

[22] A German proverb, *"Den der hunger aus den augen sihet."*

scarcely have bread and water, they go about naked as a jay-
bird, and they have nothing of their own. The farmer and the
burgher give them nothing, and the nobility take, so that there are
only a few of us who have something, and we cannot help everyone. This should be the purpose of monasteries and convents. If
others are stingy, then Lazarus must die of starvation [Luke 16:19-
31]. The papists laugh at this, but they only prove thereby that
we are the ancient church suffering scorn and injury at the hands
of the children of the devil.

Thus we have proved that we are the true, ancient church,
one body and one communion of saints with the holy, universal,
Christian church. Now you too, papists, prove that you are the
true church or are like it. You cannot do it. But I will prove that
you are the new false church, which is in everything apostate,
separated from the true, ancient church, thus becoming Satan's
whore and synagogue [Rev. 2:9].

First, you do not hold to the original, ancient baptism, for
you have invented many other new baptisms, teaching that the
original baptism is subsequently lost through sin, that a man must
atone by his own works, and, particularly, that by entering a
monastery a man becomes as pure as if he had been baptized
with the baptism of Christ. This is why you have filled the earth
with churches and monasteries.

And this matter of *satisfactio*, "satisfaction," is the source and
origin, the door and entrance, to all the abominations of the papacy, just as in the church baptism is the source and entrance to
all grace and forgiveness of sins. For where there is no baptism,
the sacraments, the keys, and everything else are of no avail. Had
the notion of satisfaction not arisen, then indulgences, pilgrimages,
brotherhoods, masses, purgatory, monasteries, convents, and most
abominations would not have been invented, and the papacy would
not have grown so rich and fat. Therefore they have called it
"baptism" in their church, because it has effected many baptisms,
the sacrament and forgiveness of sins, and indeed even great holiness! This is nothing but self-righteousness, a holiness based on
works, about which we have written a great deal.[23] Who has com-

---

[23] Beginning with *The Ninety-five Theses* in 1517. LW 31, 17-33.

manded you to do this? Or where is it written? Where do you find in the ancient church that you may invent such a new baptism and holiness? Who then is a heretic, apostate, and a new church?

Second, you have sent indulgences into all the world, like a baptism, indeed, like a deluge, to wash away sin, so that there is not a corner of the world where your indulgences are not sold or given. The whole world is full of seals and letters. Who has commanded you to do this? Or where is it written? Where do you find in the ancient church that you may institute such a new baptism and washing away of sins? Who then is here the new heretical church? Is it not you, the whore church of the devil?

Third, you have brought holy water and salt not only into every church, but also into every corner of the world, as a washing away (or baptism) of sins, even teaching a lot of magic about it as dist. III, "Salt Water,"[24] proves. Who has commanded you to do this? Where is it written? Where do you find it instituted by the ancient church, or by the apostles? Who then is here the new apostate church?

Fourth, you have instituted pilgrimages for the gaining of indulgences or the forgiveness of sins, and this, since it happens without the office of the keys, through one's own merit, is also a new and different baptism or washing away of sins. Who has commanded you to do this? Where is it written? Where do you find in the ancient church that you should institute this new forgiveness or baptism? Who then is here the new apostate church?

Fifth, you have founded brotherhoods without number, so many that you have filled the whole world with seals and letters, all for indulgences, forgiveness of sin, and merit, which are solely the office of holy baptism and the sacrament. Who has commanded you to do this? Where is it written? Where do you find in the ancient church that you may institute this new forgiveness or merit? And who can tell how many new ways you have invented in order to forgive sin through money and one's own merit? Who then is here the new church with new doctrines and

---

[24] *Aquam sale,* a section of canon law. See p. 168, n. 422.

sacraments, of which neither Christ, the apostles, Scripture, nor the ancient church knew anything?

Sixth, who can tell all the abominable innovations you have devised in the sacred and holy sacrament of the body and blood of Christ? Who has commanded you to do this? Where is it written? Where do you find in the ancient church, first, that you can take and plunder this sacrament of the whole church, and allow only one kind, and make the whole sacrament the property of the priests; second, that this same one kind is not for instructing and increasing faith, but is turned into a work of obedience to the church; and third, that the whole sacrament (provided it is still a sacrament) is not an open proclamation of Christ as a remembrance of him, or a thanksgiving for his suffering, but is turned into a priestly sacrifice and a means for scoundrels to acquire merit, to sell it to others, and to impart it to souls in purgatory? In the most abominable and blasphemous way it has been turned into something to serve any worldly need, like some heathen idolatry, indeed, like some vile flea market.[25] You have silenced and obliterated the remembrance of Christ—the purpose for which he instituted it. And if you were in other respects as pure a church as that of the apostles themselves, and even purer, this one abominable, dreadful thing, which you have newly devised at the devil's instigation, makes you a new apostate heretical church, yes, the arch-whore of the devil and the synagogue of hell [Rev. 2:9]. For this thing is so hopelessly and abysmally evil that in this life no tongue can fully describe it and no heart comprehend it, till the day of judgment.

Read, collect, put together all the evil that the devil and the lot of you can devise against us, and then lie ten thousand times again, and it would not even be a speck of sawdust compared with the plank on which not one devil, but without any doubt every devil and every arch-knave has been performing his carpentry for six centuries. That is truly one of the things Christ calls an abomination in the holy place [Matt. 24:15]. Therefore we not only ought and must flee from you, as from the mighty wrath of God, but heaven and earth also fear and shrink from such a mur-

---

[25] *Grempelmarckt*, i.e., *Trödelmarkt*.

derer's den [Matt. 21:13], for this thing not only ruins every church, but makes of it the vilest cesspool that the devil has on earth. The Turks, the Tartars, and the Jews are in no way such a den of murderers as the papal church is in this matter, for they only deny Christ and turn their back on him; but these take him and then spit upon, mock, revile, besmirch, and torture him, and inflict a more terrible suffering upon him than was physically inflicted upon him by the Jews. Well, go on now and boast that you are the holy church, from which we have apostatized. May the devil remain with you in such a church, and all those who want to be like Harry. May God save us from that—as he has already delivered us from it in his mercy, for which may he be praised and thanked into eternity.

Seventh, who has commanded you to innovate and make new keys, indeed, two false skeleton keys, with which you neither forgive nor retain sins, as the ancient keys do with us and as they did in the whole of the ancient church? But in your new, apostate, murderous church you institute sin and murder anew where there was none before, by chaining, binding, terrorizing, and killing the Christian conscience with countless unbearable laws concerning food, drink, clothes, homes, days, and external things like these in which Christ gave freedom, Colossians 2 [:16], and which the ancient church held to be without sin and danger. In addition, you have deposed kings and princes as if you were God himself. Who is here the new and apostate church? May the devil stay with you in this blasphemous, murderous, sinful, pernicious thing. What is more, he does stay with you. We, however, have returned to the ancient church, God be praised and thanked!

Eighth, who has commanded you, contrary to the custom of the ancient church and the command of Christ, to preach differently than Christ commanded you? Matthew 28 [:20] says, "Go and teach them to observe all that I have commanded you," and not, "What you think is right and good"; John 14 [:26] says, "The Holy Spirit will teach you all things and bring to your remembrance all that I have said to you." You have so fully defiled all the churches and schools with the filth of your lies, that is, with human doctrines and lies, and you have spewed out so much of

202

your vomit that, as Isaiah [28:8] says, there is no more room left; and yet you still want to be honored as the church. Besides, the private mass is one of the worst abominations, whose harm and trouble can neither be measured nor fathomed. With it you have built the devil a new church and worshiped him, thereby turning into murderers of souls, just like Molech, the devourer of children.[26] But (unlike that Molech) you do not save the souls of the children after their bodies are burned, but on the contrary you keep the body alive for a short while and burn the soul in eternity. I am afraid to let my thoughts dwell much on the wretchedness of the countless, false, idolatrous, murderous doctrines within the papacy, that is to say, of your new lovely church.

Ninth, who has commanded you to make this sacrilegious innovation in the church, which is a spiritual kingdom, of giving it a bodily head, whom you call His All-Holiness, when there can be no other head than a spiritual one, that is, Christ? This is the third most malicious abomination in your all-holiest, indeed, all-hellish, church. The ancient church knows nothing of this. It stayed with its head, just as we have. It knew this to be the devil's own creation coming on account of sin, and it clearly declared this in II Thessalonians 2 [:4], "The man of sin and the son of perdition will take his seat in the temple of God, proclaiming himself to be God." For he lets himself be called an earthly god by you. Daniel also said [Dan. 11:37] that he would despise the ancient church and the God of his fathers and would institute a new god and a new church (which would help him to strengthen his new god). Who then is the new apostate church? Is it those in the ancient church, and we, who have stayed with the true ancient church and have avoided and fled from this new devil's head? Or is it those who worship the new devil's head, kiss his feet, are blessed by his two fingers, raise his doctrines above the word of God, and do not honor the ancient true head of the church with a bending of the knee, indeed, never think of him, not esteeming his blessing, which he has won for us with his whole body and blood? But this abomination is too abominable, so that

---

[26] Molech is the name of a Canaanite deity associated with the cult of sacrificing children, frequently by fire. See, for example, II Kings 23:10; Jer. 7:31; Ezek. 16:20-21.

to speak a little about it does not help at all, and yet no angel tongue is sufficient to speak of it adequately. What God's own mouth pronounces an abomination must be a greater abomination than any tongue could describe.

Tenth, who has commanded you to set up this new idolatry of worshiping the saints, canonizing them, and appointing fast days and feast days on which to honor them, just as if they were God himself, so that men rely on and trust in their merit more than in Christ himself, his blood and his merit? You have portrayed him for us as a judge, whom we must appease, and whose grace we must win through the merit and intercession of his mother and all the saints, together with our worship of the saints. The result is that your church has become in this matter nothing less than a heathen church, praying to Jove, Juno, Venus, Diana, and other dead men. Just as the Romans built a Pantheon in their city of Rome, so you have built a pantheon in the church, which is the church of all devils. You will not find this in the writings of the apostles, nor in the nascent church, which in former times would not even allow pictures of the saints—and a lot of blood was spilt over this[27]—not to mention invocations or prayers to them, things that belong to God alone.

Eleventh, who has commanded you to innovate by damning, reviling, and condemning marriage as impure and incapable of serving God? Have you got that from the apostles or from the original ancient church? Yes, indeed, for St. Paul says in I Timothy 4 [:1-3] that in later times you would come and would separate and depart from the ancient church and the faith. You would be like the devil's own whore, you would receive such teaching from the devil and would preach against marriage, and yet you would live in false, hypocritical chastity, that is, in every kind of unchastity. We see this innovation with its noble fruits in that the earth will no longer bear you, and God has already begun to strike with his judgment and to dedicate this new holy church to

---

[27] The iconoclastic controversy, which originated from contradictory interpretations of the Decalogue (Exod. 20:23), reached its climax in 726 when the Byzantine emperor Leo III (716-741) prohibited the use of images in the church. The seventh ecumenical council of Nicaea (787) finally decreed that images should be "revered" but not "worshiped." Cf. PNF² 14, 549-574.

the fires of hell, and he will not let you escape. We know that—
God be praised!

Twelfth, who has commanded you to make such innovations
as to rule with the secular sword and to wage war, and that chiefly
for the sake of shedding innocent blood? You sharp-eyed bats,[28]
when did you see the apostles or the ancient church coerce men
by the sword or enlarge the church by war? Where do you come
from, you who boast of being the heirs of the ancient church,
calling us the new apostate church—we who hold what the ancient
church held and are descended from her, whereas you are descended from that apostate devil's whore, your new murderous, lying church?

There are still more innovations, like purgatory, relics, consecration of churches, swarms of decrees and decretals,[29] and many
more countless books full of vain, new inventions, of which neither
the ancient church nor the apostles knew anything. For who can
tell the whole extent of this dirt or filth, indeed, poison, and of
these devilish lies? In this matter it is enough for the present to
demonstrate how shamefully the papists lie, through their Harrys,
when they call us the new, apostate, heretical church. For their
poisoned sword pierces their own heart [Ps. 37:15]; and it is evident that as the arch-whore of the devil they have abandoned the
ancient church and its ancient bridegroom and have not only become apostate and heretical (for that word is too light and too
honorable for such a hussy),[30] but Antichrist and "antigod," indeed, the last and most shameless bride of the devil, setting herself up even above God (just as her bridegroom in heaven wanted
to do) [II Thess. 2:3-4]. But we, because we flee from and avoid
all such deviltry and novelty and hold fast once more to the ancient church, the virgin and pure bride of Christ—we are certainly
the true, ancient church, without any whoredom or innovation.
This church has therefore remained till now, and it is out of it
that we have come. Indeed, we have been born anew of it as the

---

[28] An ironic remark, since Luther was quite familiar with the fact that bats
are nearly blind and shy away from light. Cf. WA 30ᴵᴵᴵ, 284.

[29] *Drecket* and *Dreckental*, a pun in German on "decretal." Luther frequently
employs it. Cf., for example, WA 47, 492; 50, 77.

[30] *Schandbübin.*

Galatians were of St. Paul [Gal. 4:19]. We too were formerly stuck in the behind of this hellish whore, this new church of the pope. We supported it in all earnestness, so that we regret having spent so much time and energy in that vile hole. But God be praised and thanked that he rescued us from the scarlet whore [Revelation 17].

If such innovations in the papacy were or could be simply novelties, they could to some extent be borne for the sake of peace, just as one bears or puts up with a new coat. But now this devilish poison and hellish murder is glued to it—it is the command of the church, the holy worship of God, the good and spiritual life, for which one deserves grace and life (if one obeys) or wrath and death (if one doesn't). That is to make truth out of falsehood, God out of the devil, heaven out of hell, and vice versa. For this reason the pope's church is full and swarming with falsehood, devils, idolatry, hell, murder, and every kind of calamity. Thus it is time to hear the voice of the angel in Revelation 18 [:4-5], "Come out of her, my people, lest you take part in her sins, lest you share in her plagues; for her sins are heaped high as heaven," etc.

When the painters of old painted the Last Judgment, they pictured hell as a great dragon's head with vast jaws, in the middle of which, in the fire, stood the pope, cardinals, bishops, priests, monks, emperors, kings, princes, all kinds of men and women, but never a young child.[31] I really do not know how one should, or could, paint or describe the church of the pope better, more to the point, or more clearly. It represents indeed the jaws of hell, and through the mouth of the devil, that is, through its devilish preaching and teaching, it swallows into the abyss of hell first and foremost the pope himself, and then all the world. It must have been by no means a simple man who devised it, perhaps on the basis of Isaiah 5 [:14], where he says, "Therefore Sheol has enlarged its appetite and opened its mouth beyond measure, and the nobility of Jerusalem and her multitude go down, her throng and he who exults in her." Whether it has been ex-

---

[31] Cf. Christian Rogge, *Luther und die Kirchenbilder seiner Zeit* (Leipzig, 1912), p. 27.

pressed like this by accident or as a joke, it is a very apt picture to delineate the papal church to a simple man, so that he may be on guard and flee from it, as something which has swallowed up everything except young baptized children. But more of that later.

Here they might say and probably will say, "Why do you depict us shamefully as a new, apostate church, when we have baptism, the sacrament, the keys, the creed, and the gospels, just like the ancient church from which we derive? Haven't you already admitted above that we, as well as you, derive from the ancient church?" I answer, "It is true, I admit, that the church in which you sit derives from the ancient church as well as we, and that you have the same baptism, the sacraments, the keys, and the text of the Bible and gospels. I will praise you even further and admit that we have received everything from the church before you (not from you). What more do you want? Are we not devout enough? Will you not call us henceforth unheretical? We do not regard you as Turks and Jews (as was said above) who are outside the church. But we say you do not remain in it but become the erring, apostate, whorelike church (as the prophets used to call it), which does not remain in the church, where it was born and brought up. You run away from this church and from your true husband and bridegroom (as Hosea says of the people of Israel [Hos. 1:2]) to the devil Baal,[32] to Molech and Astaroth.[33] Do you understand that?" I will explain.

You were indeed all baptized in the true baptism of the ancient church, just as we were, especially as children. Now if a baptized child lives and then dies in his seventh or eighth year, before he understands the whorelike church of the pope, he has in truth been saved and will be saved—of that we have no doubt. But when he grows up, and hears, believes, and obeys your preaching with its lies and devilish innovations, then he becomes a whore of the devil like you and falls away from his baptism and bridegroom—as happened to me and others—building and relying on his own works, which is what you whoremongers preach

---

[32] From the Hebrew "lord." A Canaanite god whose cult threatened Israel's religion. Cf., for example, the struggle between Elijah and the prophets of Baal in I Kings 18:17-40.
[33] The female counterpart of Baal.

in your brothels and devil's churches; whereas, by contrast, the child is baptized to rely and build on his one dear bridegroom and Lord, Jesus Christ, who gave himself for us. It is as if a devout man were to bring up a poor, young, servant beggar girl as his future bride and become betrothed to her, and she were to keep herself pure until she came to womanhood, and then turn her attentions elsewhere and look at other men who pleased her better, and let herself be persuaded by them and become passionately desirous of them, thus abandoning her true, devoted bridegroom, who had rescued, nourished, educated, clothed, adorned, and treated her well, and let herself be made a whore by everyone. This whore, who before was a pure virgin and dear bride, is now an apostate, erring, married whore, a house-whore, a bed-whore, a key-whore, being the mistress of the house, having the key, the bed, the kitchen, the cellar, and everything at her command. Yet she is so evil that beside her the common unattached whores, the pimp-whores, the whores of the field, the country, and the army are almost holy. For she is the true archwhore and the true whore of the devil.

Of such a whore Hosea speaks, and Ezekiel indeed does so much more coarsely, in fact almost too coarsely, in chapter 23. You should read that if you want to know what kind of a whore your church is. For this is what I mean when I call you an apostate, erring whore—you who were baptized as children in the dear Lord and even lived some years like the ancient church. But when you grew up and reached the age of reason (as I and everyone else have done), you saw and heard the lovely ceremonies of the papal church, and also its glittering profit, honor, and power, yes, its magnificent holiness, the mighty worship, and all the yarns about the kingdom of heaven. Then you forgot your Christian faith, baptism, and sacrament, becoming the diligent pupils and young little whores (as the comedies say) the procuresses,[34] the arch-whores, until you old whores once more make young whores. Thus the church of the pope, indeed, the church of the devil,

---

[34] *Lenae.* Aristophanes (448?-380? B.C.), the Greek comic-dramatist, satirizes them in *The Clouds.* Cf. Whitney J. Oates and Eugene O'Neill (eds.), *The Complete Greek Drama* (2 vols.; New York: Random House, 1938), II, 541-599.

grew, transforming many of Christ's young virgins, who were born in baptism, into arch-whores. This, I hold, should be said in German, so that you and everyone can understand what we mean. For if you hold these innovations of yours to be a joke—you who neither have a God nor honor him—then it is something terrible and abominable before God. It is idolatry, murder, hell, and every calamity, which God cannot bear, so that he will damn the arch-whore for eternity.

St. Peter prophesies about that when he speaks of you, that is, of such new prophets and churches in II Peter 2 [:18-19], "For, uttering loud boasts of folly, they entice with licentious passions of the flesh men who have barely escaped, and who must now walk in error. They promise them freedom, forgiveness, and indulgences,[35] but they themselves are slaves of corruption." And again, "For if, after they have escaped the defilements of the world through the knowledge of our Lord and Savior Jesus Christ, they are again entangled in them and overpowered, the last state has become worse for them than the first. For it would have been better for them never to have known the way of righteousness than after knowing it to turn back from the holy commandment delivered to them. It has happened to them according to the true proverb, the dog turns back to his own vomit, and the sow is washed only to wallow in the mire" [II Pet. 2:19-22]. That is what you are, and that is what I was. There you have your new apostate erring church sufficiently described in German and portrayed clearly enough for you to see.

We acknowledge not only that you have, with us, come from the true church and been washed and made clean in baptism through the blood of our Lord and Savior Jesus Christ, as St. Peter says here, but also that you are in the church and remain in it. Indeed, we say that you sit and rule in it as St. Paul prophesied in II Thessalonians 2 [:3-4], that the accursed Antichrist would sit (not in the cowshed), but in the temple of God. But you are no longer of the church, or members of the church, for in this holy church of God you are building your own new apostate church, the devil's brothel with limitless whoredom, idolatry, and innova-

---

[35] Luther has added "forgiveness" and "indulgences" to the biblical text.

tion, by which you corrupt those who have been baptized and redeemed along with yourselves. And you swallow them down
through the jaws of hell into the abyss of hell itself, with a countless multitude, along with the terrible wailing and deep sorrow of
those who see this with spiritual eyes and recognize it.

But it is God, who by his wonderful almighty power in the
midst of so much abomination among you and the whoredom of
the devil, nevertheless still sustains the young children through
baptism, and some old people, but only a few, who at the end of
their lives have turned once more to Christ, of whom I myself have
known many. So it is that the true ancient church with its baptism and the work of God still remains with you, and your god,
the devil, has not been able to obliterate it entirely with all this
new idolatry and all your devilish whoredom. It is just like the
time of Elijah, when (although the people were called God's people, that is, the holy church, and boasted of the God who had led
them out of Egypt) everything in the land was full of Baal, idolatry, and whoredom. Yet, although God had not kept a single
altar, seven thousand men, out of all the many thousands who had
fallen and gone to the devil, still remained among the greatest
and the best [I Kings 19:9-18]. And under Moses in the wilderness, all died except two, Joshua and Caleb [Num. 26:65]. God's
work is called "consummating and cutting short,"[36] since he saves
a few by grace, whereas the whole mass perish by his wrath. Of
this Paul speaks at length in Romans 10.

Daniel 12 [:1] also foretold long ago that under the Antichrist there would be a time of wrath and trouble such as there
had never been before in the world. And St. Paul too, in II Thessalonians 2 [:8-12], taking his prophecy from that very place in
Daniel, says that God will grow angry and send powerful errors
because the truth that saves has not been accepted in love. My
dear man, let us look at our own history, that is, the history of
Christendom: under Constantius, the son of Constantine, God's
wrath was so great that the Arian heretics were in control of all
the churches in the world except two;[37] at that time, in the eyes

---

[36] *Consummans et abbrevians.* A reference to the "remnant" in Isa. 10:22.
[37] Rome and Alexandria constantly opposed Arianism. On Constantius, see p.
79, n. 210.

of the world, the bishops and the Arians themselves were learned, devout, honorable, and diligent men. What then is to happen under the papacy, when no bishop can or does exercise his office, but lives like Epicureans[38] and sows? So the fat is in the fire! The papistic Harrys and the Harryish papists, therefore, understand what the church of God is much less than a cow or a sow. The church is a high, deep, hidden thing which one may neither perceive nor see, but must grasp only by faith, through baptism, sacrament, and word. Human doctrine, ceremonies, tonsures, long robes, miters, and all the pomp of popery only lead far away from it into hell—still less are they signs of the church. Naked children, men, women, farmers, citizens who possess no tonsures, miters, or priestly vestments also belong to the church.

Here the papists might perhaps desire, indeed, would enforce, the observing and tolerating of these new articles of their new church, along with the ancient articles of the ancient church; and if we do not keep them, they would call us heretics and kill us. For the papal asses are such stupid asses that they cannot and will not distinguish between God's word and human doctrine, but hold them both as one. They prove this by frequently proposing an agreement or compromise with us and by acting as if we ought to give up something if they were willing to do likewise; thus we would both be in agreement (although this has never been their real intention, and they have only meant to divide us and take some of our followers). Here one sees so well how they have set themselves above God like blaspheming Antichrists, and how they regard doctrine as true only as long as they want it to be. If they do not want it, then it is no longer true. They want to have the power to give up or hold on to some point of doctrine, and, to the extent that they give it up or hold on to it, we are to accept or reject it. They expect such filthy blasphemy of us, without shame, openly and publicly, thereby showing that they no longer have, as they did several centuries ago, a cunning devil spurring

---

[38] Named after Epicurus (341-271 B.C.), who taught Hedonism, i.e., the doctrine that pleasure is the chief end of life. Yet his ethics frequently stress a desire for peace rather than pleasure. Cf. Whitney J. Oates (ed.), *The Stoic and Epicurean Philosophers* (New York: Random House, 1957), pp. XVII-XVIII.

them on, but a palpable blockhead, a crude devil, who in his malice can no longer disguise himself.

Since they volunteer to give something up and want us to do the same, they show that for them the word of God and the doctrines of men are of equal value. Oh, yes, to give up or change the word of God is not open even to God himself, for he cannot deny or change himself [II Tim. 2:13], and his word remains for ever [Isa. 40:8]. Whoever is to change or limit it must have a greater power than God himself, for he would not have altered the law of Moses if he had not previously promised, in his word, to alter it. No one would dare to do that except Antichrist— namely, the papacy—who, as Daniel 12 [11:36] and St. Paul [II Thess. 2:4] say, sets himself up against God.

Now what should one do with such people, with these vulgar Harrys and great asses who think God's word is a reed bent by the wind [Matt. 11:7], over which they have power? Or rather, they regard it as a counter,[39] the value of which depends on their damned wantonness, according to how they move it up and down on the board. How well they understand what the church is! Indeed, they thereby show how much they despise God and his word. Moreover, they set themselves up above God and thus cannot be his church. And that vulgar boor, blockhead, and lout from Wolfenbüttel, that ass to cap all asses, screams his heehaws, judges, and calls men heretical. Why, he could never learn if he studied a hundred years, not even if he heard his masters in the whole of the papacy tell what the church is and what a heretic is, what Christ is and what an apostate is. This would take too great a measure of understanding. But he could indeed teach his masters, and even the pope himself, what arson is.[40]

The holy Christian church (I am speaking to our own people now, for with the papal ass and with these Harrys and other blocks and stones there is no reasoning, no perception or listening) is neither a reed nor a counter. No, it does not waver or give way, like the devil's whore—the papal church—who, like an adulteress,

---

[39] *Zalpfennig.*

[40] A reference to charges of arson made against Henry of Wolfenbüttel; see the Introduction, p. 182.

thinks she need not remain faithful to her husband, but may waver, yield, and submit to the will of the whoremonger. It is (as St. Paul says) a pillar and bulwark of the truth [I Tim. 3:15]. It stands firm (he says) and is a bulwark and sure foundation. It is not a bulwark of falsehood and lies, but a bulwark of truth, neither lying nor deceiving; it has no truck with lies. But whatever wavers or doubts cannot be truth; and what would be the use or need of a church of God in the world if it wanted to waver or be uncertain in its words, or wanted to say something new every day, now asserting this, now rejecting that? Moreover, of what use would a God like this be, who wanted to teach us to waver and to doubt—just as the theology of the papists teaches that one must doubt grace? But enough has been written about that.[41] Even if the papists had won in everything else, they still lose this major point when they teach that we must doubt the grace of God if we are not already worthy enough through our own satisfaction or merit or the prayers of the saints. That is the purpose of their books, letters, seals, convents, monasteries, and even of their tonsures and masses.

Because they teach reliance on works and doubt—indeed, they cannot do otherwise—it is quite certain that they must be the devil's church. For there are not, and could not be, more than these two ways: the one which relies upon God's grace, and the other which builds on our own works and merit. The first is the way of the ancient church, of all the patriarchs, prophets, and apostles, as Scripture testifies. The other is the way of the pope and his church, and that is something no one, not even Harry and all the devils in hell, can deny. There is the testimony (as has often been said) of books, bulls, seals, letters, convents, and monasteries, so that one can prove it to all the world.

And there is the testimony of St. Peter in Acts 4 [:12], "There is no other name under heaven given among men by which we must be saved, except Jesus Christ alone." Against that, Pope Harry of Rome says, "Not at all! There are many other names by which people should be saved, in particular, my name, and after

---

[41] Cf., for example, *Disputation Against Scholastic Theology* (1517). *LW* 31, 9-16.

that those I choose—St. Francis, St. Dominic,[42] and all the works which bring me money and lay kings and emperors at my feet. Here is holiness and salvation, and there is no more need or use for Christ," etc.

But to return to our point: they must themselves admit, whether they like it or not, that the church of Christ neither lies nor deceives. Otherwise, where would they be? They themselves must say that it is a rock, Matthew 16 [:18], against which the gates of hell will not prevail, or as St. Paul says, commenting on this, a pillar and bulwark of the truth [I Tim. 3:15]. We do not (I say) congratulate them on admitting this. The children's faith[43] also says the church is holy and Christian. And St. Paul says in I Corinthians 3 [:17], "For God's temple is holy, and that temple you are. If any one destroys God's temple, God will destroy him."

Therefore the holy church cannot and may not lie or suffer false doctrine, but must teach nothing except what is holy and true, that is, God's word alone; and where it teaches a lie it is idolatrous and the whore-church of the devil. What help was it to the kings of Israel to boast that they served the God of Israel, who had led them out of Egypt? Indeed, they sought and called on the true God of their fathers, and they also held the law of Moses. But since, in addition, they honored calves and Baal, or at least instituted their own new worship in honor of the true God in their religious fervor, they lost everything. For God's command, "You shall have no other God before me" [Deut. 5:7], stood against this; and Deuteronomy 4 [:2] and 12 [:32] had strongly forbidden them to undertake anything new or different on their own, saying, "You shall not add to the word which I command you, nor take from it." And again, "You shall not turn aside to the right hand or to the left" [Deut. 5:32], that is, to make it better or worse, to limit or to change it. Therefore we read everywhere in the prophets how they rebuke the kings, priests, and people for always inventing new ways and not remaining on the one and only path.

---

[42] St. Dominic (1170-1221), founder of the Order of Friars Preachers. On St. Francis, see p. 128, n. 347.
[43] *Kinderglaube*, i.e., the catechism.

For whatever departs from the word of God (which is the only way, as Christ says, "I am the way, and the truth, and the life" [John 14:6]), however well and beautifully it may glitter, is without question error, lie, and death. It is without the word of God, that is, without the way, the truth, and the life. And what need would we have of the word if we could find ways for ourselves without it? For the word alone is the lamp to our feet, and the light to our path [Ps. 119:105], which, as St. Peter says, shines in the darkest place of this world [II Pet. 1:19]. Whoever does not hold it constantly and steadfastly before his eyes—where else can he go but into darkness? The light therefore is there in the darkness so that we can guide ourselves by it.

Now let us look in turn at each of these new things which have arisen in the pope's new church. We discover that they have all been invented without God's word, that is, without the way, the truth, and the light, but rather out of human devotion or opinion, or the malice of the pope. Therefore, as the church of the pope is full of indulgences, human merit, brotherhoods, worship of saints, monkery, masses, satisfaction, and the things we have already mentioned, such as worship, it is full of error, falsehood, idolatry, unbelief, murder, and is the epitome of the church of all the devils. They cannot say that God's word teaches such things. On the contrary, they have to confess that the holy Christian church must be holy and a bulwark of the truth, without error or falsehood, because the church cannot err.[44] But at the same time they must confess that they are not and cannot be such a holy church, since they are full of abominable errors, lies, and idolatry. In fact, they must confess that they are the true, erring, apostate, shameless whore of the devil, whom they follow and serve with such abominable lies.

Now a kindhearted man (as they say) might ask, "What harm is there if one holds to the word of God and yet lets all these matters, or at least those that are bearable, remain as well?" I answer, "They may be called kindhearted, but they are wrong-hearted and misled, for you have heard that it is impossible to teach any word other than God's word, to serve anyone other than

---

[44] *Quia ecclesia non potest errare.*

215

God, to light any light other than that which has been placed by God in the darkness" [Matt. 6:24]. It is indeed an error and a will-o'-the-wisp thing, even if it were only one single thing, for the church ought not and cannot teach lies and error. If it teaches one lie, then it is wholly false, as Christ says in Luke 11 [:35-36], "Be careful lest the light in you be darkness. If then your whole body is full of light, having no dark part, it will be wholly bright." That is to say, it must be all light, without any darkness in it. The church must teach God's word and truth alone, and not error or falsehood. And how could it be otherwise? For God's mouth is the mouth of the church, and vice versa. God cannot lie, nor can the church.

It is, of course, quite true that if judged by its way of life, the holy church is not without sin, as it confesses in the Lord's Prayer, "Forgive us our trespasses"; and John writes [I John 1:8, 10], "If we say we have no sin, we lie and make God a liar, who calls us all sinners"—also Romans 3 [:23], Psalm 14 [:3] and 51 [:7]. But doctrine should not be sinful or reproachable. It does not belong to the Lord's Prayer and its petition, "Forgive us our trespasses," because it is not something we do, but is God's own word, which cannot sin or do wrong. A preacher should neither pray the Lord's Prayer nor ask for forgiveness of sins when he has preached (if he is a true preacher), but should say and boast with Jeremiah, "Lord thou knowest that which came out of my lips is true and pleasing to thee" [Jer. 17:16]; indeed, with St. Paul and all the apostles and prophets, he should say firmly, *Haec dixit dominus*, "God himself has said this" [I Cor. 1:10]. And again, "In this sermon I have been an apostle and a prophet of Jesus Christ" [I Thess. 4:15]. Here it is unnecessary, even bad, to pray for forgiveness of sins, as if one had not taught truly, for it is God's word and not my word, and God ought not and cannot forgive it, but only confirm, praise, and crown it, saying, "You have taught truly, for I have spoken through you and the word is mine." Whoever cannot boast like that about his preaching, let him give up preaching, for he truly lies and slanders God.

If the word were to be sinful or untrue, after what would or could men guide their lives? Then, no doubt, a blind man would

216

lead a blind man, and both would fall into the pit [Matt. 15:14]. If the plumb line[45] or the T-square were false or crooked, what kind of work would or could the master-builder produce? One crooked thing would make the other crooked, without limit or measure. Life too can be sinful and untrue in the same way—unfortunately life is indeed very untrue—but doctrine must be straight as a plumb line, sure, and without sin. Therefore nothing must be preached in church except the sure, pure, and one word of God. Where that is missing, we no longer have the church, but the synagogue of the devil [Rev. 2:9], just as a godly wife (an example the prophets always use)[46] should not listen to any other word in her house or in her bed than that of her husband, and if she does listen to the word of someone who does not belong in her husband's bed, she is certainly a whore.

Now the purpose of all this is to show that the church must teach God's word alone, and must be sure of it. The church is the pillar and bulwark of the truth, built on the rock, and called holy and irreproachable [Eph. 2:21]. Thus one rightly and truly says, "The church cannot err, for God's word which it teaches cannot err." But whatever else is taught or whatever is not with certainty God's word, cannot be the doctrine of the church, but must be the doctrine, falsehood, and idolatry of the devil. The devil cannot say (since he is a liar and the father of lies), "God says this." But, as Christ says in John 8 [:44], he must speak *ex propriis*, "from and of himself," that is, he must lie; and so, without God's word, all his children speak from and of themselves, that is, they must lie.

Now observe, my dear friend, what a wonderful thing this is: we who teach God's word with such certainty are so weak, and in our great humility so timid, that we do not like to brag that we are God's church, witnesses, servants, and preachers, and that God speaks through us, etc. And yet, we do not doubt it, since we are certain to have and to teach his word. Such timidity stems from the fact that we earnestly believe God's word is such a noble and majestic thing that we regard ourselves far too unworthy of its

---

[45] A reference to Amos 7:7.
[46] See pp. 208-209, where Luther discusses Hosea and Ezekiel 23.

being spoken and done through us who are still creatures of flesh and blood. But our adversaries, the devils, the papists, the sects,[47] and all the world, are confident and intrepid, asserting with great holiness and arrogance, "Here is God, we are God's church, his servants, prophets, and apostles." It is just like every false prophet has always done, so that even Harry-wurst[48] dares to boast that he himself is a Christian prince. But the true sign of the true holy church has always been humility and fear in the word of God, whereas lust and wantonness in innovating have been the true signs of the devil—something that becomes quite evident from the pope's decretals.[49]

This we say about doctrine, which must be pure and clean, namely, the dear, blessed, holy, and one word of God, without any addition. But life, which should daily direct, purify, and sanctify itself according to doctrine, is not yet entirely pure or holy, so long as this maggoty body of flesh and blood is alive. But as long as it is in the process of purification and sanctification, being continually healed by the Samaritan[50] and no longer decaying in its own impurity, it is graciously excused, pardoned, and forgiven for the sake of the word, through which it is healed and purified; thus it must be called pure. This is why the holy Christian church is not a whore or unholy, because it continues to hold to and remain with the word (which is its holiness) without blemish and with strength. "You are already made clean (says Christ in John 15 [:3]) by the word which I have spoken to you," not on your own account.

The holiness of the word and the purity of doctrine are powerful and sure, so that even if Judas, Caiaphas, Pilate, the pope, Harry, or the devil himself preached it, or baptized truly (purely, without addition), they would still receive the true, pure word and the true, holy baptism, for there must always be hypocrites and false Christians in the church and a Judas among the apostles. Again, the impurity of doctrine that is not or is without God's word is such a poisonous evil that even if St. Peter, indeed, an

---

[47] *Rotten;* see p. 66, n. 191.
[48] *Heintz worst,* a pun on *Hanswurst.*
[49] *Dreckete.* Cf. p. 205, n. 29.
[50] Cf. Luke 10:29-37.

angel from heaven, were to preach it, he would nevertheless be accursed, Galatians 1 [:8]. Therefore those who teach, baptize, or distribute the sacrament falsely cannot be or remain in the church, as Psalm 1 [:5] says. For they act not only against the life the church must endure—particularly when it is hidden—but also against the doctrine that must gleam and shine in public to be a guide for life. This has been taught from the beginning, as St. John says, "They went out from us, but they were not of us" [I John 2:19], and, "They are in the church but not of the church";[51] or, "In number but not in merit,"[52] and the like. Accordingly, we draw this distinction: not all are Christians who pretend to be Christians. But when there is disagreement in doctrine, it becomes quite evident who the true Christians are, namely, those who have God's word in purity and refinement.

That is enough for now on the true church, about which there is much to say. If they want to hear more about who they are they should have their Harry write more on this subject because they know no one better. For he is an excellent man, as skilful, clever, and versed in Holy Scripture as a cow in a walnut tree or a sow on a harp.[53] He, as you might think, can accomplish such great feats quite well—especially when it comes to lying, slandering, and cursing. They are indeed not worthy of anyone better. "Cattle are like the cattle-shed," said the devil, and pushed a fly into his mother's rear-end![54]

Now if the papists will or can prove that they are the true holy church, and have neither taught nor held any of the above-mentioned articles and inventions of the whore-church, or if they can prove that our articles are not the articles of the true ancient church—we did not invent or devise them—then we must indeed confess that we are heretics and apostates. But if they cannot prove it, they must also, for their part, confess that they are the true whore-church of the devil that has strayed from Christ its

---

51 *In ecclesia sunt, sed non de ecclesia.*

52 *Numero, sed non de merito.*

53 A German proverb, *"Wie eine Kü auff dem Nusbaum"* and, *"Wie eine Saw auff der Harffen."* Cf. Thiele, *Luthers Sprichwörtersammlung*, No. 76.

54 The original reads, *"Es ist viehe und stal sprach der Teufel, und treib seiner mutter eine fliegen in den hindern." Ibid.*

Lord and has let the devil bring it into disgrace through new and different doctrine. This, I think, should be a certainty, even if Jews and heathen, or whoever possesses human reason, were to judge between us.

If they are not the church but the devil's whore that has not remained faithful to Christ, then it is irrefutably and thoroughly established that they should not possess church property, much less stir up this contention (with which they have till now troubled both emperor and empire) that they should be reinstated among us and have their property restored.[55] It is just as if the devils desired that the angels reinstate them in heaven, even though they know and confess that they have not remained God's angels, but have become his enemies, and belong to the fire of hell. Or, to speak of men, it is as if a thief or murderer were to insist on the return of the money or goods he had stolen or robbed which had been recovered from him and held by the court or given back to the rightful owner, and, if refused, were to threaten to become Harry the arsonist.[56]

But since there is no judge on earth in this matter—for the judges have become a party in the case since they previously had appointed themselves the chief judges, and thus their judgment is not valid according to all law; indeed, it has as little value as ours has with them because we are the other party—we must let it pass and wait for the true judge. Otherwise, if there were a judge on earth in this matter, it would be his judgment that they (for their part) not only have no right to demand restitution, but deserve to be expelled from the world, and treated as King Jehu treated the followers of Baal [II Kings 10:24-25], and as King Josiah treated the priests at Samaria and Bethel [II Kings 23:20]. For they are (as proved above) before God and in the judgment of Holy Scripture the true den of robbers and devil's whore. Consequently, they (as the arch-robbers of the church and thieves of God) have seized the churches, that is, the property of poor Christendom, and wantonly withheld it; and as compensation for this they then per-

---

[55] On the various negotiations concerning control over ecclesiastical property, cf. Köstlin, *Martin Luther*, II, 559-575.
[56] See p. 182.

secute and harm it, destroying themselves in body and honor for time and eternity.

A seven-year-old child, indeed, a silly fool, can figure it out on his fingers—although that stupid ass, the pope, together with his damned Harrys cannot understand anything—that the worthy emperors, princes, lords, and pious people of former days undoubtedly neither intended nor desired to give their property for the purpose of adorning and honoring nothing but the devil's whores and idolatry, much less to educate and to support murderers of men's souls, robbers of churches, Harrys, and arsonists. On the contrary, they desired to support good churches and schools, that is to say, the holy word of God, the office of preaching and other services, theologians, ministers, preachers, in addition to the poor, the widows, the orphans, and the sick—all this to the praise and glory of God.

It is not called the property of whores, murderers, blasphemers, the devil, or arsonists named Harry, but it is called the property of the church. Yet it is now not only bought, sold, stolen, robbed, and wasted by the spiritual whores of the devil in the papal den of murderers in the most shameful way by simony and every kind of vice, but it is also dissipated and squandered by real whores and scoundrels in the most shameless way. This is much worse than what happened at Sodom and Gomorrah; they do not even give a penny's help to a poor priest, a schoolboy, or a poor man, for they are not good enough to do such a small thing, but rather, like the wicked Epicureans, they both mock and deride God himself, his word, and his church. That indeed is the beautiful, holy church that still boasts of being holy, regards church property as its own, and demands restitution. But he who will give true restitution to such desperate, wanton mockers and such raging murderers will soon come.

But as long as we have no judge on earth, we shall, for the moment, use the judgment and testimony of the papists themselves on our own behalf and against them, in addition to the judgment of God, the highest judge, in his Holy Scripture. Even Duke George,[57] of unhappy memory, said that he knew perfectly

---

[57] Duke George was the ruler of Albertine Saxony (1500-1539). In 1485 Sax-

well many abuses had spread within the church; but that one single monk from some obscure place should attempt a reformation, that he could not endure. Now then, he confesses (and undoubtedly not he alone) that your church is full of abuses—which means that it is not the true, pure church, for the church must be pure and holy, without any additions, not to mention abuses. As the creed says, "I believe in one, holy, Christian church."

Thus you, for your part, entreated the emperor at the Diet of Augsburg[58] to persuade the pope to prevent any further sending of indulgences to Germany, because they were held in contempt. Here you yourselves confess that indulgences are contemptible, that is, an abuse and idolatry. If you held them to be right and good, a pure service of God, you could not in good conscience hold them in contempt, nor ask to have them abolished. Your conscience here testifies, by your own word, that your church is a pagan temple and impure and that it served, and still serves, the devil and not God, with false, worthless, and deceitful indulgences.

Third, the cardinal of Mainz[59] has said, "What is the point of a lot of disputation? They have an article which we know and cannot deny is right, namely, marriage, but which we cannot accept."[60] And even if the cardinal had never said that, you yourselves are by this time so convinced of it that any of you who want to be the best openly confess it. Now tell me: do you think it was a little whore of the devil who set up, instituted, taught, honored, and held this dreadful article (that is, idol) in the church, so that God's creatures, his work and ordinance of creation, and his blessing might be damned, accursed, and thought of as the greatest sin? What evil could the devil himself, the enemy of God, institute if he wanted to institute something against God? How could your church have been holy if you had served such an idol (even though you had lived like pure virgins) with such an abomination? For God forbade such as a doctrine of the devil, II

ony had been divided into two parts because there were two heirs, Ernest and Albert. Cf. Schwiebert, *Luther and His Times*, pp. 81-85. Duke George's statement is recorded in *WA*, TR 2, 542.

[58] Luther refers to the Diet of Augsburg in 1530.

[59] Cardinal Albrecht; see p. 15, n. 12.

[60] *WA*, TR 4, 299.

Timothy 4 [:1-4]. And you yourselves must bewail the kind of fruit and holiness which this idol and its idolatrous worship have brought forth in your church. For Rome, the monasteries, and the entire clergy[61] bear witness; indeed, their sin has filled heaven and earth with shame and cries of bloodshed. Where then is your holy church which with such abomination has been so abominably made into a whore by the devil?

And what have you yourselves done that you now desire a council, now promising it, then again postponing it, and at other times refusing it?[62] If your church is holy, why does it fear a council? Why does it fear a reformation or a council? If it needs a council, how can it be holy? Do you want to reform your holiness too? We, for our part, have never desired a council to reform our church. God and the Holy Spirit already sanctified our church through his holy word and, indeed, purged away all papal whoredom and idolatry, so that we have everything (God be praised) pure and holy—the word, baptism, the sacrament, the keys, and everything which belongs to the true church—without the addition and filth of human doctrine. Life (as was said above) is not lived completely according to our insight and wishes, a fact bewailed by the prophets and apostles themselves; for this belongs to the time when we shall be like angels [Matt. 22:30].

But we desire a council so that our church may be examined and our doctrine come freely to light—and your whoredom in the papacy be recognized and condemned. Thus everyone who is misled by it may, together with us, be converted to the true holy church and sustained in it. But you, and your god the devil, have no desire for this. You bats, moles, horned owls, night ravens, and screech owls who cannot bear the light do all in your guile and power to prevent, by all means, the truth from being heard and discussed in the light. Yet God never stops his activity: the more you seek to prevent it, the sooner he brings it to light, so that at last you will have to bear it with all its shame and hurt. And let your conscience and your own heart tell you whether your timid,

---

[61] *Geistlicher Stand*, literally, "the spiritual estate." This term has been variously translated as, for example, "order," "estate," or "vocation."

[62] The possibility of holding a council had first been mentioned by Luther in 1518. On the many delays, see pp. 5-6.

fearful, desperate shunning of the light could either frighten us or give you confidence.

Because now, as I say, you yourselves confess and, indeed, must confess, what a vile church you have—I do not here speak of life, but of doctrine; you have so many abominable lies and so much false doctrine which you do not wish to abandon—you must further admit that you are not the holy church, but the devil's church, especially those who uphold the doctrine and compel others to do the same, for they knowingly worship the devil in his lies because they admit that these articles are untrue. But that is what you do from the pope on down to the lowest priest and monk. That is the essence, the core, of what you call your church, not counting the lay members, who represent the temporal estate.[63] They who regret these things do not belong to your devil's whore-church but to our church, that is, the true ancient and holy church.

Moreover, since we have your own testimony and judgment, you cannot call us heretics and apostates, but must agree with us; as the true church we reject your known abominations and your untrue articles of faith and, conversely, abandon you, the true church of the devil, because you defend abominations and untrue articles of faith, as you yourself have confessed, and compel others to hold them. Moreover, you have to admit that church property is not yours to dispose of like spoils[64] that ought to be returned to you, but that as thieves of God and robbers of churches, it is your duty to give up, restore, and surrender to the true church all the property you still possess. And even if you had a harlot's brow (as the prophets say [Jer. 3:3]), incapable of shame, you yourselves would nevertheless have to say that such a verdict is a true one. For in the end, wood, stone, mud, and dung would cry out against you, because it is impossible for a desperate whore to be a chaste and pious virgin. Therefore she ought not to be a church or rule a church or have any church property—that is the sum of it all!

That Harry goes on to call the elector, that is, all of us, rebellious,[65] can be refuted in the same way, namely, that this in-

---

[63] *Weltlichen stenden.*
[64] *Spolium.*
[65] For the passages in the *Rejoinder*, see WA 51, 532, n. 1.

famous liar boxes his own ears,[66] or, rather, as was said above in the words of Psalm 37 [:15], his sword entered his own heart. But I know quite well that he has never in his life known or experienced what obedience or disobedience is and therefore cannot know what rebellion or public peace are,[67] as his writings and his whole life prove; nevertheless, even if he knew how evil it is, he is so full of demons that he would still dare to do it and to involve others in it. But so that we may serve God and spite this Harry-like devil, we confess this truth: our princes and lords have always obeyed the emperor truly and sincerely, as the whole empire must publicly testify. Wherever they have been summoned, whether to imperial diets or to battle, they have been the first to go, so that you, devil and Hanswurst, are in this matter a particularly silly *wurst* to lie so shamefully against the testimony of the empire.

But if your Harry means that our princes do not obey imperial edicts, in which our church and our doctrine are damned, then we boast and thank God, who has mercifully supported us, that we are not to be found with you in such damned obedience. God stands in the way, forbidding us and saying, "Render to Caesar the things that are Caesar's, and to God the things that are God's" [Matt. 22:21], and Psalm 115 [:16] says, "The heavens are the Lord's heavens, but the earth he has given to the sons of men." Heaven, the kingdom of heaven, is not an imperial fief, and God cannot be a vassal of the emperor, but the emperor ought to be and be called God's vassal, as Sirach 17 [Ecclus. 17:17] also says, "In other lands God has appointed rulers, but in Israel he is himself Lord." God himself, and he alone, will teach and rule in the church. Such rule he has never surrendered to another or let fall from his hand, as Psalm 60 [:6] testifies, "God has spoken in his sanctuary."

Therefore you papists must fight out such matters of obedi-

---

[66] A German proverb. See p. 113, n. 305.

[67] *Landfriede.* A temporary truce (*pax publica*), secured by law in 1495 in Germany. It was an attempt to curb the feuds between princes after the medieval church was unsuccessful in preventing war through the similar Truce of God. See *O.D.C.C.*, p. 1378.

ence with God himself, not with us; or else you must fully convince us beforehand, so that we (as you do) may give to the emperor what belongs to God. Otherwise, we will not do it, but rather we will accept your blaspheming and lying with great delight, for thereby you testify and confess that we do not take from God what is his and give it to the emperor. And with your poisonous lies you help us to boast the truth that we do not live in your accursed obedience. For God has prohibited the emperor and, indeed, all angels and creatures from teaching any word other than his in his heavenly kingdom, that is, in the church, as Paul declares like a thunderclap in Galatians 1 [:8], "If an angel from heaven should preach to you a gospel contrary to that which we preached to you, let him be accursed." Now we have related above several of the countless pieces of new and different doctrine (that is, as St. Paul calls it here, *anathema*, "cursing, damnation, execration") of which your new papal whore and devil's church is full. Therefore neither the emperor nor any other creature can compel us to such accursed obedience. Indeed, he ought, with us, to keep himself from it, if he does not want to be cursed and dashed to the depths of hell by St. Paul's thunderbolt.

God has committed enough to the emperor, more indeed than he can manage, namely, the earthly kingdom, that is, men's bodies and goods. There his office ends. If he reaches beyond that into God's kingdom, then he robs God of what is his, and that is called *sacrilegium*, "stealing from God," or as St. Paul calls it in Philippians 2 [:6], "grasping equality with God."[68] When someone desires to be equal with God, which he cannot be, then he must want to steal this equality, for it cannot be given to him. There is only one single inheritor of it, having neither stolen nor desired to steal it [Phil. 2:6] (as did the devil in heaven and Adam in paradise), but having received it from the Father in eternity was born with it by nature. Those who now entice the pious Emperor Charles[69] to do this, or who do so under his seal, are creatures as pious as the serpent in Paradise. The emperor should remain under God and act according to his distinct command (just like all

---

[68] *Rapinam divinitatis.*
[69] Charles V.

226

other creatures). For here, that is, in the church, God wants to speak himself, and will suffer no one else.

It is (if I may make it plain in this way) like a husband or bridegroom who can indeed appoint many an office in his home; he may call one servant emperor, another king, and he may commit all his property to them—his field to this one and his vineyard, cattle, fish, clothes, money, and goods to that one. Yet in his bedroom and his bed no servant may be found, be he called emperor or king, for that is death (as Solomon says in Proverbs [14:12]); the bridegroom alone belongs there, and the bride should not hear or know any word other than her bridegroom's alone, as John the Baptist says, "He who has the bride is the bridegroom" [John 3:29]. Thus God cannot and will not suffer anyone besides himself in the church. One ought to hear nothing except God himself and his word there, otherwise, the church becomes a whore, not his bride.

It becomes quite evident, from all this, what you Harrys and little Harrys do when you call us rebels because, unlike you, we do not obey the imperial edicts. For this is what you do: you confess that we keep the bride of Christ and the bridal bed pure for our Lord Christ alone, serving outside in our appointed offices as faithful and obedient Josephs [Gen. 39:2-23]; whereas you, lustful pimps and adulterers, that is, robbers of God and rebels against heaven, burst in on the Lord in his bedchamber and want to turn his bride into a whore. But he will strike you with blindness, like the Sodomites, so that you cannot find the door [Gen. 19:11], and he lets you find your own kind, whores and adulterers, who obey you and go to the devil with you. In a word, as I have said, fight it out first with God if you want us to hear and teach something other than God's word in the church. Likewise, if your above-mentioned innovations are God's word, and you are the holy church, then you are right, and we will gladly obey. But what is the use of your shouting out the "conclusion" so emphatically, leaving the "premise"[70] alone? The conflict is not over the conclusion you senseless fools shout about, but over the premise. "If the church is established with certainty, then obedience follows of necessity. Conversely, if the church is not established, then obedience does

---

[70] *Consequens; antecedens.*

not follow. It is a relative question"[71]—as you can see if there is still a spark of "dialectics"[72] in you.

That is enough about the church now in answer to the slanderous mouth of the papists, though someone else could no doubt say it better, and I, if I live, could say more. Yet Harry the arsonist still goes on to defame the way we live in several ways. He denounces my gracious lord and the landgrave[73] with a heap of gross invectives, but, as is the way with liars, he does not prove a single point. But I have confessed above, and must unfortunately confess, that although we have the pure doctrine of the divine word, and a fine, pure, holy church like that of apostolic times in all matters profitable and necessary for salvation, we are neither holier nor better than Jerusalem, God's own holy city, where there were so many wicked people, yet where God's word was always kept pure by the prophets.

Thus we are still creatures of flesh and blood, and the devil is indeed to be found among the sons of Job [Job 1:6]. The peasant is wild, the burgher covetous, the nobleman acquisitive. With God's word we shout and rebuke with confidence, and we prevent all we can, and, God be praised, it is not without success. For those peasants, burghers, nobles, and lords who listen and let themselves be taught are (God be praised) very good, and do more than one desires, some more than they are able. Even if there are few of them, it does not matter. God can help a whole country for the sake of one man, as with the Syrian Naaman [II Kings 5:1] and the like. In a word, there is no need to quarrel about the way we live, for we gladly and freely admit that we are not as holy as we ought to be. But we have the advantage that these Harrys cannot, in good conscience, reprove us before God or the world, unless they are first more godly than we; otherwise, Christ has already damned them by saying, "You hypocrite! First take the log out of your own eye" [Luke 6:42]. If they have to take the log out of their own eye first and prove they are more godly than we, then

---

[71] *Ponatur ecclesia certo, et obedientia sequetur necessario. E contra: non positar ecclesia, nulla sequitur obedientia, ex natura relativorum.*

[72] *Dialecticae,* a term used in medieval scholastic argument. Cf. *O.C.D.,* p. 271.

[73] Philip; see p. 181, n. 2.

we are safe eternally. For, as we have related above, what we have against them is not only the speck (that is, the way of life), but also the big log (that is, doctrine). And for us it is not a laughing matter that there is evil in our midst, as it is for them in their church, as Solomon says in Proverbs 2 [:14], "They rejoice in doing evil, and delight in the perverseness of evil." Moreover, they would defend it with sword and fire.

Oh, why so many words! He upon whom God's wrath has so mightily fallen that he must revile and curse his God and Lord (as Isaiah 8 [:21] says of the Jews) will indeed let nothing that God creates or does or speaks go unreviled and uncursed, for such a man has in fact become a devil. Now it is certain that these Harrys must admit that we teach God's word and that our church teaches nothing but what God has commanded. That is quite evident, and neither Harry nor the devil can deny it. And yet they slander and curse our church and its doctrine, calling us heretics and rebels, etc. That is nothing less than calling God himself (whose doctrine and church it is) a heretic, slandering and cursing him. Now if God himself and his holy word have to be slandered like this by such devils, what won't they do to our life and works? If God exposes himself, his word and doctrine, to the insults of these Harrys, we should expose our lives, which by contrast are not entirely holy, even more.

But to give a short answer for our people's sake (not for the sake of Harry, the devil of Wolfenbüttel, who does not deserve the trouble a pious man would take in answering his brazen lies), I will answer him as briefly as I can in one or two points. First, when he writes that this rumpus, which was so stirred up by Luther, was caused by Duke Frederick because he did not want Bishop Albrecht to be bishop of Magdeburg, etc.,[74] I must excuse the worthy and godly prince and say that in this not only Harry but also Mainz[75] (from whom come such lies in other places as well) lie like desperate scoundrels, as their own conscience is witness. According to my knowledge at the time, Duke Frederick took pains to help the present bishop of Magdeburg become

---

[74] For the passages in the *Rejoinder*, cf. WA 51, 537, n. 1.

[75] A German rhyme, *"Heinz und Mainz,"* i.e., "Harry and Albrecht."

bishop. Moreover, there was at that time no duke of Saxony on whose account Duke Frederick would have had to scheme to get him made bishop.[76]

However, be this as it may, I know that I once heard in Lochau[77] (for I have never in all my life heard his voice, or seen his face, except at the Diet of Worms)[78] that the same pious Duke Frederick so praised Bishop Albrecht and was so pleased with him as one who would make a promising prince for the empire that it was really astonishing. For when he came back from Zerbst, where a discussion took place between von Lüneburg and Braunschweig,[79] after the battle in which Harry had taken to his heels and fled as fast as his legs would carry him[80] (for those there were not poor, unarmed cooks and messenger boys who would let themselves be run through unawares)[81]—now (I say) when Duke Frederick himself, as a representative of the empire after the death of Maximilian,[82] had negotiated with Bishop Albrecht and come home, he was so pleased with him and had such high hopes for him that he spoke of him genially in this way, "Leave him

---

[76] Frederick the Wise was the sole ruler of Saxony from 1486 to 1500, when Duke George inherited Albertine Saxony. On Albrecht's election as archbishop, cf. Schwiebert, *op. cit.*, pp. 306-314.

[77] A town in Saxony where Frederick the Wise hunted.

[78] The Diet of Worms was held in 1521. Luther usually communicated with Duke Frederick through George Spalatin (1484-1545), Luther's good friend at the elector's court.

[79] A reference to the conflict between the houses of Lüneburg and Braunschweig, known as the feud of Hildesheim (*Hildesheimer Stiftsfehde*). When Bishop John of Hildesheim intensified his quarrel with several of his fiefholders, Henry joined an alliance against him. John of Hildesheim defeated this alliance in the battle of Soltau on June 28, 1519. Despite his involvement, Henry escaped imprisonment. For a more detailed account, see *Allgemeine Deutsche Biographie*, ed. Historische Kommission bei der Königlichen Akademie der Wissenschaften (56 vols.; Leipzig, 1875-1912), XI, 492-495.

[80] A German proverb, *"Das hasen panir ergriffen und mit fersen hinder sich gehawen."* Cf. Thiele, *Luthers Sprichwörtersammlung*, No. 119.

[81] Possibly a reference to the ambassador of Goslar, Konrad Dellingshausen, who was on the side of Henry's enemies and who was not an inexperienced soldier, that is, an "unarmed cook" or a "messenger boy." Cf. Koldewey, *op. cit.*, p. 10.

[82] Maximilian I (1493-1519). Frederick the Wise and Albrecht of Mainz were two of seven electors involved in negotiations concerning the election of a new Holy Roman Emperor. They supported Charles I of Spain, who became emperor Charles V in 1519; the dukes of Braunschweig/Wolfenbüttel favored Francis I of France.

alone,[83] and he'll do it." But soon thereafter, when he got to know this little weed, he said to his friends, "No one in all my life has deceived me like this cleric"; he was really annoyed that he had first praised the cleric and had been so deceived in the end.

And I might say too that no lord, not even my own most gracious lord the elector of Saxony, has at all times answered me as graciously or thought as excessively well of me as has Bishop Albrecht.[84] I thought, indeed, he was an angel. He had the master-devil all right, who can make himself look so beautifully clean, and yet at the same time call us Lutheran scoundrels. Nor has he omitted doing anything he could against our doctrine. I really think that I also have been deceived in the high trust I placed in such an evil man. Well, what is past is past,[85] and so must he be. My Lord Christ is above him, and so am I.

Since he does not want to know who caused this Lutheran rumpus (as he calls it) I will announce it publicly, and not just to Harry or to him, for he knows it much better than I do. It happened, in the year 1517, that a preaching monk called John Tetzel, a great ranter, made his appearance. He had previously been rescued in Innsbruck by Duke Frederick from a sack—for Maximilian had condemned him to be drowned in the Inn (presumably on account of his great virtue)—and Duke Frederick reminded him of it when he began to slander us Wittenbergers; he also freely admitted it himself. This same Tetzel now went around with indulgences, selling grace for money as dearly or as cheaply as he could, to the best of his ability. At that time I was a preacher here in the monastery, and a fledgling doctor fervent and enthusiastic for Holy Scripture.

Now when many people from Wittenberg went to Jütterbock and Zerbst for indulgences, and I (as truly as my Lord Christ redeemed me) did not know what the indulgences were, as in fact

---

[83] A German proverb, "Lasst mir den man mausen." Cf. Thiele, Luthers Sprichwörtersammlung, No. 88. For a detailed account of the historical background of this section, cf. Paul Kalkoff, Die Miltitziade (Leipzig, 1911), pp. 39-40, and the brief summary in Schwiebert, op. cit., pp. 371-379.

[84] Cf., for example, Albrecht's humble correspondence with Luther in WA, Br 2, 421.

[85] A German proverb, "Hin ist hin!" Cf. Thiele, Luthers Sprichwörtersammlung, No. 387.

no one knew, I began to preach very gently that one could probably do something better and more reliable than acquiring indulgences.[86] I had also preached before in the same way against indulgences at the castle and had thus gained the disfavor of Duke
Frederick because he was very fond of his religious foundation.
Now I—to point out the true cause of the Lutheran rumpus—let
everything take its course. However, I heard what dreadful and
abominable articles Tetzel was preaching, and some of them I shall
mention now, namely:

That he had such grace and power from the pope that even
if someone seduced the holy Virgin Mary, and made her conceive,
he could forgive him, provided he placed the necessary sum in the
box.

Again, that the red indulgence-cross, bearing the papal arms,
was when erected in church as powerful as the cross of Christ.

Again, that if St. Peter were here now, he would not have
greater grace or power than he had.

Again, that he would not change places with St. Peter in
heaven, for he had rescued more souls with indulgences than St.
Peter had with his preaching.

Again, that if anyone put money in the box for a soul in purgatory, the soul would fly to heaven as soon as the coin clinked
on the bottom.

Again, that the grace from indulgences was the same grace as
that by which a man is reconciled to God.

Again, that it was not necessary to have remorse, sorrow, or
repentance for sin, if one bought (I ought to say, acquired) an indulgence or a dispensation; indeed, he sold also for future sin.

He did an abominable amount of this, and it was all for the
sake of money. I did not know at that time who would get the
money. Then a booklet appeared, magnificently ornamented with
the coat of arms of the bishop of Magdeburg, in which the sellers
of indulgences were advised to preach some of these articles.[87] It

---

[86] See, for example, a sermon Luther preached on February 24, 1517. *LW* 51,
26-31. See also two Lenten sermons he preached in March, 1518. *LW* 51,
35-49.

[87] This was the *Summary Instruction* (*Instructio Summaria pro Subcommis-
sariis*) of Albrecht of Mainz, written for the sub-commissioners in the indul-

became quite evident that Bishop Albrecht had hired this Tetzel because he was a great ranter; for he was elected bishop of Mainz with the agreement that he was himself to buy (I mean acquire) the pallium[88] at Rome. For three bishops of Mainz, Berthold, Jakob, and Uriel,[89] had recently died, one shortly after the other, so that it was perhaps difficult for the diocese to buy the pallium so often and in such quick succession, since it cost twenty-six thousand gulden according to some, and thirty thousand according to others, for the most holy father of Rome can charge as much as that for flax[90] (which otherwise is hardly worth six cents).

Thus the bishop devised this scheme, hoping to pay the Fuggers[91] (for they had advanced the money for the pallium) from the purse of the common man. And he sent this great fleecer of men's pockets[92] into the provinces; he fleeced them so thoroughly that a pile of money began to come clinking and clattering into the boxes. He did not forget himself in this either. And in addition the pope had a finger in the pie as well, because one-half was to go toward the building of St. Peter's Church in Rome. Thus these fellows went about their work joyfully and full of hope, rattling their boxes under men's purses and fleecing them. But, as I say, I did not know that at the time.

Then I wrote a letter with the *Theses* to the bishop of Magdeburg,[93] admonishing and beseeching him to stop Tetzel and prevent this stupid thing from being preached, lest it give rise to public discontent—this was a proper thing for him to do as archbishop. I can still lay my hands on that letter; but I never received an answer. I wrote in the same manner to the bishop of Branden-

---

gence traffic. Cf. Schwiebert, *op. cit.*, pp. 303-330, and Walther Köhler, *Dokumente zum Ablassstreit von 1517* (Tübingen and Leipzig, 1902), pp. 104-124.

[88] See p. 168, n. 421.

[89] Berthold, count of Henneberg (1484-1504); Jakob of Liebenstein (1504-1508); and Uriel of Gemmingen (1508-1514).

[90] The material of which the pallium was made.

[91] Internationally known bankers in Augsburg. They were the pope's financial representatives in Germany. On their financial involvement with the papacy, cf. Aloys Schulte, *Die Fugger in Rome, 1495-1523* (Leipzig, 1904), pp. 98-104.

[92] *Beuteldrescher.*

[93] For Luther's letter to Cardinal Albrecht, see *LW* 48, 43-49. For the *Ninety-five Theses*, see *LW* 31, 25-31.

burg as my ordinary;[94] in him I had a very gracious bishop. He answered that I was attacking the authority of the church and would get myself into trouble. He advised me to leave it alone.[95] I can well imagine that they both thought the pope would be much too powerful for me, a miserable beggar.

So my theses against Tetzel's articles, which you can now see in print, were published. They went throughout the whole of Germany in a fortnight, for the whole world complained about indulgences, and particularly about Tetzel's articles. And because all the bishops and doctors were silent and no one wanted to bell the cat (for the masters of heresy, the preaching order,[96] had instilled fear into the whole world with the threat of fire, and Tetzel had bullied a number of priests who had grumbled against his impudent preaching), Luther became famous as a doctor, for at last someone had stood up to fight. I did not want the fame, because (as I have said) I did not myself know what the indulgences were, and the song might prove too high for my voice.

This is the first, real, fundamental beginning of the Lutheran rumpus, which the bishop of Mainz, not Duke Frederick, began with that fleecer and pickpocket, Tetzel. Indeed, it goes back rather to Tetzel's blasphemous preaching, which (as you have heard) was aimed at stealing and robbing the people of their money to pay for the bishop's pallium and pomp. Yet after having been admonished by me, he would not stop Tetzel, but rather increased the price and wanted to steal far more money than he had already stolen under the guise of indulgences; thus he showed regard for neither the truth nor the salvation of men's souls. This shameless cleric, who knows all this perfectly well, now wants to lay the blame at the feet of a worthy prince who has since died.[97] He shamelessly breathes and instills these lies into his Harrys. Now if a rumpus has come out of this, and discontent with these slanderous Harrys, these infamous Mainzes, these effeminate cowards, these desperate scoundrels and their whole hellish crew, they may

---

[94] Jerome Sculteus, bishop of Brandenburg. This letter was probably written on February 13, 1518. WA, Br 1, 138-140.
[95] Sculteus' answer is not extant.
[96] The Dominican Order.
[97] Frederick the Wise died on May 5, 1525.

thank the bishop of Mainz for it. He began it with his execrable thieving greed and his blasphemous Tetzel, whom he sent out and defended. And if Luther had not attacked Tetzel's blasphemous preaching, which at that time had gone so far and with such power, wood and stones would have cried out against it; not a gentle Lutheran rumpus, but an abominably devilish one would have been the result. If they were to tell the truth, they have been safe until now under our protection, that is, under God's word. Otherwise, the sects[98] would indeed have taught them manners.

The other cause for the beginning of this rumpus was the most holy father, Pope Leo, with his untimely ban.[99] Doctor Sow[100] and all the papists helped him with it, as did a number of silly asses, indeed, everyone who wanted to win his spurs at my expense. They wrote and ranted against me, that is, whoever could hold a pen in his hand. But I hoped the pope would protect me because I had so secured and armed my disputation with Scripture and papal decretals that I was sure the pope would damn Tetzel and bless me. I also dedicated the *Explanations*[101] to him with a humble essay, and this book of mine greatly pleased even many cardinals and bishops. For I was at that time a better papist than Mainz and Harry have ever been, or could possibly be, and the papal decretals[102] say quite clearly that indulgence sellers cannot redeem souls from purgatory with indulgences. But while I waited for the blessing from Rome, thunder and lightning came. I had to be the sheep who troubled the water for the wolf. Tetzel went free, but I had to be eaten.[103]

In addition, they treated me in such a fine popish way that I was, to be sure, damned in Rome sixteen days before the citation came to me.[104] But when Cardinal Cajetan came to the diet in

---

98 *Rottengeister.* A reference to the Peasants' War of 1525.

99 Leo X (1513-1521) issued the bull *Exsurge, Domine,* in 1520.

100 John Eck.

101 *Explanations of the Ninety-five Theses* (1518). *LW* 31, 83-251.

102 See *Clementis Papae Constitutiones,* V, tit. IX, C. II. *CIC* 2, 1190-1191. See also Luther's analysis in *LW* 31, 170.

103 A reference to one of Aesop's fables published by Luther in 1530. See *About the Wolf and the Sheep* (*Vom Wolff und Lemlin*). *WA* 50, 441.

104 See Schwiebert, *op. cit.,* pp. 337-357.

Augsburg,[105] Dr. Staupitz arranged for that same good prince, Duke Frederick, to go to the cardinal and obtain a hearing with him for me. Thus I came to the cardinal in Augsburg. He himself appeared friendly, and after much discussion I offered to be silent thereafter, if my opponents would also be compelled to be silent. Since I did not succeed in that, I went from pope to council, and left. Thus the matter came before the diet, and was often discussed there—but I cannot write about that now since it is too long a story. In the meantime there have been written exchanges of the most violent kind, until the point is now reached that they unashamedly avoid the light, indeed, they now teach many things that formerly they damned. Moreover, they would have had nothing to teach if our books had not existed.

Now if a rumpus has arisen out of this which causes them pain, they have only themselves to thank. Why did they handle matters so imprudently and clumsily, contrary to all justice and truth, and contrary to Scripture and their own decretals? They should blame no one except themselves. We, however, shall laugh up our sleeves[106] at their complaints and ridicule them, and console ourselves that their hour has come. Even now they still deal with the matter like blind, hardened, senseless fools, as if they wilfully desired to perish. God's wrath has come upon them as they have deserved.

For now (God be praised) that it has become evident how devilish a lie indulgences are, they do not repent or think of improving or reforming themselves; but with that simple word "church" they want blindly to defend all their abominations. And if they had done nothing else wrong, these indulgences would be enough for God to damn them to the fires of hell, and for all men to drive them from the world. Just think, dear Christian, how, first, the pope, the cardinals, the bishops, and all the clergy have filled and deceived the world with these lying indulgences; second, how they have blasphemously called them the grace of God, though they are and can be nothing except a remission of satisfaction, that is, nothing. For we know now that satisfaction is noth-

---

[105] Cajetan (1469-1534), vicar-general of the Dominican Order, was the papal legate at the Diet of Augsburg.
[106] See p. 193, n. 17.

ing. Third, think how they have, with abominable simony and Iscariotry,[107] sold them for money as the grace of God, whereas God's grace must be given freely [Matt. 10:8]. Fourth, think how they have taken and stolen money and property from the whole world—and all in the name of God. Fifth, and worst of all, think how they have made these blasphemous lies into a terrible idolatry. Many thousands of souls who have died relying on them as though they were God's grace are lost because of these murderers of men's souls, since whoever trusts and builds on lies is a servant of the devil.

Such souls eternally scream their verdict over the papacy, which ought to reinstate them before God. Moreover, they ought to give back all the money and property they stole. Above all, they ought to restore to God his honor, of which they shamefully robbed him with their indulgences. When will they do that? When indeed will they care about it? But if they will not do it, by what pretense would they call themselves a Christian church, and possess or demand church property? Should that be called a church which, as we have seen, is full of indulgences, that is, of devilish lies, idolatry, simony, Iscariotry, robbery, and the murder of souls? Well then, whether they like it or not, they must. He is strong enough to wrest it from them, at any rate, with the eternal fires of hell. Meanwhile they ought not to be or to be called a church, but a synagogue of the devil [Rev. 2:9], even if all the Harrys and Mainzes rage and foam at the mouth about it.

Likewise, when devil Harry slanders the elector and calls him a drunkard, a Nabal [I Samuel 25], etc., and, as though he were himself a sober Christian, quotes Scripture, "Do not get drunk with wine, for that is debauchery,"[108] then—although I do not like praising my lord, for this Harryish devil can easily retort, "His praise I sing whose bread I eat"—I cannot leave the devil uncensored, but must tell him that, true to character, he lies even when he speaks the truth.[109] First, I cannot wholly excuse the fact that my gracious lord sometimes takes a glass too many at the table, especially with guests. We do not like to see that either, though he

---

[107] A pun on Judas Iscariot.
[108] Eph. 5:18. The passage from the *Rejoinder* is quoted in WA 51, 547, n. 1.
[109] See p. 37, n. 82.

can hold his liquor better than others. But when Harry says that he is a drunkard or debauched as a result of this, he is lying and cannot prove what he says. Harry, Mainz, and every devil must confess (however much they regret it) that the elector has a large realm to rule, many things to deal with, and is moreover so over-burdened with religious and imperial affairs in addition to other matters that he has little leisure or rest, but only work and more work—that is quite evident and is public knowledge throughout the entire empire. No drunkard is skilled or competent to deal with so many great, high, and important matters, which come up incessantly every day, and any child or fool can understand that, even if this poisonous liar from Wolfenbüttel cannot. For God has punished him by making him incapable of understanding truth, virtue, or honor, thus handing him over to the devil [I Cor. 5:5] to tell nothing but lies, indeed, to do all that is evil, and to upset all that is good.

We have here (God be praised) one whose way and manner of life is modest and honorable, whose tongue is truthful, and whose hand is gentle in helping churches, schools, and the poor; one whose heart is earnest, constant, and true to honor God's word; one who punishes the wicked, protects the pious, and maintains peace and good government. And his marriage is so pure and praiseworthy that it is a fine example to all princes, lords, and in-deed everyone. The quiet Christian life of his lady resembles a convent (as people are given to say) where they hear God's word daily, go to church, pray, and praise God—not to mention how much the elector himself reads and writes every day. Do you hear that, devil Harry and Harry devil? You will not be able to call such a Christian, noble, and honorable life a debauched or drunken life, unless you would do it with a tongue that dishonors and blas-phemes man and God himself. For, barring the drink at the table, you will find nothing but the pure gifts of God and the virtues of a worthy Christian prince and pure, chaste husband; the fruits bear witness to the tree [Matt. 7:16-20]. One just has to put up with a wart or a scab somewhere on a beautiful body, which one cannot change however much one would like to.

On the other hand, when you hear such things, what does

your heart (if you have one) say of the sober, holy, chaste, and orderly life you lead? For you know that everybody realizes how you treat your worthy princess—not only like an utterly mad brute and drunkard, but also like a senseless raving tyrant, who daily and hourly gorges and fills himself up, not with wine, but with the devil, like Judas at the Last Supper [John 13:27]. Out of your whole body, in all you do and are, you simply spew out the devil, with blaspheming, cursing, lying, committing adultery, raving, flaying, murdering, setting fires, etc., so that one cannot find your like in history (as we shall see). Moreover, you cannot carry out your shameful whoredom and adultery except by insulting and dishonoring the divine name, and hiding the wretched whore, like one dead, beneath your sacred worship, mass, and vigils.[110] You have learned that from your comrade at Mainz, who also has to commit his whoring and adultery in the guise of holy things, though you are probably able to invent such virtue by yourself.[111] Truly, you are well-behaved people, who know how to preach about drunkenness and debauchery.

How like the elector, in whom every virtue shines, are you now? Only a splinter, drinking at the table, must make you (who are otherwise full of the devil and without a single wretched little virtue) a sober, holy, Christian man. I do not hereby seek to have court life, which they themselves call a sow's life,[112] excused. It is unfortunately not just this court but all of Germany which is plagued with excessive drinking. We preachers speak and preach against it; unfortunately that does not help much. It is an old and evil custom in Germany, as the Roman Cornelius wrote,[113] which has grown worse and is getting worse still. The emperor, kings,

---

[101] A reference to Duke Henry's affair with Eva von Trott. See p. 183.

[111] There was a rumor that Cardinal Albrecht of Mainz hid the corpse of his mistress in a casket shown as a relic and supposedly occupied by the body of St. Margaret. Luther used this rumor against the archbishop in *Against the Bishop of Magdeburg, Cardinal Albrecht* (*Wider den Bishof zu Magdeburg, Albrecht Kardinal*) (1539). WA 50, 386-431. Cf. also Paul Redlich, *Cardinal Albrecht und das Neue Stift zu Halle 1520-1541* (Mainz, 1900), p. 294.

[112] Cf. *Exegesis of Psalm 101* (*Auslegung des 101. Psalms*) (1534-1535). WA 51, 256-257.

[113] Cornelius Tacitus (*ca.* 55-*ca.* 120), Roman historian, in *Germania*, 22. John Church and William J. Brodribb (trans.), *The Complete Works of Tacitus* ("The Modern Library" [New York: Random House, 1942]), p. 720.

princes, and nobles ought to see that it is checked. Moreover, it will get even worse (no doubt as a punishment) now that Italian customs are beginning to spread in Germany through our accursed cardinals and Harrys, so that it is to be feared that Germany is no longer what it was. But there is not time to speak of that now.

Where does this restlessness in the empire come from? Not from the elector, who is quiet and obedient, but from you (and your devilish comrades), who with your raving, raging, and arson are the cause of all the empire's misfortune, devouring your own subjects and thinking day and night of nothing else but of committing murder and all other evils. That is what you call peace, and sober orderly existence. Whoever does not want to be like you in this must be called rebellious, restless, disorderly, and drunk. Indeed, your father[114] does the same; because God would not do in heaven what he wanted, he persisted and did not want to let God be God, and he still doesn't want to. You do the same thing, you lovely image of your angelic (hellish) father.

I have spoken above about church property. The elector (God be praised) has used what he himself owned most Christianly, and he still does, for churches, schools, the poor, etc.; and he may need even more of it to meet the heavy expenses which now face him. But Harry, this holy and obedient child of the holy church, has devoured the bishopric of Hildesheim,[115] and would like to devour Magdeburg and Halberstadt as well. Yet he would not give a farthing to a poor man, not to mention that he should help schools and churches. But he has an excellent excuse: the churches and schools are heretical, whereas he is a holy and Christian man. This is why he may devour what he will, although this angers his own church, which now announces that it will force him, under threat of excommunication, to restore these properties. But I shall not worry about whether the battle is serious or sham. Let the knaves do what they like among themselves; all that the devil does is lie and murder.

---

[114] The devil.

[115] After the battle of Soltau in 1519 (see p. 230, n. 79) the dukes of Braunschweig-Wolfenbüttel managed to defeat Bishop John of Hildesheim and take most of his land. By 1523 Henry and his brother William had divided the bishopric of Hildesheim between them. Cf. Koldewey, *op. cit.*, p. 3.

He depicts the landgrave as a bigamist and an Anabaptist, indeed, as one who has himself been rebaptized.[116] But he does so with words as underhanded and changeable as a cardinal's, so that, if any proof should be demanded, he can talk out of the other side of his mouth and say he had not declared this as a fact but rather had suspected it. For he is a murderer, a liar, and a double-dealer, and lies, murders, and is double-tongued in everything he says and does. But I shall not say much about that at this time. The landgrave is man enough himself, and he has learned men about him. In Hesse I know of a landgravine, who is and should be called a wife and mother in Hesse, and there is probably no one else who would bear or suckle young landgraves—I mean the duchess, daughter of Duke George of Saxony.[117] But because some of you princes have gone astray, you have with your bad example unfortunately brought it to pass that even the peasant refuses to be responsible for a sin, and you have made it difficult for us to maintain marriage as a worthy and honorable estate, or indeed to re-establish it as such.

But from the very beginning no one has more shamefully dishonored marriage than Harry of Wolfenbüttel—that holy, sober man who cloaks and hides his shameless, impenitent, and brazen adultery under the terrible judgment and wrath of God (namely, death, which devours all men so that God's Son had to help us from it) with services, masses, and vigils, using them as a magic hood behind which to hide his immorality. Indeed, he makes a jester's cap out of both God and the Christian faith, as if death, resurrection, and eternal life were nothing but a joke or a piece of tomfoolery; as if God were not mocked enough when men despise his command not to commit adultery, but must also be traduced as a cloak for dishonor. It would be no wonder if God caused the land to be swallowed up like Sodom and Gomorrah. And this blasphemer and defamer dares to judge and slander other honorable princes. Turks (they say) have more than a hundred wives, but their behavior is not defamed with the name and work of God used like a jester's cap as is this Harry's.

---

[116] Philip. Cf. the passage in the *Rejoinder*. WA 51, 549, n. 10.
[117] Christina, Philip's first wife. See p. 183, n. 6.

As for rebaptism, I will let this poisonous loudmouth be answered by the books in which you can read what the landgrave and the elector have done against the madmen of Münster.[118] If he is or can be called an Anabaptist on the basis of this, then he is and can be called something much greater and much worse. And what could not the holiest man on earth become among such scandalmongers, when our doctrine, which they themselves must admit to be God's word, is called heresy, disobedience, and rebellion, and has to endure every kind of reproach? For since they have become devils they want to make everything else, like themselves, into devils. But thereby they do not (as we have already said) make our case any worse, or theirs any better.

Now—so that I may come to an end—this, I myself think, is the reason Harry the devil undertook to write such evil, slanderous, and deceitful books: he knows that throughout the world he has a most infamous name and that he stinks like devilish filth flung into Germany. Perhaps he would like not to stink so much himself, but would like to make other princes stink as well, so that it is not his stench alone which fills everyone's nostrils, particularly since this year the cry of arson was raised against him. He cannot drown these cries with soft words. Hence he must shriek and scream in his struggle to escape, cursing, slandering, lying, raving, and raging, just to see whether that would help. But it does not, Harry, you rave in vain, even if you could thunder and storm like God himself. That mass of innocent blood shed at Einbeck[119] and elsewhere by your arson cries so strongly to heaven that (if God wills) it will soon cry you and your associates down into the abyss of hell; and it will not cease till then.

Were you to whitewash yourself,[120] saying that rogues and scoundrels say this about you to impugn your honor, you would

---

[118] Radical reformers, associated with Anabaptism, attempted to transform Münster in Westphalia into the "kingdom of Zion." On June 25, 1535, an army led by Catholic and Protestant princes sacked the city. Cf. Williams, *The Radical Reformation*, pp. 362-381, and Luther's *Preface to the New Newspaper about the Anabaptists of Münster* (*Vorrede zur Neuen zeitung von den Wiedertäufern zu Münster. 1535*). WA 38, 341-350.

[119] See Koldewey, *op. cit.*, p. 11. See also in this volume, p. 182.

[120] Proverbial German, *"Das du aber das maul woltest wischen."* Cf. Thiele, *Luthers Sprichwörtersammlung*, No. 315.

indeed be right in calling them by your own true name. They
have been asphyxiated in fire for having been such rogues and
scoundrels as to serve their head and arch-arsonist, and the hangman who has passed sentence on them has thereby depicted for
you what you would deserve if you were to receive your due.
Well, you must think it just as well to run into hell as to walk,
for you have made it your purpose to remain the enemy of God
and man. And if you could murder God you would indeed spare
him as little as you would men. Your own word testifies to this,
for when Duke George died[121] you said, "Well now, I would rather
God in heaven had died." But enough of that for now—it is too
horrid to go into all the details. You have in other respects quite
adequately established for yourself an eternal memorial, so that
Judas, Herod, Nero, and all the scoundrels in the world will have
to be canonized, compared to you.

For though Nero set fire to Rome, he at least did it publicly
and risked the outcome like a man. And other arsonists write
threatening letters, openly display their names, warn their enemies,
and take the risk of falling into the hands of the hangman. But
this timid wretch and coward does everything underhandedly. He
would do better as a guardian of women—he should do nothing
but, like a eunuch who is a guardian of women, stand in a fool's
cap with a fly swatter[122] and protect the women and that which
makes them women (as the vulgar Germans put it). I have heard
from good soldiers what a timid wretch he is. He has never been
known to have acted like a real man; rather, what he has done
has either been done secretly and underhandedly so that it could
later be denied, or else against those to whom he is superior in
numbers or power. He lets his equal, or a man, well alone, proving this not only with his dishonorable and underhanded adultery,
but also with this wretched underhanded arson, not to mention all
the other things.

For that is what all the books say, "He who is an assassin is
timid and strikes no man honestly"—as the emperor Maurice said

---

[121] In 1539. The origin of Henry's saying is unknown.
[122] *Fliegenwedel.*

of his murderer Phocas, "If he is timid, it is homicide."[123] A real man is ashamed to undertake anything underhanded or to act against a man who is unarmed or not his equal—but that is Harry's prize virtue. And I think that if he were alone in the field, an angry cat would be enough to scare him away. Therefore when such Thrasons[124] have committed their treachery they stick their snouts in the air like bold braggarts, and with oaths and curses revile and profane both God and man. But their boldness is in their mouths, in the shameful words they speak, and only there. For you can imagine what a manly Achilles he must be who can curse God (whom he considers a nonentity) in heaven and wish him dead; or he, who, when several hundred remain on the field of battle from which he has boldly fled, afterward becomes a hero and a most esteemed knight with the words, "Ha! Such people are reared with a pailful of milk," or when he leads them onto the field saying, "The mother of all soldiers is not dead yet," or, "God with us, and the devil take the hindmost," and the like. What Christian, indeed, what reasonable man, does not understand what kind of heart it is from which such words come? Is not what I said before true, that he has eaten and drunk himself full of devils, and so spews vainglorious devils out of his hellish gorge?

Suetonius writes of Nero[125] that when another inhuman monster stood talking with him, saying, "I would like the whole world to be destroyed by fire after my death," he replied, "I should like it to happen while I live." This Nero, however, is so bold and manly that he would like to share this destruction with others. Our timid guardian of women would like to throw others to the devil, but secure his own flight and save his life, like the bold hero he is, who with words can kill even God, not to mention men. But the last hour has come,[126] as we Christians know, and in it the pa-

---

[123] *Si est timidus, est homicida.* Cf. Schäfer, *Luther als Kirchenhistoriker,* pp. 330, 405.

[124] Plural of the Greek *Thraso,* the name of the bragging soldier in the comedy *Eunuchus* by Publius Terentius Afer (*ca.* 185-159 B.C.), a Roman poet. Cf. Henry T. Riley (trans.), *The Comedies of Terence* (New York, 1868), pp. 63-131.

[125] Gaius Tranquillus Suetonius (*ca.* A.D. 75-160), Roman historian, in *Nero,* 38. Cf. Alexander Thomson (trans.), *The Lives of the Twelve Caesars* (London, 1884), p. 367.

[126] See p. 13, n. 6.

pacy and its members, as Daniel [11:36] and Paul [II Thess. 2:3-4] say, will be the most terrible example of God's wrath, and the true and final abomination. No power on earth, not even the holy church itself, shall slay and destroy it, but only the Lord Christ himself, for by the spirit of his mouth he will slay it, and by his coming he will destroy it [II Thess. 2:8]. Therefore this final abomination must have as its servant the most shameful man on whom the sun has ever shone. For a church worker and saint like this belongs to such a church. And we know well (thank God) whom Harry serves with his underhanded incendiarism, and whence the money comes. But we, on the contrary, shall be bold and undaunted, since we know to whom they are doing this, that is, to the right Man.[127] Just let them speed and hasten confidently to their damnation, as St. Peter says [II Pet. 2:1]. It is not only Harry who will be repaid for such arson—this I know for a certainty (for he is not worth bothering about); and we shall one day see that our weeping and mourning are turned into joy which they will not laugh over as they do now. Shall we bet on that?

Harry and all of them rely on the fact that the pope has damned us and the emperor has published an edict[128] against us, so that no one can blame or condemn them for being obedient to the pope and emperor, and therefore they may do us what harm they will. This is a pair of cobweb trousers (as Isaiah [59:6] puts it) for them to wear, like the man who being naked put on a net to hide his shame. Now we have often torn off these trousers. But since they are mad and stupid we will now tear them off once more, not for the sake of these Harrys—who do not understand anything and who really think their cobweb is golden cloth or, indeed, a cuirass and a harness—but to give comfort to our own people and to instruct (those who do not know).

We say in German that justice is always an honest man, but the judge is often a rogue.[129] I remember how Duke Frederick

---

[127] A reference to the second stanza of Luther's hymn, "A Mighty Fortress Is Our God."

[128] The Edict of Worms (1521). On its origins, cf. Schwiebert, *op. cit.*, pp. 509-512.

[129] *"Das Recht ist allzeit ein from Man, Der Richter ist offt ein Schalck."* The origins of the proverb are unknown.

once got a letter of complaint from a poor woman, in which she begged that His Grace the Elector would help her get just justice. The good prince was quite amused that the woman indicated two sorts of justice, for he knew nothing about an unjust justice. But he soon understood that she meant to say the judge was a scoundrel. O Lord God, if this life were so blessed that the judge were really as honest as justice, we should need no lawyers, no kings, no emperor. But ask the lawyers why it is that their books think so little of judges that they must be there to help and defend wherever and by whatever means they can. Indeed, ask the princes and lords themselves what they do when they dismiss and punish their officials. Is not the office just and honest? And why did princes in former times depose some of the emperors, if the office of emperor is of God? For it is (justly) called the Holy Roman Empire by the grace of God, who is holy and who has ordained it; and all princes extol their estate as coming from God's grace, that is, as holy.

Indeed, why do people call the whore's body God's creature, since she is an evil whore and all honest women, who are not better creatures as far as the body goes, avoid her? All of nature is full of such examples. The reason is that there is a difference between the thing and the person,[130] that is to say, "the thing itself,"[131] justice, is always an honest man, but "the person,"[132] the judge, is often a rogue. Now these Harrys brag about the fact that not justice but the pope and emperor, that is, the persons, have damned us, so that we have lost and they have won. That is the sort of dialectic[133] for which in school one beats a boy of ten; their own sophists call it, "From the cane to the corner,"[134] or to put it in German so that even the papal asses can understand it, "The woman is beautiful, therefore she is not a whore." Thus Harry is a prince, therefore he is not an adulterer, murderer, or arsonist. Caiaphas is a high priest, therefore he did not crucify Christ. Judas is an apostle, therefore he is not a traitor. My dear

---

[130] *Quod est differentia inter Rem et Personam.*
[131] *Res illa.*
[132] *Persona.*
[133] Cf. p. 228, n. 72.
[134] *A Baculo ad Angulum.* The origins of the saying are unknown.

246

man, what shall we call people who talk like that? Are they not mad and foolish?

And all this I still say about the state of things here on earth, namely, that justice and the judge, the thing and the person, are not one and the same, but should be distinguished and not mixed together. Moreover, we should not give regard or attention to what the judge does, but to what justice does, as the heathen Seneca says, "Pay attention to what is said, not to who says it."[135] And all of Scripture forbids us to give regard to the person. Now they have learned from our books that government and authorities are to be honored, and they take this to mean that what Harry the person does is to be honored; whereas we meant and understood the office and justice, and, as an example, we have reprimanded (and still do) many princes and lords for not carrying out their office. They mix things so shamefully that they think everything the person wishes or thinks is the work of the government or the office—just as Duke George deceived himself and many with him in thinking that he could issue any decree he wanted in religious matters and that his subjects were obliged to obey. That is precisely the pope's idea and way of acting.

But God's Ten Commandments, which demand obedience not only of kings and emperors, but also of prophets, apostles, and all creatures, stand against this, and compel them to do what is right according to their office, not what they want to do as persons. Dear God, is the world still so blind when such light has been so clearly revealed in the catechism?[136] What is the point of our preaching when people still will not or cannot learn this? If what the person who holds an office wills and does is justice, then all is over, and we are ruled simply by the devil and these Harrys, while God and his commandment are utterly dead and nonexistent. That is what Albrecht the hangman did at Giebichenstein when he mur-

---

[135] *Non quis sed quid dicatur attende.* Lucius Annaeus Seneca (*ca.* 4 B.C.-A.D. 65), Roman philosopher, in *Epistola 108*, 4; *118*, 12: *Attende, quid dicam.* Luther's quotation is not exact. Cf. Richard M. Gummere (trans.), *Seneca Ad Lucilium Epistulae Morales* (3 vols.; Cambridge: Harvard University Press, 1943), III, 232, 336.

[136] Cf. Luther's *Large Catechism* and *Small Catechism.* Tappert (ed.), *The Book of Concord,* pp. 227-461.

dered Hans Schönitz;[137] he wanted to be both judge and justice, and so God had to be nothing and dead.

But to put it simply for the simple, there is more on earth than imperial law (by which I understand the whole jurisdiction of the temporal power, and what the lawyers teach). For the emperor should and must be under the second table of the law, [beginning with] the fourth commandment. He cannot be above it (unless the devil leads him). Moreover, as I have said, he is entirely subject to the second table and bound to hold what God commands in it, just as much as the least man on earth. But he has no business in the first table (no more than any angel or creature has). He can do nothing but fear and tremble before God, his name and his word—let alone change anything—for here God alone rules. And although he has no power to change the commandments in the second table, he can nevertheless govern both the life and property (which are subject to him) so that they are used in accordance with, not contrary to, these commandments, just as father and mother have authority in the home.

Now when the Harrys cry, "The pope and emperor, to whom one ought to be obedient, have commanded it," then the answer is, "With the exception of the Ten Commandments and the gospel, which the pope and emperor, like us, are bound to obey and be subject to." If they do not do this, then the proverb, "The judge is a rogue,"[138] holds, and the devil and his Harrys may obey him; we choose to obey the honest man, justice. Twist yourself all you like, you must at last come back to justice, and if that damns you, the person will not be able to help you at all, even though you had a hundred thousand emperors and popes behind you. For no one who is sentenced and damned by justice as a scoundrel and arsonist can be proclaimed pious by any emperor or pope. And it does not help him one bit to set the imperial crown on his head,

---

[137] Hans Schönitz, a banker employed by Cardinal Albrecht, was hanged in 1535 because he was involved in embezzlement. Luther criticized the archbishop for this act of cruelty in *Against the Bishop of Magdeburg, Cardinal Albrecht* (*Wider den Bishof zu Magdeburg, Albrecht Kardinal*) (1539). WA 50, 395-431. For the complex story of Luther's involvement in the Schönitz case, see WA 50, 386-393.

[138] See p. 245, n. 129.

for that would only be like cobweb trousers, that is, a judge without justice.

But since this year Harry has been revealed and proven by God's judgment to be an arch-assassin and bloodhound, the like of which has never been seen under the sun, it does not help him in the slightest that the pope, the emperor, and the supreme court[139] cannot or will not declare him to be such; for God's judgment is over all, and tramples on pope and emperor. But it is God's revealed judgment that in a judicial examination not one but many have confessed and solemnly sworn that God's eternal judgment—that is, sudden death—should overtake them if that miserable scoundrel and underhanded arsonist of Wolfenbüttel is not the one who set the murderous fire. No crying, no shrieking and struggling, no cursing or reviling, no adultery or despair, no emperor or pope, no devil or angel will be able to save you from this verdict and condemnation, even if they were to canonize you. For there stands the word and judgment of God, which says one shall and must believe two or three witnesses [Matt. 18:16; Deut. 19:15] (even more must we believe the many in their last agony), if one is to believe God himself. If there had been only one, or only one court, or if, as at Metz,[140] someone had been tortured by a hangman, a mistake might have been made, but not for long. But here are many who must be believed, as God himself who commands it to be believed as a true judgment. And it comes from many jurisdictional courts, which must be regarded as right and as courts ordained by God. They have done right, and those who confessed have rightly testified against you.

There you are in the chains of divine judgment, bound in hell like all the devils. Now let Duke George, your idol, and Mainz, your Holy Spirit, help and counsel you. Or if you like, come once more and take to yourself all the spitters and bawlers so that you may do well. If you cannot understand this, then, God willing, I will tell it to Mainz and to others with him so that he must understand it, for he is not such a *wurst* or such a senseless fool

---

[139] *Kamergericht.*
[140] Luther is referring to a story about a merchant who was robbed and whose family was killed by a hangman in the French city of Metz. Luther recalls it in his *Against the Bishop of Magdeburg;* cf. WA 50, 412-413.

as Harry. He knows quite well what he ought to do, if only he had the grace, and he could bring the empire more profit (as Duke Frederick also found out) than you have done it harm, you godless, underhanded guardian of women and pusillanimous scoundrel. But he is not worth it, and I am sorry that I have wasted that true-hearted prayer to convert him, which like Samuel for his Saul [I Sam. 15:35] I prayed so earnestly and often for that godless cleric.

And you, infamous Harry, you allow yourself to be used not only for lamentable arson, but also for writing these books dealing with and vilifying such elevated things as churches, heretics, faith, unbelief, rebellion, obedience, while both they themselves and you too know that you are a fool with no understanding for this, which remains deep even for us who have occupied ourselves with it day and night for many years. You should not write a book before you have heard an old sow fart;[141] and then you should open your jaws with awe, saying, "Thank you, lovely nightingale, that is just the text for me!" Take note of that, Rüdem,[142] that would be good to print in a book—nowhere but in Wolfenbüttel—against writers and the elector. Oh, how they will then hold their noses and have to admit that Harry, the guardian of women,[143] has also become a writer. Yes, that is how you should write books; these you could understand.

Finally, I first ask all pious Christians and honorable hearts who read or hear this to remember most earnestly that the Lord God (as is right) has, through so many legal examinations and judgments, condemned this Harry as a murderer, bloodhound, and arch-assassin to the fires of hell, since he cannot be overcome by fire here. And I ask that every man do God this service: glorify and praise his divine judgment wherever he can, both in public and in private; spit on the ground, to the glory of God, wherever he sees Harry; and hold his ears closed whenever he hears him named, just as he would do against the devil himself. And es-

---

141 A reference to proverbial German. Cf. Thiele, *Luthers Sprichwörtersammlung*, No. 398.

142 *Rüdem*, the name of Duke Henry's publisher in Wolfenbüttel, is used here as a pun on *Rüde*, a German word used when calling a hunting dog.

143 *Potzenhüt*, a phonetic pun on *Fotzenhut*, a German slang term meaning "guardian of women."

pecially you ministers and preachers, confidently let your voices resound in this, and know that we are duty-bound to do this, by divine authority, and do God a service thereby. One should and must praise and glorify God's judgment and work, as the psalms teach us to do, for God has revealed himself concerning Harry, as he did concerning Pharaoh in Egypt [Exod. 6:1] so that we are certain it is his judgment and work. And you preachers are to add to this by telling the people that with such judgments God means not only Harry, but also the pope, the cardinals, the bishops, the priests, the monks, and all their followers. Harry is the servant of them all in that he boasts about their church and their obedience in his books (although we should know it quite well without that). And all who serve him are condemned by the same verdict, whether they be spewers, printers, nobles, or whoever has consented to this or has pleasure in it. This is no papal or imperial excommunication, but God's ban, as against the devil himself.

Our need compels us to shout out and glorify this judgment and work of God, so that God does not charge us (because we knew of it and wanted to keep silent) with this welter of blood and distress which happened among us through these accursed bloodhounds and sneaky, murderous arsonists, these Harryish papists and popish Harrys. Remember how earnestly God, in Moses, commanded the nearest towns to claim and purify the dead man found in the field [Deut. 21:1-9]. What would become of us when he himself, through his public judgment and work, informs us about these horrible murderous Harrys and their associates and points them out to us? The earth should indeed swallow us up [Num. 16:30], or the Turks devour us, if we did not repudiate this welter of blood and murder with earnest, loud cries about injustice, pointing to Harry, whom God singles out for our eyes, to test whether we will shout out, or whether with our silence we wish to become participants.

They have heretofore always been big bloodhounds and have murdered many people, until God truly exposed and condemned them in their Harry. For previously they always did it as judges, since God held his peace. But now they are doing it as furtive arsonists, as they are not judges but partisans and enemies, now con-

251

demned by God to be handed over to the judge. Thus will God overthrow his enemies, who have murdered and blasphemed unceasingly, and against their conscience, too.

On the other hand, I beg our princes and lords to be less anxious and troubled from now on and instead be more cheerful and patient, as they see now how God himself intervenes and grants our prayer; as the gospel says, he will soon give the papacy its just dessert [Luke 23:41]. For this Harry has, with his murderous arson, done them a true service, and they have given him a true reward. God's verdict is clear; he has brought the arsonists, Harry's servants, into court despite all our care and diligence, and, as Harry and the pope deserve, condemned them. God be praised for this, he who does not allow murder to go unavenged or his commandments to be despised. These timid guardians of women wanted to do it secretly, so God has brought it to light, dumbfounding them. May his divine grace go on to complete the work he has begun; to him be praise and glory for ever. Amen.

This is the place for Psalm 64, which we should preach and sing to the glory of God against such murderous underhanded Harrys, for here you see them portrayed as accurately as if David had intended to preach about these last Harrys in advance.

Psalm 64

Hear my voice, O God, in my complaint;
    preserve my life from dread of the enemy,
hide me from the secret plots of the wicked,
    from the scheming of evildoers,
who whet their tongues like swords,
    who aim bitter words like arrows,
shooting from ambush at the blameless,
    shooting at him suddenly and without fear.
They hold fast to their evil purpose;
    they talk of laying snares secretly,
thinking, "Who can see us?"
They search out crimes and have thought out a cunningly
    conceived plot.
But God will suddenly shoot his arrow at them;
    they will be wounded suddenly.

Because of their own tongue he will bring them to ruin;
    all who see them will wag their heads.
They will tell what God has wrought,
    and ponder what he has done.
Let the righteous rejoice in the Lord,
    and take refuge in him!
Let all the upright in heart glory!

For many years these Harrys have concocted various plots with Duke George and have intrigued secretly against us, until finally, boldly and brazenly, without fear or awe of God, they pulled the trigger and suddenly shot with this murderous arson and thought that no one would see such knavery and plotting, as though no one could see such treachery. These Harrys thought: the emperor will do nothing to us, the supreme court even less, for the pope, whom we serve, would not like it. Who then will do anything to us? Here on earth there is no higher court over us. Thus did God die, cursed to death by these Harrys. Therefore let us suddenly shoot, burn, and murder, but stealthily, for then we shall have a twofold advantage. They cannot place the guilt on us, or accuse us. Even if they could accuse us, the judge, our most holy father the pope, is on our side; thus we are happy and confident.

But meanwhile, what did this dead God, who has been cursed to death by these Harrys, think? The other psalm [2] says he laughed and derided such arsonists. Thus this psalm also says he thought of suddenly shooting at them and felling them through their own tongues so that they would be shamed and disgraced before all the world. For when he saw that there was no judge there, he himself assumed the office and presided at many supreme courts—at Wittenberg, in the Mark,[144] at Einbeck, at Nordhausen, and here and there. Since there were no plaintiffs, no lawyers, and no witnesses there, he made short work of it and let justice take its swift course—but the arsonists had to be their own plaintiffs, lawyers, and witnesses, using their own words as evidence. Thus God felled them through their own tongues and said, "Out of your

---

[144] *Marck,* a popular name for Mark Brandenburg, whose capital was Berlin.

own mouth," and again, "Out of your own mouth are you condemned" [Matt. 12:37].

What does God care about pope, emperor, kings, supreme court, lawyers? If they do not wish to speak they may keep silence; if they do not wish to proceed with their case they may withdraw. He is a mighty Lord who can make men out of earth and stones and, again, make stones and earth out of men. He can make fools wise, and wise men fools. In the same way he now and then made imperial supreme courts here in prison, and let the one at Spires[145] convene and be surprised by the work done. And best of all, pope, emperor, and the supreme court must regard such courts as imperial courts, for they are the courts of temporal princes and lords, who hold them as fiefs from the emperor (though everything is from on high, from God). Thus Harry is sentenced and condemned by papal, imperial, and supreme courts (before which he presumed he was safe). For I bet their heads they cannot deny that these courts are nothing else but imperial, indeed, divine courts. If the intermediate courts[146] have not done anything, then the high courts of God and the lower courts of the emperor have.

These are the miracles of God, which this psalm glorifies and commands to be glorified—that he has suddenly shot these Harry arsonists and felled them through their own tongues. For the very same tongues which previously took secret counsel with each other and decided on treacherous arson have charged, accused, sentenced, and brought themselves into the fire; and they have exposed the chief scoundrel, their leader, and charged that he deserved the same fire and could no longer be called a prince with any honor before men, but rather has been declared, by the judgment of God, to be an arch-treacherous, murderous arsonist and should be regarded as such.

And now to guard myself against contradictions: since it is written in the psalm that they are bold and fearless, and since I have previously said that Harry is a cowardly scoundrel, he or his followers might use their asinine dialectic and assert that this psalm is against me and that it proves my words to be lies, be-

---

[145] A reference to the Diet of Spires in 1526, which was unable to enforce the Edict of Worms (1521).
[146] *Mittelgerichte.*

254

cause it says they are bold. I say to that what I have said before: no assassin is a man, and no man is an assassin; but whoever assassinates is a pusillanimous Harry and a timid guardian of women, as all histories testify. They do not stand up and resist where there is danger, or where they are uncertain there cannot or will not be any opposition. But where they are sure one cannot defend oneself, or where they outnumber their opponents, they are bold—but only to do harm, not to do good.

For example, Scripture everywhere admits that the godless are intrepid toward God, and do not fear God, for God sleeps and hides himself, and is indeed so weak in his people as to be cursed to death by Harry. Then they are very bold, and hunt the suffering, fleeing, dead God, for they experience no punishment, resistance, or wrath of God. [They are] like Pharaoh, who was intrepid against the God of Israel in the Red Sea, saying, "I do not know of any God" [Exod. 5:2], and chased him into the middle of the sea. But when God just turned and looked around, they did it in their shoes and the sea and cried, "Let us flee, for God fights against us" [Exod. 14:25]—so I think that that stealthy Harry would not be bold enough to blow at a farmer's fence if he knew that there were a flail behind the door; he would lift his heels in quite a manly way, as though it were snowing flails behind him. But he can well curse God in heaven, for he is certain that there is no God who could or would defend himself—meanwhile not paying any attention to the hour that will come.

So be it! They are impenitent and blinded, delivered to the wrath of God. We must give room to the wrath [Rom. 12:19] and let God's judgment run its course. Nor shall we any longer pray for their sin (as St. John teaches us [I John 5:16]), but pray about them and against them, and to the praise and glory of God we shall sing the Judas song,[147] pointing thus to Harry.

O villainous Harry, is this your deed,
So many a saint by fire to have burned?

---

[147] A parody of a German folk song frequently quoted by Luther: "Oh, You Poor Judas, What Did You Do" (*'O Du Armer Judas, Was hast du getan'*). Cf., for example, WA 39, 412; 36, 136. On the history of the song, cf. Rochus Freiherr von Liliencron, *Deutsches Leben im Volkslied* (Berlin, 1885), p. 227.

Great torment in hell shall then be your meed;
To dwell ever with Lucifer, this you have earned.
Lord have mercy.[148]
O damned papists, is this your deed,
That no true Christian life you were willing to spare?
From this weight of shame you shall never be freed,
With your crime widely known, and great suffering to bear.
Lord have mercy.
When I complete this song I will also find a verse to deal with
the fellow in Mainz.[149]

Let them go now in the hope that since the emperor, pope,
and supreme court have not yet condemned them, they are safe.
Here is God's clear judgment commanding pope, emperor, and
everyone to be silent. If Christ had had to wait for vindication, or
Judas and the Jews for condemnation, until Pilate, Herod, and the
priestly high court in Jerusalem had done it, then Christ would
still be forced to hang on the cross, and Judas would perhaps
have become high priest a long time ago. But since no one wanted
to vindicate Christ, and the judges themselves condemned him, the
Father had to do it himself.

Thus the preachers, when they teach the people, should indeed exhort them to fear God and not undertake any secret murder or wrongdoing. For God sees it and does not remain aloof;
when one does it too obviously and even, impenitently, wants to
defend it as right, then he surely intervenes and acts. Thus may
these stealthy murderous arsonists, together with Harry and Judas,
be used as an example. For it is written, "Nothing is covered that
will not be made known. To God who shows mercy and judgment
to those who suffer harm be praise and glory for ever and ever.
Amen."[150]

---

[148] *Kyrieleison.*
[149] Cardinal Albrecht.
[150] *Nihil opertum, quod non reveletur. Deo sit laus et gloria, in saecula saecu-
lorum, qui facit misericordiam et iuditium inuriam patientibus, Amen.* Cf.
Matt. 10:26 and Ps. 103:6.

AGAINST THE ROMAN PAPACY
AN INSTITUTION OF THE DEVIL

1545

Translated by Eric W. Gritsch

INTRODUCTION

This treatise, the most bitter of Luther's polemic writings, is intimately related to the political power struggle between pope and emperor. The struggle reached its climax when Charles V made many concessions to the German Protestant princes at the Diet of Spires in 1544 in order to gain their support for his war against Francis I of France and the Turks. The *Recess* of June 10, 1544,[1] guaranteed ecclesiastical revenues to holders of Protestant benefices, the suspension of lawsuits against Protestants already in progress at the supreme court (*Reichskammergericht*), and the abolition of *Recesses* passed by previous diets against Protestants. Moreover, it announced plans for another German diet at which a "Christian reformation by devout and peace-loving men" would be discussed. The *Recess* did not even mention the pope or ecclesiastical authority.

When the contents of the *Recess* became known in Rome, Pope Paul III immediately convoked a consistory and had an admonitory brief drawn up against the emperor.[2] He charged Cardinal Giovanni Morone, who was at that time in Lyons, France, with its delivery to the imperial court. The brief, originally consisting of two drafts[3]—the first was more radical than the second—was completed on August 24. It accused the emperor of interference in the rights of the Apostolic See, demanded the withdrawal of all concessions made to Protestants, and threatened, in careful terminology, stern papal action if the emperor should refuse to comply. Finally, the assertion was made that the general council, rather than an imperial diet, should create a settlement of the religious issues dividing Germany, thus repeating the fundamental principle

---

[1] For the text of the *Recess of the Imperial Diet*, cf. J. C. Lünig, *Deutsches Reichsarchiv* (24 vols.; Leipzig, 1710-1722), II, 721-744. A detailed account of the events between the Diet of Spires and the Council of Trent is given in Ernest Graf (trans.), Hubert Jedin's *A History of the Council of Trent* (2 vols.; St. Louis: Herder, 1957), I, 494-544.

[2] Jedin, *op. cit.*, pp. 497-499.

[3] Cf. Stephanus Ehses, *Concilii Tridentini Actorum Pars Prima* (Freiburg im Breisgau, 1904), Nos. 276, 277.

of medieval papalism, that Rome is to be arbiter in temporal affairs and judge in religious affairs.

The admonitory brief, however, never accomplished its purpose, due to a series of diplomatic mishaps:[4] Cardinal Morone could not be located by the papal emissary at the imperial court in Brussels, whence Charles V was directing his war against France. When the emperor refused to see the emissary, the brief was returned to Rome, and a copy was left in Brussels. By the time the emperor learned the contents of the document, it was outdated; a peace had been negotiated on September 18, 1544, between Charles V and Francis I, in which they agreed that a general council should be held at Trent, and Pope Paul III felt compelled to congratulate them in two further briefs composed in October, 1544. The consistory then proposed, on November 14, to convoke the general council March 25, 1545, at Trent.

Both drafts of the papal admonitory brief were already known to German Protestants by December, 1544, through friends in Venice. Rumors of its existence had reached Elector John Frederick of Saxony in October; copies of both drafts were delivered to him on December 27, through Philip of Hesse, the leader of the Smalcald League. Luther received them sometime before January, 1545, and immediately started a furious refutation, which was published on March 25, the day the Council of Trent was to convene. Thus *Against the Roman Papacy, an Institution of the Devil* became a key instrument of Protestant propaganda against papal diplomacy.[5]

The treatise was meant to propagate political Protestantism, although Luther would certainly have written it even without the encouragement of the elector and the leaders of the Smalcald League. Within two months of publication it was praised by Landgrave Philip of Hesse, delivered to King Christian III of Denmark, and read with anger by papal legates to the Diet of Worms and Trent. A series of cartoons by Lucas Cranach, created in the same

---

[4] For a more detailed account, see Jedin, *op. cit.*, pp. 499-504.

[5] In March, 1545, John Calvin also produced a propaganda tract by publishing the text of the brief with sarcastic comments. His *Paternal Admonition of Pope Paul III* (*Admonitio Paterna Pauli III Romani Pontificis*), published in Geneva, is available in *C.R.* 35, 249-288.

year and probably intended to serve as illustrations of the treatise, also appeared.[6] Justus Jonas, Luther's friend, translated the treatise into Latin in November, 1545, thus assuring its international distribution. Luther meant to edit the translation and send it to Trent, but was prevented from doing so by his illness; he died on February 18, 1546.

The treatise is Luther's last great testimony against the papacy, which he called "my great anguish" (*meine grosse Anfechtung*). He dealt here with three questions: (1) whether it is true that the pope is supreme lord over Christendom, councils, angels, and everything else; (2) whether it is true that no one can judge or depose him; and (3) whether it is true that he brought the reign of the Roman Empire from the Greeks to the Germans, that is, whether German emperors could receive the title "Holy Roman Emperor of the German Nation" only from the pope—a fiction fostered by the popes since the coronation of Charles the Great by Leo III in 800.[7] Luther seemed to know that he had not much time left—death would come soon, but not before the fiercest enemy of his cause, the papacy, received his scorn and violent condemnation.

This polemical tract, like *Against Hanswurst*, reveals the faith and wrath of the old Luther. Yet one should not forget that his tracts usually originated as replies against equally abusive and violent attacks.[8] "Dogmatic, superstitious, intolerant, overbearing, and violent as he was, he yet had that inscrutable prerogative of genius of transforming what he touched into new values."[9]

The first edition of the treatise was printed by Hans Lufft in

---

[6] The picture series is found in Fritz Hermann (ed.), *Lutherbibliothek des Paulus-Museums der Stadt Worms* (2nd ed.; Darmstadt, 1922). Cf. the description of the pictures and their origins in WA 54, 346-373, and Hartmann Grisar and Franz Heege (eds.), *Luthers Kampfbilder*, Vol. IV of *Die "Abbildung des Papsttums" und andere Kampfbilder in Flugblättern 1538-1545* (Freiburg im Breisgau, 1923). Cranach (1472-1553) also produced woodcuts for Luther's German Bible and many of his pamphlets.

[7] Luther had already dealt with the question in *An Open Letter to the Christian Nobility* (1520). PE 2, 57-164.

[8] Earlier collections of Luther's works usually printed these attacks and replies together. See, for example, *St. L.* 15 and 18.

[9] Quoted in Schwiebert, *Luther and His Times,* p. 747, from Preserved Smith, *The Age of the Reformation.*

Wittenberg. The title page carried a woodcut showing the pope in the jaws of hell.[10] Four German editions and two Latin translations appeared in the first year, followed by two more German editions in 1565. The translation is based upon the first edition; the text is given in *WA* 54, 206-299. I want to thank Miss Doris Jackson for her help in the preparation of this translation.

---

[10] Cf. the description of cartoon No. 8 in *WA* 54, 351.

AGAINST THE ROMAN PAPACY
AN INSTITUTION OF THE DEVIL

The Most Hellish Father, St. Paul III, in his supposed capacity as the bishop of the Roman church, has written two briefs[1] to Charles V, our lord emperor, wherein he appears almost furious, growling and boasting, according to the example of his predecessors, that neither an emperor nor anyone else has the right to convoke a council, even a national one, except solely the pope; he alone has the power to institute, ordain, and create everything which is to be believed and done in the church. He has also issued a papal bull[2] (if one may speak like that) for about the fifth time; now the council is once again to take place in Trent, but with the condition that no one attend except his own scum, the Epicureans and those agreeable to him—whereupon I felt a great desire to reply, with God's grace and aid. Amen!

First, I beg you, for God's sake, whoever you are, a Christian, indeed, even if you still have natural reason, tell me whether you can understand or comprehend what kind of a council that would be, or whether it could be a council, if that abominable abomination in Rome, who calls himself pope, has such reservation, power, and authority to tear up, change, and ruin everything that is decided in the council, as most of his decrees bellow. Doesn't it seem to you, my dear brother in Christ, or my dear natural-reason friend, that such a council would have to be nothing but a farce, a carnival act put on to amuse the pope.

What is the use of spending such great pains and effort on a council if the pope has decided beforehand that anything done in the council should be subjected to him, that nothing should be

---

[1] The two drafts of the admonitory brief. See p. 259.

[2] The *Bull of Convocation*, proposed on November 14, 1544, by the consistory and read on November 19. Cf. Ehses, *op. cit.*, No. 283, and Jedin, *op. cit.*, p. 504.

done unless it pleased him very much, and that he wants the power to condemn everything? To avoid all this trouble it would be better to say, "Most Hellish Father, since it makes no difference at all what is or will be decided before or in or after the council, we would rather (without any council) believe in and worship Your Hellishness. Just tell us beforehand what we must do; "Good Teacher, what shall I do?" [Mark 10:17]. Then we shall sing the glad hymn to Your Hellishness, "Virgin before, in, and after childbearing,"[3] since you are the pure Virgin Mary, who has not sinned and cannot sin for ever more. If not, then tell us, for God's sake, what need or use there is in councils, since Your Hellishness has such great power over them that they are to be nothing, if it does not please Your Hellishness. Or prove to us poor, obedient "simple Christians"[4] whence Your Hellishness has such power. Where are the seals and letters from your superior that grant such things to you? Where is written evidence which will make us believe this? Won't Your Hellishness show us these things? Well then, we shall diligently search for them ourselves, and with God's help we shall certainly find them shortly.

Meanwhile, we see and hear what a masterly conjurer the pope is. He is like a magician who conjures gulden into the mouths of silly people, but when they open their mouths they have horse dirt in them. So this shameful fop Paul III calls for a council now for the fifth time, so that anyone who hears the words must think he is serious. But before we can turn around, he has conjured horse dirt into our mouths, for he wants to have a council over which he can exercise his power, and whose decisions he could trample on. The very devil himself would thank him for such a council, and no one but the miserable devil, together with his mother, his sister, and his whoring children, pope, cardinals, and the rest of his devilish scum in Rome will get there.

It is now the twenty-fourth year since the first imperial diet was held at Worms under Emperor Charles, at which I person-

---

[3] *Virgo ante partum, in partu, post partum.*

[4] *Bon Christian,* an Italian term used by papal courtesans to describe the uneducated, common man, especially in Germany. Luther probably became acquainted with it during his stay in Rome in 1510. Cf. Heinrich Boehmer, *Luthers Romfahrt* (Leipzig, 1914), p. 143.

ally stood before the emperor and the whole empire. It was the common wish of all estates of the empire in this same diet that several great and intolerable abuses (which were there named and afterward pointed out to Pope Adrian at the Diet of Nürnberg and printed, a copy of which is still available)[5] should be eliminated by the pope and clergy, or the estates would do it themselves. Moreover, it was desired that His Imperial Majesty should ask the pope to call for and hold a general free Christian council in Germany or set up a national council, which the good emperor has until now done diligently; but he has been unable to accomplish anything with the popes. This is why the three words, "free, Christian, council," have remained on everyone's lips in the German lands.

These three words, "free, Christian, German," are to the pope and the Roman court nothing but sheer poison, death, devil, and hell; he cannot stand them, nor see or hear them. That's the way it is! It is certain that he would rather let himself be torn to pieces and would rather become Turkish or devilish or whatever else would help him. This is the reason: in the year 1415 a council was held in Constance, Germany, wherein John Huss and Jerome[6] were martyred; three popes were deposed;[7] and a fourth, Martin V,[8] elected. But the worst and most abominable item which so horrifies the pope is the one decided and established

---

[5] A reference to a combined Latin-German edition of the most significant records of the Diet of Nürnberg in 1522, printed by Peypus in 1523. It contains the *Gravamina*, the grievances of the German nation against the curia. The *Gravamina* was first presented at the Council of Constance in 1417, and thereafter was constantly referred to in German diets. Pope Adrian VI (1522-1523) had a brief sent to the Diet of Nürnberg which Luther published with marginal notes in 1538. See the *Preface, Epilogue, and Marginal Notes to the Brief of Pope Adrian VI (Vorrede, Nachwort und Marginal glossen zu Legatio Adriani Papae VI)*. WA 50, 352-363. The content of Peypus' records is listed in WA 50, 353.

[6] Jerome of Prague, a friend and disciple of John Huss, was executed in 1416, while the Council of Constance was in session (from November 5, 1414, to April 22, 1418). Huss was martyred in 1415.

[7] John XXIII was deposed May 29, 1415; Gregory XII abdicated July 4, 1415; and Benedict XIII, deposed on July 26, 1416, claimed the papal throne until his death in 1424. For the records of the council, cf. John H. Mundy and Kennerly M. Woody (eds.), *The Council of Constance* (New York: Columbia University Press, 1961), pp. 52-65.

[8] Martin V (1417-1431).

there that a council is superior to the pope, not the pope to the council; also, that a council has the power to judge, sentence, punish, elect, or depose the pope, and not the contrary, that the pope could judge, sentence, or change the council. Ow, ouch, oh! That little item hurts them, that sting sticks deep in their heart, that stone nearly flattens their heart; this time they got burned, they won't come back for more, they would rather let the whole world bathe and drown in blood, as Pope Eugene did when he brought about great murder and bloodshed through the French Dauphin at Strassburg, so that he could break up the Council of Basel, which had started, according to the example and order of the Council of Constance, and had already chosen a pope—Amadeus, count of Savoy, called Felix V.[9] But if there was to be peace, this same pope had to abdicate and the council fall, for they cannot and will not again risk the terrible experience they suffered at Constance.

Now the Council of Constance, which was unholy enough, nevertheless had great and inescapable needs and compelling reasons to establish and resolve that a council must be above the pope and not the pope above a council, for there were three popes, not one of whom wished to yield to the others. Thus there was great disorder, and chaos reigned in the whole Roman church, as one pope banned the other, one took the other's endowments and prebends, for each wanted to be the sole pope over everything—no good could come of this. This confusion lasted for about thirty-nine years,[10] so that the whole world cried and begged for a council in order to have a single pope again. For at that time men were of the opinion that Christendom could not exist without a

---

[9] Eugene IV (1431-1447) was compelled to convoke the Council of Basel (1431-1449), but disagreed with its decisions. When it elected Felix V (1439-1449), Eugene IV managed to remain in power, supported by Emperor Frederick III (1440-1493). The "great murder and bloodshed at Strassburg," however, had nothing to do with Eugene IV. It was caused by Louis XI (called "Dauphin" as the eldest son of King Charles VII of France), who assisted Frederick III in the war against the Swiss (1443-1450). His mercenaries plundered Strassburg on their way to Basel in the summer of 1444. Cf. Schäfer, *Luther als Kirchenhistoriker*, pp. 460-461.

[10] The papal schism lasted from 1378 until 1417, when the Council of Constance elected Martin V. Cf. Alexander C. Flick, *The Decline of the Medieval Church* (2 vols.; New York: Knopf, 1930), I, 249-313.

pope. Thereupon the five nations of Germany, Italy, France, England, and Spain joined to help bring about a council at Constance, which the emperor Sigismund[11] convened after great effort.

Now if the council were to depose the popes, it had to reach an agreement beforehand and resolve that a council is to be above the pope and has the power and right to depose him, for papal law prohibits an inferior to depose a superior. Thus their great need compelled them—as one had to depose at least two popes, whereas the third would remain—to decide beforehand that they had the power and the right to depose the popes. So it was then and there decided that the pope was under the council and not above the council, despite the fact that for so many centuries beforehand the pope had cried himself hoarse and bellowed until he nearly died through all his decrees and decretals that said he was above all councils, above all the world, even above all the angels in heaven; that is, he was God's vicar on earth and an earthly god, and so many other abominable things that are terrible for a Christian heart and ears to hear.

Thereupon one pope, named Gregory, abdicated voluntarily and handed his papacy over to the council, albeit in the hope that the council would appreciate his ready humility and re-elect him pope; since this did not happen he died of regret and sorrow.[12] The second pope, named John,[13] was with great difficulty persuaded to go to Constance to the council, in the same and much greater hope that he would remain the only pope because he had sat on the Roman throne. The third, Benedict,[14] remained stiff-necked in his position and was justly and forcefully deposed according to the law and statute of the council. This is the horrible item that has until now so annoyed the popes, and this is why they will not and cannot tolerate a council among the beasts in Germany. They fear that the example of the Council of Constance may be used against them, and that perhaps Paul III would ride into Trent as pope, but ride out again as a poor fool. So it is to his interest, and according to their plan, to stay in Rome without coun-

---

[11] Holy Roman emperor (1410-1437).
[12] Gregory XII. He remained a cardinal and died in 1417.
[13] John XXIII.
[14] Benedict XIII.

cils and above councils, even if the world should come to an end.

For the histories tell of when one Pope John visited Germany; there someone began to examine his life and administration—up to then no one had dared to speak up against him as pope—and it was found that about forty articles were proved against him, all of them worthy of death.[15] Thereupon he fled and tried to get back to Rome, but Emperor Sigismund caught him on the way and he was placed in the custody of the count of the Palatinate.[16] When he was then rebuked with the articles he answered each one with, "Oh, I have done something much worse than that!" This reply amazed the delegates, for, among other articles, it was written he had strangled his father, had practiced black magic, simony, and many more scandalous vices. How could he have done worse things than that? He answered that the worst thing he had ever done was to have allowed himself to be persuaded to cross the Italian mountains from Rome into Germany. By this he meant that if he had stayed in Rome and kept the papacy he would have been free of such accusations and would have remained the Most Holy Father Pope, even if he had done a thousand times as much evil.

Now the popes have learned a lesson from this and take the greatest care not to commit such great folly and sin as to travel across the mountains into Germany like that same Pope John had done. And who can blame them for it? Out of great love and concern for poor Christendom they love the papacy and hate to abandon it, for the pope is the head of all Christendom and lord of the whole world, moreover an earthly divinity whom Christ made his vicar on earth to teach and save all souls. You will understand the rest very well if you just think, "Yes, devil and hell-fire!"

According to that, just look at the writing of this fop, Paul III, when he writes to the emperor, "Do you want a council? We shall grant it to you. Do you want it in Germany? See, we shall even dare to do this. But in such a way that it is a free and Christian

---

[15] Cf. Mundy and Woody (eds.), op. cit., pp. 246-247.
[16] Louis of the Palatinate, German elector (1410-1436). Cf. Frederick I. Antrobus (trans.), Ludwig Pastor's History of the Popes from the Close of the Middle Ages (40 vols.; St. Louis: Herder, 1891-1954), I, 191-200.

council, in which the heretics have no part, as they can have no part in the church; moreover, you should order the arms withdrawn, that is, you should create safety and peace. You should also know that you have no right to judge who shall be ordered to the council—that is the prerogative of our temporal authority."[17] There you see now what kind of language the pope and his holy school of scoundrels in Rome have, and how he teaches us to interpret the three words, "free, Christian, German"; namely, that he wishes to grant a council, which he is certain can never be held, for he knows and senses quite well that he and his accursed school of scoundrels would fare far worse than Pope John did in Constance.

The princes and estates of the empire have been working these twenty-four years, through the emperor, for a free, Christian, German council, with the honest intention—according to the commonly accepted meaning of these words, devoid of all sophistry, namely, that "free" in German and *liberum* in Latin mean that tongues and ears should be free in the council—that everyone, especially those appointed by all sides to speak, listen, and act, may freely say, complain, or respond to whatever is pertinent to reform the church and abolish offenses and abuses. This is how the Germans and imperial estates meant it, and still mean it—but particularly and above all, that God's word, or Holy Scripture, should, free and without strings (as it must be), have its way and its rights, according to which one decides and judges everything. That is why there must also be good theologians there, who have understanding of and experience in the Scriptures. It means "free" because the council is free, and the Scriptures, that is, the Holy Spirit, are free.

But the Roman school of scoundrels and its schoolmaster twist and falsify the word so that "free" should mean that he and his school of scoundrels are free; that nothing shall be said, changed, or undertaken against them; but that absolutely everything, the way they now live and act, will be ratified; that therefore the pope would be free against the council, not the council against

---

[17] Cf. Ehses, *op. cit.*, No. 277. The passage is also quoted in WA 54, 210, n. 6. Luther's translation is not quite accurate.

the pope. This is the pope's old story, of all his decrees and decretals;[18] namely, he should be lord and judge over the council, not the council over the pope, so that the pope has the power to condemn, tear up, and veto anything the council resolved against him. Indeed, before undertaking something they have to ask His Grace to see if it would please him; so that a council would be nothing but a yes-man who sits near the washbowl at the door of the council chamber upstairs and listens to what the gracious lords at the high table propose. This is what the pope calls a free council!

This is the language of the see in Rome, so that when he grants a free council, you may henceforth also understand it in Roman: when they say "free," it means "captive" with us Germans; when they say "white," you must understand "black"; when they say "the Christian church," you must understand "the scum of all the scoundrels in Rome"; when they call the emperor a "son of the church," it is as much as to say he is the most accursed man on earth, who they wish were in hell so that they would have the empire; when they call Germany the praiseworthy nation, it means the beasts and barbarians who are not worthy to feed on the pope's dung, like the Italian Campanus (as one says) did when he had been in Germany (not to his disadvantage) and, on returning to the Italian frontier, turned his back on Germany, squatted, bared his behind, and said, *"Aspice nudatas, Barbara terra, nates,"* "Look here, you beasts, look up my ass."[19]

The princes and estates of the empire also use the word "Christian" with simple, upright intent to be a council in which one should act on Christian affairs through Christian people, according to the Scriptures, for they knew full well how the pope in his canon law had dealt with belts, gowns, shoes, cassocks, tonsures, church dedications, Easter cake-blessings, benefices, prelates

---

[18] *Drecketen und drecketalen.* Cf. p. 205, n. 29.

[19] Gianantonio Campano, court poet of Pope Pius II (1458-1464), known for his satirical report about the barbaric ignorance of Germans he met during his stay at the Diet of Regensburg in 1471. Cf. L. Geiger, *Renaissance und Humanismus in Italien und Deutschland* (Berlin, 1882), pp. 146-147. It is not certain that the saying originated with him. Cf. Thiele, *Luthers Sprichwörtersammlung,* No. 290, and the description of cartoon No. 9 in WA 54, 351.

and pallia,[20] dignities, and countless follies. Instead, since weighty, important matters and disputations are being prepared about indulgences, purgatory, the mass, idolatry, faith, good works, and things like that, one should settle such things in Christian fashion, according to Holy Scripture, not in papal fashion, and help the poor simple man to know just where he stands and what should finally become of his soul. Yes, this in German, Latin, Greek, or any other language means "Christian council." The pope and his hellish scum smelled this quite well, not having a cold.[21] But he took sneezing powder to give himself a cold, and thus distorted this word "Christian" thusly:

"Christian" is to mean nothing more than "papal," and what His Hellishness, including his school of scoundrels (God forgive me, I almost said, "including his holy church"!) in Rome, judge and conclude. Anything undertaken against this should be un-Christian and heretical, namely, if the council wished to conclude that one should freely administer the sacrament in both kinds, as the heretics want to do, it must be condemned by the council at the command of its lord the pope, and those who had planned to bring it up in the council should, as heretics, not be admitted, as the Hellish Father writes to the emperor, "The heretics should have no place in the council and no part in the holy church." And if the heretics were to rebuke the emperor, saying that God the Father had, through his dear Son, instituted such an article and had commanded all the world to hear his Son, Luke 3,[22] "Hear him"; and that the Holy Spirit had maintained it in the whole of Christendom until the pope forbade it in the 1400's; that the majority of Christendom, which is not subject to the pope, still keeps this article [concerning heretics] and will continue to keep it until the end of the world—in spite of all this the emperor should burn, kill, and drive out all the heretics that keep this with God the Father, Son, Holy Spirit and Christians of all the world, even those in India, Persia, and the whole Orient. This is the reason:

---

[20] See p. 168, n. 421.

[21] A German proverb, *"Hatte den schnuppen nicht."* Cf. Thiele, *Luthers Sprichwörtersammlung*, No. 96. In the next sentence Luther reinterprets the proverb to suit his purpose.

[22] Luke 3:22; cf. Luke 9:35.

God the Father, Son, and Holy Spirit, including his holy church, are heretics and un-Christian; only the pope and his Roman school of scoundrels are Christians. Now it is really much better that God the Father, Son, and Holy Spirit, together with his holy church, are condemned as miserable heretics by the council than that the Hellish Father Pope and his hermaphrodites should be called un-Christian.

Un-Christian, heretical views like this, and many more, are taught and held by God the Father, Son, and Holy Spirit in his holy church. For example, it is held that there is no purgatory, since the Hellish Father in Rome has invented it for a fair and has stolen unlimited money and property with it. Again, [it is held] that indulgences are a filthy fraud, with which the Hellish Father has made fools of and defrauded all the world. Again, [it is held] that the mass is a sacrifice for the living and the dead, that the estate of marriage is free, and many more of these things, upon which the papacy now bases itself. I will not mention simony, greed, trading with benefices, pederasty, and other things the Holy See in Rome does and enjoys doing in its most holy life; all of which the Holy Spirit—that un-Christian heretic—and his church condemn to the utmost and cannot bear to hear mentioned.

It follows from this that God, especially the Holy Spirit, who, it is claimed, assembles the councils and directs all their dealings and decisions, cannot come to the Council of Trent or to any papal council and will have to stay out. The reason: the holy virgin, St. Paula III, writes to Emperor Charles that the heretics should have neither part nor place in his holy, free Christian council. Now, it has been shown that God the Holy Spirit is an abominable arch-heretic, as well as God the Father and Son, because against papal and Roman holiness he has instituted and ordained and still today keeps and teaches the administration of his very holy sacrament in both kinds in his churches and condemns those who do not keep it or do it in this way—all of which is contrary and hateful to the hellish see in Rome, who has frequently condemned this as heresy through his bulls, for as his apologists write, he has also become a powerful lord and judge over Scripture and over God's word, able to change what God has instituted and commanded.

272

Now there would probably be help and counsel available so that the Holy Spirit, the poor arch-heretic, might come to grace and be admitted into the holy, free, and Christian council, if he were not too stiff-necked and would humble himself, fall on his knees before the holy virgin St. Paula III, Madame Pope, and kiss her sweet feet, confess his heresy then and there, repent, and recant. He would undoubtedly receive a bull of indulgence, without charge and absolutely free, for both himself and his holy church. But St. Paul, also a great heretic (who confused the whole world, Acts 17 [:6], as the Jews in Thessalonica screamed about him), says in Romans 11 [:29], "The gifts and calling of God are irrevocable," that is, he will change them for no one's sake. This same heretic Paul also confuses the Holy Spirit so that he must remain unrepentant and can find neither grace nor forgiveness for his sin and heresy. That is why he will just have to stay out of the holy, free, Christian council of the holy Madame Pope Paula III. He may, meanwhile, duck and hide himself in his own heretical church, so that Paula III does not catch him; otherwise, he would surely have to be burned to ashes as an arch-heretic. St. Paula, the holy virgin pope, will no doubt find a better, more beautiful, much more Christian, freer, and holier spirit in his holy, free, Christian council.

Someone may think here that I am satisfying my own desire with such scornful, wounding, stinging words to the pope. O Lord God, I am far, far too insignificant to deride the pope. For over six hundred years now he has undoubtedly derided the world, and has laughed up his sleeve at its corruption in body and soul, goods and honor. He does not stop and he cannot stop, as St. Peter calls him in II Peter 2 [:14], "insatiable for sin."[23] No man can believe what an abomination the papacy is. A Christian does not have to be of low intelligence, either, to recognize it. God himself must deride him in the hellish fire, and our Lord Christ, St. Paul says in II Thessalonians 2 [:8], "will slay him with the breath of his mouth and destroy him by his glorious coming." I only deride, with my weak derision, so that those who now live

---

[23] Luther quotes the Greek and translates it into Latin, *Akatapauston amartias; Incessabilem, inquietum incorrigibilter, peccatorem.*

and those who will come after us should know what I have thought of the pope, the damned Antichrist, and so that whoever wishes to be a Christian may be warned against such an abomination.

He distorts and tortures the third word "German" or "in German lands" in this way: Emperor Charles is to see to it that no weapon is to be feared, that is, there should be peace, and no war to fear; the arms should be withdrawn. Now the Roman scoundrel knows very well that Emperor Charles, together with his brother King Ferdinand,[24] and all the German princes, are so powerful that he can keep peace not only in one city, Trent, but also in all of Germany. This scoundrel Paula knows it well (I say), but he warns him of a danger that exists nowhere so that the council cannot be held. At the same time he blames Emperor Charles and the German princes that no council can be held, as though it were not his fault but that of the emperor and estates of the empire who do not provide either peace or security because they do not lay down their sword or armor—but these neither are nor can be at hand.

With these words he obligingly confesses that he never wants to hold a council in the German lands. For when will there be a time when a pope cannot invent or allege that it would be dangerous if the armor is not put aside? Even if the emperor would have him accompanied on the highway by one hundred thousand men on both sides, he would still say, "Yes, but who can trust them?" But if the emperor does not do it, the complaint would be that it is dangerous and not safe, that the way the emperor is doing it he still cannot protect the pope; and so the armor or armaments will remain an eternal obstacle to a council, which the emperor, even if there were a hundred emperors, could not remove. The meaning of putting aside armor, of keeping armor, of free or unfree, of Christian or un-Christian lies in the will and power of the hellish pope.

Such words also provide many other excuses, which cannot be counted, but which the Hellish Father can daily invent with his mind. I shall touch upon several: he can undoubtedly drum up

---

[24] Ferdinand had been king of Austria since 1521. In 1556 he succeeded Charles and his title became Ferdinand I (1556-1564).

274

several men and horses at this time who can raise an alarm that enemies are at hand, creating a dangerous situation. For instance, the Turks have twice been his cover.[25] Or he can fall ill. Oh, who will worry about the devil finding excuses and ways out? But this is his very best one: he can goad France against the empire any time, as he did most diligently in the last twenty years, particularly when the council was due to start. Then he can claim, "Ah, Lord God, how gladly we would hold a council, but because our two sons the emperor and France are at odds, we cannot manage it." This is just what he is doing now when in his bull he sings of his great joy that the two rulers are reconciled and calls for a council in Trent. But O Lord God, how sorry the Hellish Father is that France does not keep the treaty and the split become wider than before.[26]

From this we can now understand that the word of the Hellish Father in Rome, "You are to lay down your arms,"[27] is as much as saying, "You, Emperor Charles, are to see that there is peace; you are not only to put aside your sword, but you are also to see that France puts its aside, which it neither can nor should do. For it is our wish that France give you unrest for ever and ever. That is why, before we hold a council, you Charles, shall always put out fires, and France shall always light them. And if France should get lazy in this, then we ourselves shall blow on it and blow it up, so that you always have something to extinguish and finally get tired of extinguishing. This is how we shall teach you and your German swine to covet a council from the Roman See—and still we shall continue to boast, 'Have the arms withdrawn, have the arms withdrawn!' When you establish peace, we shall grant a council, which will and shall happen when we stop warmongering—which shall never happen!"

Now you can see what a rascally answer the emperor and estates have been given to their plea, which they have now made for twenty-four years, for a free Christian council in Germany. Because those Roman rascals zealously apply themselves, as they

---

[25] A reference to Pope Paul's hesitations to hold the council at Mantua and Vicenza. Cf. Jedin, *op. cit.*, pp. 313-354.
[26] See p. 260.
[27] *Arma iubeas deponi.* See p. 269, n. 17.

have always done, confusing the languages, so that the rascal in Rome answers in gibberish,[28] whereas the emperor and estates speak exact German or Latin, they will never agree on language, to say nothing about being able to convene a council. Doesn't this mean drumming on the emperor's and estates' snouts as one drums on the snouts of fools?[29] The rascals laugh up their sleeves over this and at the same time scold and slander the emperor with the very same words, as though he had looked for a captive, un-Christian, unsafe council, but that they were the most holy people who wanted a free, Christian, safe council. Thus the pious emperor and the estates of the empire now have to have the reputation, with the rascals in Rome, of having wanted, and of still looking for, a forced, captive, compelled, un-Christian, heretical, dangerous, and troublesome council. This is the way to scrape off the tongue and horns of an emperor and an empire.[30] Now plead once more to the Most Holy Father for a council!

Some people think the cardinal of Mainz has perpetrated this rascality, but I don't believe it; it would be much too inferior an example of his craft. He would do it much better, for it seems to me he is the real master, even over those in Rome. Those in Rome have been practiced and well versed in such rascality and roguery for over four hundred years now, as one can see from the pope's decretals and all the histories of emperors. Just look how the poor lawyers are plagued, patching, unifying, and smoothing the Roman rascality with glosses before they can give it any sort of shape; it is just as though a furrier patched up a bad pelt on which neither the skin nor the fur is any good, and which is moreover full of spit, pus, and excrement!

Very well, let it continue as long as it can. The emperor and empire must swallow this kind of rascality; this is not the first emperor with whom the incorrigible rascal in Rome has played like that. They have not spared a single one since they came to power. Maximilian's[31] greatest complaint was that no pope had

---

28 *Rotwelsch.*
29 See p. 9.
30 A German proverb, *"Die Zungen und hörner schaben,"* which means "to rebuke" or "to put someone in his place." Cf. Thiele, *Luthers Sprichwörtersammlung,* No. 396.
31 Maximilian I (1493-1519), predecessor of Charles V.

ever kept faith with him. I should think this Emperor Charles has truly experienced the same thing with Clement VII,[32] Leo X, and now Paul III. In summary, they are all the creatures and heirs of the emperor Phocas, who first established the papacy in Rome, and whom they loyally follow. This same Phocas, as a regicide in Constantinople, murdered his lord, the Emperor Maurice, and his wife and children.[33]

The popes do this kind of thing too. If they could not themselves murder the German emperors, as Clement IV had the noble Conradin, the last duke of Swabia and hereditary king of Naples, publicly executed with the sword;[34] if they have not been able to kill the emperors with treachery and every diabolical wickedness, it is nevertheless their definite intention, and their regret has always been that their bloodthirsty, murderous, evil intentions have been foiled and prevented. The descendants of the emperor Phocas, their founder and regicide, are, as was said, desperate, thorough arch-rascals, murderers, traitors, liars, the very scum of all the most evil men on earth—as is said in Rome itself. They embellish themselves with the names of Christ, St. Peter, and the church, even though they are full of all the worst devils in hell— full, full, and so full that they can do nothing but vomit, throw, and blow out devils! You will say that this is true when you read the histories of how they have treated the emperors.

Very well, as I have said, the emperor Charles and his empire must swallow the gibberish of the rascal in Rome, Paul III; and it really does not yet harm us very much. But it does help the See of Rome to uncover themselves front and rear, and lets us see into their behinds, so that we can know them. Until now we had to believe that the pope was the head of the church, the most holy, the savior of all Christendom. Now we see that he, with his Roman cardinals, is nothing but a desperate scoundrel,

---

[32] Clement VII (1523-1534) opposed the election of Charles V. See Schwiebert, *Luther and His Times*, pp. 55-58.
[33] Luther frequently mentions this story. Cf. p. 90, n. 248.
[34] Clement IV (1265-1268), a Frenchman, managed to drive the Hohenstaufens from Italy with the help of King Louis IX of France. Conradin, the last of the Hohenstaufen line, was defeated and executed by order of Charles of Anjou in 1268. There is, however, no evidence to link Clement IV with the execution. Cf. the description of cartoon No. 5 in WA 54, 350.

the enemy of God and man, the destroyer of Christendom, and Satan's bodily dwelling, who, through him, only harms both church and state, like a werewolf, and mocks and laughs up his sleeve when he hears that such hurts God or man—more of this later.

I have to include a story here, from which one can tell what to think of the holy rascals and murderers of the Roman See. In the year of our Lord 1510 (if I remember correctly) I was in Rome and heard tell this story:[35] about seven German miles this side of Rome there is a spot called Ronciglione, where lived, at the time of Paul II (who reigned seventy years ago), a papal official who saw the blasphemous, devilish nature of the pope and his scum in Rome, and did not give the pope his annual tax from his office. The pope sent for him, he did not come; and whatever the pope ordered him to do, he ignored. Finally the pope put him under the ban, but he did not care about this either. After this, the pope had him tolled out with bells and thrown out and damned with lights extinguished from the pulpit, as is the custom;[36] this did not bother him either. At last, because such obstinate disobedience to the pope in his canon law must be called heresy, he had the official's portrait drawn on paper, with many devils over his head and on both sides, and had it brought to court, accused, and sentenced to the stake for heresy. Then straightaway he took the paper to the fire and burned it. The official also had a portrait of the pope amid his cardinals drawn on paper, with lots of devils above and around them, called a court into session, and the pope and cardinals were accused as the worst scoundrels living on earth, doing immeasurable harm to poor people; and if their leader were to die, they would diligently set in his place the very worst one they could find among themselves; they were surely worthy of hell-fire, and many witnesses testified to all this. Then the judge, the official, and the plaintiffs stepped forth and declared that they should be burned; and quickly, in the name of a thousand devils,

---

[35] This story of Count Deifobo of Anguillara is found in L. A. Muratori, *Rerum Italicarum Scriptores* (28 vols.; Milan, 1723-1738), XXIII, 153. Cf. Boehmer, *Luthers Romfahrt*, p. 135.

[36] A medieval custom symbolizing the exclusion of a person from the "light of the church."

he put the picture of the pope and cardinals into the fire to burn them, until the pope forcefully drove him out.

This story is perhaps ridiculous, but it nevertheless points out a horrible misfortune—that the pope, with his abominable, diabolical nature, causes extraordinarily damaging offense in Rome, and the people who see this stumble over it and become quite Epicurean, just as he himself is. Indeed, almost everyone who comes back from Rome brings along a papal conscience, that is, an Epicurean belief.[37] For this is certain, that the popes and cardinals, including his school of scoundrels, believe in nothing—they laugh when they hear something said of faith. And I myself, in Rome, heard it said openly in the streets, "If there is a hell, then Rome is built on it."[38] That is, "After the devil himself, there is no worse folk than the pope and his followers." That is why it is no wonder that they fear a free council, and shun the light. But they have one basis on which they stand, namely, they believe their estate, office, and teaching is right; so, even though the people are evil, one could neither judge nor condemn the office and the doctrine. Thus they go on and do whatever they want, convinced that nothing can happen to their office—of which we shall say more later.

And even if they would be reformed in a council—which really is not possible—and the pope and cardinals should promise in blood to observe it, it would still be wasted trouble and labor; they would only grow worse afterward than they were before, as happened after the Council of Constance. For since they believe that there is no God, no hell, no life after this life, and live and die like a cow, sow, or other animal, II Peter 2 [:12], it is to them ridiculous to keep seals and letters, and reform. That is why it would be best for the emperor and estates of the empire to let the blasphemous, abominable rascals and damned scum of Satan in Rome just go to the devil. There is no hope of achieving any good anyway; one has to handle it differently, for nothing can be accomplished with councils, as we have seen. The senseless fools imagine that we are in urgent need of their council, as if we or

---

[37] Cf. *ibid.*, p. 111.
[38] Cf. *ibid.*, pp. 145-146, 148.

Christendom could do nothing without their council or office; so they think that one must always run after them and that they can for ever make fools and monkeys out of us. But that is not what we think, and, with God's grace, I will sing them another song. If they do not want to hold a council, they needn't, as far as we are concerned—we have no need of one for ourselves. And if they are furious, they can do something in their pants and hang it around their necks—that would be a musk apple and *pacem*[39] for such gentle saints. God does not think them worthy of bettering themselves or of doing any good; therefore they have been given up to a base mind, Romans 2 [1:28]. There you find a list of papal Roman virtues, as in II Peter 2. Let this be enough.

In Pope Paul's briefs to the emperor Charles, it says further, "And you should know that it is not your prerogative to choose who shall be in the council, for that is the prerogative of our jurisdiction."[40] Gently, dear Pauli, dear donkey, don't dance around! Oh, dearest little ass-pope, don't dance around—dearest, dearest little donkey, don't do it. For the ice is very solidly frozen this year because there was no wind—you might fall and break a leg. If a fart should escape you while you were falling, the whole world would laugh at you and say, "Ugh, the devil! How the ass-pope has befouled himself!" And that would be a great crime of lese majesty[41] against the Holy See in Rome, which no letters of indulgence or "plentitude of power"[42] could forgive. Oh, that would be dangerous! So consider your own great danger beforehand, Hellish Father.

Dear one, why shouldn't the emperor have authority to name at least several who should be in the council, since the four principal councils of Nicaea, Constantinople, Ephesus, and Chalcedon were not called by the popes (as there was no pope yet at that

---

[39] A small tablet showing the image of the Virgin Mary, or a relic which was kissed by the faithful, usually before holy communion.

[40] Cf. p. 269, n. 17.

[41] *Limen Crese maiestatis*, i.e., *crimen laesae maiestatis*. Luther mutilates the Latin to emphasize the irony of his sentence.

[42] *Plenitudo potestatis*, the canonist doctrine of the papal prerogative, the extent of which was dangerously undefined. For a general description of papal jurisdiction, see Charles G. Herbermann *et al.* (eds.), *The Catholic Encyclopedia* (15 vols.; New York, 1907-1912), XII, 269-270.

time), nor by bishops, but solely by the emperors Constantine, Theodosius I, Theodosius II, and Marcian,[43] who assembled, called, and named the bishops to the council, and themselves attended it. "Yes, we afterward established in our decretals that only the pope should convoke councils and name the participants." But dear one, is this true? Who commanded you to establish this? "Silence, you heretic! What comes out of our mouth must be kept!" I hear it— which mouth do you mean? The one from which the farts come? (You can keep that yourself!) Or the one into which the good Corsican wine flows? (Let a dog shit into that!) "Oh, you abominable Luther, should you talk to the pope like this?" Shame on you too, you blasphemous, desperate rogues and crude asses— and should you talk to an emperor and empire like this? Yes, should you malign and desecrate four such high councils with the four greatest Christian emperors, just for the sake of your farts and decretals? Why do you let yourselves imagine that you are better than crass, crude, ignorant asses and fools, who neither know nor wish to know what councils, bishops, churches, emperors—indeed, what God and his word—are? You are a crude ass, you ass-pope, and an ass you will remain!

Again, besides these four great councils there have been many others, now and again, in Greece, Asia, Syria, Egypt, Africa, which did not first confer with the bishop of Rome about it, and were nevertheless good Christian councils, particularly those in which St. Cyprian and St. Augustine participated. Charles the Great too held councils in Frankfurt[44] and France, his son Louis in Aachen,[45] and other emperors held councils too. Dear one, should such bishops and emperors have done wrong and should they be damned merely because this farting ass in Rome (what else can he do?) sets up, out of his own mad head, and farts, out of his stinking belly, that it is not fitting for the emperor to convoke a council or to decide or name who shall attend? Oh, how good the

---

[43] See p. 22, n. 30; p. 23, n. 33; p. 24, nn. 39, 40.
[44] The Council of Frankfurt in 794 rejected the veneration of pictures, a decision which was approved by the Council of Nicaea in 787.
[45] The Council of Aachen in 816 and 817, under Louis the Pious (814-840), was primarily concerned with organizational reforms in the church.

crude donkey feels! He is looking for someone who will lay a stick to his sack, so that his loins will have to bend!

In the second brief[46] to Emperor Charles he wants to be a theologian (if one may call him that) and introduces the example of Eli in I Kings 2 [I Sam. 2:27-36], who was punished for not having admonished his sons for their sins. He too is obliged to admonish the emperor, as his first-born son, so that he would not also be punished—for it was to be feared that grave unrest and disagreement would arise in the church from the great evil committed by Emperor Charles at Spires, etc. Here once again the desperate rascal and scoundrel Paul, with his hermaphrodites, talks gibberish, just as though no one knew what their hellish, devilish doings in Rome were like, or how he himself, the insatiable, bottomless pit of covetousness, Paul, including his son,[47] carries on with the possessions of the church. No, his son does not sin, does nothing that his father Paul would have to punish; the cardinals, hermaphrodites, and servants of the Roman See, "in their front parts men, in their back parts women,"[48] are entirely clean and have no need of admonition. And as the poet Mantuanus writes of the curia:

> The house of Peter is decadent, defiled with
> luxury unrestrained. In this I am disclosing no
> secrets, I am telling nothing unknown, I crave
> permission to state matters of common knowledge,
> this is what the cities and peoples talk about,
> this is the scandal, the old established scandal
> throughout all Europe, that is destroying good
> sound morality: sacred land is given over to
> debauchees, the holy altar is made over to catamounts,
> and the reverend temples of the gods serve the turn
> of Ganymedes. Why be surprised that their wealth
> grows and their fallen houses are rebuilt? The
> effeminate Arab sells balls of scented incense,

---

[46] Cf. Ehses, *op. cit.*, No. 276. The passage is quoted in *WA* 54, 222, n. 5.
[47] Pier Luigi Farnese. Cardinal Alexander Farnese had four children when he became Pope Paul III in 1533. Cf. "Paul III," *O.D.C.C.*, p. 1032.
[48] *A parte ante viri, a parte post mulieres.*

the Tyrians sell raiment; temples, priests, altars,
holy things, wreaths, fires, incense, prayers are
on sale to us—heaven is on sale—and God himself.
But all this is ancient history; nowadays morals are
good and sound.[49]

We in Germany are accused of being heretics, of destroying
churches, monasteries, masses, the Roman and blasphemous idolatries. But just look at how they themselves, who teach such idolatry as true worship, deal with it in Rome. Look at the churches of
St. Agnes, which previously had one hundred fifty nuns, St. Pan-
cras, St. Sebastian, St. Paul, and all the rich monasteries and
churches inside and outside Rome.[50] The pope and cardinals have
gobbled up all of these, and now they come out to us and take
hold of our churches and monasteries too, with pallia, annates,
and many other robberies and extortions. In all of these and many
other abominations, for which God has destroyed Sodom and Gomorrah, as well as many cities in every land, by flooding water
and shaking earthquake—here, I say, the holy virgin St. Paula the
pope has no conscience, no worry, no fear of God, that they might,
like Korah [Num. 16:32], be swallowed up into the earth. St. Paul
III has no right to admonish us when they themselves invalidate
the many masses, vigils, canonical hours, and daily worship ser-

---

[49] Baptista Spagnuolo Mantovano (1448-1516), called "the Mantuanian" for
his hometown Mantua, was a vicar general of the Carmelite Order. This passage is found in *On the Calamities of Our Times or On the Seven Deadly Sins*
(*De Calamitatibus Horum Temporum Sive de VII Peccatis Capitalibus*), lib.
iii. Cf. Boehmer, *Luthers Romfahrt*, pp. 104, 152, 157.

> *Petrique domus polluta fluente*
> *Marcescit luxu. Nulla hic arcana revelo,*
> *Non ignota loquor, liceat vulgata referre:*
> *Sic urbes populique ferunt, ea fama per omnem*
> *Iam vetus Europam mores extirpat honestos*
> *Sanctus ager Scurris, venerabilis ara Cynedis*
> *Servit, honorandae divum Ganymedibus aedes.*
> *Quid miramur opes recidivaque surgere tecta?*
> *Thuris odorati globulos et cynnama vendit*
> *Mollis arabs, Tyrii vestes, venalia nobis*
> *Templa, sacerdotes, altaria, sacra, coronae*
> *Ignes, thura, preces, coelum est venale Deusque.*
> *Sed haec vetera, nunc honesti mores sunt.*

[50] Luther visited these churches in 1510. See Boehmer, *Luthers Romfahrt*, pp.
145, 151.

vices, which they so vociferously demand from us and about which they call us heretics, when they are almost all much worse than Sodom and Gomorrah and live in a way that could not be more abominable.

But there is a great uproar about what Emperor Charles did at Spires—Pope Paul is worried about his son Charles, lest some great misfortune befall him. What then has his dear son Charles done at Spires? Well, he did not want to start a bloodbath in Germany, in which the devil, the pope, and the cardinals would have loved to bathe and which would have protected their hellish scum; instead, he suspended the Edict of Worms, from which all the unrest in Germany had come, and he did this so that they could resist the Turks with a united front, as a pious Christian emperor should provide his fatherland with peace and protection. This is what the scoundrel in Rome calls "wrongdoing." Oh, dreadful sin! So what do the rascals call well done, apart from what they do in Rome? From now on the sun is weary of shining on them, and the land (as they themselves say) can bear them no longer [Gen. 13:6]. For thus I have heard it said in Rome myself, "It is impossible that it should continue like this; it must break."[51]

Then the other thing Emperor Charles did at Spires—oh, dare I mention it? *Horresco referens*, I shudder at the thought of it. Dear one, pray a Pater Noster for me, so that I may not, like Eli [I Sam. 2:12-17, 22], be punished. Oh, dear sun, do not get frightened and do not turn black at my speech, now that I tell of such a great sin. This is the sin: Emperor Charles would like to have peace and unity in religion, just as he would like to see peace in the empire. But because he has now for twenty-four years vainly worked to attain a general Christian council from the pope, and has attained nothing except that the pope has drummed on his snout and treated him as his fool, he has set about—following the worthy example of Constantine, Theodosius I and Theodosius II, Marcian, Charles the Great, Louis I, and many other emperors—calling a national council, although he really has the right and authority to call a general one, no matter what the Roman rascal spits out in his decretals. Oh, may God forgive me, if it can be

---

[51] See *ibid.*, pp. 146 ff.

forgiven, that I have dared to speak of such an appalling sin! Oh, that Emperor Charles not go out into the sunshine, for the sun might fall from heaven before such a great sinner, and we should have to pay for him, and sit in darkness for evermore! Oh, that the holy fathers, pope, and cardinals, with their horde, would support us with their good works and their virtues, like their Epicurean faith, sodomy, simony, mockery, blasphemy of God and his Christians and all their worship. Perhaps their god, whom St. Paul calls "the god of this world" [II Cor. 4:4], will have mercy on us.

Do you almost believe that the Roman See, pope and cardinals, are possessed of all the devils and their rascally gibberish has neither bottom, end, nor measure? Do you almost believe that such villains must be Epicureans and the enemies of God and man? Here you certainly see that the pope would rather see all Germany drowned in its own blood than have peace there, and would rather have all the world go to hell-fire with him than that one soul should be brought to true faith. Now that the pope's horrible, frightening will has not been carried out, but hindered by Emperor Charles, the pope cannot forgive it, but threatens him with the example of Eli. Now here you have a gloss of the C. *Si Papa*, dist. XL:[52] "If a pope is found to have forgotten his own and his brothers' salvation; to be lazy and lax in his works; and to be silent about teaching the best, which is that much more harmful to himself and others (as if such could happen in faith!),[53] and moreover drags with himself to the devil in hell countless souls in great throngs, who, with him, must eternally suffer great pain—such sin cannot be punished by any man alive, for he is the judge of all, and to be judged by none, unless he be found erring in faith (after the year of Plato!)."[54] Instead, the whole of Christendom prays all the more zealously for his office, especially when it notices that its salvation depends, next to God, on his welfare.

Everyone can see that such a decree must have been blown

---

[52] *Decreti Prima Pars*, dist. XL, C. VI. *CIC* 1, 146; *MPL* 187, 214-215.

[53] *Quasi talia fieri possint in fide!* Luther's interpolation.

[54] *Post annum Platonis!* Another interpolation, meaning a long time or never. The notion of a "year of Plato" or a "great year" (*annus magnum*) is based upon Plato's Pythagorean speculations concerning the movement of heavenly bodies. Cf. Francis M. Cornford, *Plato's Cosmology: The Timaeus of Plato, Translated with a Running Commentary* (London, 1956), pp. 115-117.

into the pope and Roman See by all the existing devils with one breath; and I, when I read this decree twenty-six years ago, thought, by God, that these were vain words, like the *Donation of Constantine*,[55] and that it was impossible for any pope to be so corrupt that he would accept such a decree or build upon it. But, since Sylvester[56] and some others wrote against me and used things like this against me, I really had to believe it; and, as you can see in Paul III's brief, he is also of this opinion, and would like to lead the whole world to hell with him. Now whoever does not want to believe that the papacy is the devil's possession and of his own realm is welcome to ride to hell with him! We hear the word of our Lord, Matthew 7 [:15], "Beware of false prophets"; I Corinthians 1 [2:15], "The spiritual man judges all things."[57] More of this later. We shall and should be the pope's judge, and no one shall stop us.

But let us also see how the ass distorts the Scriptures, as he introduces Eli and his sons. The text in I Kings [I Sam. 2:12-17, 22] says the sons of Eli were evil scoundrels and committed three offenses. First, they neither knew nor esteemed the Lord; second, they did not know what the priestly duties to the people were; and third, they lay with the spiritual women who served God in the tabernacle—these were widows who after the death of their husbands dedicated themselves to service in the temple, as it says in Luke 3 [2:37] about holy Anna, that she never again left the temple, fasted and prayed, etc.

The first item—neither to know nor to esteem the Lord—means not to believe in God, scorning his promises or word and

---

[55] A papal document of the eighth century that claimed Constantine the Great had ordered all ecclesiastics to be subject to the bishop of Rome, Sylvester, and transferred to him "the city of Rome and all the provinces, districts, and cities of Italy or of the Western regions." The Renaissance scholars Nicholas of Cues and Lorenzo Valla proved it a forgery in 1440. Luther published the *Donation* with marginal notes in 1537. See *One of the High Articles of the Most Holy Papal Faith, Called the Donation of Constantine* (*Einer aus den hohen Artikeln des Allerheiligesten Bepstlichen glaubens genant Donatio Constantini*). WA 50, 65-89.

[56] Sylvester Prierias, against whom Luther wrote several tracts; see, for example, *A Response to the Dialogue of Sylvester Prierias Concerning the Power of the Pope* (*Ad dialogum Silvestri Prieratis de potestate papae responsio, 1518*). WA 1, 644-689. See also Schwiebert, *op. cit.*, pp. 338-340.

[57] *Spiritualis omnia judicat.*

living in unbelief, roughly and ruthlessly, without any fear of God. The second—that they did not esteem their priestly office, that is, how they should sacrifice and teach the people—means, as it says in the text, that they did what they wished with the sacrifice and whatever they spoke against the law had to be right, which upset the people very much. The third is that they shamelessly committed adultery with dedicated women, for they had wives of their own, and did this in a holy place, in the temple before the face of God, who had promised that he would dwell there. Eli made himself a participant in these sins by not punishing his sons; he does speak about it for the sake of the people, but not seriously, for he did not remove them from office, does not want to shame them, and lets them carry on in their ways. That is what God says, that Eli had esteemed his sons more than God, for he preferred the honor of his sons, wishing them to remain in office, to God's word and obedience.

This is a fine example and would fit extremely well if the emperor Charles would turn it around and hold it under the pope's nose—he would then be hanged with his own rope,[58] namely, like this: do you hear, Pope Paul, first of all you have no faith, and you and your sons, the cardinals and the curia's riffraff, do not honor God, for you are Epicurean sows, just like all the popes, your predecessors. When one reads the papal decretals from the beginning to the end one cannot find a single letter which teaches what faith is or how one should believe like a Christian; nor can any iota of faith enter the heart of a pope or cardinal, that much is certain! Second, you with all of your Roman court and predecessors do not know what a priestly office is, how to instruct the people in God's word and commandments, or how to praise God, for one can find nothing of this in any decretal so that one could make a sermon; instead, all of it is human teaching and conceit, which is simply idolatry. Third, you and your children commit abominable unchastity, for the cardinals and the Sodomists[59] and hermaphrodites of your court lead such horrible lives

---

[58] The original reads, *So würde er mit seinem eigen Schwert auff seine Platten [Tonsur] geschmissen.*

[59] *Puseron*, probably from *pusiones*, "little boys."

that heaven and earth quake and tremble before them. You see, hear, and know this well, and yet you say nothing about it, punish and reform nothing, but laugh at it and find pleasure in it, Romans 1 [:32]. That is why you shall not have it as good as Eli, but will have to join your predecessors in the depths of hell. Indeed, in this way the example would correctly apply to the pope, and thus it would be found that the pope and his cardinals are crude asses, unlearned in the Scriptures.

Now along comes this bishop of hermaphrodites and pope of Sodomists, that is, the apostle of the devil, and quotes this example against Emperor Charles; and just as he and his predecessors are malicious in their gibberish, so does he also try to make God a scoundrel in Holy Scripture. He pretends that the emperor is a great sinner for having suspended the Edict of Worms for the sake of peace and for wishing to convoke a national council; he makes sin and damnation praiseworthy, high, noble, princely virtues. Another one of the idolatrous horrors of the pope is that he makes sin and damnation where God wants none, as one can see throughout the whole decretal. The reason is that he is, as the lawyers say, an earthly god, so he must make sin and damnation what the heavenly God considers virtue and innocence, as St. Paul says in II Thessalonians 2 [:3], "Man of sin and son of perdition." In Hebrew "man of sin" means one who not only is a sinner in his own right, but who through false doctrine causes others to sin with him, as Jeroboam the king of Israel sinned [I Kings 14:16], or, as Scripture says, made Israel to sin, through his idolatry.

Thus this pope of Sodomists, this founder and master of all sins, here wants to push sin and damnation off onto Emperor Charles, although he knows quite well that his rascally tongue lies abominably. And such accursed villains want to convince the world that they are head of the church, the mother of all churches, and masters of the faith. Why even if we were stones and wooden blocks, we could see by their works throughout all the world that they are lost, desperate children of the devil and also mad, crude asses in Scripture. Someone probably would like to curse them so that they might be struck down by lightning and thunder, burned

288

by hellish fire, have the plague, syphilis,[60] epilepsy,[61] the plague of St. Anthony,[62] leprosy, carbuncles, and all the plagues—but these are all caresses,[63] and God has long ago punished them with greater plagues, just like God's despisers and blasphemers should be punished, Romans 1 [:26-27], namely, that in sanity they have become so obviously mad and raving that they do not know whether they are or want to be male or female; they are not ashamed in the presence of women, and their mothers, sisters, and grandmothers are among those forced to see and hear such things of them, to their great distress. Shame on you, popes, cardinals, and whatever you are at the curia, that you are not afraid of the cobblestones upon which you ride, which would like to swallow you!

The imperial laws have much to say about how to handle furious, insane, mad people. How much greater the need is here to put into stocks, chains, and prisons the pope, cardinals, and the whole Roman See, who have not become raving mad in the usual way, but who rage so horribly that at one time they want to be men, at another women, and never know at any one time when their mood will strike them. We Christians should nevertheless believe that such raving and lunatic Roman hermaphrodites have the Holy Spirit and are the heads, masters, and teachers of Christendom! But I must stop here, or save what I could write further against the papal briefs and bulls, for my head is weak, and I feel that I might not get everything said, and yet I still have not gotten to the points I had intended to make in this book. I will do this first, before my strength gives out completely. I wanted to cover three things: first, whether it is true that the pope in Rome is the head of Christendom—above councils, emperor, angels, etc.—as he boasts; second, whether it is true that no one may sentence, judge, or depose him, as he bellows; and third, whether it is true that he

---

[60] *Frantzosen,* "the disease of the French."

[61] *St. Velten,* i.e., epilepsy. St. Valentine was revered as the mitigator of this disease.

[62] *S. Antonii,* or *plaga S. Antonii,* frequently called "the fire of St. Anthony," a disease treated in the Middle Ages especially by the Hospitalers of St. Anthony, a religious order founded in the eleventh century. Although the exact nature of the disease is unknown, it was a serious inflamation of the hands and feet.

[63] *Fuchsschwentze.*

has transferred the Roman Empire from the Greeks to us Germans,[64] about which he boasts immeasurably and beats his breast. Should I then have some strength left, I shall again take up his bulls and briefs and try to see if I can comb out the crass, crude donkey's long unkempt ears for him![65]

Part I

It is very easy to prove that the pope is neither the commander or head of Christendom, nor lord of the world above emperor, councils, and everything, as he lies, blasphemes, curses, and raves in his decretals, to which the hellish Satan drives him. He himself knows full well—and it is as clear as the dear sun from all the decrees of the ancient councils, from all the histories, from the writings of the holy fathers, Jerome, Augustine, and Cyprian, and from all of Christendom before the first pope, who was called Boniface III[66]—that the bishop of Rome was nothing more than a bishop and should still be that. St. Jerome dared to say freely, "All bishops are equal, all together they have inherited the throne of the apostles," and adds the example, "as the bishop of a small city—like Engubium[67] and Rome, Regium and Constantinople, Thebes and Alexandria."[68] He says that one is higher or lower than another because one bishopric is richer or poorer than the other. Other than this they are all equally the successors to the apostles, so he says.[69] This (I say) the pope in Rome knows perfectly well, and he also knows that St. Jerome wrote this; and as proof, it is contained in the *Decretum,* as we read in C. XCIII.[70] Still, the pope dares to

---

[64] See p. 261.

[65] Cf. the description of cartoon No. 8, used on the title page of this tract, in WA 54, 351.

[66] Boniface III convinced King Phocas to acknowledge Rome as "the head of all churches" (*caput omnium ecclesiarum*). This is why Luther calls him "the first pope."

[67] Gubbio in Italy.

[68] *Epistola 146, ad Evagrium. MPL* 22, 1194; *PNF*[2] 6, 289. The original reads *Evangelum.* Luther published the letter in 1538. *WA* 50, 338-343.

[69] *Haec ille.*

[70] *Decreti Prima Pars,* dist. XCIII, C. XXIV. *CIC* 1, 327-329; *MPL* 187, 412c-414.

lie so brazenly and blasphemously against it, and deceive the whole world.

In addition, St. Gregory, when it [the title "universal pope"] was offered to him by several great bishops, sharply refused it and writes that none of his predecessors had been so bold as to accept or wish to carry such a title,[71] although the sixth council in Chalcedon[72] had offered it to them; he closes by saying briefly and to the point that no one should call himself the highest bishop or head of the whole of Christendom, as many decrees also say, and furthermore, that the bishop of Rome too, though he is one of the greater ones, is nonetheless not to be called *universalis,* the head of "all" Christendom. This is the very plain truth, regardless of how he himself and his hypocrites martyr and crucify these words, for they are too clear and powerful. Thus their deeds are out in the open, for he has never had authority over the bishops in Africa, Greece, Asia, Egypt, Syria, Persia, etc., and never will have; indeed, at that time he did not have authority over the bishops in Italy either, especially those of Milan and Ravenna.

This St. Gregory was the last bishop of Rome, and the Roman church has not had another bishop since then, up to the present day, and will not get one either, unless a miraculous change should occur; instead, vain popes, who are masks of the devil (as you will hear), have ruled there and damaged all the churches physically and spiritually. It is certain, as was said, that at the time of St. Gregory there was no pope, and he himself, together with his predecessors, did not want to be pope; moreover, he condemned the papacy in many of his writings, although he had been painted with a papal crown and many lies have been made up about him. But he is not a pope and does not wish to be a pope, as his books testify to the disgrace of all the popes who have arisen after him and against him.

---

[71] Gregory I (590-604) refused the title "universal pope" (*universalis Papa*) and wanted to be called "servant of servants" (*servus servorum*). See, for example, *Book IX of the Epistles* (*Liber Nonus Epistolarum*), *Epistola 68, ad Eusebius Thessalonica. MPL* 77, 1004*ab; PNF*[2] 13, 18. See also Headley, *Luther's View of Church History,* pp. 190-193.

[72] Not the sixth, but the fourth, ecumenical council. There is, however, no evidence that it had offered the title to the Roman bishop. Cf. William R. Clark (trans.), Joseph Hefele's *A History of the Councils of the Church* (2nd ed.; 5 vols.; Edinburgh, 1876-1896), III, 429-438.

But after Gregory's death Sabinianus[73] was a bishop for a year and a half; I count him among the popes, for he was a big monster, like a pope is, and wanted to burn the books of St. Gregory, his immediate predecessor—perhaps because in his writings St. Gregory did not want the papacy to be tolerated. Boniface III was elected after him. This is when God's wrath began. This Boniface persuaded the regicide Phocas that he should be pope, or chief of all the bishops in the whole world. The bell was cast[74] then, and the Roman horror accepted with joy, as the one who was now lord over all the bishops in the world. For this is what several of his predecessors had sought and pined for, but had not been able to attain, because St. Gregory and several devout bishops, his predecessors, had not tolerated it. There we have the origin and beginning of the papacy, when and by whom it was founded—namely, Emperor Phocas, the regicide, who had his lord, Emperor Maurice, and his wife and children, beheaded. They themselves know very well that these things are true.

Now up to that time it had been the custom for the emperors, as patrons, to confirm all the bishops, for when St. Gregory was elected by the people and priests of Rome he asked Emperor Maurice in writing not to confirm his election,[75] for he was a humble, devout man, and did not wish to become bishop. But his writing was intercepted, and Emperor Maurice confirmed his election against his will. Thereafter the popes thought that since they had the papacy from the emperor Phocas, perhaps another emperor might take it from them again. For so it must be, in the worldly sphere, that if an emperor gives out grace, then he may take it back if the wickedness of the possessor merits it. This is how German emperors, Frederick, Lothar, and the Ottos,[76] have often taken from the princes what they had given them, and returned it after repentance. That is why the succeeding popes came along and did not

---

[73] Sabinianus was pope from 604 to 606.

[74] A German proverb, *"Da ward die Glocke gegossen,"* similar to the English expression, "The die was cast." Cf. Thiele, *Luthers Sprichwörtersammlung,* No. 124.

[75] Luther is retelling a story reported by Gregory of Tours in *The History of the Franks,* X, 1. *MPL* 71, 527d.

[76] Probably Frederick I (1152-1190), Lothar II (1125-1137), Otto I (936-973), Otto II (973-983), Otto III (983-1002).

want to have the papacy from emperor or council, but directly from God; they made one decree after another, boasting, shouting, and roaring that the Roman church and the pope were not founded by men or by councils, but instituted by Christ himself, over the whole world. They particularly like to embellish themselves with the passage in Matthew 16 [:18-19], "You are Peter, and on this rock I will build my church, and the gates of Hades shall not prevail against it. I will give you the keys of the kingdom of heaven, and whatever you bind on earth shall be bound in heaven," etc. They also quote this one, John 21 [:15], "Feed my lambs."[77] But they have achieved the most with the passage in Matthew 16, with which they have frightened the world, suppressed all the bishoprics, and trampled the emperors and the secular government underfoot.

Now these abominable liars and blasphemers of God's word knew very well and still know very well that this passage does not prove their point, nor is it relevant; every letter in it is against them, drives the papacy into the ground, and vitiates it, as I argued twenty-five years ago in the *Resolutions*[78] and in public disputation against Dr. Sow in Leipzig,[79] and intend to go on doing hereafter. But it was balm to the hearts of these desperate scoundrels in Rome that the world, both bishops and emperor, let themselves be frightened and intimidated by this passage, as befits good Christians who did not want to act against God and his word. For this is the pope's first rascality and blasphemy against God's holy words.

When they now saw that such rascality had succeeded, through God's terrible wrath over the world because of its sinfulness, and that everyone was afraid of such words, they were truly neither lazy nor sleepy, and, comforted, pressed on with every knavery and help of the devil. They began to interpret, sharpen, and strengthen their papacy or primacy, which they had founded through their own invented, lying decree, and through blasphemous, false, and rascally exegesis of the passage in Matthew 16, by

---

[77] *Pasce oves meas.*

[78] *Resolution Concerning the Lutheran Thesis XIII On the Power of the Pope* (*Resolutio Lutheriana Super Propositione Sua Decima Tertia De Potestate Papae*) (1519). WA 2, 180-239.

[79] The Leipzig Debate (1519), in which Luther and John Eck argued the authority of the pope and the jurisdiction of the church of Rome. See LW 31, 309-325. Luther frequently calls Eck Dr. Sow. See in this volume, p. 235, n. 100.

saying that the pope was the head, not only because of honor and rank (which would probably have been granted to him) and because of superintendence[80]—that he was an overseer of the teaching and heresy in the church (which is much too much for a single bishop, and impossible to do throughout the whole world)—but because with the power that he had as their lord he could force the bishops into subjection in a powerful and worldly, indeed, even a tyrannical fashion, could bind them with oaths and obligations, make them vassals, take their bishoprics, enthrone and depose, change, steal, take, give, assess, and sell them, as well as burden them most highhandedly with pallia, annates, and countless chicaneries. Whoever refused to do or tolerate this had to be condemned eternally as disobedient to the Roman church, a heretic, and one who sinned against the passage in Matthew 16.

A chancellor in Mainz named Martin Meyer wrote[81] to Eneas Silvius, later called Pope Pius II (Meyer had been a close companion of Silvius while Silvius was away from Rome at the court of Emperor Frederick III in Germany for several years),[82] and complained that the pope was burdening and plundering the convents with annates and pallia. The proud hypocrites answered him, saying, among many other wicked, cutting things, that Germany deserved to bear such a load because the pope had bestowed the Roman Empire upon the Germans; and the pope had to have a great deal of money so that he could prevent the emperor from overcoming France, or France from overcoming England. Just look at these desperate rascals and scoundrels—look at what they have in mind and at their secret intention, namely, to keep the two sovereigns at odds and in such a position that they can back now the one, now the other, as the wind blows; meanwhile they are safe from the beasts and have no need to fear either reformation or council.

---

[80] *Superattendentz*, hence the later title "Superintendent" or *Superattendent* in the Lutheran church.

[81] Meyer's letter is dated August 31, 1451. Luther had discussed the correspondence in 1537 when he edited the work of a Dominican monk, Giovanni Nanni, on the state of Christendom during the Turkish threat in 1481. Cf. *Comment on Giovanni Nanni's Disputation on the Rule of the Pope (Ioannis de monarchia papae disputatio)*. WA 50, 96-105.

[82] Pius II had been secretary in 1432 to the bishop of Fermo, who attended the Council of Basel. Frederick III hired him as secretary in 1442. Cf. Pastor, *op. cit.*, I, 343-344.

Their deeds and history testify to this over and over again, just as in our time Clement VII sent help, before Pavia in 1525, to the French against our Emperor Charles;[83] and when this misfired, he wiped his snout, like the whore in Proverbs 30 [:20], and said he had done it for the good of the emperor. Thus, to his ridicule and hurt, Emperor Charles had to let him drum on his snout, although he was later, in the year 1527, attacked in Rome and captured,[84] but did not receive his just desserts due to the emperor's goodness.

Oh, how can a pope do otherwise? Consider it yourself: when a desperate, wicked, cunning knave puts on the mask and name of Christ or St. Peter and gains such an advantage that the Christians fear him and flee, for the sake of the names of Christ and St. Peter, he has won and does what he likes, commits one rascality after another, particularly when God's wrath allows the devil to lift and push him along. Christ has warned us enough, Matthew 24 [:23], that many would come in his name and say, "I am the Christ." And Matthew 7 [:15], "Beware of false prophets, who come to you in sheep's clothing." Thus the pope too, under the mask and name of Christ and St. Peter, has intimidated and fooled the whole world, as he wanted to do; and through the devil he has put up a show of great devotion and spirituality, until he has reached the point that he now raves openly and with all his might, in every depravity, so that there is no means of stopping him from now on. But the scoundrel Eneas Silvius would have deserved to be set straight by the scholars; he really boasts quite proudly that the pope should become involved in wars between kings, so that he can rightfully plunder the convents. Why doesn't he look for other means, such as prayer and preaching, to reconcile the kings? But what are prayer and God's word to the pope? He must serve his own god the devil!

But all this, although it is unbearable and intolerable, is still the least of it. The foremost and worst scum of all the devils in hell is that he expands such power to the point that he wants authority to establish laws and articles of faith, to interpret Scripture (which

---

[83] Charles V defeated Francis I of France despite the pope's intervention. On the pope's involvement, cf. Jedin, *op. cit.*, pp. 220-232.
[84] The famous "sack of Rome" on May 6, 1525. Cf. *ibid.*, p. 232.

he never learned, does not know, and does not wish to know) according to his own mad fancy; he wants to force the whole world to believe his teaching, though he teaches nothing but pure idolatry, as we shall hear; and he destroys everything that the Son of God our Lord gained for us with his blood. He takes away faith, Christian freedom, and true good works, and calls it, in his devilish, villainous decretals, "well done and obedience to the church"; and he roars as one possessed and full of devils that whoever is not obedient to him and his Roman church cannot attain salvation. He who is obedient will be saved; the only thing that matters to him is that the whole world should be obedient and subject to him. He does not ask for obedience to God and Christ—this thought does not occur to him at all.

But you must under no circumstances understand the words "Roman church" as meaning the true Roman church, especially the one that existed before the papacy, which did not wish either to accept or tolerate the papacy, as we heard in St. Gregory[85]—also, Christ certainly still has several Lots and his daughters [Gen. 19:15] in the Roman Sodom, who are displeased by the horrible nature of the papacy—but you must instead understand it as popish, villainous, devilish. You must understand that the pope uses the name of the holy Roman church in the most abominable, blasphemous fashion and means his own school of scoundrels, church of whores and hermaphrodites, the devil's scum, just as before he meant "free, Christian, German council" in a rascally way. And if you do not interpret the pope's decretals in this way, it is impossible for you to grasp the pope's meaning, for this is his Roman church language, and whoever has anything to do with the pope and Roman See must know such things, or he will certainly be cheated. For the devil, who founded the papacy, speaks and works everything through the pope and Roman See. But a Christian should not believe the devil, that murderer and father of all lies, John 8 [:44].

Now after the pope had thus intimidated, captured, and subjected the bishops to himself—for they truly defended themselves honorably and long enough, as the histories testify—he tackled the worldly sovereigns with that very same text, Matthew 16 [:18],

---

[85] See p. 291, n. 71.

296

and could not rest until he had forced them to be under his control too. It went so far that they had to kneel before him, and kiss his feet; indeed, he even trampled on their necks with his feet, pursued them with sword and ban, robbed their lands and cities, beheaded several, set son against father, embittered one king against another, and instigated sheer conflict, murder, and bloodshed among the kings, as though he were the very devil incarnate, in the hope that if the beasts (as he calls them) devoured each other, he would then be emperor, king, and lord of the world in their stead. This is why he boasts he is emperor and has authority to depose emperors and kings as he pleases. Although by the grace of God he has not yet quite succeeded in this devilish effort, and will never succeed, he has nevertheless often and repeatedly instigated great misfortune and heartache between the emperor and France, as he is still doing and has done until now; if he were not a pope but a bishop of the true Roman church, like St. Gregory, he would in all seriousness reconcile the two sovereigns and not be able to rest until they were sincerely agreed, particularly because in our time it is vital for all Christianity that the great sovereigns be sincerely reconciled to each other. But this is not important to the Roman pope; and if he does reconcile them, as he has done several times, then it has all been rascally, popish, and devilish, the reverse of what it seems to be.

And if one had at that time asked Emperor Phocas if it were his opinion that his command should establish such trash in Rome— who subjects all bishops, institutions, and churches under his own control, tears up and devours everything there is, establishes new faith and doctrine, destroys Christ and Christian faith, institutes innumerable idolatries, thoroughly cheats the whole world and defrauds it with great treachery of vast sums of money and property; who then tramples on emperors and bans, slays, and persecutes them, who robs them of their lands and towns while he ridicules them as his fools and laughs up his sleeve, who devours [their wealth] and spends it with his whores and hermaphrodites—do you think that Phocas, no matter how wicked he is, would say yes to this? Indeed, perhaps he would so deal with them that they would no longer speak of the papacy and would forget about it.

Yes, this is what happens, and this is how it must happen, when one paints the devil above the door and asks him to be godfather.[86] It is difficult enough to have it end well (as Peter says, "The righteous man is scarcely saved")[87] when one blesses oneself in God's name before the devil and begins a thing with prayer. But what should it be and become when one begins a thing in the devil's name and against God's will? Then doors and windows are opened wide for the devil to blow in with all his might. Now then, the pope has begun his papacy in the name of the devil and with all kinds of lies and blasphemy, and has dragged the papacy down to the hellish dregs of every kind of depravity and disgrace, all of which we can see in Rome in broad daylight. We can recognize what kind of tree it is and who planted it by its fruits. For these fruits I have told of prove that the papal horror did not come from God and was not started in God's name, but was instituted by the devil through God's wrath in punishment for sins, and in his name entered the church; and so I shall go on proving it.

First—by proper division[88] and to start at the bottom—it was not instituted by the temporal authority, and even if it had been, it would still have been from the devil. The reason is this: temporal authority does not have the power to do this in the kingdom of God. Thus we heard above[89] that it was truly not the intention of Emperor Phocas to establish a power like this in the church, and he cannot do it either. Perhaps he meant the bishop of Rome to be solely a superintendent who would, for God's sake, watch over the life and doctrine of the church, as had been ordered by the Nicene council. For it is impossible to watch over the life and teaching of all the churches and bishops in the whole world. In summary, the pope himself cannot tolerate the fact that he should have it [the papacy] from the emperor; instead, emperors and kings should have their crowns and kingdoms from him. This is one point and note it well: the papacy is not from the emperor, and cannot come from the emperor; nor does the pope want to have it from him.

---

[86] Proverbial German, *"Wenn man den Teufel über die Thür malet und zu gefattern bittet."* Cf. Thiele, *Luthers Sprichwörtersammlung*, No. 356.
[87] *Vix justus salvabitur.* Cf. I Pet. 4:18.
[88] *A sufficiente divisione.*
[89] See p. 277.

Second, the papacy did not come from spiritual powers either, that is, from Christianity and bishops in the whole world, or from the councils; they neither are able nor do they have authority to create the papacy. Indeed, when one really studies the histories, one finds not one bishop or church in all the world that has willingly accepted the pope, but rather, almost all the bishops and churches struggled and fought against it, just as until the present day the bishops and churches in the whole Orient have not acknowledged the pope and still do not acknowledge him. Therefore he blasphemes and lies grossly that God set him over all the churches in the whole world, which God never said or did and does not intend to do; and thus he makes a liar out of God and heretics out of all the churches, through his evil spirit that rages in him against God, his Holy Spirit, and his church. Even when there were still bishops in Rome, before the pope, the Antichrist, was thrown there by the devil, the Nicene council entrusted the bishop of Rome with the care of the churches near Rome, but did not make him a pope and did not give him ruling authority over some of the churches. Thus we have heard above that the papacy did not exist before Emperor Phocas and Boniface III, and the churches in the whole world knew nothing of it. St. Gregory, pious Christian bishop of the Roman church, condemned it and would not tolerate it at all.

What is the use of more words? The pope himself refuses to accept that he was established by councils or spiritual sovereigns of Christianity; he rages at it. Oh, how he bellows, rages, raves, and foams, just like one possessed by many thousands of devils, in his decretals, dist. XVI, XIX, XXI,[90] etc., and in *De Electione c. Significasti.*[91] When Pope Paschalis[92] sent the pallium to the archbishop of Palermo in Sicily with the condition that he should pledge his loyalty to the pope in a formal oath, and the bishop very humbly replied with only the words that the kings (of Sicily) and their followers were really amazed that such an oath was required of him,

---

[90] *Decreti Prima Pars*, dist. XVI, XIX, XXI. *CIC* 1, 41-50; 58-64; 66-72; *MPL* 187, 81-94a, 103c-112a, 113c-122c.
[91] *Decretalium D. Gregorii Papae IX*, lib. i, tit. VI, *De Electione*, C. IV. *CIC* 2, 49-50.
[92] Paschalis II (1099-1118).

since Christ, Matthew 5 [:34], had forbidden swearing and one could find no law of the councils condoning it, the holy noble jewel Paschalis was furious. For the bishop had hit him so hard with the word of Christ that his head spun, and he did not know what to say or how to say it, and he martyred the word of Christ, Matthew 5, like a pope, against whom I wrote in Latin twenty-five years ago[93]— I intend to write in German later, if I do not forget it on account of the many things I still have to do. But at the reference to the council he opened his big mouth as though he would like to swallow heaven and earth and roared, "Do you think that the councils have authority to set goals for the Roman church? (read: 'the church of his whores and hermaphrodites'). Don't you know that all councils were convened by the Roman church and have their authority from the Roman church?"

This is the way—this is exactly the way one should lie and blaspheme if one wants to be a proper pope. Dear God, what an utterly shameless, blasphemous lying-mouth the pope is! He talks just as though no man on earth knew that the four principal councils and many others were held without the Roman church, and instead thinks like this, "As I am a crude ass, and do not read the books, so there is no one in the world who reads them; rather, when I let my braying heehaw, heehaw resound, or even let out a donkey's fart, then everyone will have to consider it an article of faith; if not, St. Peter and St. Paul and God himself will be angry with them." For God is nowhere God anymore, except solely the ass-god in Rome, where the big, crude asses (pope and cardinals) ride on better donkeys than they are.

From all this you now hear that the papal holy office is not instituted by spiritual authority or by the holy Christian churches of the whole world, that is, it is not of God, for God dwells in Christendom and works through it, nor is it of temporal authority; and papal holiness does not want to be instituted by one of them or both, as we have heard. Thus he confesses herewith that he does not derive from God, that is, from the church. And this is certainly the truth, and we accept it as such; we are in complete agreement with His Holiness on these two items, even though

---

[93] See p. 293, n. 78.

he speaks such truth unknowingly, like one possessed, for he means by this to strengthen his lies and blasphemy. Now comes the really main point: because God has ordained no estates on earth (I do not speak of the estate of marriage and whatever is connected with that) to rule, other than these two, namely, the spiritual and the temporal, through which he wishes to help the human race— through the spiritual one to eternal life in heaven, through the temporal one to finite life on earth—the real question now is, "Whence then does the papal office come, since it does not want to come either from spiritual authority (that is, from the Christian church, where Christ is) or from temporal authority (that is, from secular sovereigns)?" It cannot come from Never Never Land, for who would be so unreasonable and sin so highly against the most holy father pope?

Dr. Luther is a crude fellow; if he were to hear this asked he would jump in like a farmer with boots and spurs and say, "The pope has been thrown out of hell unto the church by all the devils," as was said above. For this same abominable, accursed heretic is drowned in the deep error of believing that what God wants to do, he surely does through the two realms, and no one is to set up another one. Well then, Joke, lie down![94] Where does the papacy come from? I repeat: it comes from the devil because it does not come from the church, which Christ rules through his Holy Spirit, and it does not come from temporal authority. I will prove this so thoroughly that even the gates of hell will not prevail against it [Matt. 16:18].

St. Peter says, I Peter 4 [:11], "Whoever speaks, let him speak as the oracles of God. Whoever renders service, let him do it as one who renders it by the strength which God supplies; in order that in everything God may be glorified through Jesus Christ," etc. Also, in many places St. Paul sharply forbids the teachings of men, especially Titus 1 [:13-14], "Rebuke them sharply, that they may be sound in the faith, instead of giving heed to commands of men who reject the truth"; and our Lord himself says in Matthew 15 [:9], "In vain do they worship me, teaching as doctrines the

---

[94] A German proverb, "*Schertz lege dich*," meaning roughly, "All joking aside." Cf. Thiele, *Luthers Sprichwörtersammlung*, No. 293.

precepts of men." Here it is firmly forbidden to preach or hear human teachings in the church, for they do not give honor and glory to God, but instead seduce people away from the faith and seek the glory of man. For God alone would speak, work, and govern in his church, so that he alone is glorified, which we have, praise God, managed to achieve in our churches; and, with God's help, it has become customary that almost everyone knows how one should beware of the teachings of men as of the devil himself, and should hear only our Lord and Savior, as the Father tells us of him at the river Jordan, "This is my beloved Son, with whom I am well pleased; him you shall hear."[95] He himself says in John 10 [:27, 5], "My sheep hear my voice. . . . A stranger they will not follow, but they will flee from him, for they do not know the voice of strangers." By going among the sheep, you may see for yourself if you wish this sweet and joyful picture that the Lord uses here about them. If a stranger calls, whistles, or coaxes them, "Hermen, Hermen,"[96] they run and flee, and the more you coax, the more they run, as if a wolf were there, for they do not recognize the strange voice; but when the shepherd lets himself be heard a little, they all run toward him, for they know his voice. Just so should all true Christians act, who hear no voice but that of their shepherd, Christ, as he says himself, John 10 [:8], "All who came before me are thieves and murderers; but the sheep did not heed them."

From these and many similar sayings it has been clearly and convincingly enough proven that God has strictly and sharply forbidden the doctrines and works of men in the church, as being contrary to faith and leading men away from the truth, that is, they are sheer lies and fraud before God. And where the devil has gotten involved—that one embellishes them with God's name or the apostles' names, and sells them under these names—then they are no longer simple lies and fraud, but also horrible blasphemy, idolatry, and abomination. For then the devil makes God a liar and deceiver, as though God had spoken such lies or done such

---

[95] Luke 3:22. C. p. 271, n. 22.
[96] A name given to wethers, frequently used in Luther's time. Cf. Karl Friedrich Wilhelm Wander, *Deutsches Sprichwörter Lexikon* (5 vols.; Leipzig, 1862-1880), IV, 1113.

works; and the people fall for it, believe it, and depend on it, as if God had said and done it, and thus they give their trust and honor, which is due to God alone, to lies and to the devil. This is what is meant by true idolatry and blasphemy in all the prophets. Isaiah 2 [:8] says, "Their land is filled with idols; they bow down to the work of their hands, to what their own fingers have made," and Jeremiah 29 [:31] says, "Because Shemaiah has prophesied to you when I did not send him, and has made you trust in a lie," etc. Now you hear: he who is not sent does not have the word of God; and by his own human doctrine he makes men trust in lies, that is, commit idolatry.

Here we come to the really important points. It is now certain that the pope and his office is merely a figment of human imagination and invention, for as we have heard, he does not come from nor wish to come from the order of temporal authority. He does not and does not wish to come from the order of the church or the councils. Thus one knows for certain that not one letter of God's word will be found by him in Scripture; instead, he placed himself this high by his own arrogance, arbitrariness, and malice, then decorated himself with God's word, thereby blaspheming abominably and making an idol of himself. He filled Christendom with his horrible idolatry, he lied, cheated, and made those who believed and trusted this into damned idolaters, as though God had commanded it in his word; thus they were compelled to fear, honor, worship, and serve the devil in the name of God. There you have the pope, what he is, whence he comes, namely, a horror (as Christ says, Matthew 24 [:15]) of all idolatry, brought forth by all the devils from the depths of hell.

"Yes," you say, "he really claims to come out of God's word and out of God, for in many decretals he quotes the passage in Matthew 16 [:18], 'You are Peter, and on this rock I will build my church. I will give thee the keys of the kingdom,' etc. That is as much as saying that the pope in Rome is lord over all Christendom." Truly, that might do it! Who could have missed such high reason in the most holy father? Someone really should have warned a poor fellow before he sinned so deeply and called the pope an ass, fool, idol, and devil. How fortunate for me that I tightened my belt; I was already getting a laughing fit from my shock over the pope's great reasoning and it might easily have happened, had I not been wearing trousers, that I would have made something people don't like to smell, so afraid and awed was I at such papal great wisdom!

Yet I wonder why His Holiness has chosen such an obscure saying when there are so many clearer sayings in Scripture to suit his purpose, such as, first, this one, Genesis 1 [:1-2], "In the beginning (that is, in Rome), God created (that is, instituted) heaven (that is, the pope) and earth (that is, the Christian church). The earth was without form and void (that is, the Christian church is subject to the pope, etc.)." This saying would have been much more effective. Again, Isaiah 1 [:3], "The ox knows its lord (that is, the pope in Rome is lord over all), and the ass its master's crib (that is, Christendom is the pope's body servant)." And Scripture is full of sayings that speak much more clearly of the papacy than Matthew 16. The *Logica* and *Parva logicalia*[97] would also help here, as, "No one and nobody bites into his own sack," that is, the pope is the lord and master of the church. Again, "The hypothetical proposition (that is, the pope) is clothed in a categorical cap (that is, in the city of Rome), sits on the porphyrian tree (that is, the head of the universal church), and devours all living things (that is, has the power to violate laws)."[98] And so it continues to be written, painted, given,

---

[97] Contained in the *Summulae Logicales* of Peter of Spain, who became Pope John XXI (1276-1277). Joseph P. Mullally (ed.), *Summulae Logicales* ("Publications in Medieval Studies, Vol. VII [Notre Dame, Ind.: The University of Notre Dame, 1945]).

[98] *Nullus & nemo mordent se in sacco, id est, Papa est Caput & Dominus Ecclesiae. Item, Propositio hypothetica (id es Papa) induta Cappa Cathegorica, (id est, in urbe Roma) Sedet in Arbore Purphyricana (id est, Caput Ecclesiae universalis) & devorat genera & species (id est, habet potestatem condendi leges).* The origin of this saying is unknown. It may be associated with the *Grammatical Analysis (Quaestio Grammaticalis)* of Crotus Rubeanus (*ca.* 1480-1539), a German humanist and theologian, rather than with Peter of Spain. Rubeanus was Luther's roommate at Erfurt, and the author of the well-known *Letters of Obscure Men.* See Frances G. Stokes (trans.), *Letters of Obscure Men* (New Haven: Yale University Press, 1925), and Schwiebert, *op. cit.*, pp. 137, 225. For a detailed analysis of the passage, cf. Julius Köstlin *et al.* (eds.), *Luthers Werke für das Christliche Haus* (8 vols.; Leipzig, 1924), IV, 481-482.

and pictured in all creatures, that the pope in Rome is chief, lord, and judge over everything in heaven and earth.

For in *Ex. c. Solite, De Maioritate*,[99] the most holy father pope, in order to interpret the Scripture in this way and defend the papacy, writes to the emperor in Constantinople, "Didn't you read that God created two great lights, the sun (that is, the pope) and the moon (that is, the emperor)? To the extent that the sun is greater than the moon, the pope is greater than the emperor"; that is, the pope is (as the gloss cleverly calculates)[100] forty-seven times greater than the emperor. That will be a fine little pope, when he is fully grown![101] Listen, reader, you must not laugh here, or you might get a laughing fit too, like me, and if your breeches do not fit tightly, you too would create a fearful smell that one would have to disperse with incense and juniper, and the most holy father would never forgive you your stinking sin, not even if you were in the throes of death. So beware of laughing in such serious matters, and remember that the pope is not joking or failing in his interpretation of Scripture, as you see here!

But before I point to the Christian understanding of this passage, I must first tell this joke: the glosses L: *c. Considerandum*[102] and *Abbas c. Significasti*[103] say that this passage in Matthew 16 does nothing to confirm the papacy, but rather [it is confirmed by] the passage in the last chapter of St. John, *"Pasce oves meas,"* "Feed my lambs" [John 21:15]. So the pope and his lawyers are in disagreement as to what the papacy is based on. The pope says it is based on Matthew 16, and screams it in many decretals. His

---

[99] *Decretalium D. Gregorii Papae IX*, lib. i, tit. XXXIII, C. VI. *CIC* 2, 196-198. It is the letter of Innocent III (1198-1216) to Emperor Alexios III.

[100] *CIC* 2, 198, par. 4.

[101] The Weimar edition reads, *"Das wil ein bepstlin werden, wens nu ausgewechst,"* and notes that this may be a typographical error. Cf. WA 54, 241, n. 1.

[102] *Decreti Prima Pars*, dist. L, C. LIII. *CIC* 1, 198; *MPL* 187, 230c.

[103] Abbas Panormitanus, i.e., "the abbot of Palermo," Nicholas of Tudescho, abbot of a monastery near Messina in 1425 and archbishop of Palermo (1434-1445) interpreted canon law in *Lecture on the Five Books of the Decretalium* (*Lectura in Quinque Libros Decretalium*). Cf. Hauck, *Realencyklopädie für protestantische Theologie und Kirche*, XIV, 626. Cf. also *Decretalium D. Gregorii Papae IX*, lib. i, tit. VI, *De Electione*, C. IV. *CIC* 2, 49-50.

305

lawyers say no, and so the servant charges the lord with lying, and the lord charges the servant. May the devil here get into their squabble. In the meantime we shall let them squabble and not recognize the pope as pope until they have reached an agreement; although, speaking legally (if I were a lawyer), it seems to me that the lawyers have a better case than the pope because they base their arguments on the fact that in Matthew 16 Christ did not give the keys to St. Peter, but only promised them; thus the pope should have to prove where they were given to him. We theologians can help out the lawyers with arguments like the following (if the pope should wish to damn them).

To Christians it is not enough that one refers to the prophets who promised Christ, but one must also present the apostles who testify that the promise was fulfilled and the promised Christ had come and was given. Thus the pope is also duty-bound not to quote the promise, Matthew 16, but to present a clear text showing that this promise has been fulfilled and St. Peter has been ordered into the office. This is where the pope's trousers will stink, for where in the world will he find a text that clearly states that Christ gave the keys to St. Peter? That is the proof he owes, according to the verdict of his own lawyers, and no letter in Scripture speaks of the keys, outside of Matthew 16.

Because the pope grabbed the keys of St. Peter for himself before he proved his claim, and he can never prove it, it follows that he has, like a villain, stolen what is not his, or that they must be false, painted keys which are nothing but a picture; and we are free to believe nothing from him, the desperate liar and scoundrel, yes, the spirit of a devil! Moreover, we may with a good conscience take his coat-of-arms, which features the keys and his crown, to the privy, use it for wiping, and then throw it into the fire[104] (it would be better it were the pope himself). To deal so falsely and blasphemously with God's word in such important things concerning all of Christendom is to instigate idolatry, which no finite punishment can avenge—God must himself punish it in deepest hell. Meanwhile, a good Christian, whenever he sees the pope's coat-of-arms, should spit and throw filth at it, just as one

---

[104] Cf. the description of cartoon No. 10 in WA 54, 351-352.

should spit and throw filth at an idol, to the glory of God. For such a papal coat-of-arms is a public lie and the devil's image, which the people have vainly feared and depended on as though it were God's commandment, when it is sheer lies, blasphemy, and arch-idolatry. This, I say, follows from the best confessions of his very own lawyers, since they say the text, Matthew 16, does not contribute to the existence of a papacy. This is like saying that the pope lies and blasphemes when he applies Matthew 16 to his worthless, blasphemous papacy, and out of this he makes his accursed coat-of-arms and crown in order to frighten the world and subject it to himself and to capture and corrupt the consciences which had been redeemed and freed through Christ's blood.

The pope makes such high claims for this text in Matthew 16 that in dist. XX [XXII], c. Omnes and c. Sacro sancta,[105] he dares to bellow that the Roman church alone (none other) was instituted by God himself. The other churches were instituted by the Roman church, and God gave the Roman church the privilege before others of having power over heavenly and earthly kingdoms; and he who breaks away from other churches does a great wrong, but he who breaks away from the Roman church is a heretic—and much more of the same. Now because his own lawyers say no to this, and regard these things as lies, what shall we theologians do, who have to see and hear such big lies, embellished with God's word? We say it is a horrible blasphemy, indeed, idolatry, for, as we heard above, there is quite a difference between false action and false teaching, and a bigger difference between simple teaching without the word of God and false teaching embellished with God's word. Whoever thus lies in teaching and quotes God's word for it makes the devil into God and God into the devil, as though God spoke the devil's lies, and seduces me to honor and worship the devil in God's name, and regard the lies as truth. The pope has filled the world with such innumerable blasphemous idolatries.

Oh, emperor, king, princes and lords, and anyone who can take hold, now take hold! God will not bring luck to lazy hands.[106]

---

[105] Decreti Prima Pars, dist. XXII, C. I, II. CIC 1, 73-74; MPL 187, 121c-124c.

[106] A German proverb, "Gott gebe hie faulen Henden kein glück," similar to the English saying, "God helps those who help themselves." Cf. Thiele, Luthers Sprichwörtersammlung, No. 186.

First, one should deprive the pope of Rome, Romagna,[107] Urbino,[108] Bologna,[109] and everything he possesses as pope, for he is "owner of the worst faith";[110] he has it through lies and fraud. Oh, why did I say lies and fraud? He has it through blasphemy and idolatry; he has abominably stolen from the empire, robbed and subjected it to himself, and as reward for this, he has seduced countless souls into eternal hell-fire through his idolatry, as he himself boasts, XL, *Si Papa;*[111] and he has destroyed Christ's realm, for which he is called a horror of desolation, Matthew 24 [:15]. Then we should take him—the pope, the cardinals, and whatever riffraff belongs to His Idolatrous and Papal Holiness—and (as blasphemers) tear out their tongues from the back, and nail them on the gallows in the order in which they hang their seals on the bulls,[112] even though all this is mild compared to their blasphemy and idolatry. Then one could allow them to hold a council, or as many as they wanted, on the gallows, or in hell among all the devils. For they did not begin this loathsome papacy in ignorance or weakness; they knew quite well that their predecessors—St. Gregory, Pelagius, Cornelius,[113] Fabian,[114] and many other holy bishops of the Roman church—never practiced such a horror, as declared above. They knew well that St. Cyprian, Augustine, Hilary, Martin, Ambrose, Jerome, Dionysius, and many other holy bishops in all the world had known nothing of the papacy, had not been subject to the Roman church. They knew well that the four great councils—Nicaea, Constantinople, Ephesus, Chalcedon—and many other councils had never acknowledged such a papal horror.

Oh, what more shall I say? They knew well—and still know well—that the whole of Christendom in the world has no sovereigns, except solely our Savior Jesus Christ, the Son of God, whom St. Paul calls the head of his body, which is all of Christendom,

---

107 Romagna is the area between Urbino and Bologna.

108 Pope Leo X gave Urbino as a fief to his nephew Lorenzo de Medici.

109 In 1506 Bologna became a papal fief after various aristocratic parties had warred against each other without success.

110 *Possessor pessimae fidei.*

111 *Decreti Prima Pars*, dist. XL, C. VI. *CIC* 1, 146; *MPL* 187, 214c-215a.

112 Cf. the description of cartoon No. 7 in *WA* 54, 351.

113 Cornelius I.

114 Fabian (236-250).

Ephesians 4 [:15-16] and many other places. They still know well today that Christians in the whole of the Orient are not subject to the pope. They know well that they have not a single word of God in their favor, but everything against them. Yet they are such out-rageous, shameless blockheads that they instigated, consciously and knowingly, the loathsome, blasphemous, idolatrous papacy, against the strong testimony and admonition of their conscience, the whole world, and all of Scripture. Moreover, they still maintain it, while at the same time they condemn as heretics all their predecessors before Boniface III, along with the whole of Christendom which existed for six hundred years before the pope, including all the holy fathers and councils, and all the Christians who have existed these fifteen hundred years, up to the present day, in the lands of the East. Where the papacy is an article of faith, and such an im-portant, necessary article as the pope bellows in all his decretals, basing [his claim] on Matthew 16, it is certain that St. Augustine and St. Cyprian, indeed, all the apostles and all of Christendom in the world for over fifteen hundred years, must be heretics and eter-nally damned; and along with them, Christ himself, who taught them these wicked heresies through his Holy Spirit—no one has been saved or become holy except the papal Christians. A pope has the perfect right to make such a judgment, and if he does not dare to speak such a verdict he should not be pope.

But enough of this juristic understanding against the pope; we want to see how Christ's words, Matthew 16, should be under-stood in a truly Christian way and how masterfully the pope quotes them as the basis of his papacy. In John 6 [:63] the Lord says, "The words that I have spoken to you are spirit and life." Accordingly, the words in Matthew 16 must also be spirit and life, namely, when he says, "On this rock I will build my church." "Build" must here mean a spiritual, living building. "Rock" must be a living, spiritual rock. "Church" must be a spiritual, living as-sembly, indeed, so alive that all of it lives eternally. For "the flesh is of no avail," etc. [John 6:63]; it dies and does not live eternally. Now this rock is solely the Son of God, Jesus Christ, of whom the Scripture is full, and no one else, and we Christians know this full well. To build or to be built on this rock is something that cannot be done with laws or good works, for Christ is not grasped by hands or works, but must come through faith and word. Thus the church cannot, through itself or its own works, make itself spiritual or living; instead, it is built on this rock, through faith, and thus is spiritual and living as long as it remains built on the rock, that is, until eternity. You see from this that Christ means in this saying exactly the same thing as he says in John 11 [:25], "I am the resurrection and the life; whoever believes in me shall never die." Again, John 8 [:51], "If a man keeps my saying, he will never die." And in summary, this text, Matthew 16, speaks of faith: he who has faith is built on this rock, as one says, "He who trusts God has built well." Note this well (I say), that in Matthew 16 Christ speaks of faith and not of our works, for thereby it will become evident what a little pious prancer[115] the pope is.

Thus St. Peter himself (whom the scoundrels would have liked to make pope in Rome, or even Christ himself, as Platina does)[116] interprets it, I Peter 2 [:3-5], "You have tasted the kindness of the Lord. Come to him, to that living stone, rejected by men but in God's sight chosen and precious; and like living stones be yourselves built into a spiritual house, to be a holy priesthood, to offer spiritual sacrifices acceptable to God through Jesus Christ." But soon afterward St. Peter proves through the prophet, Isaiah 28 [:16], that building on this stone or rock is faith in Christ, saying, "For it stands in scripture: 'Behold, I am laying in Zion a stone, a cornerstone chosen and precious, and he who believes in him will not be put to shame.' To you therefore who believe, he is precious, but for those who do not believe 'It has become the head of the corner,' and 'A stone that will make men stumble,' even to them that stumble at the word and do not believe him upon whom they have been founded" [I Pet. 2:6-8]. Peter points up the word "believe" so often that there can be no doubt that "building on this rock" is nothing else than believing in Jesus Christ.

---

115 *Frömchen.*

116 Cf. p. 7, n. 18. Luther regarded Platina as the prototype of papal historians. Cf. Schäfer, *op. cit.*, pp. 127-128.

St. Paul too, in Ephesians 2 [:19-22], agrees with St. Peter: "So then you are no longer strangers and sojourners, but you are fellow citizens with the saints and members of the household of God, built upon the foundation of the apostles and prophets, Christ Jesus himself being the chief cornerstone, in whom the whole structure is joined together and grows into a holy temple in the Lord; in whom you are also built into it for a dwelling place of God in the Spirit," etc. All this is to be noted carefully, so that we can treat with contempt the filthy, foolish twaddle that the popes present in their decretals about their Roman church, that is, about their devil's synagogue [Rev. 2:9], which separates itself from common Christendom and the spiritual edifice built up on this stone, and instead invents for itself a fleshly worldly, worthless, lying, blasphemous, idolatrous authority over all of Christendom. One of these two things must be true: if the Roman church is not built on this rock along with the other churches, then it is the devil's church; but if it is built, along with all the other churches, on this rock, then it cannot be lord or head over the other churches. For Christ the cornerstone knows nothing of two unequal churches, but only of one church alone, just as the Children's Faith,[117] that is, the faith of all of Christendom, says, "I believe in one holy, Christian church," and does not say, "I believe in one holy Roman church." The Roman church is and should be one portion or member of the holy Christian church, not the head, which befits solely Christ the cornerstone. If not, it is not a Christian but an un-Christian and anti-Christian church, that is, a papal school of scoundrels.

Now let us take up the text of Matthew 16 itself and see how strongly it supports the pope, who so proudly and firmly insists on it, even against his lawyers. Matthew 16 [:13-14][118] speaks thusly: "Jesus questioned his disciples, saying, 'Who do men say that the Son of man is?' And they said, 'Some say John the Baptist, others say Elijah, and others Jeremiah or one of the prophets.'"

This should not now be followed any further; you can read

---

[117] The Apostles' Creed.

[118] Cf. Luther's exegesis of the passage in *Annotations on the Other Chapter of Matthew* (*Annotationes in Aliquot Capita Matthaei*) (1538). WA 38, 611-639.

about it in St. Jerome,[119] who interprets it very well—how flesh and blood cannot say anything certain about Christ, even though it sees the great miracle of Christ and esteems him highly. Furthermore, Christ does not ask what the people think, but what they themselves, his disciples, think of him, and says, "Who do you say that I am?" [vs. 15]. (Notice here that he asks all of them together, "Who do you say that I am?") Then Simon Peter said, "You are the Christ, the Son of the living God" [vs. 16]. Peter gave this answer on behalf of all the apostles, for when a crowd is asked something, they cannot all reply at once; rather, one must speak for the sake of all, as is said, "Two can sing at once, but they cannot talk at once."[120] That is why the fathers—Augustine, Cyprian, and Chrysostom[121]—rightly say that St. Peter was the mouth of the apostles and answered in the name of all, for they had all been asked and owed an answer.

This is why the pope here lowers his guard[122] and builds on the rotten foundation that because St. Peter alone replied he was the lord over the other apostles and the pope over all the world. There it is clearly in the text that Christ does not ask St. Peter, "Who do you say that I am?" but he asks all the disciples, saying, "Who do you say that I am?" And St. Peter had to reply for all of them, and his reply had, at the same time, to be the reply of all; just as it happens in worldly and domestic spheres when a servant, town clerk, or secretary is the spokesman for the council, community, or domestic staff, but is not thereby the lord of the city. Or a lawyer or chancellor may speak the words of the emperor, king, or prince, but is a long way from being emperor, king, or prince himself—just as the pope, from these words of St. Peter, wants to be lord over apostles and the churches of

---

[119] *Commentary on the Gospel of Matthew* (*Commentariorum in Evangelium Matthei*). *MPL* 26, 117c-120a.

[120] A German proverb, *"Zween mügen mit einander singen, aber mit einander könenn sie nicht reden."* Cf. Thiele, *Luthers Sprichwörtersammlung*, No. 20.

[121] See, for example, Augustine's *Sermons on New Testament Lessons*, LXXVI (*MPL* 38, 479; *PNF*[1] 6, 340), Cyprian's *Epistola LV ad Cornelium* (*MPL* 4, 358; *ANF* 5, 341), and Chrysostom's *The Homilies on the Gospel of Matthew*, LXV (*MPL* 31, 622; *PNF*[1] 10, 401).

[122] Proverbial German, *"legt einen blossen,"* that is, *"gibt sich eine Bloesse,"* an expression used in fencing.

all the apostles. That is rotten, I say, and the pope will not last long if he does not bring up something better, as he will do now, as follows: "And Jesus said to him, 'Blessed are you, Simon Bar-Jona! For flesh and blood has not revealed this to you, but my Father who is in heaven. And I tell you, you are Peter, and on this rock I will build my church, and the gates of Hades shall not prevail against it. I will give you the keys of the kingdom of heaven, and whatever you bind on earth shall be bound in heaven, and whatever you loose on earth shall be loosed in heaven'" [Matt. 16:17-20].

Now, if you have eyes, don't stick them in a bag,[123] and if you have ears, don't send them across the fields, so that you can see and hear how the pope is there made lord over heaven and earth, over church and emperor. Christendom did not know of this important article of faith from the beginning until the papacy. Even the two lawyers (as said above), Johannes Teutonicus[124] and Panormitanus,[125] those desperate heretics, deny this and refuse to concede anything in the text to the pope. But what are God, Christ, church, world, and lawyers, compared to the pope?

"Simon Bar-Jona (says the Lord), you are blessed." Good for you, O Simon, that you know that I am the Messiah and the Son of the living God; your father John did not teach you this—for this is what Jesus calls him, in the last chapter of John [21:17], "Simon, son of John, do you love me?" which Matthew 16 says in Hebrew "Simon Bar-Johanna," or even shorter, "Bar-Jona," which means "son of Jonas" or "son of Johanna." No, you did not get this deep understanding from your father, nor did the other disciples, including you, get it from flesh and blood, or from their fathers or from several people; rather, my Father in heaven has revealed it to you. In these few words of Peter, which he confesses with all the other disciples (for they are all represented in Peter's reply), is included the whole of the gospel, indeed, all of Holy Scripture. What else does Scripture from beginning to

---

[123] A German proverb, "Wer nu hie Augen hat, der stecke sie nicht in Beutel." Cf. Thiele, Luthers Sprichwörtersammlung, No. 34.

[124] John Zemecke or Semeca (d. 1245), called "Teutonicus," was a canonist in Halberstadt. Cf. Allgemeine Deutsche Biographie, XIV, 475-476.

[125] Nicholas of Tudescho; see p. 305, n. 103.

end intend to say, except that the Messiah, the Son of God, should come and through his sacrifice, "like that of a lamb without blemish" [I Pet. 1:19], bear and take away the sin of the world and thus deliver from eternal death to eternal salvation? Holy Scripture, Genesis 3 [:15], "Her seed shall bruise your head." And Eve, Genesis 4 [:1], as she speaks of Cain, "I have gotten a man with the help of the Lord." In their meaning these words sound exactly like Peter's, for she wants to say, "Now I have the seed, the right Man, the Messiah, the Jehovah, that is, God and Son of God, who is to do what was promised to us." But she mistakes the person—otherwise her words at this place are very similar to the words of St. Peter. See, a great thing like this is in St. Peter's words, that is, a true apostolic speech. This is what all the apostles, not only St. Peter, afterward preached in the whole world, and preach until the end of the world, for as was heard, not St. Peter alone, but the others through his mouth answered this question the Lord had put to them.

The Lord then says, "And I tell you, you are Peter, and on this rock will I build my church." In St. John 1 [:42], he calls him Cephas, "You shall be called Cephas," *Keph* in Hebrew, *Kepha* in Chaldean, and *Petros* or *Petra* in Greek, *Rupes* in Latin, all of which mean *rock* in German—like the high rocks the castles are built on. Now the Lord wants to say, "You are Peter, that is, a man of rock.[126] For you have recognized and named the right Man, who is the true rock, as Scripture names him, Christ. On this rock, that is, on me, Christ, I will build all of my Christendom, just as you and the other disciples are built on it through my Father in heaven, who revealed it to you." In plain German one would say, "You say (on behalf of all) that I am the Messiah or Christ, the Son of the living God; very well then, I say to you, you are a Christian, and I shall build my church on a Christian." For in German the word "Christ" means both the Lord himself, as one sings, "Christ the Lord is risen, Christ ascended to heaven,"[127] and he who believes in the Lord Christ, as one says, "You are a Christ." Thus Luke in Acts 11 [:26] says that the disciples in Antioch were first

---

126 *Ein Felser.*
127 Cf. *Service Book and Hymnal,* No. 107; LW 53, 255-257.

314

called Christians, which is why names have survived such as, "Christians, Christendom, Christian faith," etc. So here our Lord gives Simon, son of Jona, the name "man of rock" or "Christian" because he, from the Father, recognized the rock, or Christ, and praised him with his mouth on behalf of all the apostles.

From this it is clear enough that by the building of his church on the rock or on himself, Christ meant nothing else but (as was said above, from the apostles Peter and Paul) the common Christian faith, that whoever believes in Christ is built on this rock and will attain salvation, even against all the gates of hell; whoever does not believe in Christ is not built on this rock and must be damned, with all the gates of hell. This is the simple, single, certain understanding of these words, and there can be no other. This the words clearly and convincingly prove, and they agree with the words in the last chapter of Mark [16:16], "He who believes and is baptized will be saved," and with John 11 [:26], "Whoever believes in me shall never die." Yes, I say, remember well and mark diligently that the Lord in Matthew 16 does not speak of laws, Ten Commandments, or the works we should or could do, but of the Christian faith or the work of the Father, which he, with the Son and the Holy Spirit, performs in us, namely, that he spiritually builds us on the rock, his Son, and teaches us to believe in Christ, that we might become his house and dwelling, as is proven in I Peter 2 [:4-7] and Ephesians 2 [:19-22].

Further, "And I will give you the keys of the kingdom of heaven, and whatever you bind on earth shall be bound in heaven, and whatever you loose on earth shall be loosed in heaven" [Matt. 16:19]. The Lord wants to provide well for his churches, built on him and believing in him. Because they should preach and confess the gospel before the whole world and govern on the basis that Christ Jesus is the Son of God, he wants to have their words honored and not scorned, as though he were speaking personally from heaven. Now he who hears the gospel from the apostles or churches and does not want to believe should be sentenced to be damned. Again, if he should fall after he has believed and will not convert back to faith, he should be sentenced in the same way—he should keep his sins and be damned. On the other hand, he who hears and believes the gospel, or turns from his sins back to faith, should have his sins forgiven and should attain salvation. And he will consider such a verdict in heaven as if he had spoken it himself. See, these are the keys of the kingdom of heaven and they should be used to give eternal retention and remission of sins in the church, not just at the time of baptism, or once in a lifetime, but continuously until the end—retention for the unrepentant and unbelievers, remission for the repentant and believers.

And here remember once again, and write it upon your heart, that the Lord does not speak here of laws or the works we should do, but of his works, namely, of retention and remission of sins. To retain or forgive sins is the work of the divine majesty alone. But he wants to perform and accomplish these works of his through his church; that is why he says that whatever it will bind or loose on earth should be bound or loosed by him in heaven. That is why, too, the two items follow one another in the Children's Creed, "I believe in one holy Christian church, the communion of saints, forgiveness of sins"; so, where the church is, namely, the building on the rock, there are the keys to the forgiveness of sins.

Second, note that the keys and the power to bind and loose sin was not given to the apostles and saints for their sovereignty over the church, but solely for the good and use of sinners. For one does not need the keys and their office where there is no sin. One should neither loose nor absolve St. Paul and saints like him from sins, for they have none except the daily and usual ones of the flesh, which remain until death; as he says, I Corinthians 3 [4:4], "I am not aware of anything against myself, but I am not thereby acquitted," and Romans 7 [:25], "I serve the law of sin with my flesh"; instead, one should let them be commended to the rock on which they are built. But they are necessary to the sinners, who are not built on the rock, or who have fallen off, so that one can build them on it again. Thus it is not a worldly power with which the bishops wish to boast and rule over the churches (it is grace, not power),[128] but is a spiritual power given for the

---

[128] *Beneficium, non dominium.*

good and salvation of sinners, so that they might seek and find these things through the bishops and churches as often as they need them, whereby the sinners should be saved. and not bishops, lords, and masters. Just as when a prince entrusts a thousand gulden to his servant to share among several poor people, these thousand gulden should not make the servant rich or lord over the poor; but rather, as the lord commanded, the gulden should be sought and found, freely and with no strings attached, by the poor people. He should show himself only a willing servant, for the consolation and benefit of the poor people. Remember this well— it applies to the pope.

Third, mark well and remember that the keys were not given to St. Peter alone, much less to the pope alone, after St. Peter. Although the Lord was speaking only to Peter, Peter nevertheless stood not only for his own person, but in the place and person of all the disciples, with whom Christ had started to talk and question—as all the teachers, before the pope was instituted by the emperor Phocas, have understood, taught, and believed, in all of Christendom, and still believe today in the Orient. Oh, what is the need of many words? Light cannot be darkness. In Matthew 18 [:18] Christ is not speaking just to Peter, but to all the disciples, "Truly, I say to you, whatever you bind on earth shall be bound in heaven, and whatever you loose on earth shall be loosed in heaven." These are the same words about binding and loosing that he used above with St. Peter [Matt. 16:19], and[129] even though there is here no mention of the keys, it is nevertheless the office of the keys, as was expressed in Matthew 16 so forcefully above. And he is furthermore clearly speaking here of sin, which one should bind and loose, for shortly before that he speaks of the sinners who do not wish to hear, and says, "Let him be to you as a Gentile and a tax collector" [Matt. 18:17], and immediately afterward, "Truly, I say to you, whatever you bind on earth," etc.

And what is more, he says in the same place, "If two of you agree about anything they ask, it will be done for them by my

---

[129] The second edition of this treatise inserts here: Yes, this is the text in which the promised keys (just as the lawyers wish) are indeed given. "I tell you" does not mean "I shall give you," but "I tell you and give you now." WA 54, 250, l. 37.

Father in heaven. For where two or three are gathered in my name, there am I in the midst of them" [Matt. 18:19-20]. Now we hear that even two or three, assembled in Christ's name, have the same power as St. Peter and all the apostles. For the Lord himself is there, as he says in John 14 [:23], "If a man loves me, he will keep my word, and my Father will love him, and we will come to him and make our home with him." This is how it has happened that a person who believed in Christ has often resisted a whole crowd, like Paphnutius in the Council of Nicaea,[130] and as the prophets resisted the kings, priests, and all the people of Israel. In short, God will not be bound by numbers, greatness, importance, power, or whatever is personal in people, but rather wants to be only with those who love and keep his word, even if they should be mere stable boys. What does he care about high, great, powerful lords? He alone is the highest, greatest, and mightiest.

Now if the pope could still stand stiffly and proudly, which he cannot, on the passage in Matthew 16, then we on the other hand stand even more proudly and stiffly on Matthew 18. It is not another Christ who speaks in Matthew 16 with St. Peter, and then in Matthew 18 with the other disciples, saying the same words and giving power to bind and loose sin. So let the pope go ahead with his St. Peter, binding and loosing what he can. We shall consider the power of the other apostles to bind and loosen to be the same as St. Peter's—even if a thousand St. Peters were one Peter, and the whole world were a pope, and, in addition, an angel from heaven were on his side! For we have here the Lord himself, over all angels and creatures, who says, "They shall all have the same power, keys, and office"—even two simple Christians assembled only in his name. The pope and all the devils shall not make a fool, liar, and drunkard out of this Lord for us; instead, we shall kick the pope with our feet and say he is a desperate liar, blasphemer, and idolatrous devil, who, in the name of St. Peter, has snatched the keys for himself, though Christ has given them to everyone in common, and who wants to make the Lord, in Matthew 16, a liar; indeed, this one should praise!

---

[130] See p. 43, n. 10.

Again, in John 20 [:21-23], the Lord speaks not only to St. Peter, but to all the apostles or disciples, "'As the Father has sent me, even so I send you.' And when he had said this, he breathed on them (not only on St. Peter), and said to them, 'Receive the Holy Spirit. If you forgive the sins of any, they are forgiven; if you retain the sins of any, they are retained.'" I would really like to hear what the ass-pope could say against this; if he had a thousand villainous tongues, they would all still have to break down here! For the words of the Lord are clear, "As the Father has sent me, even so I send you," you, you!—not thee alone, Peter; that is, what I have preached at the Father's command and have built upon myself, the rock. You should preach and build on just this and nothing else, and you shall all have the same power and keys to forgive and to retain sin. These are just the same words about binding and loosing that he said in Matthew 16 to St. Peter about keys. This is the Lord himself who says these things; that is why we don't care what the ass-pope raves in his decretals.

And here—so that we help the poor lawyers John Teutonicus and Panormitanus, too—is the text in which the promised keys, Matthew 16 (as they think), are indeed given to St. Peter and he is restricted in his possession of them in order to make it clear that the promised keys, Matthew 16, were not promised to St. Peter alone, for the fulfilment of this promise is not given to St. Peter alone, but to all the disciples. I say this as a favor to the poor lawyers. We theologians have stronger reasons and do not dispute "about the future and present word"[131] in such high matters. That is why the words that our Lord says to all of them, "If you forgive the sins of any, they are forgiven," mean just as much as though he addressed each one separately—"See here, Peter, receive the Holy Spirit, if you forgive the sins of any," etc.; "See here, Andrew, receive the Holy Spirit, if you forgive the sins of any," etc.; "See here, James; see here, John, Thomas, Bartholomew, Philip, Simon, Judas," etc. It is just as much (I say), when he addresses them collectively as if he had addressed each one individually. Each one had to accept it at the same time as the

---

[131] *De verbo futuro und praesenti,* a reference to the exegesis of Matt. 16:18 by the canonists.

others, because it was said to all at the same time. That is why St. Peter cannot be understood to have the common keys and the common office of the keys, which is the forgiveness and retention of sin, for himself alone or peculiar to himself over the other apostles; and there is no exclusiveness here, as the Roman asses patch and invent. It does not say, "To you alone, Peter"[132]—and even if it were so, the excluded[133] would still not be the apostles, but perhaps Caiaphas and the Mosaic priesthood. In any case, Peter stands for all the apostles, as these two passages, Matthew 18 and John 20, prove forcefully and mightily. That is certain.

Finally, there are the deeds and events. St. Matthias was made an apostle not by St. Peter, but by lot, confirmed by Christ in heaven, and ordained to join the other eleven apostles, Acts 1 [:26]. But if it is an article of faith, which is the lie the Roman asses like to threaten us with, that St. Peter alone has the keys as a privilege (that is what the fools in Rome call it), then St. Peter and all the apostles and Matthias are sheer heretics here for acting contrary to this article and for not allowing St. Matthias to be ordained and confirmed solely by St. Peter, who alone should have the keys over the whole world; and Christ himself will have to be under the pope's ban because he confirmed the heresy committed with St. Matthias. Oh, that poor sinner Christ, how can he ever attain forgiveness for his heresy and sin from the Roman See?—I almost said "from those mules."

And even though His Papal Holiness conceded to Christ, as to a prince who is subject to no law, the power to call, after his ascension, more apostles than he had on earth, none of these apostles can preach on earth or ordain bishops, but rather must go from the world into Never Never Land to preach, build churches, and ordain bishops. The reason is: the most holy father, with his St. Peter, is—as his decrees declare—the bishop of the whole world, and no one may preach or ordain bishops except the pope; that is why St. Matthias and the other ten apostles must not have either room or position in the whole world to preach, build churches, or ordain bishops, but only His Papal Holiness—you understand well what I mean!

132 *Tibi Petro soli.*
133 *Exclusiva.*

Or, if it should be that each apostle had equal power with St. Peter and each one had preached, built churches, and ordained bishops in his own part of the world, without the knowledge or command of St. Peter, but on the command of Christ, as was heard above, John 20, then it would follow that the papal holiness would have to do three things: first, condemn his decretals as desperate, stinking lies and hit himself on his own lying, blaspheming mouth, since he boasts of being the high priest and sovereign of all the churches in the whole world, and makes Christ, in Matthew 18, John 20, and Acts 1, a liar and heretic. Second, he should first seek to ascertain in which churches of the world St. Peter had preached, and which bishops he had ordained, so that he would not interfere with the churches and bishops of the other apostles, who are all together as good and holy as the Roman bishop. For all of them have been ordained by those apostles whom Christ made equal in all things with St. Peter. Oh, here the most holy father would have so much to do that he would not even be finished after Judgment Day. And where would the Roman See and the mulish reign in Rome be in the meantime?

Third, he should also make sure that St. Peter had founded no churches, ordained no bishops, and preached in no churches except in Rome. If this is not the case, the pope should also lose St. Peter, with keys and all, but if St. Peter should have preached in other parts of the world, founded other churches, and ordained more bishops, then the one in Rome cannot claim that he alone is the heir to St. Peter's throne; rather, all the others can claim just as much as the Roman, "St. Peter is our apostle, he has ordained our churches and bishops, therefore his keys are ours and not those of the bishop of Rome." Now it is certain that St. Peter was an apostle in Jerusalem, Antioch, and, as his epistle testifies, in Asia, Pontus, Cappadocia, Bithynia, and Galatia [I Pet. 1:1]. All these could boast, against the bishop of Rome (and much more so against the pope, who came after the bishops, being neither bishop nor Christian), "Dear bishop, St. Peter is our apostle; we have the keys from him, and are superior to the Roman church, for he has written his beautiful long letters to us. But he did not even write the shortest stem of the shortest letter to the Roman church." How do you like that snub,[134] ass-pope?

"Yes, but St. Peter was martyred in Rome with St. Paul, as the decretals claim." That is beside the point. Thousands of martyrs lie in Rome who were martyred there, and yet none of them was bishop of Rome. St. Stephen was martyred in Jerusalem [Acts 7:59-60], but that did not make him bishop of Jerusalem. When one asks about St. Peter's office, his preaching, and how he ordained bishops in Rome, they quote Matthew 16 in justification of their actions. There are, however, several scholars who maintain that St. Peter never came to Rome—and may the pope get indigestion defending himself against such evidence. I do not want to be the judge as to whether or not St. Peter was in Rome; for probably only St. Paul, who certainly was there (as Luke writes in Acts [28:14] and he himself writes in his epistles), can have ordained the church and the bishop in Rome. But I can cheerfully say, as I have seen and heard in Rome, that in Rome one doesn't know where the bodies of St. Peter and St. Paul lie, or if they lie there at all![135] Pope and cardinals know very well that they do not know that.

And yet, on SS. Peter and Paul's day, they display two heads, pretend, and let the common man believe that these are the natural heads of the apostles; so the reverent mob comes running, along with John Doe of Jena.[136] But the pope, cardinals, and their riffraff know quite well that they are two wooden, carved, and painted heads; it is just the same as they do with the cloth of St. Veronica[137]—they pretend it is our Lord's face imprinted on a handkerchief. All it is is a small black square board with a shred of cloth[138] hanging on it, and over that hangs another shred of cloth which they pull up when they show St. Veronica's; but poor John

---

[134] *Schnitzer.*

[135] While in Rome, Luther was told that parts of Peter's and Paul's bodies were buried in San Paolo. Cf. Boehmer, *Luthers Romfahrt,* pp. 124-125.

[136] *Hansen von Ihnene,* i.e., Jena. A reference to the symbol of the city of Jena, a head on the face of the big clock at the town hall, trying to reach an apple which is offered by a bearded man whenever the bell-hammer strikes.

[137] Cf. *O.D.C.C.,* p. 1414.

[138] *Klaretlin,* derived from *Klaterlin.* The origin of the word is obscure. See *WA* 54, 255, n. 7.

Doe can see nothing anymore but a shred of cloth in front of a black board—that is called showing and seeing the cloth of Veronica—and there is much pious reverence and many indulgences for such crude lies.

This damned ass-pope and his accursed school of scoundrels in Rome take such great, immeasurable pleasure in making a monkey, fool, and laughingstock of the poor Christian man, indeed, in blaspheming against God in heaven and causing such idolatry in his holy church—he laughs up his sleeve to see such blasphemous, idolatrous lies worshiped, and robs and steals the goods and obedience of the whole world for it—that one is forced to understand that the papacy is (as was said above) the very image of the devil set in the church by the devil to do nothing but instigate lies, blasphemy, and idolatry in order to destroy faith and God's word, and thus rob the world under him of all it has and owns and lead all the souls to the devil.

Well, as was said, the apostles St. Peter and St. Paul may or may not lie in Rome; not this, but who founded the church and bishopric there is relevant. For St. Paul does not lie in Corinth, Philippi, Thessalonica, Colossae, or other churches where he nevertheless established and ordained churches, so that, as far as St. Peter is concerned, there is almost no other church that has an uncertain beginning, except the Roman. They do write that St. Peter sat in Rome for twenty-five years, but a lie like this devours itself. For he was still in Jerusalem when St. Paul came to him more than eighteen years after our Lord's ascension, Galatians 1 [:18] and 2 [:11], and is said to have sat in Antioch for seven years, from which the Festival of St. Peter's Throne[139] is known. All together that makes forty-five years. Thus Peter seems to have lived eight years after Nero, who is supposed to have martyred him, for Nero stabbed himself thirty-seven years after Christ's ascension. They lie and invent such confusions about St. Peter, from the hundreds to the thousands, that I have got the delusion that neither Peter nor Paul laid the first stone of the church in Rome.

---

[139] *Festum Cathedrae Petri Antiochenae*, celebrated on February 22. It is a traditional holy day that dates back to the fourth century, when the church of Rome introduced it to counteract the pagan ancestry cult.

Instead, possibly a disciple of the apostles of Jerusalem or Antioch came to Rome and preached faith in Christ in a few houses; or, as was usual at that time, some Jews living in Rome, like Aquila and Priscilla, etc., went to Jerusalem for Easter and Pentecost, learned the faith there, and brought it home to their relations, both Jews and Gentiles in Rome. I am led to this by Romans 16, wherein St. Paul greets many saints in Rome by name, although neither he nor St. Peter had come there yet, for Aquila and all the Jews were driven from Rome by Claudius,[140] Acts 18 [:2], and yet were greeted first.

Now this is nothing for the Roman church to be ashamed of, for when Paul came there later he undoubtedly organized and improved everything, as he promised, Romans 1 [:8-15], wherein he praised their faith highly, which neither he nor St. Peter had planted. St. Peter did the same thing, though he came to Rome at another time. In Crete, too, St. Paul's disciple Titus ordained bishops and founded churches, as St. Paul commands him to do in Titus 1 [:5].

Well, what happens to St. Paul, the great apostle, in Acts 9 [:3-6]? When heaven had struck St. Paul down near Damascus, the Lord told him to go into the city, where he would be told what to do. Isn't this a miracle? Such an apostle is not first referred to Jerusalem, to St. Peter and other apostles, but to an ordinary disciple, Ananias, who lays his hand on him that he might receive the Holy Spirit. What does that lying ass in Rome have to say to this—he who, with his Peter, claims to be lord and master of all the world's churches? This Apostle Paul gives him a greater push than St. Matthias and the other ten apostles, whom the pope drives into Never Never Land together with their apostolic office because he wishes to be the teacher of the whole world. Paul uncovers the rogue completely, front and back, so one sees beneath his lies as into the realm of hellish Satan.

For there are his epistles—about fourteen—which clearly show how many churches and bishops in the world he ordained without St. Peter, and certainly without the pope, all of whom can say that St. Paul and not St. Peter is their apostle. Therefore, the pope,

---

140 Emperor Claudius (41-54).

with his Peter—yes, with his devil—has no authority or power over them, and his lying mouth should be cursed, since he claims to be the head of all the churches and master of the Christian faith, or, to speak Roman, master of all lies, blasphemy, and idolatry.

Oh, what more can one say? It is said, as St. Paul says, "God shows no partiality."[141] The church in Antioch was founded by none of the apostles, but by Barnabas, or, as is written in Acts 13 [:1], by the prophets and teachers Barnabas, Lucius, Symeon, Manaen, and Saul, so it is certain that at this time Saul was not yet ordained an apostle among the Gentiles (which occurs soon afterward in the same chapter [vss. 2-3]). Now the church in Antioch was an exemplary church, far superior to the Roman one, and also had (as is written) as many martyrs as stones in the city wall, although Rome too had more than the usual number of martyrs; but it never had schools and learned scholars like this—that is true— and never will get them. Therefore it is pointless to say, "This church was founded by an apostle." Those are thoughts of the flesh which God does not respect—moreover, they are lies. To contradict this, there is Antioch, which was founded by no apostle, and surpasses many others, even those founded by apostles.

The church in Alexandria was not founded by an apostle either, but by St. Mark, whom some call "the Evangelist" and others call something else; but it is certain that no apostle went there, and yet this church is far superior to the Roman church. There was an excellent school there, which helped many countries— Athanasius and many other great teachers come from it. There never was a school in Rome, nor did any particularly learned people come from there. These two churches, Antioch and Alexandria, were the best and most useful—as one knows from all the histories[142]—yet they were never subject to the Roman church, much less to the master (I wanted to say liar) of all the world, the pope.

Hippo[143] was a town perhaps as big as Wittenberg; it had a bishop—namely, St. Augustine—who did more for the churches than all the popes and bishops of Rome melted into one pile; from

---

[141] *Non est apud Deum personarum respectus.* Acts 10:34.
[142] See p. 7.
[143] Hippo Regius in North Africa.

his school many fine bishops, here and there in many lands, have been ordained; and St. Gregory admits that his writings, compared with St. Augustine's writings, are as chaff compared with wheat. And that is true. Furthermore, this bishop St. Augustine was never subject to the bishop of Rome, much less to the murderer of souls and devourer of the world, the pope. That is why it means nothing to judge these things according to persons or externals, and allege, "This church is greater, this one has an apostle, this one is richer, this one is nobler, this is the church of an imperial city." Worldly and finite matters may and must be determined by these things; God sets no store by them—he wants to be independent, with his Spirit and gifts, and have freedom, as is right, to give to a small church such people as he does not give to all the great churches, such as our example of Hippo, and our Wittenberg too. The Holy Spirit and his gifts are not inheritable goods, subject to worldly law, or tied to a place. His motto is, "It blows where it wills,"[144] not, "It blows where we want it."[145]

The pope probably thinks the Holy Spirit is tied to Rome. If he could produce reliable seals and letters to prove it, he would have won. If he wants to be head of all the churches (which is impossible), then he must first prove to us that he and his descendants must, beyond a doubt, be the possessors, by inheritance, of the Holy Spirit, and cannot err. Yes, I would like to see those seals and briefs! For his allegation, based on Matthew 16, that the Roman church is built on the rock so that the gates of hell shall not overcome it has been clearly enough proven above to have been said of the whole of Christendom and not of the Roman papal see. And the summation is, as was said, that God sets no store in his realm by the great, high, powerful, many, wise, noble, etc., but, as Mary sings, "He has regarded the low estate of his handmaiden" [Luke 1:48]. And as he says to his apostles in Matthew 18 [20:26-28] and on many other occasions, "Whoever would be great among you must be the least, and whoever would be first among you must be your slave; even as I did not come to be served but to serve among you."

But in the papacy and all the decretals the main point is that

---

[144] *Spirat, ubi vult.* Cf. John 3:8.
[145] *Spirat, ubi nos volumus.*

he alone is the greatest, highest, and mightiest, to whom no one is equal, whom no one should condemn or judge, but to whom everyone should be subject, and by whom everyone should let himself be judged. And yet, at the same time, he claims to be a servant of all the servants of God—that is, in a Roman and popish way, lord of lords, king of kings, and set above all Christians, that is, above God, Christ, and the Holy Spirit, who lives and dwells in all Christians, John 15 [14:17, 23]. It is he whom St. Paul calls in II Thessalonians 2 [:3], "The man of sin and the son of perdition," the Antichrist, who has rebelled against God and set himself up above him. Christendom has no head and can have none, except the only Son of God, Jesus Christ, who has seals and briefs so that he cannot err, and who is tied neither to Rome nor any other place.

Now, to return to the passage in Matthew 16, tell me, how could the pope show and deliver into our hands a finer, more powerful passage in all of Scripture against himself, so that we can damn his blasphemous papacy into the ground and destroy it? In his decretals he interprets the rock on which Christ wants to build his church thusly: "rock" does not mean Christ, but the power and lordship of St. Peter—that is, his own invented, untrue sovereignty over the whole world—which Christ is said to have given to St. Peter and the pope with the word "rock." That all the churches are built on such a rock means that they must all obey the pope, or be eternally damned, so that not even the blood of Christ could help prevent it. Isn't this beautiful exegesis? The Lord says, "I am the rock; the building on it is faith in me." Against this, hear the pope, "The rock is my power and authority; the building on it is the obedience of all Christians to me"; thus he leads Christians from faith in Christ to himself, and teaches them instead of faith obedience to him, which is a work instituted by man, indeed, by the devil—upon which Christians should depend, that is, have the devil as an idol, and worship him. We Christians know that even the works of God's commandments, to which the holy devout are obedient, are not enough if the building on this rock, that is, faith in Jesus Christ, does not sustain us. How then can obedience to the pope, which is something invented by man and, what is more, is devil's work and idolatry, help us?

327

For the pope, or rather, the evil spirit in him, knows quite well that if the rock, Christ, and the building on it, faith in Christ, were to remain, and if the words, "On this rock I will build my church" should be understood as, "My Christians should and shall believe in me," then he could have done nothing, nor could he have made a pope. What can you do with these words, "My church will be built on me, the rock; it will believe in me, trust in me, and depend on me"? What can you make of these words (I say) except that all Christians, or the whole of Christendom, and anyone claiming to be a Christian, will believe in Jesus Christ, and put their trust in him, as on a rock, so that even the gates of hell, that is, all the devils, may not harm them? No pope can admit or tolerate this meaning, since it does not refer us either to pope, bishops, or to any human being, be he king or emperor, but assembles us all under the only Son of God, the true rock of our salvation—assembles us so completely upon Christ alone that we have to forsake even ourselves and our good works and be made just and holy solely through faith in him.

This is why the evil spirit had to invent a different, false meaning for this passage, and say, " 'Rock' means St. Peter and the pope, or their authority (which is the same thing); 'to build on it' means to be obedient to the pope." If it no longer means "whoever believes in Christ shall be saved," but "whoever is obedient to the pope shall be saved," a pope could result; but he, the pope himself, as the rock, should be neither obedient nor subject to anyone. There you have the summary and complete meaning of the canon law and all the decretals, from which you can obviously see that the pope and his papacy is the spirit of the devil and derives from a distorted, falsified interpretation of Matthew 16, that is, out of lies and blasphemies—born out of the rear end of the devil.[146] That is why no good has come of the papacy; rather, what has come is the ruin of faith, false legends, blasphemous idolatry of our own works, as well as corruption of worldly estates, murder, every kind of trouble, and such abominable fornication as can now be seen openly in Rome, for which he has stolen bishoprics and all the possessions of Christendom, and even

---

[146] Cf. the description of cartoon No. 1 in WA 54, 350.

from kings. Now what would the pope, who has made such a horror and furor of confusion out of this blessed and comforting passage regarding faith in Christ, have earned? He belongs in the court of hell; all the torments on earth would be too mild.

Further, that which follows, "I will give you the keys of the kingdom of heaven. Whatever you bind on earth shall be bound in heaven and whatever you loose on earth shall be loosed in heaven" [Matt. 16:19], can, as we have heard, mean nothing else but that the dear Lord and true bishop of our souls left us the power to bind and loose sin. There must be discipline and punishment in the church for the sake of the wild, impudent people; but also hope and consolation for the sake of the fallen ones, so that they do not think their baptism is now invalid, as the Novationists,[147] but even more the pope, have taught. Now, this binding and loosing is not enough for the pope, since he cannot rule over the others thereby because even ordinary ministers and chaplains must have such binding and loosing. In summary, it belongs to faith too, and not to obedience to the pope, as was said above. That is why he has interpreted it differently and better, like this, "Whatever you bind, command, establish, and will on earth shall be commanded, established, and willed in heaven; and whoever does not obey you and keep these things shall not attain salvation," etc. What do you think of this fellow? Just look whether the Roman church—that is, the papal hellish scum—does not rightly boast of being the mother of all churches and mistress of the faith, when we are supposed to do what one of the most malicious rogues on earth commands and wills to be done, irrespective of whether God forbids it or doesn't wish it.

He now forces the word of Christ, our dear Lord, in Matthew 16 (*Quodcunq*, "everything") into this meaning and makes much use of it in his decretals. "Whatever you bind," etc.—"whatever" should mean not sin, which is the only thing Christ speaks of, but everything that is on earth, churches, bishops, emperors, kings,

---

[147] Named after Novatian, a presbyter in Rome who was elected counterbishop against Cornelius in 251. He and his followers insisted upon the permanent exclusion of those church members who had committed a "deadly sin" or had left the church under the pressure of persecution. He was martyred in 257 or 258.

perhaps also all the farts of all the donkeys and his own farts too! Oh, my dear brother in Christ, when I here or elsewhere speak so coarsely about the loathsome, accursed, atrocious monster in Rome, be sure to credit it to me. He who knows my thoughts must say that I do far far too little to him, and that I can with neither words nor thoughts do justice to the abominable, desperate blasphemy he commits with the word and name of Christ, our dear Lord and Savior; and afterward he laughs up his sleeve, as though he had successfully mocked Christ, the fool, and his Christians, who believe his glosses; and yet he pretends to pomp, as though he were the vicar of Christ and wanted to save the whole world with his sanctity.

He martyrs the word "on earth" in the same way—"As far as the earth extends, that far I have to bind, that is, to command, to establish, and to order, and the whole world owes me obedience." The dear Lord and Bishop of our souls Jesus Christ, as I Peter 3 [2:25] says, meant it this way, "What you bind or loose here below shall be bound or loosed up there in heaven. For here on earth I am with you until the end of the world" [Matt. 28:20]; he did not mean that the whole earth, physically, should be obedient to the pope, but, what we Germans call "here below,"[148] he calls "on earth"; what we call "up above,"[149] he calls "in heaven." No sovereignty is thereby given to either bishops or churches here on earth. For Christ's kingdom is a spiritual and heavenly kingdom and, although it is on earth and must live in the flesh, it nevertheless does not rule in the flesh, as St. Paul says in I Corinthians 10 [:4]. But here one must except the most holy father, who has a higher spirit than Christ himself; therefore we must believe only his decretals, and not the Holy Spirit or Christ, or even God his Father. For he is against and above God, as St. Paul says in II Thessalonians 2 [:3-4].

And here it becomes quite evident that the pope must be possessed and full of devils to have so completely lost all sense and reason. For Christ's words about the keys are without doubt a divine, strong promise, "Whatever you bind shall be bound."

---

[148] *Hie niden.*
[149] *Droben.*

330

This must be fulfilled, for God must not and cannot lie, since he is not pope or cardinal; what he promises, he will firmly and surely keep [II Tim. 2:13]. Now ask the histories whether St. Peter was lord over the whole world, as the pope interprets the words. Here either Christ must be a liar who did not keep his word, or the pope must be a desperate, blasphemous villain who has put the lies into our Lord's mouth—that he gave St. Peter and him temporal power over the whole world, although the Turk is still strong enough now to say no to this, to say nothing about what the rest of the world does. Now should I, as a Christian, and all the lovers of our Lord Christ, not rightfully be impatient, angry, and intolerant, and moreover curse the accursed pope and call him the most abominable things, since he is not ashamed to blaspheme our Lord most abominably and make his promises into lies? It is not only untrue that Christ with the words, "Whatever you bind on earth," promised Peter power over all the world, but it is also untrue that St. Peter or the popes actually received, brought into being, or took possession of such power.

And just so that no one thinks I say such things about the pope out of emotions of fury, let us hear his own words. In dist. XXII, *Omnes*,[150] Pope Nicholas[151] says (which has been mentioned above), "The Roman church has founded and instituted all the churches, be they patriarchates, archbishoprics, primates, or of whatever dignitaries or orders they are. But it, the Roman one, was instituted and set on the rock of newborn faith solely by him who gave Peter, the key-bearer of eternal life, the power and authority over both earthly and heavenly kingdoms. Thus the Roman church was not instituted by any earthly verdict, but by the word, through which heaven and earth and all the elements were created. It has its privilege from him who established it. Hence there is no doubt that whoever takes away a right from other churches does wrong, but whoever intends to take away the privilege of the Roman church, which the supreme head of all the churches has given it, falls into heresy; and just as the former should be rebuked as a wrongdoer, so the latter should be rebuked as a heretic."

---

[150] See p. 307, n. 105.
[151] Nicholas II (1058-1061).

You hear there that Christ's words, "On this rock I will build my church," ought not mean that the whole of Christendom should believe in Jesus Christ, but rather, "Only the Roman church was instituted by Jesus Christ." All the other churches, that is, all of Christendom, were instituted not by Christ, but by the Roman church. The dear Lord Christ knows of no more than one church in the whole world, which he builds on himself, the rock, through faith; but the pope makes two kinds of churches—the Roman, which alone was instituted on the rock by Christ; and the other churches, which were instituted not by Christ, but by (perhaps the devil, or to put it not much more mildly) the Roman church. Again, the keys should not bind and loose sin, as our Lord said, but give the pope power and authority over all earthly and heavenly kingdoms. I must stop: I can no longer rummage in the blasphemous, hellish devil's filth and stench; someone else may read too. He who wants to hear God speak should read Holy Scripture. He who wants to hear the devil speak should read the pope's decretals and bulls. Oh, woe, woe, woe unto him who comes along and becomes pope or cardinal; it would be better for him if he had never been born [Matt. 26:24]. Judas betrayed and killed the Lord, but the pope betrays and brings ruin upon the Christian church, which the Lord held more precious and dearer than himself or his blood, for he sacrificed himself for it. Woe unto you, pope!

This is the origin of the fearful raving and raging after the time of the Roman Empire; there they call themselves emperors and lords over kings and emperors, depose and dethrone them, let them kiss their feet, ban, murder, and curse them. How they treated our German emperors, Frederick I and II—until they openly executed the sole heir Conrad with the sword[152]—Philip,[153] Henry IV and Henry V,[154] and Louis the Bavarian![155] They always

---

[152] See p. 277, n. 34.

[153] Philip of Swabia, elected emperor in 1198, had to fight Otto IV (1209-1215) who, with the support of Pope Innocent III and several German princes, also claimed the imperial crown.

[154] Henry IV and Henry V were involved in the famous investiture controversy with Pope Gregory VII.

[155] Louis the Bavarian, emperor from 1314 to 1347. Pope John XXII (1316-1334) banned him after Frederick of Austria (1314-1330), another contender

wanted to make the empire headless so that the pope could be emperor. But King Philip of France[156] made a fine example of Pope Boniface VIII, the great chief rogue among the popes. This savage ruffian deposed King Philip, forbade France to honor or obey the king, and alleged that the kingdom had now reverted to the See of Rome because he would not do what the pope willed. But the forces of King Philip followed him, through a Columnese[157] who caught him in Anagni in the very room where he had been born, led him to Rome, and threw him into the dungeon, where he died like a dog from great suffering and inability to bear it.[158] But such punishment is still far too mild—except that it would be good to do the same thing to the other popes and cardinals. For it is a blasphemous, accursed office, so that even if one should wish to be pious, one would still have to be a blasphemer and enemy of Christ, because of one's office.

But they have greater and much nastier hypocrites who goad them to such ravings and write that the pope has every right to be king of kings and lord of lords. Among these is one who writes that the emperor Nero ought to have given the Roman Empire to St. Peter and that Constantine the Great was responsible for handing the empire over to Sylvester, bishop of Rome, against the will of the Roman senate; that is why those great lies, *De Donatione Constantini*, dist. XCVI,[159] and *Ludovici Primi* and *Ottonis Primi*, dist. LXIV,[160] and *Tibi Domino Johanni*[161] were invented. The popes like this kind of lie and titillation; it tickles them, and so one fool robs the other of sense. Not that they believe it to be true—they know perfectly well that it is otherwise—but they would

---

for the imperial crown, had lost the war over possession of the throne.

[156] Philip IV (1294-1303), called the Fair. Luther loved to tell the story of Philip, which he associated with the *Donation of Constantine*. See in this volume, p. 286, n. 55, and WA 50, 76. See also Flick, *op. cit.*, I, 15-30.

[157] A member of the Sciarra or Colonna family, which had been driven out of Rome and had found refuge in France.

[158] Actually Boniface was liberated by the people of Anagni, and died shortly thereafter at the age of eighty.

[159] *Decreti Prima Pars*, dist. XCVI, C. XIII. *CIC* 1, 342-345.

[160] *Decreti Prima Pars*, dist. LXIII, C. XXX and C. XXXIII. *CIC* 1, 244-245, 246; *MPL* 187, 539c-540b, 541b. Like the *Donation of Constantine*, these two documents are famous forgeries dealing with papal property.

[161] *Decreti Prima Pars*, dist. LXIII, C. XXXIII. *CIC* 1, 246.

like it to be spread among the people and believed by the whole world so that the emperors and kings might feel guilty of possessing their kingdoms unjustly and against God's will, kingdoms insolently taken and robbed from the pope, to whom they should hand over their possessions and abdicate. Perhaps it might turn out that the kings would fear the pasteboard devil, or their own vision[162]— or the pope's farts—and beg the pope to take over their kingdoms! The pope does not display the keys with the three crowns (in his coat-of-arms) because he cares much about binding and loosing sins, but because in doing so he attracts the kings' attention to the decretal Omnes,[163] and preaches and threatens that they should consider with what great insolence they withhold their kingdoms from the pope. For all the earthly crowns are his, given to him through the keys, by Christ, as Nicholas raves and farts in Omnes.

This is why the papal crown in Rome is not called a bishop's miter, but Regnum Mundi, "the world's empire," of which St. Gregory and pious bishops of the Roman church knew nothing before the pope came. The world is divided into three parts—Europe, Africa, and Asia—which are the three crowns of the pope. All the kingdoms of these three continents belong to the pope, as the chapter Omnes and his hypocrites (I nearly said, "as the devil's farts") boast that he is lord over all the world. This is the crown the devil offered our Lord, Matthew 4 [:8-10], when he led him up the high mountain and showed him all the kingdoms of the world and their splendor, and said, "All these I will give you, if you will fall down and worship me." But the Lord said to him, "Begone, Satan!" But what does the pope say? "Come here, Satan! And if you had more worlds than this, I would accept them all, and not only worship you, but also lick your behind." These are the words of his decrees and decretals wherein nothing is taught about faith in Christ, but all and everything about his greatness, majesty, power, and lordship over churches, over councils, over emperors, over kings, and over the whole world, even over heaven. But all of this is sealed with the devil's own dirt, and written with the ass-pope's farts.

---

[162] A German proverb, "Sie fürchten sich fur frem eigen Star." Cf. Thiele, Luthers Sprichwörtersammlung, No. 15.
[163] Cf. p. 307, n. 105.

Well then, this has dealt briefly with the first damage the pope has caused with his binding. For who can recount everything that the devil, through the pope, has been able to accomplish with the murder and betrayal of kings and emperors? They are temporal lords, ordained by God. Why do they tolerate such things from such a rotten paunch, crude ass-pope and fart-ass in Rome? Why don't they ask God's word and true preachers? But God's wrath has punished the world in this way.

The second damage the devil has caused through the pope's— no, through the devil's—keys is much worse and much bigger, for the worldly goods of all kingdoms are nothing in comparison with the spiritual eternal goods. Here he has extended his binding or commanding into the spiritual realm, in the name of all the devils, so that it should mean establishing laws regarding the conscience of all of Christendom, as Mr. Nicholas, lord ass-pope, claims in *Omnes;* he also has *Jura coelestis Imperii,* "power to act in the kingdom of heaven." And it is true to a certain extent; he does have a great deal to do in the heavenly kingdom, that is, in the church, and has accomplished much (just as his god, the devil, has too)—for he has his work cut out for him, to break down and destroy all that Christ has built up and is still building. Thus his god had his work cut out for himself too, in the house of Job, when he slew all his children, servants, and cattle, and tormented Job himself. His holy child, the pope, has just the same kind of work to do in Christ's kingdom—we shall now illustrate with some examples.

First, as heard above, the Lord wishes to have his church built on himself, the rock, that is, he who wishes to be a Christian should believe in him. "No," says the ass-pope, "it means that one should obey me and regard me as a lord; works like this save— and disobedience or refusal to consider me a lord damns." Again, the Lord gives the whole of his sacrament to his Christians. "No," says the fart-ass pope, "one element is enough for the layman; the whole belongs to the priests."

Again, the Lord wants to have his sacrament given to strengthen the poor consciences through faith. "No," says pope fart-ass, "one should sacrifice it for the dead and the living, sell it, and make a profitable business and market out of it so that we can expand our belly with it and devour all of the world's goods."

Again, the Lord wills that whoever dies in the true faith shall certainly attain salvation. "No," says the papal ass, "one must first go to purgatory and atone for sin. For without works—the atonement for sin—which I bind or command, one must go into purgatory. Nobody but me, with keys and masses, can help there; Christ and faith can do nothing here."

Again, the Lord wills that the efficacy of his baptism shall remain as often as we repent, as long as we live here. "No," says the ass-fart pope, "the baptism is soon lost. That is why I have let it be preached that the holy monastic orders are to be considered as good, if not better, than baptism, although I myself neither long for nor need such a baptism."

Again, the Lord wills that whoever confesses his sins and believes the absolution should be forgiven. "No," says ass-pope fart, "faith does nothing; but your own repentance and atonement do, as well as the recounting of all your secret, forgotten, and unrecognized sins."

Again, the Lord wills that according to faith and brotherly love, the customs of all creatures should be free, and no sin or justification be looked for therein. "Oh, no," speaks the most hellish father, "Christ is drunken, raving, and mad; he has forgotten what great power he, with the keys, gave me to bind—namely, I have the authority to bind and to forbid that:

"Whoever drinks milk on Friday, Saturday, on the eve of Apostles' Day or of my saints' days, which I have made, is guilty of a deadly sin and eternal damnation; except that I am not bound to observe this.

"Whoever eats butter, cheese, or eggs on those same days is guilty of a deadly sin and hell.

"Whoever eats meat on these days, however, is damned far more deeply than hell—except me and my cardinals, who are not subject to such binding, because he who has the authority to bind will undoubtedly not bind himself but others.

"Whoever does not fast and celebrate the saints I have created is guilty of a deadly sin and damnable disobedience. The reason for this is that I have authority to bind and loose. Perhaps even:

"Whoever does not worship my fart is guilty of a deadly sin and hell, for he does not acknowledge that I have the authority to bind and command everything.

"Whoever does not kiss my feet and, if I were to bind it so, lick my behind, is guilty of a deadly sin and deep hell, for Christ has given me the keys and authority to bind all and everything.

"Whatever king, emperor, or prince does not hand over to me his kingdoms and authority is guilty of a deadly sin and eternal damnation, for I have the authority to bind and command such things.

"Whatever bishop does not buy the pallium from me commits a deadly sin and is damned. The reason: I have the power to bind, and to command such things.

"Whoever calls such a purchase (it is not robbery) simony is guilty of a deadly and damnable sin, for it is I who should bind and loose.

"Whoever complains of the burden of annates, papal months,[164] and many more commits a deadly sin, for I have authority to bind such things." That is what he means, dist. XIX, *In memoriam*,[165] that one must bear and suffer everything the See of Rome imposes, even if it is unbearable.

And, so that I return to the real points, Christ wanted marriage to be free. "No," says the farter in Rome, "priests, monks, and nuns should not be married; and it is much better to live chastely (according to the Roman, papal, cardinal chastity, compared with which Sodom and Gomorrah were virgins) than to get married."

Again, laymen should not get married or have weddings during the closed seasons,[166] for the hellish father has closed and forbidden it, on pain of deadly sin and damnation.

After this he scraped all the sects of monks and nuns to-

---

[164] "Papal months" refers to the right of the pope to nominate persons for ecclesiastical offices during certain months of the year. This "right of reservation," as canon law calls it, had been practiced since the twelfth century. Cf. Hauck, *Realencyklopädie*, XII, 629-632.

[165] *Decreti Prima Pars*, dist. XIX, C. III. *CIC* 1, 60-61; *MPL* 187, 106d-107b.

[166] *Verbunden Zeiten*, such as Advent and Lent.

gether, with all their statutes on clothes, food, gestures, etc.—and whatever a fool like this invented—confirmed these countless and unbearable laws, and crowned them with indulgences and grace so that Christian freedom and faith were no longer known. Instead, the whole world, all the corners, all the clothing, all the people, all the foods, have been overwhelmed and filled with strings and bonds, so that had it gone on any longer it might have had to be sin and hell if someone had coughed, blown his nose, sneezed or otherwise relieved his need. I won't mention now what he has instituted with his false indulgences, jubilee year, holy water, Agnus Dei, holy oil, fire, wax, herbs—oh, who can recount it all?—and pilgrimages, brotherhoods. There is almost no creature left around whom he has not hung his snares and poison, so that whenever someone walked, stood, or did anything, he came into danger of sin and death.

But he did not do all these things to establish discipline and good government in the church, as are done by the office of preacher, the father of the family, and the temporal sword. For discipline has no need or use for such fine bonds and snares; instead, all of this must bear a noble title so that it defames, blasphemes, and desecrates God—namely, it must be called service to God and holy good works, through which forgiveness of sins and eternal life may be achieved.

This is to say that herewith Christians are forced to believe that the pope has the authority and power, as a god over the churches, to bind and do whatever he wants. Indeed, he has thus strengthened his own power and subjected us to obedience to himself; he has robbed the whole world of its money and goods to do so—and afterward quite softly and joyfully laughed up his sleeve to see that the Christians are such great, crude fools as to let themselves be fooled and deceived so easily out of their faith, liberty, body and soul, goods and honor, temporally and eternally. That was the devil's chief aim, for (as was said) the worst damage is not that he has subjected our bodies, goods, and honor to himself, with his accursed bonds, but that he has bound and tied up the consciences or souls with them, as though they were divine ordinances, service to God, and works to attain salvation, and

338

makes sin where there is none—that is when consciences became frightened and timid, faith weakened and finally strangled and suffocated, and Christian freedom was lost.

Thus was fulfilled what St. Paul said in Colossians 2 [:20-21], "Why do you live as if you still belonged to the world? Why do you submit to regulations? (There are those who say) Do not handle, Do not taste, Do not touch." These are the strong errors which God sends to those who do not love the truth, but believe the lie [II Thess. 2:11]. And if the devil himself were to rule in Rome, he could not make it any worse anyway. Indeed, if he himself ruled, we could cross ourselves before him and flee so that he could accomplish nothing. But now that the pope has given himself to him, embellished himself with the mask of God's word, under which one was unable to recognize him, it is the wrath of God that everything his bitter, devilish, hellish hatred of Christ and his church could think of has happened. So he has become our god, whom we have worshiped, under the name of St. Peter and Christ, with all his lies, blasphemies, and idolatries. This can truly be called being bound and using the keys for power, not for faith.

Here you may read II Thessalonians 2 [:4] yourself and see what St. Paul means when he says, "The Antichrist sits in the very temple of God," that is, in Christ's church, as though he were God and Christ himself, as his hypocrites blaspheme, saying that the pope is not purely man, but a mixture of God and man, just as our Christ alone is. And you can easily gather from the previous items what a man of sin is who is not only a sinner by himself, but fills the whole world, particularly God's temple, the church, full, full of sin, false service to God, blasphemy, unbelief, and lies, thus also being a child of perdition, that is, taking himself and countless souls to hell and eternal damnation.

The Turk leads the world astray too, but he does not sit in the temple of God, nor does he use the names of Christ, St. Peter, or Holy Scripture; instead, he attacks Christendom from the outside and boasts of being its enemy. But this inward destroyer claims to be a friend, wants to be called father, and is twice as bad as the Turk. That is called "the desolating sacrilege" [Matt. 24:15] or destruction—an idol who in opposition to Christ makes a shambles of everything Christ built and has given us. Oh, how

339

terrible it is to watch and hear such horror! This shall be said briefly of the second damage wrought by the pope's binding, murder of souls, idolatry, lies, and the destruction of faith, the imprisoning of Christian freedom, and the corruption of conscience.

Now when the devil had established himself in such immeasurable power and occupied himself with nothing but binding, capturing, lying, robbing, murdering, and blaspheming (as his works are, John 8 [:44], he began the second part, namely, loosing—not forgiving sin, but offering these fine laws for sale and selling them. For he also has the power to loose, that is, to sell for money, so he has set up a market and business in the whole world, which (I am sure) he would not exchange for the market in Venice or Antwerp. Thus he offers for sale butter-letters, egg-letters, milk-letters, cheese-letters, meat-letters, letters of indulgences, mass-letters, and marriage-letters. And everything he has bound abominably, he now looses more abominably for money. There you have the swarm and vermin of his business—indulgences, privileges, immunities without measure and number. Thus his laws are not only snares for the soul and bonds for poor consciences (as was said), for which he has robbed and stolen all the money and goods, but they are also fish-lines and nets for money so that he may rob and steal whatever is left over. Now we have to buy, with our money, our Christian freedom, earned for us by Christ's blood and given in grace, as Lamentations 5 [:2, 4] also complains.

And yet we could never be certain whether we were doing the right thing, for there was no faith that could have given us any assurance. The pope does not care about that, just as long as he gets his money and confirms his power. What should the pope and his god the devil care about the welfare of souls? I, who have seen much, was in this myself. I guess there are probably still many in the papacy who would not have built upon this selling and loosing of the pope's even though they had made a large fortune. And often it was a greater sin, and a deeper hell, if someone ate meat on Friday than if he had committed murder or adultery. But if a monk had [not?][167] bought his tonsure, cap, and

---

[167] The sense of Luther's argument seems to require this addition, although no edition of the original text included it. See WA 54, 270.

monkhood (as often happened) from the pope, he was considered an apostate, backsliding Christian whose soul was hopeless.

Thus human teaching is a desperate, deep, devilish poison when it really grasps the conscience, especially when long habit and God's name are falsely added so that God's commandment falls by the wayside in comparison with these iron chains of human, devilish teachings. Very well, this is indeed called masterfully interpreting the words of Christ, "Whatever you bind and loose on earth shall be bound and loosed in heaven." Friend, draw me the ass-pope with his bagpipes here,[168] but let us also thank God, who has delivered us from such bonds of the devil so that nothing worse happens to us.

The third damage in the church wrought by the pope with his keys is first: he should bind, ban, and punish the real sin against God's commandment, which is the only reason the Lord gave the keys to his church, Matthew 16 and 18. The pope has no binding keys here, but only loosing keys, since he lets such free living go on in Rome and all the monasteries, in all kinds of outrages and whoring that even Sodom is holy, compared with them. And he himself is the abbot of such a holy order—the worst rascal of all the rascals on earth! The dreadful fear of a just, free council comes from this, for he wishes to be unreformed, and will probably remain so in all eternity. He will not tolerate the keys above him, rather, he wants them under him; as he rants in many decretals, no one should or would bind or judge him. So it is impossible to hold a useful, fruitful council, for he will afterward carry on as before and will loosen himself from the council, as he has always done and as he freely claims to have the power to do henceforth.

Oh, why do we plague ourselves with the accursed pope! How can he bind sins? The crude crass ass and fool does not even understand what sin is, and is not able to, and does not wish to know. I know that our children or catechumens, that is, those who know their catechism, are more learned than pope, cardinals, and the whole curia with its followers. You need not worry that the papal ass, with his Roman school of scoundrels, understands

---

168 Cf. the description of cartoon No. 4 in WA 54, 350.

one single commandment out of the ten, one petition in the Lord's Prayer, one article of faith, or how baptism and the sacrament are to be understood and used, how a Christian should live, what good works are—God grant that he could recite (I won't speak of understanding) the Ten Commandments, one after the other, as our children of four or five years can. For they do not read them and do not occupy themselves with them, so they do not include them in their large books, decrees, decretals, *Sexti, Clementinae, Extravagantes*,[169] or bulls. You cannot find one word in all these books, including their writings, which would teach you to understand the first commandment or to pray one petition of the Lord's Prayer. And it is no wonder—they consider what we Christians believe fraud and sheer foolishness; they call us "simple Christians,"[170] that is, great fools, who would believe such things.

For just think, if he should understand the first commandment, "You shall have no other gods," and, on the other hand, what to call sin, he would then have to burn all his decrees, decretals, and bulls, and, along with them, himself and all his cardinals. As heard above, his decretals are sheer, supreme lies, fearful blasphemies, and horrible idolatries. How could he not have other gods—he who originates idolatry, blasphemy, and lies in the whole world, as a man of sin and child of perdition must? That is why there is nothing here about keys, about binding, banning, and punishing sin; for there is no one here who would know or recognize what sin is. One must let him go, as he is possessed and always turns toward the devil; God's wrath has come down upon them, and they sin impenitently against the Holy Spirit.

Second, now that he has come to the loosing of the real sin, that is, to the forgiveness of sin committed against God's command, he makes the consoling loosing key worthless and powerless in the whole world. He and his school teach that this key does not loose and sins are not forgiven where repentance, confession, and atonement are not present; thus he points us away from faith

---

[169] The *Sextus Decretalium Liber,* the *Clementinae,* and the *Extravagantes* comprised that part of canon law which was collected in the thirteenth and fourteenth centuries. They are, together with the *Decreti Prima Pars,* called the *Corpus Iuris Canonici.*

[170] *Bon Christian;* see p. 264, n. 4.

to our works, so that we can never again be certain beforehand that we are worthy of forgiveness and have earned it. This is a vain and impossible thing. Oh, it is a terrible plague in Christendom to make people uncertain and leave them to their own uncertain works!

Our dear Lord and Savior, with the words, "Whatever you loose shall be loosed," gives us a particularly comforting promise, as was said above, that what we loose will be loosed with him, as is more clearly written in John 20 [:23], "If you forgive the sins of any, they are forgiven." These are words (I say) of promise, with which he promises forgiveness of sins. Such a promise does not demand our works, as the law does, but our faith. God does not want to give us the kingdom of heaven for the sake of our merit, but out of sheer grace and mercy through Christ. And it should not mean (as they teach) that repentance should be so great that one could rise from the mouth to heaven[171]—yes, like Judas with the rope on the tree [Matt. 27:5], and Saul on his own sword [II Sam. 1:10]. But the papal ass also knows nothing about faith, promises, or God's commandments; he regards the church as an ass's stable or pigsty, where he can reign with his filth.

That is enough about this passage in Matthew 16; I have written too much and at too great length, but the popish horror has no limits or end. And here you see (I think) how well the pope can interpret Christ's words and how well he has based his papacy on them; this means, as Christ said, "By your words you will be condemned" [Matt. 12:37], and as I Corinthians 3 [:19] says, "He catches the wise in their craftiness." The Holy Spirit is an expert at taking the very same words used by the raving spirits for their own purpose and using them against them, toppling them with their own weapons.[172] I could not, on the spot, think of a more powerful passage in Scripture to use against the pope (as already shown) than just the one with which he wants to base, set, build, and defend himself, and with which he is so quickly trapped and caught, through his own craftiness. In German it is called

---

[171] A reference to the medieval teaching that the immortal soul leaves through the mouth when it rises to heaven. See J. A. MacCulloch, *Medieval Faith and Fable* (Boston: Marshall Jones Co., 1932), pp. 100-101.

[172] Ps. 37:15; cf. Ps. 64.

"pelting oneself with one's own wisdom."[173] The pope lies in his own filth, and thus one finds out that his rule and rank[174] come neither from God nor man, but from all the devils in hell, sheer idolatry, blasphemy, lies, murder of souls, murder, robbery, disorder, and enmity against God, emperor, king, and all men, especially against Christendom—all far worse than the Turk.

"Well," you say, "he doesn't care about your screaming and writing; he remains safe from you—he is too powerful." I am quite satisfied with that; it is enough for me that I myself am safe, that I know how to judge him according to God's word, which speaks against him, and that I can with good conscience consider him a fart-ass and an enemy of God. He cannot consider me an ass, for he knows that I, by God's special grace, am more learned in the Scriptures than he and all his asses are—not only I, but a great many more of his people in almost every country. He has the devil on his side—but we have God's word. Let it come to the point of open warfare; if we die, then we shall live in that much greater glory with Christ; if he survives, then he will die that much more horribly with all the devils. *Quia Emmanuel,* here "God is with us" [Isa. 8:10], there the devil is with him. Happy is he who will have the final victory!

The second saying which is supposed to prove that the pope has come from God is in the last chapter of John 21 [:15], "Feed my lambs." Here in Pope Clement III's *Extra de Elect. c. Significasti* is this gloss, "Christ's sheep are entrusted to us in St. Peter, since our Lord says, 'Feed my lambs,' and makes no distinction between these sheep and those sheep, so that everyone should know that he does not belong to his sheepfold if he does not acknowledge Peter and the heirs to his see as his shepherd and master," etc.[175] I was frightened and thought I was dreaming, it was such a thunderclap, such a great horrid fart did the papal ass let go here! He certainly pressed with great might to let out such

---

173 A German proverb, *"In seiner Klugheit sich beschmeissen."* Cf. Thiele, *Luthers Sprichwörtersammlung,* No. 391.

174 *Regiment und stand.*

175 *Decretalium D. Gregorii Papae IX,* lib. i, tit. VI, *De Electione,* C. IV. *CIC* 2, 49. The decretal, however, is not from Clement III (1080-1100), but from Paschalis II (1100-1118).

a thunderous fart—it is a wonder that it did not tear his hole and belly apart!

If I were to ask here, "But what did all the other apostles, especially St. Paul, pasture?" perhaps the big fart of the papal ass will say that maybe they pastured rats, mice, and lice, or, if it went well, sows, just so that the papal ass remains the shepherd, and all apostles swineherds.

Yes, but what happens, since Christ spoke not to St. Peter, but to all the disciples, as Mark 16 [:15] says, "Go into all the world and preach the gospel to the whole creation"? So Christ's sheep are entrusted not just to St. Peter, indeed, not just to the apostles, but also to the seventy-two disciples. Here you must hear the Master and Shepherd of all the sheep and understand the text properly. For it depends on a good interpreter whether one says, as you have heard above, that "rock" means the pope, "to build on it" means to obey him, "to bind" means to catch emperors, kings, and the whole world. You must learn and understand in the decretals of the most holy father not Latin, Greek, or Hebrew, but the new Roman language, just as, above, the virgin Paula III presented in excellent Roman the words "free, Christian, German" to the emperor and the empire.[176] Thus the Roman meaning now is, "Go you (that is, you, Peter, go alone) into all the world (that is, to Rome) and preach (that is, set up a pope to be God and lord) to the whole creation (that is, who will have authority over bishops, emperors, and kings, over heaven and earth; c. Omnes).[177] He who believes (that is, is obedient to the pope) and is baptized (kisses the pope's feet) will be saved (will not be damned). He who does not believe (is not obedient) will be damned (is a heretic)."

But you have now heard enough out of this passage, Matthew 16, to know that when Christ our Lord speaks of the word and faith it is to be understood as the pope's power, greed, idolatry, and horror. This is the rule and trick of interpreting Scripture; thus the Roman See does not unjustly boast of being "master of faith,"[178] that is, he who knows it and does it far better than

---

[176] See pp. 265-266.
[177] See p. 307, n. 105.
[178] *Magistram Fidei.*

Christ himself and the Holy Spirit, who are his poor abecedarians. Therefore whenever Scripture speaks of faith or God's word it is to be understood as the power of the pope and our prison; as Romans 1 [:17] says, "The just shall live by his faith (that is, the pope is lord over all)." Or as John 1 [:14] says, "The Word became flesh (that is, the pope is lord over all) and dwelt among us (that is, we and the whole world are his prisoners, in body, soul, goods, and honor)." For if this passage, Matthew 16 [:18], "Upon this rock I will build my church," accomplishes nothing but to make the pope lord and god over heaven and earth, then no letter in Scripture can help but do the same—yes, even Virgil, when he says, "You, Tityrus, lie under your spreading beech's covert (that is, you, pope, reignest in Rome), wooing the woodland Muse on slender reed (that is, you are lord over the whole of Christendom)."[179] And Ovid, "This missive your Penelope sends to you, O Ulysses, slow of return that you are (that is, the pope is lord and god over heaven and earth); yet write nothing back to me, yourself come! (that is, he who is not subject, with body and soul, goods and honor, to the pope, is lost)."[180] Does this seem to you to be ridiculous? Why don't you laugh much more over the crude ass Clement III's *c. Significasti*, which applies Christ's saying, "Feed my lambs," to his power, which makes as much sense as all the verses of Virgil and Ovid? Thus this little song will serve us too: "The cuckoo's fallen to his death (the pope is master of all churches), from off a hollow tree (that is, in Rome). Who'll while away the summer hours (that is, it is the Christian's duty), for us as well as he? (that is, to kiss his feet)."[181]

We have heard above that even if St. Peter alone had been ordered to pasture all the sheep of Christ—which is not so, and is

---

[179] *Tityre, tu patulae recubans sub tegime fagit . . . Sylvestram tenui meditaris arundine Museam* in *Eclogues* I, 1. Fairclough (trans.), *Virgil: Eclogues, Georgics, Aeneid I-III*, p. 3.

[180] *Hanc tua Penelope lento tibi mittit, Ulysses . . . Nihil mihi rescribas, attamen ipse veni.* See Grant Showerman (trans.), *Ovid: Heroides and Amores* ("The Loeb Classical Library" [Cambridge: Harvard University Press, 1958]), p. 241.

[181] *"Der Kuckuck ist zu tod gefallen,"* a German folk song. Cf. Ludwig Uhland, *Alte Hoch- und Niederdeutsche Volkslieder* (3rd ed.; 4 vols.; Stuttgart, 1893), I, 241-242.

impossible, for we must not let the other apostles, especially St. Paul, be mice- or lice-herders just because of the pope's farts and decretals—it still does not follow that the pope also, like St. Peter, was ordered to pasture all the sheep. And the good bishops of the Roman church before the devil spewed out the pope never claimed or undertook it (they should all be heretics and eternally damned because they did not believe the shameless papal ass's article). Rather, the very opposite would follow, namely, since St. Peter ordained not only the Roman church but many others—in Bithynia, Asia, Pontus, and Cappadocia [I Pet. 1:1]—these same ones, and each one in particular, could boast of being the shepherd of all the sheep just as well as the Roman church because they come from the same apostle and can just as well claim, "St. Peter the apostle founded us, not the Roman church; moreover, he wrote his letters to us, not to the Roman church," as was said. Now if these same churches are not the shepherds of all the sheep of Christ, whence does the papal ass get his claim—who does not have such strong testimony from St. Peter, indeed, cannot prove any testimony at all?

We have heard above that they are very unsure of St. Peter, and that the Roman church was first planted by neither St. Peter nor St. Paul, but by the least of the disciples, Aquila and others, who lived and had probably been born in Rome, since they lived in all the lands, Acts 2 [:5]. They all say that St. Paul was converted the same year that Christ suffered and rose again, "in the same astronomical, not legal year,"[182] namely, that Christ suffered on March 25, and Paul was converted on the following January 25, as it is in the calendar, so the year was not yet up. Whether or not this is so, it cannot be very far off, perhaps barely a year. It follows from this that the Roman church had the gospel and faith twenty-seven years before St. Paul or St. Peter came to Rome, and my opinion will be verified that Aquila and others who are mentioned in Romans 16 came to Jerusalem for the great feast, heard the apostles there, and brought the word back to Rome with them.

---

[182] Luther here switches into Latin: *Eodem anno astronomico, non legali.* There were many calendars in the Middle Ages; in Luther's time the calendar year began March 25. Cf. p. 61, n. 166. Cf. also Hauck, *Realencyklopädie,* IX, 718.

For St. Paul says, Romans 16 [:7], that his blood relatives Andronicus and Junias were famous apostles and Christians before he was. He then praised a woman, Mary, who had worked with particular zeal among the Roman Christians [Rom. 16:6]. Now if Andronicus and Junias were Christians before St. Paul, they must have become believers in the year of Christ's suffering in Jerusalem, shortly after Pentecost; and they must have first preached here and there to Jews on their journey home, along the way, and thus become famous apostles. They could well have been among the three thousand who were converted by St. Peter's first sermon, Acts 2 [:41]. Now there are twenty-seven years from the year of Christ's passion to the second year of Nero,[183] when Paul came to Rome, Acts 28 [:14]. That is why he praised the faith of the Romans, Romans 1 [:8], which nevertheless he had not planted. Thus it can be assumed that the founders and first bishops or preachers of the Roman church were St. Paul's relatives, Junias and Andronicus. Whence can the pope bring testimony like this about St. Peter? And it is credible that during those twenty-seven years many Christians, young and old, were baptized and died, and that the first Roman saints who went to heaven had never seen either St. Peter or St. Paul.

But if a disciple or apostle institutes a church, then it is a true church and does not depend on the person, Galatians 2 [:6]. God does not give a better or different baptism, gospel, or faith through Peter or Paul than through Andronicus, Junias, Aquila, or however insignificant an apostle one may be. We also said above that the churches in Alexandria and Antioch were excellent churches, better than the one in Rome, gifted with special talents and people, even though they were not planted by apostles—especially the one at Antioch, which was, as Acts 11 [:19] says, planted by the scattered disciples during the trouble that arose over St. Stephen, but which nevertheless grew so much that the believers here were the first to be called Christians [Acts 11:26]. Oh, if the pope had the advantage that the disciples in Rome were the first to be called Christians, then all the ten heavens, as the astronomers

---

[183] About 55 or 56. Luther's chronology is not exact. Cf. p. 23, n. 36; cf. also his *Supputatio*. WA 53, 127.

348

count them, would be too small to encompass the glory of the arrogant paunch in Rome! And it still is worth nothing, for in Christ all churches are equal. There is neither Greek nor non-Greek, neither male nor female, neither Roman nor Antiochian, neither slave nor free man—we are all one in Christ, Galatians 3 [:28].

But of course the pope has to instigate sects and scream, "I am of Peter, and he who is not of Peter is damned," which is just what St. Paul, I Corinthians 3 [:3-4], strictly forbade, calling carnal those who say, "I am of Peter, I am of Paul, I am of Apollos." Oh, why am I speaking so amicably and mildly about such matters? Pope Clement III says that all of Christ's sheep in the world should be subject to, and let themselves be pastured by, him. May God punish you (I dare not say dishonor, for you are already much too dishonored because you ceaselessly dishonor God, his apostles, church, and Scripture)—may God punish you, I say, you shameless, barefaced liar, devil's mouthpiece, who dares to spit out, before God, before all the angels, before the dear sun, before all the world, that you alone are the shepherd of all Christ's sheep, regardless of the gospels and the epistles of the apostles Peter and Paul, against whom you so knowingly spit and throw your devil's filth. There is not a single child who could not tell you about twelve apostles and St. Paul.

My dear brother, what is it that is meant by, "I alone am the shepherd of all of Christ's sheep and master of all churches," but this—"St. Paul and all the other apostles are not apostles, or, if they are something, they must be heretics, damned and false teachers, for they have, in opposition to the article that St. Peter alone, and the heir to his see the pope, should pasture all the sheep, dared to pasture more sheep than St. Peter, when nothing was entrusted to them"? I would very much like to say a word in German here: may this and that befall you, pope, for you can do nothing but lie, deceive, blaspheme, dishonor the apostles, curse, devour churches, desolate bodily and spiritually, execrate kings, trample with your feet, bring idolatry, gobble up all the world's goods—and all this in the name of St. Peter—this and that befall you, pope! But I dare not speak such good German, the papal ass might get angry. Anyway, it is not fitting for a preacher, who is called to bless, to curse.

But I express my great anguish with clumsy words; my Lord Christ, for whose sake I do and say everything, will pardon it.

"Yes," says Clement III, "Christ simply said, 'Feed my lambs,' making no distinction between these and those; therefore 'my lambs' must mean 'all my lambs.'" Ah! There is a sharp lawyer and sophist—but not among the sharpest, you holy virgin St. Clement! If only someone would stroke you, you ass, abecedarian, and bacchanal, with a whip until the blood flowed from your arse, and teach you the *Donat*[184] and to decline the pronoun *meum*. I must give crass examples to the crass ass: if Emperor Charles were to say to one of his captains, perhaps in Brabant or Flanders, "I entrust my people to you; make sure that they are protected and that everyone receives justice; and remember that they are my lands and my people, not your people to do with as you like, as often happens." Then if the captain went off and boasted that Emperor Charles had simply entrusted all his people to him, and tried to be captain wherever Emperor Charles was lord, in Spain, Italy, Germany, etc., and yet knew very well that Emperor Charles had many more officers—wouldn't he be a nice, ideal captain? In the same way, if every prince and lord were to say to one of his officers, "I entrust my people or my subjects to you; make sure that you take good care of everything, and remember that they are not your lands and people but mine," would that officer then try to be over all the people of that same prince?

Again, every minister—I'll use myself as an example. I am a preacher of the church in Wittenberg; now I must take to heart Christ's command, "Feed my lambs," for it applies to all the pastors and preachers in the whole world, in general and in particular. But because my Lord Christ did not say to me specifically "Feed my lambs in Wittenberg," but just "Feed my lambs," suppose I set out to make Christ's sheep in all the world serve me, and make myself lord over them, regardless of the fact that he has many other preachers in other places. What should one do to me? One would have to come running with bonds and chains and say that I had become stark, raving mad. In the same way, although the pope knows, or at least should know, that Christ did not send Peter

---

[184] A Latin grammar used in schools. Cf. Schwiebert, *op. cit.*, p. 111.

alone, but twelve apostles and St. Paul into the world as his stewards to pasture his sheep, he nevertheless sets out to apply the words of Christ to St. Peter alone, because Christ did not say specifically, "Feed my lambs in Rome." Christ could not speak so specifically, otherwise, it might have sounded as if there were Christians only in Rome and nowhere else; and St. Peter is not only the apostle of the church in Rome, but also in Cappadocia, Asia, Pontus, Bithynia, etc. And still the senseless fool and papal ass wants to have St. Peter all to himself, to be his only heir to the see; moreover, he wants to have all the sheep in the world, which St. Peter never had. And even if he had had them—which is impossible, and to which the other apostles and Christ say no—the bishop of Rome could still not be St. Peter's only heir. Bring chains, ropes, fetters, and stocks—we have here a delirious, senseless fool, the very ass-pope!

But God's grace is not entirely left out in such great wrath, and he did not let the devil speak with a completely free tongue; instead, it was tied, so that he was forced to stumble, stammer, and babble with a deceitful tongue through the pope. In this way his elect had a sign and warning by which they could see that the devil dwelt in the pope, spoke through him, and, with his babbling, interpreted the Scriptures so abominably to lead the world astray. The devil must manage to leave his stench behind, by which one can tell he has been there.

Oh, the dear Lord Christ had other intentions with the passage (feed my lambs) than setting up a pope or devil against himself and his church, as even the Roman church's pious holy bishops, before the pope arose in the name of all the devils, believed and taught. He speaks with St. Peter and says, "Simon, son of John, do you love me?" (which Pope Clement wisely says nothing about, for it is poison to him); "then feed my lambs." Here it is clear that whoever should feed Christ's sheep must love Christ; or, even if he could tend them, and did not do it out of love, this passage which demands love of and pleasure in Christ would not apply to him. Now all you devils of hell, help your pope—this passage on which he insists so strongly and bases himself will stab out his heart [Ps. 37:15]. If he does not love Christ, he is not pope—as they themselves must admit because they apply this saying to themselves. As long as he does not prove he loves Christ, he can neither tend nor be pope, and the whole world is at liberty to care nothing for the pope and to ignore him. With this saying he has trapped himself through his own mouth and his own verdict, sentenced, condemned, and dethroned himself, so that he is nothing at all.

Just see once again how God traps the wise in their own craftiness [I Cor. 3:19], so that they in their wisdom must dirty themselves. As we heard above, the passage Matthew 16 [:18], on which the pope bases himself, plunges him into the abyss. This passage [John 21:15] does the same thing, so that once again I would not know how to find a passage that would topple the pope more powerfully. That is why it is said in Scripture, "Do not touch me";[185] leave Scripture in peace if you do not want to find the true meaning, and leave it untwisted or it will twist you into the abyss of hell-fire and twist you in complete disgrace here on earth, as now happens to the pope. It is a consuming fire;[186] if you think you have caught it to your advantage, you are reduced to ashes before you can turn around. So what has the pope won with these two passages? First, eternal hell-fire. Second, eternal shame, here and hereafter, for he has been publicly exposed as a forger of Scripture, a liar, a blasphemer, a desecrater of all the apostles and the whole of Christendom, a lying villain, a tyrant over emperor, kings, and the whole world, and a thief, knave, and robber of both the goods of the church and the goods of the world. Indeed, who can tell it all? All these things he has originated and perpetrated through these two passages, as has been brought to light.

"Feed" does not mean here, as the pope-devil says, to be pope, to be supreme lord, to have power, to force Christians into subjection, to trample on emperors, to ensnare kings and bishops with duties of fealty and to subject them (such works befit the Turk and the devil). Rather, it means the great service of preaching the gospel and the faith, or seriously seeing to it that it is preached, and thus building the church on the rock, Matthew 16 [:18], of helping souls with baptism and the sacrament, admonishing and punishing

---

185 *Noli me tangere.* Cf. John 20:17.
186 Cf. Heb. 4:12.

the unruly, as Paul says, "Admonish the idle, encourage the faint-hearted, help the weak, be patient with them all" [I Thess. 5:14]. Again, "Praise and thank God always" [Eph. 5:19-20]. Again, "Pray constantly for all the world, and lead a chaste life, as good examples," I Peter 5,[187] so that many may be saved through this service or "pasturing." Yes, this is the kind of shepherd the Lord wants. But nobody will do this unless he loves Christ. This is why the passage, "Peter, do you love me? Then tend my sheep," is such an important one. Such shepherds are rare, and not as common as the two-legged bulls and papal asses in Rome.

Moreover, because one should do such great service freely, as he says, Matthew 10 [:8], "You received without pay, give without pay," one should not seek profit, honor, sensual pleasure, and power on earth through the preaching office; we have a rich reward in heaven. But of course Christians should also, without charge, nourish and honor their shepherds for Christ's sake, as he himself said, "Eat and drink whatever there is, for the laborer deserves his food" [Matt. 10:10], and as I Corinthians 9 [:14] says, "The Lord commanded that those who proclaim the gospel should get their living by the gospel"; not as though they were selling and the Christians buying the gospel from them, but rather, both should do it for nothing, and for Christ's sake. These preach, and those feed. The treasure is too great—it cannot tolerate the buying and bargaining necessary in worldly affairs.

And what is more, not only should the shepherds tend gratuitously, but they should also expect the prophets' reward for it, as the Lord tells Peter as an example to all others, "Peter, if you love me, tend my sheep! The reward you should expect here on earth shall be this: you girded yourself and walked where you would; but when you are old, another will gird you and carry you where you do not want to go" [John 21:17-18]. See, dear brother, what it is to tend Christ's sheep: to serve and preach the gospel freely, and to expect for it to be girded and carried—that is, to hazard and wager body, wife, child, goods, and everything. Who would do this unless he loved Christ and did it for his sake? A miser, an inordinately ambitious man, or a paunch-knave would undoubtedly leave

---

[187] A conflation of I Thess. 5:17, Luther, and I Pet. 5:3.

it alone! This is how the apostles and prophets tended, as well as the holy bishops of the Roman church—Fabian, Cornelius, Sixtus, and their like[188]—they shed their blood for it, and became martyrs. This is also how we pasture now. For the pope and his gang have girded and carried many of us in these twenty years to fire, water, sword, dungeons, into exile, from house and home, wife and family—solely because of the pasturing and the gospel—and they have not stopped yet. They have condemned us to death long ago, just because of this pasturing; they are anxiously hoping for the hour, if God would permit it just once, when they (as they have often strongly attempted) will be able to gird and carry us all—including our princes with lands and people, schools, and churches—in such a way that one could sweep up after us with a feather duster. We shall just have to accept this danger, and see, know, and expect their bitter, venomous, devilish wrath, their gnashing of teeth, and their flashing of knives. If we are doing this for money or goods, for honor or sensual pleasures, then we are the most senseless people upon whom the sun has shone for over five thousand and five hundred years, that is, since the beginning of the world.[189]

If only emperors and kings would once be Christians and do a service to the Lord Christ, which they certainly owe him, and make sure that the pope would have to be a bishop of the Roman church—like those before the papacy were, who were not popes but true bishops, as was mentioned above—and make him really fulfil the passage, "Tend my sheep," and, "Build my church on the rock," namely, pasture and build. Because he almost demands and claims this, he should thereupon expect the storms of hell's gates, or the girding and carrying where he does not want to go. And so that he would not be overburdened at the beginning, it would be enough for him to take over his foremost parish church in Rome, St. John Lateran,[190] and there begin to pasture—or in any case keep a shepherd there for himself—and attempt to tend the sheep of Christ

---

[188] Roman bishops who were martyred during the persecution under the Roman emperor Decius in 250-251 and thereafter: Fabian in 250, Cornelius I in 253, and Sixtus II in 258.

[189] See p. 65, n. 190.

[190] S. Giovanni in Laterano had been praised as the "mother church" ever since the time of Constantine the Great, who had given the palace of the Laterani family to Bishop Sylvester. The palace was turned into a church.

which are there, and expect to be girded. What is the use? He would not want to tend a single soul for a single hour, he who now wants to tend the whole world and curses all who do not want to let themselves be tended, even though the world is crying and calling for such shepherds who can pasture. And the Lord Christ himself complains that he is lacking such shepherds—"The harvest is plentiful (he says), but the laborers are few; pray therefore the Lord of the harvest to send out laborers into his harvest" [Matt. 9:37-38].

Indeed, the whole world stands open, if only someone would want to pasture it, as St. Paul says, "If one aspires to the office of bishop, he desires a noble task" [I Tim. 3:1]. One must not compel, run after, and look for (I mean the Christians who would like to be saved) such shepherds; and one cannot find enough of them. For the burghers and peasants too say now, "Why should I let my son go on with his studies? He will be a beggar if he becomes a parson. I would rather let him learn a trade or become a merchant." Well then, if churches and schools too become barren of God's word, then those who have given the cause for such desolation, be it through the theft of church goods or the keeping away of children from the schools or however they hinder, or help to hinder—they will have to assume the responsibility here and at the Last Judgment. God the Father, Son, and Holy Spirit testify that pasturing the sheep was his dearest work, for which the Son became man and shed his blood, so that the people should be saved. He who does this work or helps in it (which cannot happen without schools and churches) shall be a great saint in heaven, with the patriarchs, prophets, apostles, martyrs, and all the saints. Does this mean nothing to you, and have you neither hope nor faith for it? Then may God grant you that you become a pope, cardinal, or member of the Roman See, thus getting what you deserve.

"Well," says the pope, "I don't understand the pasturing that way." Dear little virgin pope, how do you understand it then? "This way: I thought that I would terrify all the kings and the whole world, in St. Peter's name, so that they would submit themselves to be pastured under me and serve me, and I would thus become sovereign of the world; and in that way I could rebuild the

355

old Roman Empire in Rome, mightier and greater than it was at the time of Augustus or Tiberius;[191] and I would be called the true Roman emperor, lord of lords, king of kings, Revelations 19 [:16], as my prophets told me." Yes, yes, little virgin pope, if you are torn there, then let the devil and his mother patch you.[192] But are you not afraid of God, that he will sink you with lightning and thunder from heaven through the earth into the abyss of hell, for such abominable forgery and blasphemy of his word? "Ha, ha, ha! Your health, Mr. Sow![193] Do you drunken German fools[194] think we are idiots like you, and will believe in such gasps and buffoonery about God and your dead Christ?" Oh, then why do you use his words about the rock, keys, and pasturing? "Oh, dear one, it is better to govern beasts than to be governed by beasts. Don't you know—to catch a titmouse, one must blow a titmouse whistle,[195] and to catch a Christian, one must learn to talk like a Christian. That is why, 'simple Christian,'[196] we must grasp you by your faith, and with this we can hold and lead you German beasts wherever and however we want—like one leads bears by their nose-ring—so that you don't again get too big for your britches and play with us, as your ancestors, the Goths and Lombards, and some emperors have done." Thank you very much, My Lord Ass, for the excellent information, Most Hellish Pope.[197]

Well then, if I were emperor I know well what I would do: I would link and gird all the blasphemous scoundrels together—popes, cardinals, and the whole papal riffraff—and lead them no farther than three miles out of Rome toward Ostia (for they would not go, ungirded and unled, where they did not want to go); there is a small body of water there, called in Latin *Mare Tyrrhenum*[198]—

---

[191] Augustus (30 B.C.-A.D. 14) and Tiberius (14-37).

[192] A German proverb, *"Bistu da zurissen, so flicke dich der Teufel und seine mutter."* Cf. Thiele, *Luthers Sprichwörtersammlung,* No. 483.

[193] *Bon profacit, miser porko,* from the Italian Latin, *Buon pro le factia, mi ser (signor) porco.*

[194] *Todeske Embrigek,* from the Italian, *tedesche ubbriacchezze.*

[195] A German proverb, *"Wer Meisen fahen wil, mus ein Meisen bein pfeiffen."* Cf. the variation in Thiele, *Luthers Sprichwörtersammlung,* No. 362.

[196] *Bon Christian;* see p. 264, n. 4.

[197] *Gremmerze, Miser Asine, porlabon informatione, satanissime Papa,* from *Gran merci, mi ser asine, per la buona informazione.*

[198] The Tyrrhenian Sea, that part of the Mediterranean Sea southwest of Italy.

a wonderful spa against all the infections, damages, and weaknesses of papal holiness, of all cardinals, and of his whole see—in which I would carefully set them and bathe them. And if they were frightened of the water, since usually possessed and insane people fear water, I would give them, for safety, the rock upon which they and their church are built, and the keys with which they can bind and loose everything in heaven and on earth so that they could command the water as much as they wished. They should also have the shepherd's crook and club, so that they could beat the face of the water until its mouth and nose bleed. Finally, they should also have this pasture along for a tonic and pleasure drink—all the decrees, decretals, *Sexti, Clementinae, Extravagantes*,[199] bulls, indulgences, and butter-, cheese-, and milk-letters—hung around their necks so that they would be quite safe. What will you bet? If they had bathed one half-hour in these baths, all their infections, afflictions, and infirmities would be over and done with. I would vouch for this, and give my Lord Christ as a pledge.

Meanwhile, this book has grown too large under my hand; and, as one says, age is forgetful and talkative—perhaps this is what happened to me. Although the papacy's diabolical horror is itself an unspeakable disorder, I have nevertheless, I hope—to whoever is willing to be told, for I am sure of it for myself—so clearly and powerfully developed my first point, which I took up above (whether the pope is head of Christendom, lord over emperors, kings, and all the world),[200] that, praise God, not one good Christian conscience can believe anything but that the pope is not and cannot be the head of the Christian church and cannot be God's or Christ's vicar. Instead, he is the head of the accursed church of all the worst scoundrels on earth, a vicar of the devil, an enemy of God, an adversary of Christ, a destroyer of Christ's churches; a teacher of lies, blasphemies, and idolatries; an arch church-thief and church robber of the keys and all the goods of both the church and the temporal lords; a murderer of kings and inciter to all kinds of bloodshed; a brothel-keeper over all brothel-keepers and all vermin, even that which cannot be named; an Antichrist, a man of sin and child of

---

[199] See p. 342, n. 169.
[200] This part begins on p. 290.

perdition [II Thess. 2:3]; a true werewolf. Whoever does not want
to believe this may keep on riding with his god, the pope; I, a qualified teacher and preacher in the church of Christ responsible for
telling the truth, have herewith done my share. He who wants to
stink may stink; he who wants to be lost, may be lost—his blood is
on his own head.

We know that in Christendom it has been so arranged that all
churches are equal, and there is only one single church of Christ
in the world, as we pray, "I believe in one holy, Christian church."
The reason is this: wherever there is a church, anywhere in the
whole world, it still has no other gospel and Scripture, no other
baptism and communion, no other faith and Spirit, no other Christ
and God, no other Lord's Prayer and prayer, no other hope and
eternal life than we have here in our church in Wittenberg. And
their bishops are equal to our bishops, pastors, or preachers; none
is lord or servant of the other; they all have the same mind and
heart; and everything belonging to the church is equal. Except
that, as I Corinthians 12 [:4-11] and Romans 12 [:3] say, a preacher
or a Christian can have a stronger faith, other or more gifts, than
another. For example, one can interpret Scripture better, this one
govern better, that one preach better, this one cast out spirits better,
another console better, one know more languages, and so on. But
such gifts do not make for unequality or lordship in the church;
indeed, they certainly do not make a Christian, Matthew 7 [:22-23],
for one must first be a Christian. But the papal ass wants to be lord
of the church, although he is not even a Christian, believes nothing,
and can no longer do anything but fart like an ass.

Hear St. Peter himself, who is an apostle, not the pope's Peter
(who is the hellish devil under St. Peter's name, like the pope's
Christ is the devil's mother under Christ's name), but the true holy
St. Peter, who writes in his epistles to his bishops in Pontus, Galatia,
Cappadocia, Asia, Bithynia, I Peter 5 [:1-2], "I exhort the elders
among you, as a fellow elder and a witness of the sufferings of
Christ as well as a partaker in the glory that is to be revealed. Tend
the flock of God that is your charge," etc. Look at that—Peter calls
himself a fellow elder, that is, equal with pastor or preacher; he
does not want to rule over them, but to be equal with them, al-

though he knows that he is an apostle. The office of preacher or bishop is the highest office, which was held by God's Son himself, as well as by all the apostles, prophets, and patriarchs. God's word and faith is above everything, above all gifts and personal worth. The word "elder," in Greek "presbyter," is in one case a word for old age, as one says, "an old man"; but here it is a name for an office because one took old and experienced people for the office. Now we call it pastor and preacher or minister.

Part II

This time I cannot deal at length with whether it is true that the papal ass can neither be sentenced nor judged by anyone, as he raves in his decretals; but I intend to do it later, if I live and God wills.[201] To put it briefly, you have heard above, in Part I, what a devil's spirit, blasphemer, instigator of all kinds of idolatry, man of sin, and child of perdition the pope is. That is why the answer here to this point is briefly: of course no one on earth has the right to judge or condemn the pope—except only everyone who is baptized, or still in possession of human reason, and all God's creatures. For when a person is baptized, he, or his godparents in his stead, must first swear that he renounces the devil and all his works and all his nature. Now the nature and works of the pope are nothing but the devil's works and nature, as has been amply proved. That is why every baptized child is not only a judge over the pope, but also over his god, the devil. Moreover, he is commanded to avoid, flee, and trample the pope, the devil, and all his creatures, as Psalm 91 [:13] says, "You will tread on the lion and the adder, the young lion and the serpent you will trample under foot." And I Corinthians 6 [:2-3], "Do you not know that the saints will judge the world? And if the world is to be judged by you, are you incompetent to try trivial cases? Do you not know that we are to judge angels?" etc. Ephesians 2 [:6], "God has raised us up with him, and made us sit with him in the heavenly places in Christ Jesus." I hope that in the heavenly life one can judge devil, pope, world, sin, death, and hell.

Second, all human reason says that he who neither understands something nor is able to, cannot judge it or decide, praise, scold,

---

[201] Luther died before he could write more on this subject.

condemn, or evaluate it. Whatever one is to judge must be recognized and understood. Now, it was proved above and it is the plain truth that the pope, cardinals, and the whole curia and gang are nothing but a stable full of crass, crude, clumsy, blaspheming asses, who have no knowledge of Scripture, do not know what God, what Christ, what church, what bishop, what God's word, what Spirit, what baptism, what sacrament, what keys, what good works are; there are enough strong witnesses of this available—their books, decrees, decretals, *Sexti, Clementinae, Extravagantes,* bulls, and countless books. So I live, Dr. Martin, besides many others, I who was raised in the pope's school and donkey stable and became Doctor of Theology—indeed, was praised as a learned good doctor and was one too—so that I trust I know very well and can truly prove very well how deep, high, broad, and long their knowledge of Holy Scripture is, namely, that they are inimical asses!

Their lawyers themselves testify in public that canon law stinks of sheer greed, ambition, and power, and that a canonist is an ass. And both are true. Now tell me, where do they get such a judgment if not from human natural reason, whereby they judge the pope to be an ambitious, proud, insatiable miser, a paunch-knave and servant of mammon, which St. Paul calls service to idols and idolatry [Eph. 5:5]. If the lawyers judge, praise, and commend the pope in this way, where shall we theologians find the words to condemn and rebuke him? Isn't this called a true likeness of the pope? Isn't he in works and teachings possessed and driven by the devil? And it turns out that he is "master of faith, lord of the churches,"[202] that is, a teacher of mammon, greed, and sheer idolatry, a doctor in the school of scoundrels. So, dear lawyers, go ahead and praise the pope well and in comfort, and do it so spitefully that we theologians won't have room to judge him worse! Well, that is what reason does when it judges like this.

Third, a natural donkey, which carries sacks to the mill and eats thistles, can also judge the holy Roman curia—indeed, all creatures can! For a donkey knows it is a donkey and not a cow. Again, it knows it is a male, not a female. A stone knows it is a stone; water is water, and so on through all the creatures. But the mad

---

[202] *Magister fidei, Regula Ecclesiarum.*

papal asses in Rome do not know they are asses—they do not even know whether they are women or men. In summary, they can do nothing but devour endowments, convents, and the world's goods, rob and steal the crowns of kings, and lead vain, unnatural, perverted, devilish lives, over which all creation is frightened, trembles, shakes, and cries out about the donkey stable to him who made them subject to such corruption, Romans 8 [:21], that he should deliver them, which he will soon do.

"Yes, what does the pope care about such a verdict, since no one dares to punish or depose him?" Well then, I don't want him to care. He is not worthy of caring about it. Balaam did not care that he was punished by his donkey and afterward by the angel [Num. 22:21-35]. The Sodomites did not care either that they were punished by Lot. "How (they said) are you to be judge over us?" [Gen. 19:9]. It is enough for us that we know the pope is damned by God himself, by all angels, by all Christians, by all of human reason, by all creatures, by their own conscience, even by all devils. So, free of him, his idolatry, and his blasphemy, we with a good conscience teach and pray against him, dare to spit at him, avoid him and flee from him as from the devil himself, remove him from our hearts, and sink him into the depths of hell; and we can turn his accursed teaching around where he screams, "Whoever is not obedient to the See of Rome cannot be saved," and claim just the opposite, saying, "Whoever is obedient to the pope cannot be saved. But whoever would be saved must avoid, flee, and damn the pope, his works and nature, like the devil himself, as our holy baptism teaches and exhorts us." Let this verdict go forth—the judge that follows will not hesitate with his verdict, as St. Paul says in II Thessalonians 2 [:8], "The Lord Jesus will slay him with the breath of his mouth and destroy him by his appearing and his coming."

"Yes, but you and your followers are damned heretics; your judgment is nothing against the Roman See's judgment, as St. Paula III wrote Emperor Charles that you should not be admitted to the council."[203] First, I shall answer in Latin, "I ask and demand, in the name of all of us, from the Roman See, namely, from the one which decides whether the popes are men or women: if they are

---

[203] See p. 259.

men, they should produce witnesses against us heretics; if they are women, I will quote the saying of Paul, 'The women should keep silence in the churches' [I Cor. 14:34]. It is necessary to demand this in view of the old rumor—known throughout Europe—that morality is in decay. It is said that kings and queens in the Roman curia are nothing but hermaphrodites, androgynites, cynoideans, pedicons,[204] and similar monsters in nature. These are all incompetent to judge heretics."[205]

Second, I have proven above that the papal asses of the Roman See are crass, crude asses, ignorant beyond measure of Holy Scripture, and, as their books testify, they also do not understand the Lord's Prayer, the Ten Commandments, or the Children's Creed.[206] That is why they have no right to judge what is heretical or Christian. To make such a judgment requires an understanding of the Scriptures because heresy, according to the testimony of all ancient and modern teachers, is nothing but an obstinate error against Holy Scripture.

Third, when our confession[207] was examined before the emperor and the whole empire at Augsburg in 1530, some princes of the other side asked their theologians if one could disprove this with Scripture. They answered, "No, one could not disprove it with Scripture, but with the fathers and councils." Thereupon some of the noblemen smilingly said, "Our theologians defend us excellently—they say the other side has Scripture in their favor, but we do not have Scripture in our favor."[208] Out of such admission and testimony of our opponents we gather that we cannot be heretics because we have, believe, and confess Scripture. If those who believe and confess Holy Scripture should be heretics and not Chris-

---

204 A list of sexual perverts.

205 *Provoco et appello omnium nostrum nomine ad sanctam sedem Romanum, illam scilicet, in qua explorantur Papae, an sint viri vel mulieres. Si sint vires, ostendant testes contra nos Hereticos. Si sunt mulieres, dicam illud Pauli: Mulier in Ecclesia taceat. Hoc facere cogit vulgata fama per omnem Iam vetus Europam, quae mores extirpat honestos. Reges enim et Reginae in Curia Romana dicuntur, ut plurimum, esse palam Hermaphroditae, Androgyni, Cynedi, Pedicones et simila Monstra in natura. At illis non competit iudicium de Hereticis facere.* Luther uses Latin to imitate the language of the lawyers.

206 The Apostles' Creed.

207 *The Augsburg Confession.* Tappert (ed.), *Book of Concord*, pp. 23-96.

208 Cf. p. 190, n. 12.

tians, who are those who would be Christians? Is it those who read Markolf, or Dietrich of Bern, or Eulenspiegel?[209] Or is it those who read the pope's filth and stench, which is the same thing and even worse? Very well then, we are not heretics—our opponents themselves testify to this—and so they have not dared to call us heretics thenceforth. Instead, some have called us schismatics; some, the disturbers; some, the innovators; until now they call us the protesting estates.[210] They have to avoid the word "heretic" because they know perfectly well it would be an obvious lie and calumny, which they could not prove with a single letter and which would arouse opposition.

And here the pope is judged and called a liar even by his own theologians for calling us heretics, which they do not accept; just as he was condemned and called a liar by his own lawyers—that he did not have the keys from Matthew 16 because they were solely promised and not given therein. Thus it is quite certain that no one can judge or punish him. I would not dream of judging or punishing him either, except to say that he was born from the behind of the devil,[211] is full of devils, lies, blasphemy, and idolatry; is the instigator of these things, God's enemy, Antichrist, desolater of Christendom, church-robber, key-thief, brothel-keeper, steward of Sodom; and everything else that was said above. But this is not a verdict, judgment, or condemnation; rather, these are sheer eulogies and pledges, so that no one is to be praised and honored except the most satanic,[212] the pope. It would be a good thing if he had to carry them engraved and branded on his crown and forehead—that would fit His Satanty much more honorably (because it is the simple, clear truth) than his letting his feet be kissed.

And if the pope had done nothing but set himself above all the churches and bishops to be judge of all and let himself be

---

[209] Characters of medieval German sagas. Markolf appears as the opponent of King Solomon in a twelfth-century poem; Dietrich of Bern is the pseudonym of the Ostrogothic king Theodoric the Great (d. A.D. 526) in the *Nibelungenlied;* Till Eulenspiegel is the adventurous fool in a Low German satirical work of 1500. Luther mentions these characters elsewhere. See, for example, LW 34, 235, 236. Cf. Maurice O. Walshe, *Medieval German Literature* (London, 1962), pp. 67-68, 243-249.

[210] *Protestirende Stende.*

[211] Cf. the description of cartoon No. 1 in WA 54, 350.

[212] *Satanissimus.*

judged or punished by no one—and thus give and allow the devil and flesh free rein to practice all their mischief, as we see and as Jude says in his epistle, "They are ungodly persons who pervert the grace of our God into licentiousness and deny our only Master and Lord, Jesus Christ" [Jude 4]—this one thing alone would be sufficient token by which one could recognize the pope, that he certainly must be the true, final horror, the Antichrist. Figure it out for yourself: the holy Christian church has the Holy Spirit and the gospel or God's word—as no one can deny—so that it should teach the good and punish the evil, which it does and has always done, according to Christ's words, "The Holy Spirit will come and reprove the world of sin," etc., John 16 [:8]. The pope would like to sit in judgment over this word and remain unpunished by the Holy Spirit. That means sitting in judgment over God, whose word it is, as St. Paul says, "He who opposes and exalts himself against every so-called god or object of worship" [II Thess. 2:4]. Now, one cannot serve God better than with his word, over which the pope sits in judgment and against which he rages, as all his decretals roar and rage.

What more does the Lord himself say to this? He says in Matthew 18 [:15-18], "If your brother sins against you, go and tell him his fault, between you and him alone. But if he does not listen, take one or two others along with you. If he refuses to listen to them, tell it to the church; and if he refuses to listen even to the church, let him be to you as a Gentile and tax collector. Truly I say to you, whatever you bind on earth," etc. What shall develop from this? Here the Lord throws all those who sin into punishment by first his nearest Christians, and wills, in short, that he should let himself be punished; if he refuses to let himself be punished, the congregation should punish him; if he refuses to listen to them too (now mark what the Lord says), then we are to consider him a Gentile and a tax collector. Not only all the churches or every single church is commanded here, but also you and I, to judge, sentence, and condemn the pope with a verdict of being publicly condemned by the church's throne of judgment—a Gentile and a tax collector. He will not listen and won't let himself be punished, either by one or two, or by the congregation, indeed, not by the whole of Christendom, as he rages in many decrees and decretals—he even wants to be praised for such things, be told "well done," and to force Christians to obey, praise, and worship such a horror as divine truth.

There is no need here for a trial or a long lawsuit, an "objection" or an "appeal";[213] all that is notorious according to fact and law;[214] the deeds of the pope are obvious, the mandate of our Lord Jesus Christ is obvious. Ah, be silent, lawyers, theologians, emperors, kings—yes, even angels in heaven and all creatures. Here speaks and judges one who did not suck woman's milk but virgin's milk, and was so poor on the cross he had nowhere to lay his head [Matt. 8:20], and yet in that very place gave Paradise and the kingdom of heaven to the thief [Luke 23:43], and in the manger was worshiped by all the angels in heaven.[215] Yes, it is this same Lord who here judges and speaks, "The pope shall be a heathen because he will not listen, but even claims this obstinate disobedience of his as a great holiness." He commanded the apostles in the same manner to punish the whole world because of the idolatry which was openly there, and not first to go to court with the idolatrous heathen, otherwise they would never get to the preaching office.

Thus I accept the verdict of the holy Christian church—yes, of the Lord Jesus Christ—and proclaim it with this document, as I have often done already, to all who do not know or have not understood that the pope, yes, the papacy itself, who will not and cannot listen, has been damned by God and thrown out of his church because of his decretals, those sheer pagan, heathenish, sinful things; that is, he is of the devil and of an un-Christian realm, before which everyone should bless himself, flee, and against which everyone should pray and act.

If we now know this verdict, we really are not doing well, especially emperors and kings, princes and lords (for the preachers and bishops of the churches will surely handle themselves correctly in this, so that they will embellish, praise, and decorate the pope as a devil), to so ignominiously allow him to rummage in their mouths, drum on their snouts, and make monkeys of them, when they (if

---

[213] *Exception, appelation,* juridical terms.
[214] *Notoria de facto et iure.*
[215] Cf. Luke 2:13-14.

they claim to be Christians) should rightfully acknowledge their duty to handle this accursed pagan in Rome like he deserves to be handled. They make themselves a party to all the sins the heathenish devil in Rome has practiced in the church for so many centuries, and to all the books, decretals, *Sexti, Clementinae, Extravagantes,* bulls—that is, to all the devil's filth and stench with which Christendom has been suffocated and strangled. I am certain that if the pope did not exist, the Turk (whose devil is the cousin, brother-in-law, and sister of the pope's devil) would not have received such great power.

Now, since the pope is not a Christian and is not called such, but rather has been thrown out of the church through the verdict and command of Christ—an accursed heathen should be neither judge nor lord in the church of Christ, much less such a bedeviled man of sin and child of perdition [II Thess. 2:3]—all the emperors, kings, and bishops are duty-bound to take back their sworn oaths and duties (which the pope too, even if he were a bishop in Rome, would have neither the right nor the power to demand) and act against them with all their might. A bishop of the church cannot accept either oaths of allegiance or duties from alien, free, worldly lords, nor from another bishop, since all bishops and churches are equal (unless he had some temporal subjects of his own). The pope has less right and power to do so, he who cannot be and never was a Christian or a bishop, but rather is the devil's fruit, an accursed, damned, alien rule, which is nothing but the ruin and devastation of Christendom. No one can swear an oath against God—and if he does, it is the same as doing it to the devil himself, which one should, when it is recognized, tear up immediately, as the lawyers themselves say, and act to oppose it out of the power of the first and second commandments, "Thou shalt have no other God, and thou shalt not take the name of the Lord in vain." Thus emperors, kings, and bishops are rid of the oaths they made to the pope, and because of this they are duty-bound to oppose the pope in all his works, for such an oath is made to the devil—as though the sheep had sworn allegiance to the wolf, in the name of their pious shepherd.

And here the lawyers should (for the pope claims to be a lawyer and teacher of all lawyers) play "action for damages"[216] with him. For he is neither a bishop nor a Christian, but a pagan, yes, a savage werewolf, who tears up and devastates everything in his way and has snatched for himself the keys of churches—which were really never entrusted to him, but only promised to St. Peter, as the words in Matthew 16 [:18] clearly say, and which the lawyers understand "in terms of the future."[217] But we theologians add to this: even if the keys had been promised to St. Peter and also given to him, there is still no proof that only the Roman church could have such keys because St. Peter founded other churches besides the Roman church (if he did found it at all, which is not certain and can never be proved) to which the keys of St. Peter, their apostle, should have been given, just as well as to the Roman church. But the pope, since there were no more bishops in Rome, stole and robbed these keys before St. Peter gave them, and attempted to act as though they were his exclusively, even though he has forced himself into the church like a foreign animal and werewolf, and is damned by Christ, as was heard.

So now the lawyers should admonish their lords, emperors, kings, bishops, princes, and lords of their duty (if they want to be Christians and saved) and not stop until they have forced the accursed pope "into restitution"[218]—to return and restore all that he has with the keys stolen, robbed, and done in the church, from the beginning of the papacy. It is certainly true that the pope's keys are "a sacrilege and unspeakable despoilment,"[219] a church robbery which has never been equaled since the beginning of the world, even if all the church robberies were placed in one pile. Here the emperor should take Rome, Urbino,[220] Bologna,[221] and everything the pope stole from the empire, for it was all stolen and robbed through the falsified keys; after this, he should force him to restore all the souls he has led into hell through the keys, although this will be impossible for him, and restitution must be made in eternal hellfire.

---

[216] *Repetundarum,* another legal term, by which Luther means the pope should be sued.
[217] *De futuro.*
[218] *Ad restitutionem.*
[219] *Sacrilegium & ineffabile spolium.*
[220] See p. 308, n. 108.
[221] See p. 308, n. 109.

But we could probably take the finite goods away from him and add to it what this key-thief and church-robber has used up, dissipated, spent, whored up, and squandered out of the goods he had stolen for so many years. If he could not repay or restore those things, one could play the law of the fox with him, all the cardinals, and the whole curia—that is, pull off their skin over their heads and thus teach them to pay with their skin; then throw their rumps into the springs at Ostia,[222] or into the fire. See, see how my blood boils, how gladly I would see the papacy punished, even though my spirit knows that no finite punishment is enough for this, even for one bull or decretal! But anyway, this is the summary: the poor Roman church and all the churches under the pope can neither be advised nor helped, unless the papacy and its rule, including its decretals, are removed and a proper bishop again instituted in Rome, who would preach the gospel purely and properly or see that it was preached—and would leave crowns and kingdoms in peace, which are not entrusted to his rule, and not try to subject them to himself by oaths; who would be one bishop equal to other bishops, not their lord; and who would not tear their churches apart, rob them of their goods, trap them with oaths, or increase their burden with pallia, annates, and papal months.

One can surely be bishop in Rome and in the whole world even if one does not sell the pallium, steal annates, and commit other extortions, trample on kings, and let one's feet be kissed. St. Peter was an apostle, in my opinion as good as a bishop and without a doubt better than a pope, yet he would not allow the centurion Cornelius to fall down before him, but raised him up and said, "Stand up; I too am a man," Acts 10 [:26]; and he gladly let himself be corrected and punished by St. Paul and by the apostles and all the disciples, Acts 11 [:3]. Because I have the pallium in mind, I must tell you the story of what it accomplished: this squabble that has arisen between me and the pope arose over the pallium. A pallium is made of hemp or flax, knitted and worked in the shape of a cross, which one can throw over the back and front of the chasuble, as the crosses on chasubles usually are. It is about the width of three fingers, and should be worth, all in all, about six or

---

[222] See p. 356.

seven lion-pennies[223] or one sword-penny;[224] this is how costly it is! This is what the pope blesses on the altar in Rome and then lies that it was consecrated over the bodies of St. Peter and St. Paul—for they have the bodies of neither St. Peter nor St. Paul. Then he sells it to the bishops, charging one more than another, depending on the size and wealth of the bishoprics. In former times the popes bestowed it without cost and ordered it to be given at no cost, as the decretals still say;[225] they were satisfied to thus gain lordship and power over other bishops. But later, like desperate scoundrels, they added compulsory oaths of allegiance and money to it.

Now it is said that the pallium in Mainz cost twenty-six thousand gulden—this is how expensive hemp thread is in Rome. Some say that one could not bring it from Rome for less than thirty thousand gulden. The bishop[226] could not pay for such an expensive pallium, so he let some pickpockets go out with indulgences to raise money from the people. They were so obvious about it that it was too much, so I was forced to preach and write against it. Thus the game started over a hemp thread—and no one knows the end of the game yet.[227] May it come to the pope's being strangled and suffocated by that same thread! May my dear Lord Jesus Christ, the Savior of us all, praised in eternity, help in this. Amen. Yes, I say, one can certainly be a bishop without the pallium, and it is not necessary to let the arch-robber of churches, the robber of monasteries, convent-devourer, and murderer of souls in Rome steal so much money in plain sight and repay us with his devil's filth and stench, sheer lies, blasphemy, idolatry, and eternal damnation. We Germans intend to invest this money in other ways so that the pope may not steal it from us so shamefully.

This, then, is a brief statement concerning the second point—whether no one or someone can judge, sentence, and depose the

---

223 *Lawen pfennig,* small silver coins showing the Thuringian-Meissen lion, part of the coat-of-arms of the Wettin line. Cf. Schwiebert, *op. cit.,* pp. 78-85.

224 *Schwert grosschen,* a silver coin used in Electoral Saxony, showing the swords of the electoral marshal. See *WA* 30^{II}, 368, n. 5.

225 Cf., for example, *Decreti Prima Pars,* dist. C, C. III. *CIC* 1, 352-353; *MPL* 187, 474*b*.

226 Albrecht of Mainz.

227 Cf. Luther's earlier account of the beginning of the "game," in this volume, pp. 231-236.

pope. And it has been found beyond a doubt that not only the churches, but every baptized Christian may judge, condemn, and at least depose him from his heart—as an antichrist and werewolf, as the enemy of God, of Christ, of all Christians, and of all the world—and whoever wants to be a true Christian and wants to attain salvation should judge and teach, sing and say, that whoever wishes to obey the pope should know that he is obedient to the devil, in opposition to God, and helps strengthen the pope in his horror, as II John [11] says, "For he who greets him, shares his wicked work." Besides, the Lord himself, in Matthew 18 [:17], has openly judged him and thrown him out of the church and the company of Christians. He should not be called a Christian, as was heard, because he wants to be unjudged and unpunished, that is, be a free devil and werewolf—therefore he must be damned publicly by God and all the creatures.

Yes, indeed, God's Son should have died and shed his precious blood so that a despotic scoundrel in Rome could boast in the name of all the devils that he had been freed through Christ's blood and death and had thereby received the power to sin, to rant, to rage, and to do whatever he wished. Against this no Christian, not even the Holy Spirit in his church, has anything to say or judge as *dis.* XL, *Si Papa*,[228] teaches us—even though St. Paul, Galatians 1 [:8], delegates to Christians the power to judge and condemn even an angel of heaven, if he should preach another gospel. But what are the pope, cardinals, and all the devils together, compared to a heavenly angel; except that the pope thus not only has to reveal his blasphemy, accursed lies, and idolatry, but also must show his gross ass's head to all the world, as one who does not understand at all what a Christian, a church, God's word, the Spirit, or God himself is. If he understood it he would surely know that God's word is the highest judge, over all creatures; and he who possesses it in true faith is called, I Corinthians 2 [:15], "the spiritual man" who can judge all things, yet can be judged by no man—not because of his own person, but because of the word and Spirit dwelling in him and speaking and judging through him, as St. Paul says in the same place, "But we have the mind of Christ" [vs. 16]. That is why, with

---

[228] See p. 285, n. 52.

pope and cardinals, it is nothing but crude Roman asininity.

Thus the pope brings about his own downfall, judges, condemns, and ousts himself from the Christian church, exactly because he doesn't want to be judged—and makes himself a pagan—and goes on, as the Lord says, "I will condemn you out of your own mouth" [Luke 19:22]. For because you don't want to be punished, like all the other Christians, Matthew 18 [:17], you are certainly not a Christian; if you are not a Christian, then you must certainly be, in the name of all the devils, Antichrist or pope among the Christians. Yes, this is how the pope wanted it, this is what he was striving for—whoever wants to be a Christian should and must consider the pope the devil's spirit, invention, and property, before whom one should flee, against whom one should pray, and against whom one should in all earnestness live and act as against the devil himself. He has entrenched himself so securely with his decretals that no one could do him as much harm as he does to himself, since he wishes to base and defend himself upon the very best, just as he toppled himself above with the two passages—about building on the rock, Matthew 16 [:18], and about feeding the sheep, John 21 [:15]—upon which he had based himself, so that no writing against him could have toppled him as well. This has been said about the second point, this time briefly.

Part III

Whether the pope transferred the Roman Empire from the Greeks to us Germans[229]—this is quite plainly a crude, obvious lie, which everyone can see and grasp. First, where would the pope get such an empire? And how could he give what he did not himself have? He himself, in Rome, was not safe from the Lombards, who had at that time ruled in Italy for two hundred years. What a fine present that would be for me, if I, a preacher in Wittenberg, were to give the kingdom of Bohemia or Poland to the Elector of Saxony. And, to give an example from our day, wasn't it a fine gift when Pope Leo X gave King Francis of France the empire of Constantinople?[230] If the king had not been smarter than the pope and had

---

[229] See pp. 289-290.
[230] In 1517 Leo X advocated a crusade against the Turks. He especially ad-

not despised his foolishness, what a comedy and what laughter he would have created with the empire of Constantinople! They are truly quite mad and silly, these Roman asses—with sane reason, which is a monstrosity.

The devil, through God's wrath over our sins, has fertilized us with big, bad fools and big, crude asses in Rome, who think only in this way, "We read no books, so nobody else will read them either; instead, the beasts will have to regard as articles what we asses fart and dung. The reason: they believe we are St. Peter's heirs and cannot err."

The histories, against which the pope's farts count for nothing, say this: when Constantine the Great moved the imperial residence from Rome to Constantinople (which was a sign that Rome was nearing its end), Rome decreased from day to day, until the Goths, under Emperor Honorius,[231] came and conquered Rome with all of Italy. Then came the Vandals, and then the Lombards, so that Rome was conquered and plundered four times within one hundred years by the Goths and Vandals alone—you must read the histories about this. The Goths and Lombards were Germans. Since Rome and Italy were nearing their end and were in their death throes, and the emperors in Constantinople could no longer rescue or help them because they had enough to do with Goths, Persians, and Saracens; and since the German lands, France, and Spain were gone from the Roman Empire, and Italy too was subject to the Lombards, so that Rome was nothing anymore—they attached themselves to the pope. When they heard that Charles the Great was a powerful king who had united France and Germany under one crown, they coaxed him to their side against the Lombard kings, who had now been ruling Italy cleanly and moderately for two hundred years and had become cousins, aunts, sons, daughters, and in-laws to each other—the land Lombardy is still called after them.

---

vised Francis I of France to attack Constantinople as soon as possible, promising him the conquered land. The crusade, however, never took place. Instead, Francis I tried to become Holy Roman Emperor when Maximilian I died in 1519. Though favored as a candidate, he lost the crown to Charles V. On Luther's sources, see Schäfer, *op. cit.*, pp. 345-347. Luther dealt with the problem of papal political authority in 1520 in *An Open Letter to the Christian Nobility. PE* 2, 107-111.

[231] Roman emperor of the West (395-423).

Then Charles came to the aid of the pope against the Lombard kings (listen, and read the histories) and Charles was now a pious, devout Christian. While Charles was in church in Rome on Christmas day, the pope called out that he was Roman emperor—without his knowledge and consent. Charles said afterward that if he had forseen this, he would not have gone to church. Nor would he accept or bear the title "Roman Emperor" from the pope's screaming until those in Constantinople had been consulted and had consented to it. So Charles was given the name of Roman emperor "of the West," as those in Constantinople were called "of the East" because those in Constantinople had now lost the Western empire and were unable to support it. Such a division of the Roman empire was neither new nor the first at that time, for previously Theodosius had divided the empire between his two sons, Arcadius and Honorius,[232] and Constantine the Great had divided it between his sons Constantius, Constans, and Constantine;[233] indeed, also Augustus and Antonius,[234] Julius and Pompeius,[235] Diocletian and Maximianus,[236] and so on, so that the Roman Empire was divided between two or three heads most of the time and rarely came under a single head.

But the pope's words sound as though he had taken the empire from the Greeks and turned it over to the Germans. That is a lie and pure papal twaddle. In the first place, he could not take anything from the Greek empire and give it away. On the contrary, the Roman Empire of the East remained in Constantinople, and the emperor in Constantinople has always called and signed himself "Roman Emperor," just as our emperor signed himself "Roman Emperor," except that the one is called Constantinopolitan and ours the German emperor. The reason for this is that neither one had his residence in Rome—but both were of the same Roman Empire, divided (as was said), one part in the East and the other in the

---

[232] Theodosius I, Arcadius (395-408), and Honorius (395-423).

[233] Constantius II, Constans I, and Constantine II divided the empire at the death of Constantine I in 337. In 350 Constantius II became sole ruler.

[234] Antonius was involved in the civil war following the death of Caesar in 44 B.C.

[235] Caesar (ca. 102 B.C-44 B.C.) and Pompey (106 B.C-48 B.C.).

[236] Diocletian, Roman emperor from 284-305, appointed Maximian joint emperor in 286.

West. And both agreed to this. For Charles had an embassy in Constantinople and the other had his embassy in Aachen. Empress Irene first made such an agreement with Charles, and, following her, Nicephorus and Michael.[237] As proof, Venice was excepted in the agreement so that it could be autonomous, subjected neither to this nor to that emperor.[238] The pope's historians write the same thing—such as Platina, etc.

They say further that Otto II, our German Roman emperor, the son of Otto the Great, had married Theophania, the Roman emperor John of Constantinople's sister, from whom Otto III was born, and that Otto II moreover reinstated his brother-in-law, Emperor John, in Constantinople after he had been dethroned,[239] so that Otto III could, from his mother, also have inherited the Roman Empire in Constantinople. That is why the pope has not transferred a hairsbreadth from the Greeks to the Germans, as he dupes us into believing with his vain words.

Second, much less did the pope transfer or give the Roman Empire of the West to the Germans. What could he give, who himself had nothing? Charles had inherited France and Germany from his father Pepin, and had fought for thirty years against the Saxons. For the lands of Germany, France, and Spain (as was said) had long since broken away from the Roman Empire, and Charles had to win Italy from the Lombards with the sword and save the pope. After this he also conquered Hungary, so it is true that Charles received nothing from the pope, except the mere name "Roman Emperor"—which in any case he did not want to accept behind the

---

[237] Luther's source is Platina (see above p. 7, n. 18). Irene, empress of the East (780-802), Nicephorus I (802-811), and Michael I (811-813) tried to maintain the political balance between East and West, but became more and more dependent upon Charlemagne. See Hans von Schubert, *Geschichte der christlichen Kirche im Frühmittelalter* (2nd ed.; Darmstadt, 1962), pp. 355-356, 481.

[238] The city of Venice, originally subject to Constantinople, joined Charlemagne in 805.

[239] The sources for this period are scant. See Bruno Gebhardt, *Handbuch der deutschen Geschichte* (4 vols.; 8th ed. rev.; Stuttgart, 1954-1959), I, 187-188. Otto II (974-983) did not reinstate the Greek emperor John I (969-976). John took the throne after his predecessor Nicephorus II (963-969) had been assassinated, possibly with the help of Theophania, his niece. She was married to Otto II in 972, a political marriage which strengthened Otto II's influence in the East.

back of the empire in Constantinople, as we have heard. But this mere name has cost the Germans much, for the popes afterward made our emperors into vassals. If the pope and Italy lacked something, our emperors have had to assist them at their own expense. They then rewarded and thanked them with knavery and villainy—poisoned some emperors, beheaded some, or otherwise betrayed and killed them, as the papal holiness and devil's spirit should and was forced to do.

But with a mere name and empty titles they have nevertheless dug in their claws more and more, later strengthening this with the coronation and anointment, longing more and more for the empire, so that they, the robbers of convents and regicides, could take what the Germans had inherited or won with the sword—according to the proverb of our Lord, John 4 [:37], "One sows and another reaps." Yes, I say, these rotten, abominable paunches would like to be emperors through the property and blood of our Germans! They would also like to have had the election for themselves, *Ex De Electio c. Venerabilem.*[240] Again, Cajetan is trying it with this emperor, Charles, too.[241] They have created great misfortune by deposing the emperors through the ban and, in the most despotic way, commanding the election of others. Finally, they have also subjected the emperors to themselves through sworn duties, which the devil ordered them to do. But all this is because they want to be emperors themselves over strangers' property. They have also often tried to transfer the mere title from the Germans to France, so that they could play with this king as they did with the German emperors.

But it would really have been good if the emperors had let the pope's paste[242] and crowning alone. Indeed, they can be emperors without the pope's paste or crown, which do not make an emperor; rather, electors make an emperor, even though he were never again smeared by the pope—like Louis III, Conrad I, Henry I, Conradus

---

240 *Decretalium D. Gregorii Papae IX,* lib. i, tit. VI, *De Electione,* C. XXXIV. *CIC* 2, 79.

241 A reference to the curia's attempts to influence the emperor during and after the Diet of Augsburg in 1530 through Cajetan's diplomatic moves. For a detailed account, see Schwiebert, *op. cit.,* pp. 339-370.

242 *Schmir.* A reference to the anointing of emperors.

Sueus,[243] Rudolph,[244] Maximilian, and many others who stayed un-smeared by the pope. The pope brings too much displeasure and misfortune into the empire with his paste. There are surely also some bishops who survived without the pallium. Only the vote of the chapter makes a bishop, as is only right, and it would be enough for the neighboring bishop to lay his hands on him, and leave the blasphemous, devouring, werewolfish monster in Rome to use his paste and hemp thread where he could.

Here now, papal ass, with your long donkey ears and accursed liar's mouth! The Germans have the Roman Empire not by your grace, but from Charles the Great and from the emperors in Con-stantinople—you have not given a hairsbreadth of it, but you have stolen immeasurable amounts of it with lies, fraud, blasphemy, and idolatry, just as you have handled the bishops too, like a devil, first through lies, then with pallia, oaths, and taxes. But I must leave it here. If God wills, I shall improve it in the second pamphlet.[245] If I should die meanwhile, may God grant that someone else make it a thousand times worse, for this devilish popery is the last mis-fortune on earth, nearest to that which all the devils can do with all their might. God help us. Amen.

---

[243] Conrad of Swabia, who ruled as Conrad II (1024-1039).
[244] Rudolph I (1273-1291).
[245] Luther did not write this second book.

INDEXES

INDEX OF NAMES AND SUBJECTS

389

INDEX TO SCRIPTURE PASSAGES

5:14 – 353
5:17 – 353 n. 187
5:21 – 47

II Thessalonians
2:3 – 288, 327, 358, 366
2:3-4 – 205, 209, 245, 330
2:4 – 203, 212, 339, 364
2:8 – 245, 273, 361
2:8-12 – 210
2:11 – 339

I Timothy
3:1 – 355
3:2 – 154 n. 399, 159, 161
3:15 – 213, 214
4:1-3 – 204
4:4-5 – 168
4:5 – 149, 164
6:16 – 116

II Timothy
2:4 – 130
2:13 – 212, 331
4:1-4 – 223
4:3 – 128 n. 346

Titus
1:5 – 324

1:6 – 154 n. 399
1:13-14 – 301
3:5 – 151
3:10-11 – 50
3:11 – 12 n. 5, 193 n 18

Hebrews
4:12 – 352 n. 186
13:13 – 190 n. 14

I Peter
1:1 – 321, 347
1:19 – 314
2:3-5 – 310
2:4-7 – 315
2:6-8 – 310
2:25 – 330
3:7 – 155
4:11 – 301
4:18 – 298 n. 87
5:1-2 – 358
5:2 – 85
5:3 – 131, 353 n. 18'
5:5 – 117
5:9 – 197

II Peter
1:19 – 215
2 – 280
2:1 – 245
2:10 – 197
2:12 – 279

2:14 – 273
2:14-22 – 129
2:18 – 151
2:18-19 – 209
2:19-22 – 209
3:18 – 166

I John
1:8, 10 – 216
2:19 – 219
5:16 – 255

II John
11 – 370

Jude
4 – 364

Revelation
2:9 – 199, 201, 217, 237, 311
6:11 – 175 n. 431
13:5 – 90
17 – 206
18:4-5 – 206
19:16 – 356

APOCHRYPHA
Ecclesiasticus
12:10 – 80
17:17 – 225
28:12 – 89

Type, 10 on 13 Caledonia
Display, Bulmer and Caledonia
Paper, Standard White Antique 'RRR'